The final result
is a state called
mental well-being never before achieved
by man. Read what these people have
to say about Dianetics technology and
Clear.

Dianetics technology helped me get my career under control and gain confidence.

Christina Kumi-Kimball
Dancer, Actress

My father died and when I went back to work at my advertising agency, I found myself having difficulty communicating and handling executive problems. After just one session of Dianetics counseling I was able to understand my relationship with my father, and to cope with the loss and help my family cope. It answered questions I always had about life and death and who I was.

I've been involved with Dianetics technology for six years now. Each day, I become more causative over life.

Marion Redman
Advertising Executive

I wanted to use Dianetics technology to change my life—to REALLY change it—within a year's time. It only took a week. I set a new mark, and another one, and so on—with complete success. How good can YOU get? Try it and see!

Ray Bernard
Design Engineer

After writing over three hundred scripts for television, I cannot emphasize enough the value of *Dianetics* to a writer, or any other creative person. The state of Clear took all the stops off my creative imagination, and totally blew away those self-invalidations and doubts that can destroy one's ability to create. With *Dianetics* I learned what makes people tick. In my professional career this is vital because I write about people. And in my personal life, this data is even more valuable because I can use it to help my friends improve *their* abilities as well.

Jeffrey Scott
Emmy-award winning
TV writer

I feel that the *Dianetics* book should be a vital part of every person's personal library and its reading is a definite first step in the achievement of sanity, health and self-respect.

Paul Jaconello, M.D.

Studying and applying Dianetics technology has been the most useful action I have ever done. It has assisted my health and happiness and enhanced my understanding of human relationships. What could be more vital?

Lee Purcell
Actress

DIANETICS

The Modern Science of Mental Health

L. RON HUBBARD

DIANETICS

The Modern Science of Mental Health

A Handbook
of Dianetics™ Procedure

Bridge

PUBLICATIONS, INC.

Published by

Bridge Publications, Inc.
1414 North Catalina Street
Los Angeles, CA 90027

ISBN-0-88404-269-3

This book is part of the works of L. Ron Hubbard, who developed
Dianetics™ spiritual healing technology. It is presented to the reader
as a record of observations and research into the human mind and
spirit, and not as a statement of claims made by the author. The
benefits and goals of Dianetics technology can be attained only by
the dedicated efforts of the reader.

The Hubbard™ Electrometer, or E-Meter, is a device sometimes used
in Dianetics technology. In itself, the E-Meter does nothing. It is not
intended or effective for the diagnosis, treatment or prevention of
any disease, or for the improvement of health
or any bodily function.

Dianetics™, Hubbard® and

are trademarks and service marks owned by
Religious Technology Center and used with its permission.

Printed in the United States of America

Dedicated
to
Will Durant

Important Note

In reading this book, be very certain you never go past a word you do not understand.

The only reason a person gives up a study or becomes confused or unable to learn is because he or she has gone past a word that was not understood.

The confusion or inability to grasp comes *after* a word was not understood. Have you ever had the experience of coming to the end of a page and realizing that you didn't know what you had read? Somewhere earlier on that page you passed a word that you didn't understand.

Here's an example. "It was found that when the crepuscule arrived the children were quieter and when it was not present, they were much livelier." You see what happens. You think you don't understand the whole idea, but the inability to understand came entirely from the one word you could not define, *crepuscule,* which means twilight or darkness.

If, in reading this book, the materials become confusing or you can't seem to grasp it, there will be a word just earlier that you haven't understood. Don't go any further, but go back to *before* you got into difficulty. Find the misunderstood word and get it defined.

Footnotes and Glossary

As an aid to the reader, words that are sometimes misunderstood have been defined in footnotes where they occur in the text. Words sometimes have several meanings. The footnote definitions given in this book only give the meaning that the word has as it is used in the text. A glossary including all the footnoted definitions is included at the back of this book. Other definitions can be found in various dictionaries.

Contents

"I AM ALWAYS HAPPY TO HEAR FROM MY READERS."

L. Ron Hubbard

These were the words of L. Ron Hubbard, who was always very interested in hearing from his friends, readers and followers. He made a point of staying in communication with everyone he came in contact with over his fifty-year career as a professional writer, and he had thousands of fans and friends that he corresponded with all over the world.

The publishers of L. Ron Hubbard's literary works wish to continue this tradition and would very much welcome letters and comments from you, his readers, both old and new.

Any message addressed to the Author's Affairs Director at Bridge Publications will be given prompt and full attention.

BRIDGE PUBLICATIONS, INC.
1414 North Catalina Street
Los Angeles, CA 90027

How to Read This Book

Dianetics is an adventure. It is an exploration into *terra incognita*,[1] the human mind, that vast and hitherto unknown realm half an inch back of our foreheads.

The discoveries and developments which made the formulation of Dianetics possible occupied many years of exact research and careful testing. This was exploration, it was also consolidation. The trail is blazed, the routes are sufficiently mapped for you to voyage in safety into your own mind and recover there your full inherent potential, which is not, we now know, low but very, very high.

As you progress in therapy, the adventure is yours to know *why* you did what you did when you did it, to know *what* caused those dark and unknown fears which came in nightmares as a child, to know *where* your moments of pain and pleasure lay. There is much which an individual does not know about himself, about his parents, about his "motives." Some of the things you will find may astonish you, for the most important data of your life may be not memory but engrams[2] in the hidden depths of your mind, not articulate[3] but only destructive.

---

1. *terra incognita:* an unknown land; a region or subject of which nothing is known.

2. engram: during moments when the conscious mind is suspended in operation—by injury, anesthesia, illness such as delirium—there is a more fundamental level still in operation, still recording; anything said to a man when he is unconscious from pain or shock is registered in its entirety; it then operates, on the return of consciousness, as a positive suggestion, with the additional menace of holding in the body the pain of the incident.

3. articulate: well formulated; clearly presented.

You will find many reasons why you "cannot get well" and you will know at length, when you find the dictating lines in the engrams, how amusing those reasons are, especially to you.

Dianetics is no solemn adventure. For all that it has to do with suffering and loss, its end is always laughter, so foolish, so misinterpreted were the things which caused the woe.

Your first voyage into your own *terra incognita* will be through the pages of this book. You will find as you read that many things "you always knew were so" are articulated here. You will be gratified to know that you held not opinions but scientific facts in many of your concepts of existence. You will find, too, many data that have long been known by all, and you will possibly consider them far from news and be prone to under-evaluate them: be assured that underevaluation of these facts kept them from being valuable, no matter how long they were known, for a fact is never important without a proper evaluation of it and its precise relationship to other facts. You are following here a vast network of facts which, reaching out, can be seen to embrace the whole field of man in all his works. Fortunately you do not have to concern yourself with following far any one of these lines until you are done. And then these horizons will stretch wide enough to satisfy anyone.

Dianetics is a large subject, but that is only because man is himself a large subject. The science of his thought cannot but embrace all his actions. By careful compartmenting and relating of data, the field has been kept narrow enough to be easily followed. Mostly this handbook will tell you, without any specific mention, about yourself and your family and friends, for you will meet them here and know them.

This volume has made no effort to use resounding or thunderous phrases, frowning polysyllables or professorial detachment. When one is delivering answers which are simple, he need not make the communication any more difficult than is necessary to convey the ideas. "Basic language" has been used, much of the nomenclature is colloquial; the pedantic has not only not been employed, it has also been ignored. This volume communicates to several strata of life and professions; the favorite nomenclatures of none have been observed since such a usage would impede the understanding of others. And so bear with us, psychiatrist, when your structure is not used, for we have no need for structure here; and bear with us, doctor, when we call a cold a cold and not a catarrhal[4] disorder of the respiratory tract. For this is, essentially, engineering, and these engineers are liable to say anything. And "scholar," you would not enjoy being burdened with the summation signs and the Lorentz-FitzGerald-Einstein equations,[5] so we shall not burden the less puristic reader with scientifically impossible Hegelian[6] grammar which insists that absolutes exist in fact.

The plan of the book might be represented as a cone which starts with simplicity and descends into wider application. This book follows, more or less, the actual steps of the development of Dianetics. First there was the dynamic principle of existence,[7] then its meaning,

---

4. catarrh: inflammation of a mucous membrane, especially of the nose or throat, causing an increased flow of mucous.

5. Lorentz-FitzGerald-Einstein equations: mathematical equations in the field of physics, developed by Albert Einstein, Hendrik Lorentz and George Francis FitzGerald.

6. Hegelian: after Hegel, Georg Wilhelm Friedrich: (1770–1831) German philosopher.

7. dynamic principle of existence: survival. The goal of life can be considered to be infinite survival. Man, as a life form, can be demonstrated to obey in all his actions and purposes the one command "Survive!" No behavior or activity has been found to exist without this principle. It is not new that life is surviving. It is new that life has as its entire dynamic urge *only* survival.

then the source of aberration,[8] and finally the application of all as therapy and the techniques of therapy. You won't find any of this very difficult. It was the originator who had the difficulty. You should have seen the first equations and postulates[9] of Dianetics! As research progressed and as the field developed, Dianetics began to simplify. That is a fair guarantee that one is on a straight trail of science. Only things which are poorly known become more complex the longer one works upon them.

It is suggested that you read straight on through. By the time you get into the appendix, you should have an excellent command of the subject. The book is arranged that way. Every fact related to Dianetic therapy is stated in several ways and is introduced again and again. In this way, the important facts have been pointed up to your attention. When you have finished the book you can come back to the beginning and look through it and study what you think you need to know.

Almost all the basic philosophy and certainly all the derivations of the master subject of Dianetics were excluded here, partly because this volume had to stay under half a million words and partly because they belong in a separate text where they can receive full justice. Nevertheless, you have the scope of the science with this volume in addition to therapy itself.

You are beginning an adventure. Treat it as an adventure. And may you never be the same again.

---

8. aberration: a departure from rational thought or behavior. Aberration is opposed to sanity, which would be its opposite.

9. postulate: something assumed to be true, especially as a basis for reasoning.

The Goal of Man

The Scope of Dianetics

A science of mind is a goal which has engrossed thousands of generations of man. Armies, dynasties and whole civilizations have perished for the lack of it. Rome went to dust for the want of it. China swims in blood for the need of it. And down in the arsenal is an atom bomb, its hopeful nose full-armed in ignorance of it.

No quest has been more relentlessly pursued or has been more violent. No primitive tribe, no matter how ignorant, has failed to recognize the problem as a problem, nor has it failed to bring forth at least an attempted formulation. Today one finds the aborigine of Australia substituting for a science of mind a "magic healing crystal." The shaman[1] of British Guiana makes shift for actual mental laws with his monotonous song and consecrated[2] cigar. The throbbing drum of the Goldi[3] medicine man serves in the stead of an adequate technique to alleviate the lack of serenity in patients.

The enlightened and Golden Age of Greece yet had but superstition in its principal sanataria[4] for mental ills, the Aesculapian[5] temple. The most the Roman could do for peace of mind for the sick was to appeal to the

---

1. shaman: a priest or witch doctor among certain peoples, claiming to have sole contact with the gods, etc.

2. consecrate: to set apart or declare as holy.

3. Goldi: a Mongoloid people of eastern Siberia.

4. sanitaria: plural of sanitarium: an establishment for treating chronic diseases.

5. Aesculapian: of or relating to medicine or the art of healing. (Aesculapius: *Roman mythology*. The god of medicine and healing.)

penates, the household divinities, or sacrifice to *Febris,* goddess of fevers. And an English king, centuries after, could have been found in the hands of exorcists who sought to cure his deliriums by driving the demons from him.

From the most ancient times to the present, in the crudest primitive tribe or the most magnificently ornamented civilization, man has found himself in a state of awed helplessness when confronted by the phenomena of strange illnesses or aberrations. His desperation, in his efforts to treat the individual, has been but slightly altered during his entire history; and until this twentieth century passed midterm, the percentages of his alleviations, in terms of individual mental derangements, compared evenly with the successes of the shamans confronted with the same problems. According to a modern writer, the single advance of psychotherapy was clean quarters for the madman. In terms of brutality in treatment of the insane, the methods of the shaman or Bedlam[6] have been far exceeded by the "civilized" techniques of destroying nerve tissues with the violence of shock and surgery—treatments which were not warranted by the results obtained and which would not have been tolerated in the meanest primitive society, since they reduce the victim to mere zombiism, destroying most of his personality and ambition and leaving him nothing more than a manageable animal. Far from an indictment of the practices of the "neurosurgeon" and the ice pick which he thrusts and twists into insane minds, they are brought forth only to demonstrate the depths of desperation man can reach when confronted with the seemingly unsolvable problem of deranged minds.

In the larger sphere of societies and nations, the lack

---

6. Bedlam: hospital of St. Mary of Bethlehem, London, an insane asylum.

of such a science of mind was never more evident; for the physical sciences, advancing thoughtlessly far in advance of man's ability to understand man, have armed him with terrible and thorough weapons which await only another outburst of the social insanity of war.

These problems are not mild ones; they lie across every man's path; they wait in company with his future. As long as man has recognized that his chief superiority over the animal kingdom was a thinking mind, so long as he understood that his mind alone was his weapon, he has searched and pondered and postulated in efforts to find a solution.

Like a jigsaw puzzle spilled by a careless hand, the equations which would lead to a science of the mind and, above that, to a master science of the universe, were stirred round and round. Sometimes two fragments would be united; sometimes, as in the case of the Golden Age of Greece, a whole section would be built. Philosopher, shaman, medicine man, mathematician: each looked at the pieces. Some saw they must all belong to different puzzles. Some thought they all belonged to the same puzzle. Some said there were really six puzzles in it, some said two. And the wars went on and the societies sickened or were dispersed, and learned tomes[7] were written about ever-increasing hordes of madmen.

With the methods of Bacon,[8] with the mathematics of Newton,[9] the physical sciences went on, consolidating and advancing their frontiers. And, like a derelict battalion, careless of how many allied ranks it exposed to destruction by the enemy, studies of the mind lagged behind.

---

7. tome: a large or scholarly book.

8. Bacon, Francis: (1561–1626) English philosopher and author.

9. Newton, Isaac: (1642–1727) English mathematician and astronomer. Discoverer of the law of gravitation.

But after all, there are just so many pieces in any puzzle. Before and after Francis Bacon, Herbert Spencer[10] and a very few more, many of the small sections had been put together, many honest facts had been observed.

To adventure into the thousands of variables of which that puzzle was composed, one had only to know right from wrong, true from false, and use all man and nature as his test tube.

Of what must a science of mind be composed?

1. An answer to the goal of thought.

2. A single source of all insanities, psychoses,[11] neuroses,[12] compulsions,[13] repressions[14] and social derangements.

3. Invariant scientific evidence as to the basic nature and functional background of the human mind.

4. Techniques, the art of application, by which the discovered single source could be invariably cured; ruling out, of course, the insanities of malformed, deleted or pathologically[15] injured brains or nervous systems and, particularly, iatrogenic psychoses (those caused by doctors and involving the destruction of the living brain itself).

5. Methods of prevention of mental derangement.

6. The cause and cure of all psychosomatic[16] ills,

---

10. Spencer, Herbert: (1820–1903) English philosopher. One of few modern thinkers to attempt a systematic account of all cosmic phenomena, including mental and social principles.

11. psychosis: any major form of mental affliction or disease.

12. neurosis: an emotional state containing conflicts and emotional data inhibiting the abilities or welfare of the individual.

13. compulsion: an irresistible impulse to act irrationally.

14. repression: a command that the organism must not do something.

15. pathological: of or concerned with a disease.

16. psychosomatic: *psycho* of course refers to mind and *somatic* refers to body; the term *psychosomatic* means the mind making the body ill or illnesses which have been created physically within the body by derangement of the mind.

which number, some say, 70 percent of man's listed ailments.

Such a science would exceed the severest terms previously laid down for it in any age, but any computation on the subject should discover that a science of mind ought to be able to be and do just these things.

A science of the mind, if it were truly worthy of that name, would have to rank, in experimental precision, with physics and chemistry. There could be no "special cases" to its laws. There could be no recourse to authority. The atom bomb bursts whether Einstein gives it permission or not. Laws native to nature regulate the bursting of that bomb. Technicians, applying techniques derived from discovered natural laws, can make one or a million atom bombs, all alike.

After the body of axioms and technique was organized and working as a science of mind, in rank with the physical sciences, it would be found to have points of agreement with almost every school of thought about thought which had ever existed. This is again a virtue and not a fault.

Simple though it is, Dianetics does and is these things:

1. It is an organized science of thought built on definite axioms (statements of natural laws on the order of those of the physical sciences).

2. It contains a therapeutic technique with which can be treated all inorganic mental ills and all organic psychosomatic ills, with assurance of complete cure in unselected cases.

3. It produces a condition of ability and rationality for man well in advance of the current norm, enhancing rather than destroying his vigor and personality.

4. Dianetics gives a complete insight into the full potentialities of the mind, discovering them to be well in excess of past supposition.

5. The basic nature of man is discovered in Dianetics rather than hazarded or postulated, since that basic nature can be brought into action in any individual completely. And that basic nature is discovered to be *good*.

6. The single source of mental derangement is discovered and demonstrated, on a clinical or laboratory basis, by Dianetics.

7. The extent, storage capacity and recallability of the human memory is finally established by Dianetics.

8. The full recording abilities of the mind are discovered by Dianetics with the conclusion that they are quite dissimilar to former suppositions.

9. Dianetics brings forth the nongerm theory of disease, complementing biochemistry[17] and Pasteur's[18] work on the germ theory to embrace the field.

10. With Dianetics ends the "necessity" of destroying the brain by shock or surgery to effect "tractability"[19] in mental patients and "adjust" them.

11. A workable explanation of the physiological effects of drugs and endocrine[20] substances exists in Dianetics, and many problems posed by endocrinology are answered.

12. Various educational, sociological, political, military and other human studies are enhanced by Dianetics.

---

17. biochemistry: the chemistry of living organisms.

18. Pasteur, Louis: (1822–95) French chemist and bacteriologist. Proved that decay and putrefaction are caused by bacteria; developed serums and vaccines for such diseases as cholera and rabies.

19. tractable: easy to manage or deal with; docile.

20. endocrine: designating or of any gland producing one or more internal secretions that are introduced directly into the bloodstream and carried to other parts of the body whose functions they regulate or control.

13. The field of cytology[21] is aided by Dianetics, as well as other fields of research.

This, then, is a skeletal sketch of what would be the scope of a science of mind and of what is the scope of Dianetics.

---

21. cytology: the scientific study of cells.

CHAPTER TWO

The Clear

Dianetically, the optimum individual is called the *clear*. One will hear much of that word, both as a noun and a verb, in this volume, so it is well to spend time here at the outset setting forth exactly what can be called a *clear*, the goal of Dianetic therapy.

A *clear* can be tested for any and all psychoses, neuroses, compulsions and repressions (all aberrations) and can be examined for any autogenetic (self-generated) diseases referred to as psychosomatic ills. These tests confirm the *clear* to be entirely without such ills or aberrations. Additional tests of his intelligence indicate it to be high above the current norm. Observation of his activity demonstrates that he pursues existence with vigor and satisfaction.

Further, these results can be obtained on a comparative basis. A neurotic individual, possessed also of psychosomatic ills, can be tested for those aberrations and illnesses, demonstrating that they exist. He can then be given Dianetic therapy to the end of clearing these neuroses and ills. Finally, he can be examined, with the above results. This, in passing, is an experiment which has been performed many times with invariable results. It is a matter of laboratory test that all individuals who have organically complete nervous systems respond in this fashion to Dianetic clearing.

Further, the clear possesses attributes, fundamental and inherent but not always available in an uncleared state, which have not been suspected of man and are not included in past discussions of his abilities and behavior.

First there is the matter of perceptions. Even so-called normal people do not always see in full color, hear in full tone or sense at the optimum with their organs of smell, taste, tactile[1] and organic sensation.

These are the main lines of communication to the finite world which most people recognize as reality. It is an interesting commentary that while past observers felt that the facing of reality was an absolute necessity if the aberrated individual wished to be sane, no definition of how this was to be done was set forth. To face reality in the present, one would certainly have to be able to sense it along those channels of communication most commonly used by man in his affairs.

Any one of man's perceptions can be aberrated by psychic[2] derangements which refuse to permit the received sensations to be realized by the analytical portion of the individual's mind. In other words, while there may be nothing wrong with the mechanisms of color reception, circuits can exist in the mind which delete color before the consciousness is permitted to see the object. Colorblindness can be discovered to be relative or in degrees in such a way that colors appear to be less brilliant, dull or, at the maximum, entirely absent. Anyone is acquainted with persons to whom "loud" colors are detestable and with persons who find them insufficiently "loud" to notice. This varying degree of colorblindness has not been recognized as a psychic factor but has been nebulously assumed to be some sort of a condition of mind when it was noticed at all.

There are those persons to whom noises are quite disturbing, to whom, for instance, the insistent whine of a violin is very like having a brace and bit[3] applied to the

---

1. tactile: of or using the sense of touch.

2. psychic: of the soul or mind.

3. brace and bit: a tool for boring, consisting of a removable drill (bit) in a rotating handle (brace).

eardrum; and there are those to whom fifty violins, played loudly, would be soothing; and there are those who, in the presence of a violin, express disinterest and boredom; and, again, there are persons to whom the sound of a violin, no matter if it be playing the most intricate melody, is a monotone. These differences of sonic (hearing) perception have, like color and other visual errors, been attributed to inherent nature or organic deficiency or assigned no place at all.

In a like manner, from person to person, smells, tactile sensations, organic perceptions, pain and gravity vary widely and wildly. A cursory check around amongst his friends will demonstrate to a man that there exist enormous differences of perception of identical stimuli.[4] One smells a turkey in the oven as wonderful, one smells it with indifference, another may not smell it at all. And somebody else may maintain that roasting turkey smells exactly like hair oil—to be extreme.

Until we obtain *clears* it remains obscure why such differences should exist. For in the largest measure, such wild quality and quantity of perception is due to aberration. Because of pleasurable experiences in the past and inherent sensitivity, there will be some difference amongst clears; and a clear response should not be assumed automatically to be a standardized, adjusted middle ground, that pallid[5] and obnoxious goal of past doctrines. The clear gets a maximum response compatible with his own desire for the response. Burning cordite[6] still smells dangerous to him, but it does not make him ill. Roasting turkey smells good to him if he is

---

4. stimuli: plural of stimulus: something that rouses a person or thing into activity or energy or that produces a reaction in an organ or tissue of the body.

5. pallid: faint in color; pale.

6. cordite: a smokeless explosive used as a propellant in bullets and shells.

hungry and likes turkey, at which time it smells very, very good. Violins play melodies, not monotones, bring no pain and are enjoyed to a fine, full limit if the clear likes violins as a matter of taste—if he doesn't, he likes kettledrums, saxophones or, indeed, suiting his mood, no music at all.

In other words, there are two variables at work. One, the wildest, is the variable caused by aberrations. The other, and quite rational and understandable, is caused by the personality.

Thus, the perceptions of an aberree (noncleared individual) vary greatly from those of the cleared (unaberrated) individual.

Now there are the differences of the actual organs of perception and the errors occasioned by these. Some of these errors, a minimum, are organic: punctured eardrums are not competent sound-recording mechanisms. The majority of perceptic (sense message) errors in the organic sphere are caused by psychosomatic errors.

Glasses are seen on noses everywhere around, even on children. The majority of these spectacles are perched on the face in an effort to correct a condition which the body itself is fighting to uncorrect again. Eyesight, when the stage of glasses is entered (not because of glasses), is deteriorating on the psychosomatic principle. And this observation is about as irresponsible as a statement that when apples fall out of trees they usually obey gravity. One of the incidental things which happen to a clear is that his eyesight, if it had been bad as an aberree, generally improves markedly, and with some slight attention will recover optimum perception in time. (Far from an optician's argument against Dianetics, this assures rather good business, for clears have been known, at treatment's end, to have to buy, in rapid succession, five pairs of glasses to compensate adjusting eyesight; and many aberrees, cleared late in life, settle down ocularly[7] at a maximum a little under optimum.)

The eyesight was reduced in the aberree on an organic basis by his aberrations so that the perceptic organ itself was reduced from optimum operating function. With the removal of aberrations, repeated tests have proven that the body makes a valiant effort to reconstruct back to optimum.

Hearing, in addition to other perceptics, varies organically over a wide range. Calcium deposits, for instance, can make the ears "ring" incessantly. The removal of aberrations permits the body to readjust toward its reachable optimum; the calcium deposit disappears, and the ears stop ringing. But far and beyond this very specific case, there are great differences in hearing on the organic basis. Organically, as well as aberrationally, hearing can become remarkably extended or closely inhibited so that one person may hear footsteps a block away as a normal activity and another would not hear a bass drum thundering on the porch.

That the various perceptions differ widely from individual to individual on an aberrational and psychosomatic basis is the least of the discoveries outlined here. Ability to recall is far more fantastic in its variation from person to person.

An entirely new recall process which was inherent in the mind but which had not been noticed came to light in the process of observing clears and aberrees. This recall process is possible in only a small proportion of aberrees in its fullest sense. It is standard, however, in a clear. Naturally, no intimation is made here that the scholars of past ages have been unobservant. We are dealing here with an entirely new and hitherto nonexistent object of inspection, the *clear*. What a clear can do easily, quite a few people have, from time to time,

---

7. ocular: of or relating to the sense of sight.

been partially able to do in the past.

An inherent, not a taught, ability of the remembering mechanisms of the mind can be termed, as a technical word of Dianetics, *returning*. It is used in its dictionary sense, with the addition of the fact that the mind has it as a normal remembering function, as follows: the person can "send" a portion of his mind to a past period on either a mental or combined mental and physical basis and can reexperience incidents which have taken place in his past in the same fashion and with the same sensations as before. Once upon a time, an art known as hypnotism used what was called "regression" on hypnotized subjects, the hypnotist sending the subject back, in one of two ways, to incidents in his past. This was done with trance techniques, drugs and considerable technology. The hypnotic subject could be sent back to a moment "entirely" so that he gave every appearance of being the age to which he was returned with only the apparent faculties and recollections he had at that moment: this was called *revivification* (reliving). *Regression* was a technique by which part of the individual's self remained in the present and part went back to the past. These abilities of the mind were supposed native only in hypnotism and were used only in hypnotic technique. The art is very old, tracing back some thousands of years and existing today in Asia as it has existed, apparently, from the dawn of time.

Returning is substituted for *regression* here because it is not a comparable thing and because *regression*, as a word, has some bad meanings which would interrupt its use. *Reliving* is substituted for *revivification* in Dianetics because, in Dianetics, the principles of hypnotism can be found explained and hypnotism is not used in Dianetic therapy, as will be explained later.

The mind, then, has another ability to remember. Part of the mind can "return" even when a person is wide-awake and reexperience past incidents in full. If you want to test this, try it on several people until one is discovered who does it easily. Wide-awake, he can "return" to moments in his past. Until asked to do so, he probably will not know he has such an ability. If he had it, he probably thought everybody could do it (the type of supposition which has kept so much of this data from coming to light before). He can go back to a time when he was swimming and swim with full recall of hearing, sight, taste, smell, organic sensation, tactile, etc.

A "learned" gentleman once spent some hours demonstrating to a gathering that the recall of a smell as a sensation, for instance, was quite impossible since "neurology had proven that the olfactory[8] nerves were not connected to the thalamus."[9] Two people in the gathering discovered this ability to *return* and despite this evidence, the learned gentleman continued the dispute that olfactory recall was impossible. A check amongst the gathering on this faculty, independent of returning, brought forth the fact that one-half of those present remembered smell by smelling it again.

Returning is the full performance of imagery recall. The entire memory is able to make the organ areas resense the stimuli in a past incident. Partial recall is common, not common enough to be normal, but certainly common enough to have merited considerable study. For it, again, is a wide variable.

Perception of the present would be one method of facing reality. But if one cannot face the reality of the past, then, in some part, he is not facing some portion of reality. And if it is agreed that facing reality is desirable, then one would have to face yesterday's reality as well if

---

8. olfactory: of or relating to the sense of smell.

9. thalamus: the interior region of the brain where sensory nerves originate.

he were to be considered entirely "sane" by contemporary definition. To "face yesterday" requires a certain condition of recall to be available. One would have to be able to remember. But how many ways are there of remembering?

First there is the *return*. That is new. It gives the advantage of examining the moving pictures and other sense perceptions recorded at the time of the event with all senses present. He can also return to his past conclusions and imaginings. It is of considerable aid in learning, in research, in ordinary living, to be able to be again at the place where the data desired was first inspected.

Then there are the more usual recalls. Optimum recall is by the *return* method of single or multiple senses, the individual himself remaining in present time.[10] In other words, some people, when they think of a rose, see one, smell one, feel one. They see in full color, vividly —with the "mind's eye" to use an old colloquialism. They smell it vividly. And they can feel it even to the thorns. They are thinking about roses by actually recalling a rose.

These people, thinking about a ship, would see a specific ship, feel the motion of her if they thought of being aboard her, smell the pine tar or even less savory odors and hear whatever sounds there were about her. They would see the ship in full color-motion and hear it in full tone-audio.

These faculties vary widely in the aberree. Some, when told to think of a rose, can merely visualize one. Some can smell one but not see it. Some see it without

---

10. present time: the *time* which is now and becomes the past as rapidly as it is observed. It is a term loosely applied to the environment existing in now. When we say someone should be in *present time* we mean he should be in communication with his environment. We mean, further, that he should be in communication with his environment as it exists, not as it existed.

color or in very pale color. When told to think of a ship some aberrees only see a flat, colorless, still picture, such as a painting of a ship or the photograph of one. Some perceive a vessel in motion without color but with sound. Some hear the sound of a ship but fail to see any picture whatever. Some merely think of a ship as a concept that ships exist and that they know about them, and fail to see, feel, hear, smell or otherwise sense anything on a recall basis.

Some past observers have called this "imagery" but the term is so inapplicable to sound and touch, organic sensation and pain that *recall* is used uniformly as the technical Dianetic term. The value of *recall* in this business of living has occupied such scant attention that the entire concept has never been formulated previously. It is therefore detailed at some length here, as above.

It is quite simple to test recalls. If one will ask his fellows what *their* abilities are, he will gain a remarkable idea of how widely varied this ability is from individual to individual. Some have this recall, some have that, some have none but operate on concepts of recall only. And remember, if you make a test on those around you, that any perception is filed in the memory and therefore has a recall which is to include pain, temperature, rhythm, taste and weight with the above-mentioned sight, sound, tactile and smell.

The Dianetic names for these recalls are *visio* (sight), *sonic* (sound), *tactile* (touch), *olfactory* (smell), *rhythmic*, *kinesthetic* (weight and motion), *somatic* (pain), *thermal* (temperature) and *organic* (internal sensations and, by new definition, emotion).

Then there is another set of mental activities which can be summated under the headings of *imagination* and *creative imagination*. Here again is abundant material for testing.

Imagination is the recombination of things one has

sensed, thought or intellectually computed into existence, which do not necessarily have existence. This is the mind's method of envisioning desirable goals or forecasting futures. Imagination is extremely valuable as a part of essential solutions in any mental problem and in everyday existence. That it is recombination in no sense deprives it of its vast and wonderful complexity.

A clear uses imagination in its entirety. There is an imagination impression for sight, smell, taste, sound—in short, for each one of the possible perceptions. These are manufactured impressions on the basis of models in the memory banks combined by conceptual ideas and construction. New physical structures, tomorrow in terms of today, next year in terms of last year, pleasure to be gained, deeds to be done, accidents to avoid: all these are imaginational functions.

The clear has full color-visio, tone-sonic, tactile, olfactory, rhythmic, kinesthetic, thermal and organic imagination in kind.[11] Asked to envision himself riding in a gilded coach-and-four,[12] he "sees" the equipage, moving, in full color, he "hears" all the noises which should be present, he "smells" the smells he thinks should be there and he "feels" the upholstery, the motion and the presence in the coach of himself.

In addition to standard imagination there is *creative imagination.* This is a very wide undimensional ability, quite variable from individual to individual, possessed in enormous quantity by some. It is included here, not as a portion of the operation of the mind treated as a usual part of Dianetics, but to isolate it as an existing entity. In a clear who possessed *creative imagination,* even if inhibited as an aberree, it is present and demonstrable. It is inherent. It can be aberrated only by prohibition

---

11. in kind: in the same manner or with something equivalent.
12. coach-and-four: a coach pulled by four horses.

of its general practice, which is to say, by aberrating the persistence in its application or encysting[13] the whole mind. But creative imagination, that possession by which works of art are done, states built and man enriched, can be envisioned as a special function, independent in operation and in no way dependent for its existence upon an aberrated condition in the individual, since the examination of its activity in and use by a clear possessing it adequately demonstrates its inherent character. It is rarely absent in any individual.

Finally, there is the last but most important activity of the mind. Man is to be regarded as a sentient being. His sentience depends upon his ability to resolve problems by perceiving or creating and understanding situations. This rationality is the primary, high-echelon function of that part of the mind which makes him a man, not just another animal. Remembering, perceiving, imagining, he has the signal[14] ability of resolving conclusions and of using conclusions resolved to resolve further conclusions. This is rational man.

Rationality, as divorced from aberration, can be studied in a cleared person only. The aberrations of the aberree give him the appearance of irrationality. Though such irrationality may be given the gentler names of "eccentricity" or "human error" or even "personal idiosyncrasy," it is, nevertheless, irrationality. The personality does not depend upon how irrationally a man may act. It is not a personality trait, for instance, to drive while drunk and kill a child on a crosswalk—or even to risk killing a child by driving while drunk. Irrationality is simply that—the inability to get right answers from data.

Now, it is a curious thing that although "everybody

---

13. encyst: to enclose in or as if in a cyst or sac.

14. signal: not average or ordinary; remarkable; notable.

knows" (and what a horrible amount of misinformation *that* statement lets circulate) it is "human to err," the sentient portion of the mind, which computes the answers to problems and which makes man man, is *utterly incapable of error.*

This was a startling discovery when it was made, but it need not have been. It could have been deduced some time before. For it is quite simple and easy to understand. The actual computing ability of man is never in error even in a very severely aberrated person. Observing the activity of such an aberrated person, one might thoughtlessly suppose that that person's computations were wrong. But that would be an observer error. Any person, aberrated or clear, computes perfectly *on the data stored and perceived.*

Take any common calculating machine (and the mind is an exceptionally magnificent instrument far, far superior to any machine it will invent for ages to come) and put a problem on it for solution. Multiply seven times one. It will answer, properly, seven. Now multiply six times one but continue to hold down the seven. Six times one is six but the answer you will get is forty-two. Continue to hold down seven and put other problems on the machine. They are wrong, not as problems, but as answers. Now fix seven so that it stays down no matter what keys are touched and try to give the machine away. Nobody will want it because, obviously, the machine is crazy. It says ten times ten is seven hundred. But is the calculating portion of the machine really wrong or is it merely being fed the wrong data?

In the same way, the human mind, being called upon to resolve problems of a magnitude and with enough variables to confound any mere calculating machine a thousand times an hour, is prey to incorrect data. Incorrect data gets into the machine. The machine gives wrong answers. Incorrect data enters the human memory banks, the person reacts in an "abnormal manner." Essentially, then, the problem of resolving aberration is the problem of finding a "held-down seven." But of that, much, much more later. Right now we have accomplished our immediate ends.

These are the various abilities and activities of the human mind in its constant task of resolving and putting into solution a multitude of problems. It perceives, it recalls or returns, it imagines, it conceives and then resolves. Served by its extensions—the perceptics and the memory banks and the imaginations—the mind brings forth answers which are invariably accurate, the solutions modified only by observation, education and viewpoint.

And the basic purposes of that mind and the basic nature of man, as discoverable in the clear, are constructive and good, uniformly constructive and uniformly good, modified only by observation, education and viewpoint.

Man is good.

Take away his basic aberrations and with them go the evil of which the scholastic and the moralist were so fond. The only detachable portion of him is the "evil" portion. And when it is detached, his personality and vigor intensify. And he is glad to see the "evil" portion go because it was *physical pain*.

Later there are experiments and proofs for these things and they can be measured with the precision so dear to the heart of the physical scientist.

The clear, then, is not an "adjusted" person, driven to activity by his repressions now thoroughly encysted. He is an unrepressed person, operating on self-determinism.[15]

---

15. self-determinism: is the state wherein the individual can or cannot be controlled by his environment according to his own choice. He is confident in his interpersonal relationships. He reasons but does not need to react.

And his abilities to perceive, recall, return, imagine, create and compute are outlined as we have seen.

The clear is the goal in Dianetic therapy, a goal which some patience and a little study and work can bring about. Any person can be cleared unless he has been so unfortunate as to have had a large portion of his brain removed or to have been born with a grossly malformed nervous structure.

We have seen the goal of Dianetics here. Let us now inspect the goal of man.

CHAPTER THREE

The Goal of Man

The goal of man, the lowest common denominator of all his activities, the dynamic principle of his existence, has long been sought. Should such an answer be discovered, it is inevitable that from it many answers would flow. It would explain all phenomena of behavior; it would lead toward a solution of man's major problems; and, most of all, it should be workable.

Consider all knowledge to fall above or below a line of demarcation. Everything above this line is not necessary to the solution of man's aberrations and general shortcomings and is inexactly known. Such a field of thought could be considered to embrace such things as metaphysics[1] and mysticism.[2] Below this line of demarcation could be considered to lie the finite universe. All things in the finite universe, whether known or as yet unknown, can be sensed, experienced or measured. The known data in the finite universe can be classified as *scientific truth* when it has been sensed, experienced and measured. All factors necessary to the resolution of a science of the mind were found within the finite universe and were discovered, sensed, measured and experienced and became scientific truth. The finite universe contains **time, space, energy** and **life.** No other factors were found necessary in the equation.

---

1. metaphysics: a branch of philosophy that deals with the nature of existence and of truth and knowledge.

2. mysticism: any doctrine that asserts the possibility of attaining knowledge of spiritual truths through intuition acquired by fixed meditation.

Time, space, energy and life have a single denominator in common. As an analogy it could be considered that time, space, energy and life began at some point of origin and were commanded to continue to some nearly infinite destination. They were told nothing but *what* to do. They obey a single order and that order is "Survive!"

The Dynamic Principle of Existence Is Survival

The goal of life can be considered to be infinite survival. Man, as a life form, can be demonstrated to obey in all his actions and purposes the one command: "Survive!"

It is not a new thought that man is surviving. It is a new thought that man is motivated *only* by survival.

That his single goal is survival does not mean that he is the optimum survival mechanism which life has attained or will develop. The goal of the dinosaur was also survival and the dinosaur isn't extant anymore.

Obedience to this command, "Survive!" does not mean that every attempt to obey is uniformly successful. Changing environment, mutation and many other things militate[3] against any one organism attaining infallible survival techniques or form.

Life forms change and die as new life forms develop just as surely as one life organism, lacking immortality in itself, creates other life organisms, then dies as itself. An excellent method, should one wish to cause life to survive over a very long period, would be to establish means by which it could assume many forms, and death

---

3. militate: to be directed (*against*); operate or work (*against* or, rarely, *for*): said of facts, evidence, actions, etc.

itself would be necessary in order to facilitate the survival of the life force itself, since only death and decay could clear away older forms when new changes in the environment necessitated new forms. Life, as a force, existing over a nearly infinite period, would need a cyclic aspect in its unit organisms and forms.

What would be the optimum survival characteristics of various life forms? They would have to have various fundamental characteristics, differing from one species to the next just as one environment differs from the next.

This is important, since it has been but poorly considered in the past that a set of survival characteristics in one species would not be survival characteristics in another.

The methods of survival can be summed under the headings of food, protection (defensive and offensive) and procreation.[4] There are no existing life forms which lack solutions to these problems. Every life form errs, one way or another, by holding a characteristic too long or developing characteristics which may lead to its extinction. But the developments which bring about successfulness of form are far more striking than their errors. The naturalist and biologist are continually resolving the characteristics of this or that life form by discovering that need rather than whim governs such developments. The hinges of the clam shell, the awesome face on the wings of the butterfly, have survival value.

Once survival was isolated as the only dynamic[5] of a life form which would explain all its activities, it was

---

4. procreate: to bring (a living thing) into existence by the natural process of reproduction.

5. dynamic: the tenacity to life and vigor and persistence in survival.

In order to establish nomenclature in Dianetics which would not be too complex for the purpose, words normally considered as adjectives or verbs have occasionally been pressed into service as nouns. This has

30

necessary to study further the action of survival. And it was discovered that when one considered pain and pleasure, he had at hand all the necessary ingredients with which to formulate the action life takes in its effort to survive.

As will be seen in the accompanying graph, a spectrum of life has been conceived to span from the zero of death or extinction toward the infinity of potential immortality. This spectrum was considered to contain an infinity of lines, extending ladderlike toward the potential of immortality. Each line as the ladder mounted was spaced a little wider than the last, in a geometric progression.

The thrust of survival is away from death and toward immortality. The ultimate pain could be conceived as existing just before death and the ultimate pleasure could be conceived as immortality.

Immortality could be said to have an attractive type of force and death a repelling force in the consideration of the unit organism or the species. But as survival rises higher and higher toward immortality, wider and wider spaces are encountered until the gaps are finitely impossible to bridge. The urge is away from death, which has a repelling force, and toward immortality, which has an attracting force; the attracting force is pleasure, the repelling force is pain.

For the individual, the length of the arrow could be

---

been done on the valid principle that existing terminology, meaning so many different things, could not be used by Dianetics without making it necessary to explain away an old meaning to bring forth a new. To remove the step of explaining the old meaning and saying then that one doesn't mean *that*, thus entangling our communications inextricably, and to obviate the ancient custom of compounding ponderous and thundering syllables from the Greek and Roman tongues, this principle and some others have been adopted for nomenclature. *Dynamic* is here used as a noun and will so continue to be used throughout this volume. *Somatic, perceptic* and some others will be noted, defined when used.

Descriptic Graph of Survival

POTENTIAL IMMORTALITY—ULTIMATE PLEASURE

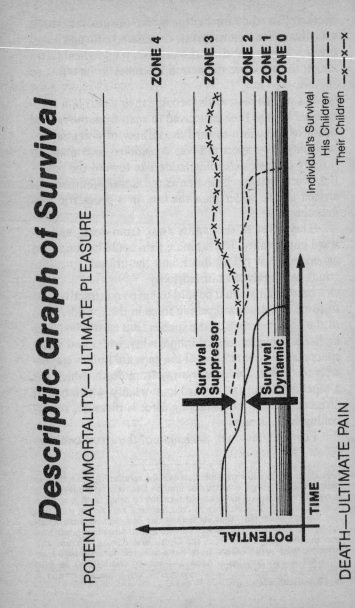

ZONE 4

ZONE 3

ZONE 2
ZONE 1
ZONE 0

Survival Suppressor

Survival Dynamic

Individual's Survival ——————
His Children — — — — —
Their Children —x—x—x—

POTENTIAL

TIME

DEATH—ULTIMATE PAIN

considered to be at a high potential within the fourth zone. Here the survival potential would be excellent and the individual would enjoy existence.

From left to right could be graphed the years.

The urge toward pleasure is dynamic. Pleasure is the reward, and the seeking of the reward—survival goals—would be a pleasurable act. And to ensure that survival is accomplished under the mandate **Survive!** it seems to have been provided that reduction from a high potential would bring pain.

Pain is provided to repel the individual from death, pleasure is provided to call him toward optimum life. *The search for and the attainment of pleasure is not less valid in survival than the avoidance of pain.* In fact, on some observed evidence, pleasure seems to have a much greater value in the cosmic scheme than pain.

Now, it would be well to define what is meant by *pleasure,* aside from its connection with immortality. The dictionary states that pleasure is "gratification; agreeable emotions, mental or physical; transient enjoyment; opposed to pain." Pleasure can be found in so many things and activities that a catalogue of all the things and activities man has, does and may consider pleasurable alone could round out the definition.

And what do we mean by *pain?* The dictionary states: "physical or mental suffering; penalty."

These two definitions, in passing, are demonstrative of an intuitive type of thought which runs through the language. Once one has a thing which leads to the resolution of hitherto unsolved problems, even the dictionaries are found to have "always known it."

If we wished to make this graph for a life-form cycle, it would be identical except that the value of the years would be increased to measure eons. For there is no difference, it seems, except magnitude, in the scope of the individual and the scope of the species. This inference could be drawn even without such remarkable evidence as the fact that a human being, growing from zygote[6] to adult, evolutes through all the forms which the whole species is supposed to have evolved through.

Now, there is more in this graph than has been remarked as yet. The physical and mental state of the individual varies from hour to hour, day to day, year to year. Therefore, the level of survival would form either a daily curve or the curve of a life on a measure of hourly or yearly position in the zones. And there would be two curves made possible by this, the physical curve and the mental curve. When we get toward the back of the book, the relationships between these two curves will be found vital and it will also be seen that, ordinarily, a sag in the mental curve will precede a sag in the physical curve.

The zones, then, can apply to two things: the physical being and the mental being. Therefore, these four zones can be called zones of the states of being. If a person is happy mentally, the survival level can be placed in zone 4. If the person is extremely ill physically, he might be plotted, on estimation of his illness, in zone 1 or close to death.

Very unprecise, but nevertheless descriptive, names have been assigned to these zones. Zone 3 is one of general happiness and well-being. Zone 2 is a level of bearable existence. Zone 1 is one of anger. Zone 0 is the zone of apathy. These zones can be used as a tone scale[7] by which a state of mind can be graded. Just above death, which is 0, would be the lowest mental apathy or lowest level of physical life, 0.1. A tone 1, where the body is fighting physical pain or illness or where the

---

6. zygote: the first cell of a new individual.
7. tone scale: a scale which shows the emotional tones of a person. These, ranged from the highest to the lowest, are, in part, serenity (the highest level), enthusiasm (as we proceeded downward), conservatism, boredom, antagonism, anger, covert hostility, fear, grief, apathy.

being is fighting in anger, could be graded from 1.0, which would be resentment or hostility, through tone 1.5, which would be a screaming rage, to a 1.9, which would be merely a quarrelsome inclination. From tone 2.0 to tone 3.0 there would be an increasing interest in existence, and so forth.

It so happens that the state of physical being or mental being does not long remain static. Therefore, there are various fluctuations. In the course of a single day an aberree may run from 0.5 to 3.5, up and down, as a mental being. An accident or illness could cause a similar fluctuation in a day.

These are, then, figures which can be assigned to four things: the mental state on an acute basis and the mental state on a general, average basis, and the physical being on an acute basis and the physical being on a general basis. In Dianetics, we do not much employ the physical tone scale. The mental tone scale, however, is of vast and vital importance!

These values of happiness, bearable existence, anger and apathy are not arbitrary values. They are deduced from observation of the behavior of emotional states. A clear is usually found varying around tone 4, plus or minus, in an average day. He is a general tone 4, which is one of the inherent conditions of being clear. A norm in current society, at a wild guess, is probably around a general tone 2.8.

In this descriptive graph, which is two-dimensional, the vital data for the solution of the problem of the life dynamic are workably combined. The horizontal lines are in terms of geometric progression beginning with the zero line immediately above death. There are ten lines for each zone and each zone denotes a mental or physical state of being, as noted. Geometric progression, so used, leaves ever-increasing spaces between the lines. The width of this space is the survival potential existing at the moment the top point of the survival dynamic arrow is within that space. The further away from death the top point of the survival dynamic arrow is, the better chance the individual has of survival. Geometric progression reaches up toward the impossible of infinity and cannot, of course, reach infinity. The organism is surviving through time from left to right. Survival optimum—immortality—lies in terms of time to the right. Potential only is measured vertically.

The *survival dynamic* actually resides within the organism as inherited from the species. The organism is part of the species as a railroad tie might be said to be part of a railroad as seen by an observer on a train, the observer being always in now—although this analogy is not perhaps the best.

Within itself the organism possesses a repulsive force toward pain sources. The source of the pain is not a driving force any more than the thorn bush which tears the hand was a driving force; the organism repulses the potential pain of a thorn.

At the same time the organism has at work a force which attracts it to the sources of pleasure. Pleasure does not magnetize the organism into drawing near. It is the organism which possesses the attraction force. It is inherent.

The repulsion of pain sources adds to the attraction for pleasure sources to operate as a combined thrust away from death and toward immortality. The thrust away from death is no more powerful than the thrust toward immortality. In other words, in terms of the survival dynamic, pleasure has as much validity as pain.

It should not be read here that survival is always a matter of keeping an eye on the future. Contemplation of pleasure, pure enjoyment, contemplation of past pleasures: all combine into harmonies which, while they operate automatically as a rise toward the survival potential, by their action within the organism physically, do not demand the future as an active portion of the mental computation in such contemplation.

A pleasure which reacts to injure the body physically, as in the case of debauchery,[8] discovers at work a ratio between the physical effect (which is depressed toward pain) and the mental effect of experienced pleasure. There is a consequent lowering of the survival dynamic. Averaging out, the future possibility of strain because of the act, added to the state of being at the moment the debauchery was experienced, again depresses the survival dynamic. Because of this, various kinds of debauchery have been in indifferent odor[9] with man throughout his history. This is the equation of "immoral pleasures." And any action which has brought about survival suppression or which can bring it about, when pursued as a pleasure, has been denounced at some time or another in man's history. Immorality is originally hung as a label upon some act or class of actions because they depress the level of the survival dynamic. Future enforcement of moral stigma[10] may depend largely upon prejudice and aberration and there is, consequently, a continuous quarrel over what is *moral* and what is *immoral*.

Because certain things practiced as pleasures are actually pains—and how easy it will be to trace out why when you've finished this volume—and because of the *moral equation* as above, pleasure itself, in any aberrated society, can become decried. A certain kind of thinking, of which more later, permits poor differentiation between one object and another. Confusing a dishonest

---

8. debauchery: indulgence in harmful or immoral pleasures.

9. odor: repute; esteem.

10. stigma: a mark of shame, a stain on a person's good reputation.

politician with all politicians would be an example of this. In ancient times, the Roman was fond of his pleasures and some of the things he called pleasure were a trifle strenuous on other species, such as Christians. When the Christian overthrew the pagan[11] state, the ancient order of Rome was in a villain's role. Anything, therefore, which was Roman was villainous. This went to such remarkable lengths that the Roman love of bathing made bathing so immoral that Europe went unwashed for some fifteen hundred years. The Roman had become a pain source so general that everything Roman was *evil* and it stayed evil long after Roman paganism perished. Immorality, in such a fashion, tends to become an involved subject. In this case it became so involved that pleasure itself was stigmatized.

When half the survival potential is struck from the list of lawful things, there is a considerable reduction in survival indeed. Considering this graph on a racial scale, the reduction of survival potential by one-half would forecast that direful things lay in wait for the race. Actually, because man is after all man, no set of laws, however enforced, can completely wipe away the attraction of pleasure. But in this case enough *was* removed and banned to occasion precisely what happened: the Dark Ages and the recession of society. Society brightened only in those periods such as the Renaissance, in which pleasure became less unlawful.

When a race or an individual drops into the second zone, as marked on the chart, and the general tone ranges from the first zone barely into the third, a condition of insanity ensues. Insanity is irrationality. It is also a state in which nonsurvival has been so closely approached continually that the race or the organism engages in all manner of wild solutions.

---

11. pagan: not Christian, Moslem or Jewish.

In further interpretation of this descriptic graph there is the matter of the *survival suppressor*. This, it will be seen, is a thrust downward out of potential immortality at the race or organism represented as the *survival dynamic*. The survival suppressor is the combined and variable threats to the survival of the race or organism. These threats come from other species, from time, from other energies. These are also engaged in the contest of survival to potential immortality in terms of their own species or identities. Thus there is a conflict involved. Every other form of life or energy could be plotted in a descriptic as the *survival dynamic*. If we were to use a duck's survival dynamic in a descriptic graph, we would see the duck seeking a high survival level and man would be a part of the duck's *suppressor*.

The balance and nature of things do not permit the infinity of the goal of immortality to be reached. In fluctuating balance and in almost unlimited complexity, life and energies ebb and flood, out of the nebulous, into forms and, through decay, into the nebulous once more.[12] Many equations could be drawn concerning this, but it is outside the sphere of our present interest.

In terms of the zones of the descriptic, it is of relative concern what the extent of the force of the suppressor is against the survival dynamic. The dynamic is inherent in individuals, groups and races, evolved to resist the suppressor through the eons. In the case of man, he carries with him another level of offensive and defensive techniques, his cultures. His primary technology of survival is mental activity governing physical action in the sentient echelon. But every life form has its own technology, formed to resolve the problems of food, protection and procreation. The degree of workability of the technology any life form develops (armor or

---

12. The Veda; also Lucretius' *Nature of Things*.

brains, fleetness of foot or deceptive form) is a direct index of the survival potential, the relative immortality, of that form. There have been vast upsets in the past; man, when he developed into the world's most dangerous animal (he can and does kill or enslave any life form, doesn't he?), overloaded the suppressor on many other life forms and they dwindled in number or vanished.

A great climatic change, such as the one which packed so many mammoths in Siberian ice, may overload the suppressor on a life form. A long drought in the American southwest in not too ancient times wiped out the better part of an Indian civilization.

A cataclysm such as an explosion of the core of the earth, if that were possible, or the atom bomb or the sudden cessation of burning on the sun would wipe out all life forms *on earth*.

And a life form can even overload the suppressor on itself. A dinosaur destroys all his food and so destroys the dinosaur. A bubonic plague bacillus[13] attacks its hosts with such thorough appetite that the whole generation of *Pasteurella pestis*[14] vanishes. Such things are not intended by the suicide to be suicide; the life form has run up against an equation which has an unknown variable, and the unknown variable unfortunately contained enough value to overload the suppressor. This is the "didn't know the gun was loaded" equation.

And if the bubonic plague bacillus overloads its own suppressor in an area and then ceases to trouble its food and shelter—the animals—then the animals consider themselves benefited.

Reckless and clever and well-nigh indestructible, man has led a course which is a far cry from "tooth and

---

13. bacillus: loosely, any of the bacteria, especially those causing a disease.

14. *Pasturella pestis:* organism causing bubonic plague.

claw" in every sphere. And so have the redwood tree and the shark. Just as a life form, man, like every life form, is "symbiotic."[15] Life is a group effort. Lichens and plankton and algae may do very well on sunlight and minerals alone, but they are the building blocks. Above such existence, as the forms grow more complex, a tremendous interdependence exists.

It is very well for a forester to believe that certain trees willfully kill all other varieties of trees around them and then conclude a specious[16] "attitude" of trees. Let him look again. What made the soil? What provides the means of keeping the oxygen balance? What makes it possible for rain to fall in other areas? These willful and murderous trees. And squirrels plant trees. And man plants trees. And trees shelter trees of another kind. And animals fertilize trees. And trees shelter animals. And trees hold the soil so less well rooted plants can grow. Look anywhere and everywhere and we see life as an assist for life. The multitude of the complexities of life as affinities[17] for life is not dramatic. But they are the steady, practical, important reason life can continue to exist at all.

A redwood tree may be first out for redwood trees and although it does an excellent job of seeming to exist as redwood alone, a closer glance will show it has dependencies and is depended upon.

Therefore, the dynamic of any life form can be seen to be assisted by many other dynamics and combines with them against the suppressive factors. *None survive alone.*

---

15. symbiotic: the living together of similar or dissimilar organisms for mutual benefit.

16. specious: seeming to be good, sound, correct, logical, etc., without really being so; plausible but not genuine.

17. affinity: the attraction which exists between two human beings, or between a human being and another life organism.

Necessity has been declared to be a very wonderful thing. But necessity is a word which has been taken rather loosely for granted. Opportunism seems to have been read largely into necessity. What is necessity? Besides being the "mother of invention," is it a dramatic, sudden thing which excuses wars and murders, which touches a man only when he is about to starve? Or is necessity a much gentler and less dramatic quantity? "Everything," according to Leucippus,[18] "is driven by necessity." This is a keynote of much theorizing down through the ages. *Driven:* that is the key to the error. Driven, things are driven. Necessity drives. Pain drives. Necessity and pain, pain and necessity.

Recalling the dramatic and overlooking the important, man has conceived himself, from time to time, to be an object of chase by necessity and pain. These were two anthropomorphic (manlike) things which, in full costume, stuck spears at him. It can be said to be a wrong concept merely because it does not work to produce more answers.

Whatever there is of necessity is *within* him. Nothing is driving him except his original impetus to survive. And he carries that within himself or his group. Within him is the force with which he fends off pain. Within him is the force with which he attracts pleasure.

It chances to be a scientific fact that man is a self-determined organism to the outermost limit that any form of life can be, for he still depends upon other forms of life and his general environment. But he is self-determined. This is a matter which will be covered later. But right here it is necessary to indicate that he is not inherently a determined organism in the sense that he is driven on this wonderful stimulus-response basis which looks so neat in certain textbooks, and works so

18. Leucippus: Greek philosopher of fifth century B.C.

completely unworkably in the world of man. The happy little illustrations about rats do not serve when we are talking about *man*. The more complex the organism, the less reliably the stimulus-response equation works. And when one reaches that highest complexity, man, he has reached a fine degree of variability in terms of stimulus-response. The more sentient, the more rational an organism, the more that organism is self-determined. Self-determinism, like all things, is relative. Compared to a rat, however, man is very self-determined indeed. This is only a scientific fact because it can easily be proven.

The more sentient the man, the less he is a "push-button" instrument. Aberrated and reduced he can, of course, in a limited degree, be made to perform like a marionette; but then it is understood that the more aberrated a person is, the closer he approaches the intelligence quotient of an animal.

Given this self-determinism, it is interesting to observe what a man does with it. While he can never escape the "didn't know it was loaded" equation in terms of cataclysm or the unexpected gain of some other life form, he operates in a high zone level of survival potential. But here he is, self-determined, rational, his primary weapon—his mind—in excellent working order. What are his necessity instincts?

Necessity, according to that very sentient if rapidly subject-changing article, the dictionary, is "the state of being necessary; that which is unavoidable; compulsion." It also adds that necessity is "extreme poverty," but we don't want *that*. We are talking about survival.

The compulsion mentioned can be reevaluated in terms of the survival dynamic. That is interior in the organism and the race. And what is "necessary" to survival?

We have seen and can prove clinically that there are

two factors at work. The necessity of avoiding pain is a factor because, degree by degree, little things, not much in themselves, can amount to large pains which, compounded in that rapid geometric progression, bring on death. Pain is the sadness of being bawled out for poor work, because that may lead to being fired, which may lead to starvation, which may lead to death. Run any equation into which pain has entered and it can be seen that it reduces down to possible nonsurvival. And if this were all there were to surviving and if necessity were a vicious little gnome with a pitchfork, it seems rather obvious that there would be scant reason to go on living. But there is the other part of the equation: pleasure. That is a more stable part than pain, stoics[19] to the contrary, as clinical tests in Dianetics prove.

There is therefore a necessity for pleasure, for working, as happiness can be defined, toward known goals over not unknowable obstacles. And the necessity for pleasure is such that a great deal of pain can be borne to attain it. Pleasure is the positive commodity. It is enjoyment of work, contemplation of deeds well done; it is a good book or a good friend; it is taking all the skin off one's knees climbing the Matterhorn; it is hearing the kid first say "Daddy"; it is a brawl on the Bund[20] at Shanghai or the whistle of amour from a doorway; it's adventure and hope and enthusiasm and "someday I'll learn to paint"; it's eating a good meal or kissing a pretty girl or playing a stiff game of bluff on the stock exchange. It's what man does that he enjoys doing; it's what man does that he enjoys contemplating; it's what

---

19. stoic: a member of a Greek school of philosophy, founded by Zeno about 308 B.C., holding that human beings should be free from passion and calmly accept all occurrences as the unavoidable result of divine will.

20. Bund: a street running along the waterfront in Shanghai.

man does that he enjoys remembering; and it may be just the talk of things he knows he'll never do.

Man will endure a lot of pain to obtain a little pleasure. Out in the laboratory of the world, it takes very little time to confirm that.

And how does necessity fit this picture? There is a necessity for pleasure, a necessity as live and quivering and vital as the human heart itself. He who said that a man who had two loaves of bread should sell one to buy white hyacinth, spoke sooth. The creative, the constructive, the beautiful, the harmonious, the adventurous, yes, and even escape from the maw of oblivion: these things are pleasure and these things are necessity. There was a man once who had walked a thousand miles just to see an orange tree and another who was a mass of scars and poor-set bones who was eager just to get a chance to "fan another bronc."

It is very well to dwell in some Olympian height and write a book of penalties and very well to read to find what writers said that other writers said, but it is not very practical.

The pain-drive theory does not work. If some of these basics of Dianetics were only poetry about the idyllic[21] state of man, they might be justified in that, but it happens that out in the laboratory of the world, they work.

Man, in affinity with man, survives, and that survival is pleasure.

---

21. idyllic: peaceful and happy.

CHAPTER FOUR

The Four Dynamics

In the original equations of Dianetics, when the research was young, it was believed that survival could be envisioned in personal terms alone and still answer all conditions. A theory is only as good as it works. And it works as well as it explains observed data and predicts new material which will be found, in fact, to exist.

Survival in personal terms was computed until the whole activity of man could be theoretically explained in terms of *self* alone. The logic looked fairly valid. But then it was applied to the world. Something was wrong: it did not solve problems. In fact, the theory of survival in personal terms alone was so unworkable that it left a majority of behavior phenomena unexplained. But it could be computed and it still looked good.

Then it was that a nearly intuitive idea occurred. Man's understanding developed in ratio to his recognition of his brotherhood with the universe. That was high-flown but it yielded results.

Was man himself a brotherhood of man? He had evolved and become strong as a gregarious[1] being, an animal that hunted in packs. It seemed possible that all his activities could be computed in terms of the survival of the group. That computation was made. It looked good. Man survived, it was postulated, solely in terms of the survival of his group. It looked good but it left a majority of observed phenomena unexplained.

It was attempted, then, to explain man's behavior in terms of mankind alone; which is to say, it was

---

1. gregarious: living in herds or flocks.

assumed that mankind survived for mankind in a highly altruistic[2] way. This was straight down the sylvan[3] path of Jean Jacques Rousseau.[4] It could be computed that man lived alone for the survival of all mankind. But when addressed to the laboratory—the world—it did not work.

Finally, it was recalled that some had thought that man's entire activity and all his behavior could be explained by assuming that he lived for sex alone. This was not an original assumption. But some original computations were made upon it and it is true that, by a few quick twists of the equation, his survival activity can be made to resolve on only the sexual basis. But when this was applied to observed data, again it failed to explain every phenomenon.

An examination was made of what had been attempted. It had been assumed that man survived only for himself as an individual; it had been computed that he survived only for the group, the pack, for society; it had been postulated that he survived only for mankind; and finally, it had been theorized that he lived only for sex. *None worked alone.*

A new computation was made on the *survival dynamic*. Exactly for what was man surviving? All four of these factors—*self, sex, group* and *mankind*—were entered into a new equation. And now it was found, a theory was in hand which worked. It explained all observed phenomena and it predicted new phenomena which were discovered to exist. It was a scientific equation, therefore!

From the *survival dynamic,* in this fashion, were evolved the four *dynamics.* By *survival dynamic* was

---

2. altruistic: having unselfish concern for the welfare of others.

3. sylvan: relating to or characteristic of forests.

4. Rousseau, Jean Jacques: (1712–78) French political philosopher and author.

meant the basic command **Survive!** which underlay all activity. By *dynamic* was meant one of the four purpose divisions of the entire dynamic principle. The four *dynamics* were not new forces; they were subdivisions of the primary force.

Dynamic one is the urge toward ultimate survival on the part of the individual and for himself. It includes his immediate symbiotes,[5] the extension of culture for his own benefit and name immortality.

Dynamic two is the urge of the individual toward ultimate survival via the sex act, the creation of and the rearing of children. It includes their symbiotes, the extension of culture for them and their future provision.

Dynamic three is the urge of the individual toward ultimate survival for the group. It includes the symbiotes of the group and the extension of its culture.

Dynamic four includes the urge of the individual toward ultimate survival for all mankind. It includes the symbiotes of mankind and the extension of its culture.

Life, the atom and the universe and energy itself are included under the symbiotic classification.

It will be seen immediately that these four dynamics are actually a spectrum without sharp division lines. The *survival dynamic* can be seen to sweep out from the individual to embrace the entire species and its symbiotes.

None of these dynamics is necessarily stronger than any of the others. Each is strong. They are the four roads a man takes to survival. And the four roads are actually one road. And the one road is actually a spectrum of thousands of roads contained within the four. They are all in terms of past, present and future in that the present may be a sum of the past and the future may

---

5. The Dianetic meaning of *symbiote* is extended beyond the dictionary definition to mean "any or all life or energy forms which are mutually dependent for survival." The atom depends on the universe, the universe on the atom.

be the product of the past and present.

All the purposes of man can be considered to lie within this spectrum and all behavior becomes explained.

That man is selfish is a valid statement when one means an *aberrated* man. That man is antisocial is an equally valid statement if one adds the modifier, aberration. And other such statements resolve equally.

Now, it happens that these four dynamics can be seen to compete, one with another, in their operation within an individual or a society. There is a rational reason for this. The phrase "social competition" is a compound of aberrated behavior and sentient difficulties.

Any man, group or race may be in contest with any race, group or man and even in contest with sex on an entirely rational level.

The equation of the optimum solution would be that *a problem has been well resolved which portends[6] the maximum good for the maximum number of dynamics.* That is to say that any solution, modified by the time available to put the solution into effect, should be creative or constructive for the greatest possible number of dynamics. The optimum solution for any problem would be a solution which achieved the maximum benefit in all the dynamics. This means that a man, determining upon some project, would fare best if he benefited everything concerned in the four dynamics as his project touched them. He would then have to benefit himself as well for the solution to be optimum. In other words, the benefiting of the group and mankind dynamics but the blocking of the sex dynamic and the self dynamic would be much poorer than the best solution. The *survival conduct pattern* is built upon this equation of the optimum solution. It is the basic equation of all rational behavior and is the equation on which a *clear* functions. It is inherent in man.

---

6. portend: to be an indication of; signify.

In other words, the best solution to any problem is that which will bring the greatest good to the greatest number of beings, including self, progeny, family associates, political and racial groups, and at length to all mankind. The greatest good may require, as well, some destruction, but the solution deteriorates in a ratio to the destructiveness employed. Self-sacrifice and selfishness are alike reductive of the optimum action equation and alike have been suspected and should be.

This is entirely a matter of: *does it work?* Even on an unaberrated basis there are times when one or another of these dynamics have to be dropped from the computation of some activity or other and indeed, few problems are so entirely intense that they must take into account all the dynamics. But when a problem achieves such intensity, and time is not an important factor, serious errors can follow the omission of one or another of the dynamics from the factors considered.

In the case of a Napoleon "saving France" at the expense of the remainder of mankind in Europe, the equation of the optimum solution was so far neglected that all the revolutionary gains of the French people were lost. In the case of Caesar "saving Rome," the equation was so poorly done that the survival of Rome was impeded.

But there are special cases when the equation of the optimum solution becomes so involved with time that certain dynamics must be neglected to permit other dynamics to persist. The case of a sailor giving his own life to save his ship answers the group dynamic. Such an action is a valid solution to a problem. But it violates the *optimum* solution because it did not answer for dynamic one: self.

Many examples of various kinds could be cited where one or another of the dynamics must, of necessity, receive priority, all on an entirely rational basis.

On an aberrated basis, the equation is still valid but complicated by irrationalities which have no part of the situation. Many solutions are bad merely because of false educational data or no data at all. But these are still solutions. In the case of aberrated solutions, the dynamics are actually and actively impeded, as will later be outlined in full.

CHAPTER FIVE

Summary

The dynamic principle of existence is survival.

This survival can be graduated into four zones, each one progressively portending a better opportunity of reaching the potential of immortality. Zone 0 borders from death and includes apathy; zone 1 borders from apathy and includes violent effort; zone 2 borders from violence into mediocre, but not entirely satisfactory, success; zone 3 borders from the mediocre to the excellent chance. These zones are each occasioned by the ratio of the *suppressor* to the *survival dynamic*. In apathy, zone 0, the suppressor appears too great to be overcome. In the area of violence, zone 1, the suppressor more or less overbalances the survival dynamic, requiring enormous effort which, when expended without result, drops the organism into the zero zone. In the area of mediocrity, zone 2, the suppressor and the survival dynamic are more or less evenly balanced. In the area of zone 3, the survival dynamic has overcome the suppressor and, the chances of survival being excellent, is the area of high response to problems. These four zones might be classed as the zone of no hope, the zone of violent action, the area of balance and the area of high hope. Clinical experiment is the basis of these zones since they follow a progress of mental or physical being as it rises from the death area into high existence.

The four *dynamics* are subdivisions of the *survival dynamic* and are, in mankind, the thrust toward potential survival in terms of entities. They embrace all the purposes, activities and behavior of mankind. They could be said to be a *survival conduct pattern*. The first of these, but not necessarily the most important nor yet the one which will receive priority in various efforts, is the individual dynamic, *Dynamic one,* which includes the personal survival of the individual as a living person and the survival of his personal symbiotes. *Dynamic two* is the thrust toward potential immortality through children and includes all sexual activity as well as the symbiotes of the children. *Dynamic three* is survival in terms of the group, which term may include such things as a club, a military company, a city, a state, a nation; this would include the symbiotes of the group. *Dynamic four* is the thrust toward potential immortality of mankind as a species and the symbiotes of mankind. Embraced within these classifications are any part of existence, any form of matter and, indeed, the universe.

Any problem or situation discoverable within the activities or purposes of mankind is embraced within these *dynamics*.

The equation of the optimum solution is inherent within the organism and, modified by education or viewpoint and modified further by time, is the operating method of unaberrated individuals, groups or mankind. The equation of the optimum solution is always present even in severely aberrated individuals and is used as modified by their education, viewpoint and available time. The aberration does not remove activity from the dynamics of survival. Aberrated conduct is *irrational* survival conduct and is fully intended to lead to survival. That the intent is not the act does not eradicate the intent.

These Are the Fundamental Axioms of Dianetics:

The *dynamic principle of existence*—Survive!

Survival, considered as the single and sole purpose, subdivides into four *dynamics.*

Dynamic one is the urge of the individual toward survival for the individual and his symbiotes. (By *symbiote* is meant all entities and energies which aid survival.)

Dynamic two is the urge of the individual toward survival through procreation; it includes both the sex act and the raising of progeny, the care of children and their symbiotes.

Dynamic three is the urge of the individual toward survival for the group or the group for the group and includes the symbiotes of that group.

Dynamic four is the urge of the individual toward survival for mankind or the urge toward survival of mankind for mankind as well as the group for mankind, etc., and includes the symbiotes of mankind.

The *absolute goal* of survival is immortality or infinite survival. This is sought by the individual in terms of himself as an organism, as a spirit or as a name or as his children, as a group of which he is a member or as mankind and the progeny and symbiotes of others as well as his own.

The reward of survival activity is *pleasure.*

The ultimate penalty of destructive activity is death or complete nonsurvival, and is *pain.*

Successes raise the survival potential toward infinite survival.

Failures lower the survival potential toward death.

The human mind is engaged upon perceiving and retaining data, composing or computing conclusions and posing and resolving problems related to organisms along all four dynamics; and the purpose of perception, retention, concluding and resolving problems is to direct its own organism and symbiotes and other organisms and symbiotes along the four dynamics toward survival.

Intelligence is the ability to perceive, pose and resolve problems.

The *dynamic* is the tenacity to life and vigor and persistence in survival.

Both the *dynamic* and *intelligence* are necessary to persist and accomplish and neither is a constant quantity from individual to individual, group to group.

The *dynamics* are inhibited by engrams, which lie across them and disperse life force.

Intelligence is inhibited by engrams which feed false or improperly graded data into the analyzer.[1]

Happiness is the overcoming of not unknown obstacles toward a known goal and, transiently, the contemplation of or indulgence in pleasure.

The *analytical mind* is that portion of the mind which perceives and retains experience data to compose

---

1. analyzer: the analytical mind.

and resolve problems and direct the organism along the four dynamics. *It thinks in differences and similarities.*

The *reactive mind* is that portion of the mind which files and retains physical pain and painful emotion and seeks to direct the organism solely on a stimulus-response basis. *It thinks only in identities.*

The *somatic mind* is that mind which, directed by the analytical or reactive mind, places solutions into effect on the physical level.

A *training pattern* is that stimulus-response mechanism resolved by the analytical mind to care for routine activity or emergency activity. It is held in the somatic mind and can be changed at will by the analytical mind.

Habit is that stimulus-response reaction dictated by the reactive mind from the content of engrams and put into effect by the somatic mind. It can be changed only by those things which change engrams.

Aberrations, under which is included all deranged or irrational behavior, are caused by engrams. They are stimulus-response, pro- and contrasurvival.

Psychosomatic ills are caused by engrams.

The *engram* is the single source of aberrations and psychosomatic ills.

Moments of "unconsciousness," when the analytical

mind is attenuated[2] in greater or lesser degree, are
the only moments when engrams can be received.

The *engram* is a moment of "unconsciousness" containing physical pain or painful emotion and all
perceptions, and is not available to the analytical
mind as experience.

Emotion is three things: engramic response to situations, endocrine metering of the body to meet
situations on an analytical level, and the inhibition
or the furtherance of life force.

The *potential value* of an individual or a group may
be expressed by the equation

$$PV = ID^X$$

where I is Intelligence and D is Dynamic.

The *worth* of an individual is computed in terms of
the alignment, on any dynamic, of his potential
value with optimum survival along that dynamic. A
high PV may, by reversed vector,[3] result in a negative worth as in some severely aberrated persons. A
high PV on any dynamic *assures* a high worth only
in the unaberrated person.

---

2. attenuate: to lessen in severity, value, amount, intensity, etc.; weaken.

3. vector: a physical quantity with both magnitude and direction, such
as a force or velocity.

Book Two

The Single Source of All Inorganic Mental and Organic Psychosomatic Ills

CHAPTER ONE

The Analytical Mind and the Standard Memory Banks

This chapter begins the search for human error and tells where it is not.

The human mind can be considered to have three major divisions. First, there is the *analytical mind;* second, there is the *reactive mind;* and third, there is the *somatic mind.*

Consider the analytical mind as a computing machine. This is analogy because the analytical mind, while it behaves like a computing machine, is yet more fantastically capable than any computing machine ever constructed and infinitely more elaborate. It could be called the "computational mind" or the "egsusheyftef." But for our purposes, the analytical mind, as a descriptive name, will do. This mind may live in the prefrontal lobes[1]— there is some hint of that—but this is a problem of structure, and nobody really knows about structure. So we shall call this computational part of the mind the "analytical mind" because it analyzes data.

The *monitor* can be considered part of the analytical mind. The monitor could be called the center of awareness of the person. It, inexactly speaking, *is* the person. It has been approximated by various names for thousands of years, each one reducing down to "I." The monitor is in control of the analytical mind. It is not in control because it has been told to be but only because it is, inherently. It is not a demon who lives in the skull nor a little man who vocalizes one's thoughts. It is "I." No matter how many aberrations a person may have, "I" is

---

1. prefrontal lobes: portion of the brain directly behind the forehead.

always "I." No matter how "clear" a person becomes, "I" is still "I." "I" may be submerged now and then in an aberree, but it is always present.

The analytical mind shows various evidences of being an organ, but as we know in this age so little of structure, the full structural knowledge of the analytical mind must come after we know what it does. And in Dianetics we know *precisely* that for the first time. It is known and can be proven with ease that the analytical mind, be it one organ of the body or several, behaves as you would expect any good computing machine to behave.

What would you want in a computing machine? The action of the analytical mind—or analyzer—is everything anyone could want from the best computer available. It can and does do all the tricks of a computer. And over and above that, it directs the building of computers. And it is as thoroughly right as any computer ever was. The analytical mind is not just a *good* computer, it is a *perfect* computer. It never makes a mistake. It cannot err in any way so long as a human being is reasonably intact (unless something has carried away a piece of his mental equipment).

The analytical mind is incapable of error, and it is so certain that it is incapable of error that it works out everything on the basis that it cannot make an error. If a person says, "I cannot add," he either means that he has never been taught to add or that he has an aberration about adding. It does not mean that there is anything wrong with the analytical mind.

While the whole being is, in an aberrated state, grossly capable of error, still the analytical mind is not. For a computer is just as good as the data on which it operates and no better. Aberration, then, arises from the nature of the data offered to the analytical mind as a problem to be computed.

The analytical mind has its standard memory banks. Just where these are located structurally is again no concern of ours at this time. To operate, the analytical mind has to have percepts (data), memory (data) and imagination (data).

There are another data storage bank and another part of the human mind which contain aberrations and are the source of insanities. These will be fully covered later and should not be confused with either the analytical mind or the standard memory banks.

Whether the data contained in the standard memory banks is evaluated correctly or not, it is all there. The various senses receive information and this information files straight into the standard memory banks. It does not go through the analyzer first. It is filed and the analyzer then has it from the standard banks.

There are several of these standard banks and they may be duplicated in themselves so that there are several of each kind of bank. Nature seems generous in such things. There is a bank, or set of banks, for each perception. These can be considered racks of data filed in a cross-index system which would make an intelligence officer purple with envy. Any single *percept* is filed as a *concept*. The sight of a moving car, for instance, is filed in the visio-bank in color and motion, at the time seen; cross-indexed to the area in which seen; cross-indexed to all data about cars; cross-indexed to thoughts about cars; and so forth and so forth, with the additional filing of conclusions (thought stream) of the moment and thought streams of the past with all their conclusions. The sound of that car is similarly filed from the ears straight into the audio-bank, and cross-indexed multitudinously as before. The other sensations of that moment are also filed in their own banks.

Now, it may be that the whole filing is done in one bank. It would be simpler that way. But this is not a matter of structure but mental performance. Eventually somebody will discover just how they are filed. Right now the function of filing is all that interests us.

Every percept—sight, sound, smell, feeling, taste, organic sensation, pain, rhythm, kinesthesia (weight and muscular motion) and emotion—is each properly and neatly filed in the standard banks in full. It does not matter how many aberrations a physically intact person has or whether he thinks he can or cannot contain this data or recall it; the file is there and is complete.

This file begins at a very early period, of which more later. It then runs consecutively, whether the individual is asleep or awake, except in moments of "unconsciousness,"[2] for an entire lifetime. It apparently has an infinite capacity.

The numbers of these concepts (*concept* means "that which is retained after something has been perceived") would stagger an astronomer's computer. The existence and profusion of memories retained were discovered and studied in a large number of cases, and they can be examined in anyone by certain processes.

Everything in this bank is correct insofar as the single action of perception is concerned. There may be organic errors in the organs of perception, such as blindness or deafness (when physical, not aberrational), which would leave blanks in the banks; and there may be organic impairment, such as partial organic deafness, which would leave partial blanks. But these things are not errors in the standard memory banks; they are simply absence of data. Like the computer, *the standard memory banks are perfect, recording faithfully and reliably.*

Now, part of the standard banks is audio-semantic,

---

2. *Unconsciousness* throughout this work means a greater or lesser reduction of awareness on the part of "I"—an attenuation of working power of the analytical mind.

which is to say, the recordings of words heard. And part of the banks is visio-semantic, which is to say, the recordings of words read. These are special parts of the sound and sight files. A blind man who has to read with his fingers develops a tactile-semantic file. The content of the speech files is exactly as heard without alteration.

Another interesting part of the standard memory banks is that they apparently file the original and hand forward exact copies to the analyzer. They will hand out as many exact copies as are demanded without diminishing the actual file original. And they hand out these copies each in kind with color-motion sight, tone-audio, etc.

The amount of material which is retained in the average standard memory banks would fill several libraries. But the method of retention is invariable. And the *potentiality* of recall is perfect.

The primary source of error in "rational" computation comes under the headings of insufficient data and erroneous data. The individual, daily facing new situations, is not always in possession of all the material he requires to make a decision. And he may have been told something on "good authority" which was not true and yet which did not find counter-evidence in the banks.

Between the standard banks, which are perfect and reliable, and the computer—the analytical mind—which is perfect and reliable, there is no irrational concourse.[3] The answer is always as right as it can be made to be in the light of data at hand, and that is all anyone can ask of a computing device or a recording device.

The analytical mind goes even further in its efforts to be right than one would suppose. It constantly checks and weighs new experience in the light of old experience, forms new conclusions in the light of old conclusions,

---

3. concourse: an act of coming or flowing together.

changes old conclusions, and generally is very busy being right.

The analytical mind might be considered to have been given a sacred post of trust by the cells to safeguard the colony, and it does everything within its power to carry out that mission. It has correct data, as correct as possible; and it does correct computations on them, as correct as they can be made. When one considers the enormous number of factors which one handles, for instance, in the action of driving a car ten blocks, he can appreciate how very, very busy on how very many levels that analytical mind can be.

Now, before we introduce the villain of this piece, the *reactive mind*, it is necessary to understand something about the relation of the analytical mind to the organism itself.

The analytical mind, charged with full responsibility, is far from without authority to carry out its actions and desires. Through the mechanisms of the life function regulator (which handles all the mechanical functions of living), the analytical mind can affect any function of the body it desires to affect.

In excellent working order—which is to say, when the organism is not aberrated—the analytical mind can influence the heartbeat, the endocrines (such things as calcium and sugar in the blood, adrenaline, etc.), selective blood flow (stopping it in the limbs or starting it at will), urine, excreta, etc. All glandular, rhythm and fluid functions of the body *can* be at the command of the analytical mind. This is not to say that in a cleared person they always are. That would be very uncomfortable and bothersome. But it does say that the analytical mind can effect changes at desire when it skills itself to do so. This is a matter of laboratory proof, very easy to do.

People have long been intuitive about the "full power of the mind." Well, the full power of the mind would be the analytical mind working with the standard memory banks, the life function regulator and one other thing.

The last and most important thing is, of course, the organism. It is in the charge of the analytical mind. And the analytical mind controls it in other ways than life function. All muscles and the remainder of the organism can be under the full command of the analytical mind.

In order to keep it and its circuits free of bric-a-brac and minor activities, the analytical mind is provided with a learned training pattern regulator. Into this, by education, it can place the stimulus-response patterns necessary for the performance of tasks like talking, walking, piano playing, etc. These learned patterns are not unchangeable. Because they are selected by the analytical mind after thought and effort, there is seldom any need to change them; if new situations arise, a new pattern is trained into the muscles. None of these are "conditionings"; they are simply training patterns which the organism can use without attention of any magnitude from the analyzer. An uncountable number of such patterns can be laid into the organism by this method. And they are not the source of any trouble since they file by time and situation, and a very little thought will serve to annul old ones in favor of new ones.

All muscles, voluntary and "involuntary," can be at the command of the analytical mind.

Here, then, is the composite of a sentient being. There is no chance for error beyond the errors incident to insufficient data and erroneous but accepted data (and the last will be used by the analyzer just once if that once proves the data to be wrong). Here is the realm of pleasure, emotion, creation and construction and even destruction, if the computation on the optimum solution says something has to be destroyed.

The dynamics underlie the activities of the analytical

mind. The urge toward survival explains all its actions. That we can understand the fundamental simplicity of the functional mechanism does not, however, mean that a man operating this way alone is cold or calculating or intent on "tooth and claw." The nearer man approaches this optimum, in an individual or in a whole society, the quicker and warmer is that society, the more honest may be its moods and actions.

Sanity depends upon rationality. Here is optimum rationality and therefore optimum sanity. And here also are all the things man likes to think man should be like or, for that matter, what he has represented his better gods to be like. This is the *clear*.

This is sanity. This is happiness. This is survival. Where is the error?

CHAPTER TWO

The Reactive Mind

It is fairly well accepted in these times that life in all forms evolved from the basic building blocks: the virus and the cell. Its only relevance to Dianetics is that such a proposition works—and actually that is all we ask of Dianetics. There is no point to writing here a vast tome on biology and evolution. We can add some chapters to those things, but Charles Darwin did his job well and the fundamental principles of evolution can be found in his and other works.

The proposition on which Dianetics was originally entered was evolution. It was postulated that the cells themselves had the urge to survive and that that urge was common to life. It was further postulated that organisms—individuals—were constructed of cells and were in fact aggregations of colonies of cells.

As went the building block, so went the organism. In the finite realms and for any of our purposes, man could be considered to be a colonial aggregation of cells and it could be assumed that his purpose was identical with the purpose of his building blocks.

The cell is a unit of life which is seeking to survive and only to survive.

Man is a structure of cells which are seeking to survive and only to survive.

Man's mind is the command post of operation and is constructed to resolve problems and pose problems related to survival and only to survival.

The action of survival, if optimum, would lead to survival.

The optimum survival conduct pattern was formulated and then studied for exceptions, and there were no exceptions found.

The survival conduct pattern was discovered to be far from sterile and barren but was full of rich and most pleasant activity.

None of these postulates outlawed any concept concerning the human soul or divine or creative imagination. It was understood perfectly that this was a study in the finite universe only and that spheres and realms of thought and action might very well exist above this finite sphere. But it was also discovered that none of these factors were needed to resolve the entire problem of aberration and irrational conduct.

The human mind was discovered to have been most grossly maligned, for it was found to be possessed of capabilities far in excess of any heretofore imagined, much less tested.

Basic human character was found to have been pilloried[1] because man had not been able to distinguish between irrational conduct derived from poor data and irrational conduct derived from another far more vicious source.

If there ever was a devil, he designed the reactive mind.

This functional mechanism managed to bury itself from view so thoroughly that only inductive[2] philosophy, traveling from effect back to cause, served to uncover it. The detective work which was invested in the location of this archcriminal of the human psyche occupied many years. Its identity can now be certified by any technician in any clinic or in any group of men. Two hundred and

---

1. pillory: to hold up to public ridicule or scorn.

2. inductive: of or using induction, logical reasoning that a general law exists because particular cases that seem to be examples of it exist.

seventy-three individuals have been examined and treated, representing all the various types of inorganic mental illness and the many varieties of psychosomatic ills. In each one this reactive mind was found operating, its principles unvaried. This is a long series of cases and will soon become longer.

The reactive mind is possessed by everyone. No human being examined anywhere was discovered to be without one or without aberrative content in his *engram bank*,[3] the reservoir of data which serves the reactive mind.

What does this mind do? It shuts off hearing recall. It places vocal circuits in the mind. It makes people tone-deaf. It makes people stutter. It does anything and everything that can be found in any list of mental ills: psychoses, neuroses, compulsions, repressions . . .

What can it do? It can give a man arthritis,[4] bursitis,[5] asthma, allergies, sinusitis,[6] coronary[7] trouble, high blood pressure and so on, down the whole catalogue of psychosomatic ills, adding a few more which were never specifically classified as psychosomatic, such as the common cold.

And it is the only thing in the human being which can produce these effects. It is the thing which uniformly brings them about.

This is the mind which made Socrates think he had a "demon" that gave him answers. This is the mind that made Caligula[8] appoint his horse to a government post.

---

3. engram bank: a colloquial name for the reactive mind.

4. arthritis: a condition causing inflammation, pain and stiffness in the joints.

5. bursitis: inflammation of a bursa, a pouch between joints or between muscles or skin, etc., and bones, for lessening friction.

6. sinusitis: inflammation of one or more sinus cavities in the skull.

7. coronary: of the arteries supplying blood to the heart.

8. Caligula: (A.D. 12–41) Roman emperor (37–41). Reign marked by extreme cruelty and tyranny.

This is the mind which made Caesar cut the right hands from thousands of Gauls,[9] which made Napoleon reduce the height of Frenchmen one inch.

This is the mind which keeps war a thing of alarm, which makes politics irrational, which makes superior officers snarl, which makes children cry in fear of the dark. This is the mind which makes a man suppress his hopes, which holds his apathies, which gives him irresolution when he should act and kills him before he has begun to live.

If there ever was a devil, he invented it.

Discharge the content of this mind's bank and the arthritis vanishes, myopia[10] gets better, heart illness decreases, asthma disappears, stomachs function properly and the whole catalogue of ills goes away and stays away.

Discharge the reactive engram bank and the schizophrenic[11] faces reality at last, the manic-depressive[12] sets forth to accomplish things, the neurotic[13] stops clinging to books which tell him how much he needs his neuroses and begins to live, the woman stops snapping at her children, and the dipsomaniac[14] can drink when he likes and stop.

---

9. Gauls: any of the Celtic-speaking people of Gaul, ancient region in western Europe consisting of what is now mainly France and Belgium.

10. myopia: inability to see clearly what is far away—nearsightedness.

11. schizophrenic: the original definition of *schizophrenic* or "scissor personality" was in observation of shift of identity; an idea that one is two persons.

12. manic-depressive: an individual who climbs way up the tone scale; there is just a small peak, and he hits this peak and then dives off it again.

13. neurotic: a person who has some obsession or compulsion which overmasters his self-determinism to such a degree that it is a social liability.

14. dipsomaniac: a person suffering from an uncontrollable craving for alcohol.

These are scientific facts. They compare invariably with observed experience.

The reactive mind is the entire source of aberration. It can be proved and has been repeatedly proven that there is no other, for when that engram bank is discharged, all undesirable symptoms vanish and a man begins to operate on his optimum pattern.

If one were looking for something like demons in a human mind—such as those one observes in some inmates of madhouses—he could find them easily enough. Only they are not demons. They are bypass circuits from the engram bank. What prayers and exhortations have been used against these bypass circuits!

If one did not believe in demons, if one supposed that man were good after all (as a postulate, of course), how would the evil get into him? What would be the source of these insane rages? What would be the source of his slips of the tongue? How would he come to know irrational fear?

Why is it that one does not like his boss although his boss has always been pleasant? Why is it that suicides smash their bodies to bits?

Why does man behave destructively, irrationally, fighting wars, killing, ruining whole sections of mankind?

What is the source of all neuroses, psychoses, insanities?

Let us return to a brief examination of the analytical mind. Let us examine its memory banks. Here we find all the sense concepts on file. Or so it appears at first glance. Let us take another look, a look at the time factor. There is a time sense about these analytical mind banks. It is very accurate, as though the organism were equipped with a fine watch. But there is something wrong here about time—it has gaps in it! There are moments when nothing seems to be filed in these standard banks. These are gaps which take place during moments of "unconsciousness"—that state of being caused by anesthesia, drugs, injury or shock.

This is the only data missing from a standard bank. If in hypnotic trance you examine a patient's memory of an operation, these incidents are the only periods in the banks you will not find. You can find these if you care to look and don't care what happens to your patient—of which more later. But the point is that there is something missing which has always been considered by one and all in any age never to have been recorded.

One and all in every age have never been able to put a finger on insanity either. Are these two data in agreement and do they have relationship? They definitely do.

There are two things which appear to be—but are not—recorded in the standard banks: painful emotion and physical pain.

How would you go about the building of a sensitive machine upon which the life and death affairs of an organism depended, which was to be the chief tool of an individual? Would you leave its delicate circuits prey to every overload, or would you install a fuse[15] system? If a delicate instrument is in circuit with a power line, it is protected by several sets of fuses. Any computer would be so safeguarded.

It happens that there is some small evidence to support the electrical theory of the nervous system. In pain there are very heavy overcharges in the nerves. It may well have been—and elsewhere some Dianetic computations have been made about this—that the brain is the absorber for overcharges of power resulting from injury, the power itself being generated by the injured cells in the area of injury. That is theory and has no place here save to serve as an example. We are dealing now only with scientific fact.

---

15. fuse: a short length of wire designed to melt and thus break a circuit if the current exceeds a safe level.

The action of the analytical mind during a moment of intense pain is suspended. In fact, the analytical mind behaves just as though it were an organ to which vital supply is shut off whenever shock is present.

As an example, a man struck in the side by a car is knocked "unconscious" and, on regaining "consciousness," has no record of the period when he was "knocked out." This would be a nonsurvival circumstance. It means that there would be no volition on the part of anyone who was injured, and this is the time when the organism most requires volition. So this is nonsurvival, if the whole mind cuts out whenever pain appears. Would an organism with more than a billion years of biological engineering behind it leave a problem like this unsolved?

Indeed, the organism solved the problem. Maybe the problem is very difficult, biologically, and maybe the solution is not very good, but large provision has been made for those moments when the organism is "unconscious."

The answer to the problem of making the organism react in moments of "unconsciousness" or near "unconsciousness" is also the answer to insanity and psychosomatic illnesses and all the strange mental quirks to which people are liable and which gave rise to that fable "it is human to err."

Clinical tests prove these statements to be scientific facts:

1. The mind records on some level continuously during the entire life of the organism.

2. All recordings of the lifetime are available.

3. "Unconsciousness," in which the mind is oblivious of its surroundings, is possible only in death and does not exist as total amnesia in life.

4. All mental and physical derangements of a psychic nature come about from moments of "unconsciousness."

5. Such moments can be reached and drained of charge[16] with the result of returning the mind to optimum operating condition.

"Unconsciousness" is the single source of aberration. There is no such action as "mental conditioning" except on a conscious training level (where it exists only with the consent of the person).

If you care to make the experiment you can take a man, render him "unconscious," hurt him and give him information. By Dianetic technique, no matter what information you gave him, it can be recovered. This experiment should not be carelessly conducted because *you might also render him insane.*

A pale shade of this operation can be obtained by hypnosis, either by its usual techniques or drugs. By installing "positive suggestions" in a subject, he can be made to act like an insane person. This test is not a new one. It has been well known that compulsions or repressions can be so introduced into the psyche. The ancient Greek was quite familiar with it and used it to produce various delusions.

There is what is known as a "posthypnotic suggestion." An understanding of this can assist an understanding of the basic mechanism of insanity. The actions under both circumstances are not identical, but they are similar enough in their essence.

A man is placed in a hypnotic trance by standard hypnotic technique or some hypnotic drug. The operator then may say to him, "When you awaken there is something you must do. Whenever I touch my tie you will remove your coat. When I let go my tie, you will put on your coat. Now you will forget that I have told you to do this."

16. charge: harmful energy or force accumulated and stored in the reactive mind, resulting from the conflicts and unpleasant experiences that a person has had.

The subject is then awakened. He is not consciously aware of the command. If told he had been given an order while "asleep," he would resist the idea or shrug, but he would not know. The operator then touches his tie. The subject may make some remark about its being too warm and so take his coat off. The operator then releases his tie. The subject may remark that he is now cold and will put his coat back on. The operator then touches his tie. The subject may say that his coat has been to the tailor's and with much conversation finally explain why he is taking it off, perhaps to see if the back seam had been sewn properly. The operator then releases his tie and the subject says he is satisfied with the tailor and so replaces his coat. The operator may touch his tie many times and each time receive action on the part of the subject.

At last, the subject may become aware, from the expressions on people's faces, that something is wrong. He will not know what is wrong. He will not even know that the touching of the tie is the signal which makes him take off his coat. He will begin to grow uncomfortable. He may find fault with the operator's appearance and begin to criticize his clothing. He still does not know the tie is a signal. He will still react and remain in ignorance that there is some strange reason he must take off his coat—all he knows is that he is uncomfortable with his coat on whenever the tie is touched, uncomfortable with his coat off every time the tie is released.

These various actions are very important to an understanding of the reactive mind. Hypnotism is a laboratory tool. It is not used to any extent in Dianetic therapy, but it has served as a means of examining minds and getting their reactions. Hypnotism is a wild variable. A few people can be hypnotized, many cannot be. Hypnotic suggestions will sometimes "take" and sometimes they won't. Sometimes they make persons well and sometimes they make them ill—the same suggestion reacting differently in different people. An engineer knows how to make use of a wild variable. There is something which makes it unpredictable. Finding out the basic reason hypnotism was a variable helped to discover the source of insanity. And understanding the mechanism of the posthypnotic suggestion can aid an understanding of aberration.

No matter how foolish a suggestion is given to a subject under hypnosis, he will carry it out one way or another. He can be told to remove his shoes or call someone at ten the following day or to eat peas for breakfast and he will. These are direct orders and he will comply with them. He can be told that his hats do not fit him and he will believe that they do not. Any suggestion will operate within his mind unbeknownst to his higher levels of awareness.

Very complex suggestions can be given. One such would be to the effect that he was unable to utter the word *I*. He would omit it from his conversation, using remarkable makeshifts without being "aware" that he was having to avoid the word. Or he could be told that he must never look at his hands and he will not. These are *repressions*. Given to the subject when drugged or in a hypnotic sleep, these suggestions operate when he is awake. And they will continue to operate until released by the hypnotic operator.

He can be told that he has an urge to sneeze every time he hears the word *rug* and that he will sneeze when it is spoken. He can be told that he must jump two feet in the air every time he sees a cat and he will jump. And he will do these things after he has been awakened. These are *compulsions*.

He can be told that he will think very sexual thoughts about a certain girl but that when he thinks them he will feel his nose itch. He can be told that he has a continual urge to lie down and sleep and that every time he lies down he will feel that he cannot sleep. He will experience these things. These are *neuroses*.

In further experiments he can be told, when he is in his hypnotic "sleep," that he is the president of the country and that the secret service agents are trying to murder him. Or he can be told that he is being fed poison in every restaurant in which he attempts to eat. These are *psychoses*.

He can be informed that he is really another person and that he owns a yacht and answers to the name of "Sir Reginald." Or he can be told that he is a thief, that he has a prison record and that the police are looking for him. These would be *schizophrenic* and *paranoid-schizophrenic* insanities respectively.

The operator can inform the subject that the subject is the most wonderful person on earth and that everybody thinks so. Or that the subject is the object of adoration of all women. This would be a *manic*-type insanity.

He can be convinced, while hypnotized, that when he wakes he will feel so terrible that he will hope for nothing but death. This would be the *depressive*-type insanity.

He can be told that all he can think about is how sick he is and that every malady of which he reads becomes his. This would make him react like a *hypochondriac*.[17]

Thus we could go down the catalogue of mental ills and by concocting positive suggestions to create the state of mind, we could bring about, in the awakened subject, a semblance to every insanity.

Understood that these are *semblances*. They are similar to insanity in that the subject would *act* like an

---

17. hypochondriac: a person who continually shows unnecessary anxiety about his health.

insane person. He would not *be* an insane person. The moment the suggestion is relieved—the subject being informed that it was a suggestion—the aberration (and all these insanities, etc., are grouped under the heading of *aberration*) theoretically vanishes.[18]

The duplication of aberrations of all classes and kinds in subjects who have been hypnotized or drugged has demonstrated that there is some portion of the mind which is not in contact with the consciousness but which contains data.

It was the search for this portion of the mind which led to the resolution of the problem of insanity, psychosomatic ills and other aberrations. It was not approached through hypnotism, and hypnotism is just another tool, a tool which is of only occasional use in the practice of Dianetics and is, indeed, not needed at all.

Here we have an individual who is acting sanely, who is given a positive suggestion and who then temporarily acts insanely. His sanity is restored by the release of the suggestion into his consciousness, at which moment it loses its force upon him. But this is only a semblance of the mechanism involved. The actual insanity, one not laid now by some hypnotist, does not need to emerge into the consciousness to be released. There is this difference and others between hypnotism and the actual source of aberration; but hypnotism is a demonstration of its working parts.

Review the first example of the positive suggestion. The subject was "unconscious," which is to say, he

---

18. An injunction here. These are tests. They have been made on people who could be hypnotized and people who could not be but who were drugged. They brought forth valuable data for Dianetics. They can be duplicated only when you know Dianetics, unless you want to actually drive somebody insane by accident. For these suggestions do not always vanish. Hypnotism is a wild variable. It is *dangerous* and belongs in the parlor in the same way you would want an atom bomb there.

was not in possession of complete awareness or self-determinism. He was given something he must do and the something was hidden from his consciousness. The operator gave him a signal. When the signal occurred, the subject performed an act. The subject gave reasons for the act which were not the real reasons for it. The subject found fault with the operator and the operator's clothing but did not see that it was the tie which signaled the action. The suggestion was released and the subject no longer felt a compulsion to perform the act.

These are the parts of aberration. Once one knows exactly what parts of what *are* aberrations, the whole problem is very simple. It seems incredible at first glance that the source could have remained so thoroughly hidden for so many thousands of years of research. But at second glance, it becomes a wonder that the source was ever discovered. For it is hidden cunningly and well.

"Unconsciousness" of the nonhypnotic variety is a little more rugged. It takes more than a few passes of the hand to cause "unconsciousness" of the insanity-producing variety.

The shock of accidents, the anesthetics used for operations, the pain of injuries and the deliriums of illness are the principal sources of what we call "unconsciousness."

The mechanism, in our analogue of the mind, is very simple. In comes a destructive wave of physical pain or a pervading poison such as ether and out go some or all of the fuses of the analytical mind. When it goes out, so go what we know as the standard memory banks.

The periods of "unconsciousness" are blanks in the standard memory banks. These missing periods make up what Dianetics calls the *reactive mind bank*.

The times when the analytical mind is in full operation plus the times when the reactive mind is in operation are a continuous line of consecutive recording for the entire period of life.

During the periods when the analytical mind is cut out of circuit in full or in part, the reactive mind cuts in, in full or in part. In other words, if the analytical mind is unfused so that it is half out of circuit, the reactive mind is half in circuit. No such sharp percentages are actually possible, but this is to give an approximation.

When the individual is "unconscious" in full or in part, the reactive mind is cut in, in full or in part. When he is fully conscious, his analytical mind is fully in command of the organism. When his consciousness is reduced, the reactive mind is cut into the circuit just that much.

The moments which contain "unconsciousness" in the individual are contrasurvival moments, by and large. Therefore it is vital that something take over so that the individual can go through motions to save the whole organism. The fighter who fights half out on his feet, the burned man who drags himself out of the fire—these are cases when the reactive mind is valuable.

The reactive mind is very rugged. It would have to be in order to stand up to the pain waves which knock out other sentience in the body. It is not very refined. But it is most awesomely accurate. It possesses a low order of computing ability, an order which is submoron, but one would expect a low order of ability from a mind which stays in circuit when the body is being crushed or fried.

The reactive bank does not store memories as we think of them. It stores *engrams*.[19] These engrams are a complete recording, down to the last accurate detail, of

---

19. The word *engram*, in Dianetics is used in its severely accurate sense as a "definite and permanent trace left by a stimulus on the protoplasm of a tissue." It is considered as a unit group of stimuli impinged solely on the cellular being.

every perception present in a moment of partial or full "unconsciousness." They are just as accurate as any other recording in the body. But they have their own *force*. They are like phonograph records or motion pictures, if these contained all perceptions of sight, sound, smell, taste, organic sensation, etc.

The difference between an engram and a memory, however, is quite distinct. An engram can be permanently fused into any and all body circuits and behaves like an entity.

In all laboratory tests on these engrams they were found to possess "inexhaustible" sources of power to command the body. No matter how many times one was reactivated in an individual, it was still powerful. Indeed, it became even more able to exert its power in proportion to its reactivation.

The only thing which could even begin to shake these engrams was the technique which developed into Dianetic therapy, which will be covered in full in the third section of this volume.

This is an example of an engram: A woman is knocked down by a blow. She is rendered "unconscious." She is kicked and told she is a faker, that she is no good, that she is always changing her mind. A chair is overturned in the process. A faucet is running in the kitchen. A car is passing in the street outside. The engram contains a running record of all these perceptions: sight, sound, tactile, taste, smell, organic sensation, kinetic sense, joint position, thirst record, etc. The engram would consist of the whole statement made to her when she was "unconscious": the voice tones and emotion in the voice, the sound and feel of the original and later blows, the tactile of the floor, the feel and sound of the chair overturning, the organic sensation of the blow, perhaps the taste of blood in her mouth or any other taste present there, the smell of the person attacking her and the smells in the room, the sound of the passing car's motor and tires, etc.

These would all be considered something on the order of a "positive suggestion." But there is something else here which is new, something which is not in the standard banks except by context: *pain and painful emotion.*

These things are what make the difference between the standard banks and the reactive engram banks: physical pain and painful emotion. Physical pain and painful emotion are the difference between an engram, which is the cause of aberration—*all* aberration—and a memory.[20]

We all have heard that bad experience is helpful to living and that without bad experience, man never learns. This may be very, very true. But it doesn't embrace the engram. That isn't *experience.* That is *commanded action.*

Perhaps before man had a large vocabulary, these engrams were of some use to him. They were survival in ways which will be developed later. But when man acquired a fine, homonymic (words that sound the same but mean different things) language, and indeed, when he acquired any language, these engrams were much more a liability than a help. And now, with man well evolved, these engrams do not protect him at all but make him mad, inefficient and ill.

The proof of any assertion lies in its applicability. When these engrams are deleted from the reactive mind bank, rationality and efficiency are enormously heightened, health is greatly increased and the individual computes

---

20. In Dianetics, a *memory* is considered to be any concept of perceptions stored in the standard memory banks which is potentially recallable by the "I." A scene beheld by the eyes and perceived by the other senses becomes a record in the standard memory banks and later may be recalled by "I" for reference.

rationally on the survival conduct pattern, which is to say, he enjoys himself and the society of those around him and is constructive and creative. He is destructive only when something *actually* threatens the sphere of his dynamics.

These engrams, then, are entirely negative in value in this stage of man's development. When he was nearer the level of his animal cousins (who have, all of them, reactive minds of this same kind), he might have had use for the data. But language and his changed existence make any engram a distinct liability, and no engram has *any* constructive value.

The reactive mind was provided to secure survival. It still pretends to act in that fashion. But its wild errors now lead only in the other direction.

There are actually three kinds of engrams, all of them aberrative: First is the *contrasurvival engram*. This contains physical pain, painful emotion, all other perceptions and menace to the organism. A child knocked out by a rapist and abused receives this type of engram. The contrasurvival engram contains apparent or actual antagonism to the organism.

The second engram type is the *prosurvival engram*. A child who has been abused is ill. He is told, while he is partially or wholly "unconscious," that he will be taken care of, that he is dearly loved, etc. This engram is not taken as contrasurvival but prosurvival. It seems to be in favor of survival. Of the two this last is the most aberrative since it is reinforced by the law of affinity which is always more powerful than fear. Hypnotism preys on this characteristic of the reactive mind, being a sympathetic address to an artificially unconscious subject. Hypnotism is as limited as it is because it does not contain, as a factor, physical pain and painful emotion: things which keep an engram out of sight and moored below the level of "consciousness."

The third is the *painful emotion engram* which is similar to the other engrams. It is caused by the shock of sudden loss, such as the death of a loved one.

The reactive mind bank is composed exclusively of these engrams. The reactive mind thinks exclusively with these engrams. And it "thinks" with them in a way which would make Korzybski[21] swear, for it thinks in terms of full identification, which is to say *identities,* one thing *identical* to another.

If the analytical mind did a computation on apples and worms, it could be stated, probably, as follows: some apples have worms in them, others don't; when biting an apple one occasionally finds a worm unless the apple has been sprayed properly; worms in apples leave holes.

The reactive mind, however, doing a computation on apples and worms as contained in *its* engram bank, would calculate as follows: apples are worms are bites are holes in apples are holes in anything are apples and always are worms are apples are bites, etc.

The analytical mind's computations might embrace the most staggering summations of calculus, the shifty turns of symbolic logic, the computations requisite to bridge-building or dressmaking. Any mathematical equation ever seen came from the analytical mind and might be used by the analytical mind in resolving the most routine problems.

But not the reactive mind! That's so beautifully, wonderfully simple that it can be stated, in operation, to have just one equation: $A=A=A=A=A$.

Start any computation with the reactive mind. Start it with the data it contains, of course. Any datum is just the same to it as any other datum in the same experience.

An analytical computation done on the woman

---

21. Korzybski, Alfred: (1879–1950) American scientist and writer. Developed the subject of general semantics, a methodology that attempts to improve human behavior through a critical use of words and symbols.

being kicked, as mentioned, would be that women get themselves into situations sometimes when they get kicked and hurt and men have been known to kick and hurt women.

A reactive mind computation about this engram, as an engram, would be: the pain of the kick *equals* the pain of the blow *equals* the overturning chair *equals* the passing car *equals* the faucet *equals* the fact that she is a faker *equals* the fact that she is no good *equals* the fact that she changes her mind *equals* the voice tones of the man *equals* the emotion *equals* a faker *equals* a faucet running *equals* the pain of the kick *equals* organic sensation in the area of the kick *equals* the overturning chair *equals* changing one's mind *equals*. . . . But why continue? Every single perception in this engram *equals* every other perception in this engram. What? That's crazy? Precisely!

Let us further examine our posthypnotic positive suggestion of the touched tie and the removed coat. In this we have the visible factors of how the reactive mind operates.

This posthypnotic suggestion needs only an emotional charge and physical pain to make it a dangerous engram. Actually it *is* an engram of a sort. It is laid in by sympathy between the operator and subject, which would make it a sympathy engram—prosurvival.

Now, we know that the operator had only to touch his tie to make the awakened subject remove his coat. The subject did not know what it was which caused him to remove his coat and found all manner of explanation for the action, none of which was the right one. The engram, the posthypnotic suggestion in this case, was actually placed in the reactive mind bank. It was below the level of consciousness, it was compulsion springing from below the level of consciousness. And it worked upon the muscles to make the subject remove his coat. It was data fused into the circuits of the body below the command level of the analytical mind and operated not only upon the body but also upon the analytical mind itself.

If this subject took off his coat every time he saw somebody touch a necktie, society would account him slightly mad. And yet there was no power of consent about this. If he had attempted to thwart the operator by refusing to remove the coat, the subject would have experienced great discomfort of one sort or another.

Let us now take an example of the reactive mind's processes in a lower echelon of life: A fish swims into the shallows where the water is brackish, yellow and tastes of iron. He has just taken a mouthful of shrimp when a bigger fish rushes at him and knocks against his tail.

The small fish manages to get away but he has been physically hurt. Having negligible analytical powers, the small fish depends upon reaction for much of his choice of activity.

Now he heals his tail and goes on about his affairs. But one day he is attacked by a larger fish and gets his tail bumped. This time he is not seriously hurt, merely bumped. But something has happened. Something within him considers that in his choice of action he is now being careless. Here is a second injury in the same area.

The computation on the fish reactive level was: shallows equals brackish equals yellow equals iron taste equals pain in tail equals shrimp in mouth, and any one of these equals any other.

The bump in the tail on the second occasion *keyed in*[22] the engram. It demonstrated to the organism that something like the first accident (identity thought) could happen again. Therefore beware!

---

22. key-in: a moment when the environment around the awake but fatigued or distressed individual is itself similar to the dormant engram. At that moment the engram becomes active.

The small fish, after this, swims into brackish water. This makes him slightly "nervous." But he goes on swimming and finds himself in yellow and brackish water. And still he does not turn back. He begins to get a small pain in his tail. But he keeps on swimming. Suddenly he gets a taste of iron and the pain in his tail turns on heavily. And away he goes like a flash. No fish was after him.

There were shrimp to be had there. But away he went anyway.

Dangerous place! And if he had not turned away, he would have really gotten himself a pain in the tail.

The mechanism is survival activity of a sort. In a fish it may serve a purpose. But in a man, who takes off a coat every time somebody touches a tie, the survival mechanism has long outlived its time. *But it is there!*

Let us further investigate our young man and the coat. The signal for the coat removal was very precise. The operator touched his tie. This is equivalent to any or all of the perceptions the fish received and which made the fish turn back. The touch of the tie could have been a dozen things. Any one of the dozen might have signaled the removal of the coat.

In the case of the woman who was knocked out and kicked, any perception in the engram she received has some quality of *restimulation*.[23] Running water from a faucet might not have affected her greatly. But water running from a faucet *plus* a passing car might have begun some slight reactivation of the engram, a vague discomfort in the areas where she was struck and kicked, not enough yet to cause her real pain, but there all the same. To the running water and the passing car we add the sharp falling of a chair and she experiences a

---

23. restimulation: the reactivation of a past memory due to similar circumstances in the present approximating circumstances of the past.

shock of mild proportion. Add now the smell and voice of the man who kicked her and the pain begins to grow. The mechanism is telling her that she is in dangerous quarters, that she should leave. But she is not a fish, she is a highly sentient being, to our knowledge the most complex mental structure so far evolved on earth—organism of the species, man. There are many other factors in the problem than this one engram. She stays. The pains in the areas where she was abused become a predisposition[24] to illness or are chronic illness in themselves, minor, it is true, in the case of this one incident, but illness just the same. Her affinity with the man who beat her may be so high that the analytical level, being assisted by a normally high general tone, may counter against these pains. But if that level is low, without much to assist it, then the pains can become major.

The fish that was so struck and received an engram did not disavow shrimp. Shrimp might have made him a little less enthusiastic afterwards, but the survival potential of shrimp-eating made shrimp equal far more pleasure than it did pain.

A pleasant and hopeful life in general—and never think we intimate that the woman stays for food alone, whatever the wits say about women—has a high survival potential, and that can overcome a very great deal of pain. As the survival potential diminishes, however, the level of pain (zone 0 and zone 1) is more closely approached and such an engram could begin to be re-activated severely.

There is another factor here, however, besides pain —in fact, several more factors. If the young man with the detachable coat had been given one of the *neurotic* positive suggestions as listed a few pages back, he would

---

24. predisposition: a state of mind or body that renders a person liable to act or behave in a certain way or to be subject to certain diseases.

have reacted to it on signal.

The engram this woman has received contains a neurotic positive suggestion quite in addition to the general *restimulators*,[25] such as the faucet and the car and the overturning chair. She has been told that she is a faker, that she is no good and that she is always changing her mind. When the engram is restimulated in one of the great many ways possible, she has a "feeling" that she is no good, a faker and she *will* change her mind.

There are several cases to hand which peculiarly illustrate the sadness of this. One case in particular which was cleared had been beaten severely many times and told a similar thing each time, all derogatory. The content inferred that she was very loose[26] morally and would cohabit[27] with anyone. She was brought in as a case by her father—she had since been divorced—who complained that she was very loose morally and had cohabited with several men in as many weeks. She herself admitted that she was, she could not see how it could be and it worried her, but she just "could not seem to help it." Examination of the engrams in her reactive mind bank brought forth a long series of beatings with this content. Because this was a matter of research, not treatment—although that was given—her former husband was contacted. An examination, independent of her knowledge, demonstrated his rage dramatization[28] to contain these very words. *He had beaten his wife into*

---

25. restimulator: an approximation of the reactive mind's content or some part thereof continually perceived in the environment of the organism.

26. loose: lacking conventional moral restraint in sexual behavior.

27. cohabit: to live together in a sexual relationship when not legally married.

28. dramatization: the duplication of an engramic content, entire or in part, by an aberree in his present-time environment. Aberrated conduct is entirely dramatization. The degree of dramatization is in direct ratio to the degree of restimulation of the engrams causing it.

being a morally loose woman because he was afraid of morally loose women.

All cases examined in all this research were checked, the patient's engrams against the engrams in the donor. The contents of the incidents were verified wherever possible and were found uniformly to agree. Every safeguard was made to prevent any other method of communication between donor and patient. *Everything found in the "unconscious" periods of every patient, when checked against other sources, was found to be exact.*

The analogy between hypnotism and aberration bears out well. Hypnotism plants by positive suggestion one or another form of insanity. It is usually a temporary planting, but sometimes the hypnotic suggestion will not "lift" or remove in a way desirable to the hypnotist. The danger of running experiments with hypnosis on uncleared patients is found in another mechanism of the reactive mind.

When an engram such as our example above exists, the woman obviously was "unconscious" at the time she received the engram. She had no standard bank memory (record) of the incident beyond the knowledge that she had been knocked out by the man. The engram was not, then, an experience as we understand the word. It could work from below to aberrate her thinking processes, it could give her strange pains—which she attributed to something else—in the areas injured. But it was not *known* to her.

The *key-in* was necessary to activate the engram. But what, precisely, could key it in? At some later time when she was tired the man threatened to strike her again and called her names. This was conscious level experience. It was found to be "mentally painful" by her. And it was "mentally painful" only because there was real, live, physical pain unseen under it which had been "keyed in" by the conscious experience. The second experience was a *lock*.[29] It was a memory but it had a new kind of action in the standard banks. It had too much power and it gained that power from a past physical blow. The reactive mind is not too careful about its time clock. It can't tell one year old from ninety, in fact, when a key-in begins. The actual engram moved up under the standard bank.

She thinks she is worried about what he said in the *lock* experience. She is actually worried about the engram. In this way memories become "painful." But pain doesn't store in the standard banks. There is no place in that bank *for* pain. None. There is a place for the concept of pain and these concepts of what is painful are good enough to keep the sentient organism called man away from all the pain he believes is actually dangerous. In a clear there *are* no pain-inducing memories because there is no physical pain record left to ruin the machinery from the reactive mind bank.

The young man with the detachable coat did not know what was worrying him or what made him do what he did. The person with an engram does not know what is worrying him. He thinks it is the *lock,* and the *lock* may be a very long way removed from anything resembling the engram. The lock may have similar perceptic content. But it may be on another subject entirely.

It is not very complicated to understand what these engrams do. They are simply moments of physical pain strong enough to throw part or all the analytical machinery out of circuit; they are antagonism to the survival of the organism or pretended sympathy to the organism's survival. That is the entire definition. Great or little

29. lock: an analytical moment in which the perceptics of the engram are approximated, thus restimulating the engram or bringing it into action, the present-time perceptics being erroneously interpreted by the reactive mind to mean that the same condition which produced physical pain once before is now again at hand.

"unconsciousness," physical pain, perceptic content and contrasurvival or prosurvival data. They are handled by the reactive mind, which thinks exclusively in identities of everything equals everything. And they enforce their commands upon the organism by wielding the whip of physical pain. If the organism does not do exactly as they say (and believe any clear, that's impossible!), the physical pain turns on. They steer a person like a keeper steers a tiger—and they can make a tiger out of a man in the process without much trouble, and give him mange[30] into the bargain.

If man had not invented language, or, as will be demonstrated, if his languages were a little less homonymic and more specific with their personal pronouns, engrams would still be survival data and the mechanism would work. But man has outgrown their use. He chose between language and potential madness and for the vast benefits of the former he received the curse of the latter.

The engram is the single and sole source of aberration and psychosomatic illness.

An enormous quantity of data has been sifted. Not one single exception has been found. In "normal people," in the neurotic and insane, the removal of these engrams wholly or in part, without other therapy, has uniformly brought about a state greatly superior to the current norm. No need was found for any theory or therapy other than those given in this book for the treatment of all psychic or psychosomatic ills.

30. mange: a skin disease affecting hairy animals, caused by a parasite and characterized by intense itching, scabs and loss of hair.

CHAPTER THREE

The Cell and the Organism

The reason the engram so long remained hidden as the single source of aberration and psychosomatic ills is the wide and almost infinitely complex manifestations which can derive from simple engrams.

Several theories could be postulated as to why the human mind evolved exactly as it did, but these are theories, and Dianetics is not concerned with structure. A comment or two as a stimulation to future workers in that field might be made, however, wholly as a postulate, that there is a definite connection between any electric-like energy in the body and the energy effusion[1] of cells undergoing injury. A theory could be constructed along the lines that injured cells, further injuring their neighbors by a discharge of electric-like energy, forced the development of a special cell which would act as a conduit to "bleed off" this painful charge. The conduits of cells might have become neurons[2] and the charge might have been better distributed so through the body with less likelihood of local incapacitation at the point of the injury impact. These conduits—neurons—might have been started in formation by impacts at the extremity of the body toward the direction of locomotion. This would make the skull the greatest mass of neurons. Man, walking upright, might have had another new point of impact, the forehead, and so gained his prefrontal lobes. And maybe not. That is just theory, with only a few data to support it which have a scientific value. And it has

---

1. effusion: a pouring forth.
2. neuron: the structural and functional unit of the nervous system.

not been subjected to experiment of any kind whatever.

This much, however, has to be advanced as theory on structure. The cell is one of the basic building blocks of the body. Cells, the better to survive, seem to have become colonies which, in turn, had the primary interest, survival. And the colonies developed or recruited into aggregations which in turn were organisms, also with the sole purpose of survival. And the organisms developed minds to coordinate the muscles and resolve the problems of survival. Again, this is still theory, and even if it was the track of reasoning which led toward Dianetics, it can be completely wrong. It works. It can be pulled away from Dianetics and Dianetics will remain a science and go on working. The concept of the electronic brain was not vital but only useful to Dianetics and it could be swept away as well—Dianetics would still stand. A science is a changing affair as far as its internal theory goes. In Dianetics we have our wedge into an enormous scope of research. As Dianetics stands, it works and it works every time and without exception. The reasons why it works will undoubtedly be mulled over and changed here and there to its betterment —if they aren't, an abiding faith in this generation of scientists and the future generations will not have been justified.

Why we talk about cells will become apparent as we progress. The reason we know that past concepts of structure are not correct is because they *don't* work as function. All our facts are functional and these facts are scientific facts, supported wholly and completely by laboratory evidence. Function precedes structure. James Clerk Maxwell's[3] mathematics were postulated and electricity was widely and beneficially used long before anyone had any real idea about the structure of the atom.

---

3. Maxwell, James Clerk: (1831–79) Scottish physicist.

Function always comes before structure. The astounding lack of progress in the field of the human mind during the past thousands of years is partly attributable to its "organ of thought" lying within a field, medicine, which was and long may be an art, not a science. Basic philosophy to explain life will have to come before that art makes much further progress.

What the capabilities of the cell are, for instance, have been but poorly studied. Some work has been carried on in recent years to find out more, but basic philosophy was absent. The cell was being observed, not predicted.

The studies of cells in man have been largely done from dead tissue. An unknown quality is missing from dead tissue, the important quality—life.

In Dianetics, on the level of laboratory observation, we discover much to our astonishment that cells are evidently sentient in some currently inexplicable way. Unless we postulate a human soul entering the sperm and ovum at conception, there are things which no other postulate will embrace than that these cells *are* in some way sentient. Entering a new field with postulates which work in all directions—and the basic philosophy of survival is a pilot which leads us on and on into further and further realms, explaining and predicting phenomena on every hand—it is inevitable that data will turn up which does not agree with past theory. When that data is as scientific as the observation that when an apple is dropped under usual conditions on earth it falls, one cannot help but accept it. Abandoning past theories may do damage to treasured beliefs and one's nostalgic love of the old school tie, but a fact is a fact.

The cells as thought units evidently have an influence, as cells, upon the body as a thought unit and an organism. We do not have to untangle this structural problem to resolve our functional postulates. The cells evidently retain engrams of painful events. After all, they are the things which get injured. And they evidently retain a whip hand of punishment for every time the analyzer fails them. The story of the engram seems to be a story of a battle between the troops and the general, every time the general gets some of the troops killed off. The less fortunate this general is in protecting these troops, the more power the troops assume. The cells evidently pushed the brain on an upward evolution toward higher sentience. Pain reverses the process as though the cells were sorry they had put so much power in the hands of a central commander.

The reactive mind may very well be the combined cellular intelligence. One need not assume that it is, but it is a handy structural theory in the lack of any real work done in this field of structure. The reactive engram bank may be material stored in the cells themselves. It does not matter whether this is credible or incredible just now. Something has to be said about it to give one a mental hold on what happens during moments of "unconsciousness."

The scientific fact, observed and tested, is that the organism, in the presence of physical pain, lets the analyzer get knocked out of circuit so that there is a limited quantity or no quantity at all of personal awareness as a unit organism. It does this either to protect the analyzer or to withdraw its power in the belief that an engram is best in an emergency—with which the analyzer, by the way, on observed experience, does not agree.

Every percept present, including physical pain, is recorded during these nonanalytical moments. Whenever pain is present—physical pain, that is—the analyzer gets shut down to a small or large extent. If the duration of the pain is only an instant, there is still an instant there of analytical reduction. This can be proven very easily—just try to recall the last time you were seriously hurt and see if there isn't at least a momentary blank period. Going to sleep under anesthetic and waking up some time later is a more complicated sort of shutdown in that it includes physical pain but is initially caused by a poison (and all anesthetics are poisons, technically). Then there is the condition of suffocating, as in drowning, and this is a shut-down period to greater or lesser extent. And there is the condition caused by blood, for one cause or another, leaving the area or areas which contain analytical power—wherever they are—and this again causes a greater or lesser degree of analytical shutdown: such incidents include shock (in which the blood tends to lake in the center of the body), the loss of blood by surgery or injury or anemia,[4] and the closing of the arteries leading through the throat. Natural sleep causes a reduction of analytical activity but is actually not very deep or serious; by Dianetic therapy any experience occurring during sleep can be recovered with ease.

It can now be seen that there are many ways in which analytical power can be shut down. And it can be seen that there is greater or lesser reduction. When one burns one's finger with a cigarette, there is a small instant of pain and a small amount of reduction. When one undergoes an operation, the duration may be in terms of hours and the amount of shutdown may be extreme. The duration and the amount of reduction are two different things, related but quite dissimilar. This is not so very important but it is mentioned.

We have seen, reading in Dianetics this far, that the principle of the spectrum has been quite useful to us. And it can be seen that the amount of reduction in analytical power can be described in the same way that survival potential can be described. There can be a very little bit and there can be a very great deal. Going

---

4. anemia: a deficiency in the oxygen-carrying material of the blood, resulting in a paleness, generalized weakness, etc.

back and taking a look at the survival potential range, one can see that there would be death at the bottom and immortality at the top. There is "infinite" survival. Whether or not there can be infinite analytical power is a matter of mysticism. But that there is a definite relationship between individual tone and the amount of analytical shutdown is a scientific fact. Put it this way: with the individual well and happy and enthusiastic, analytical power can be considered to be high (zones 3 and 4). With the individual under the wheels of a truck, "unconscious" and in agony, the analytical power may be considered to be ranging in zone 0. There is a ratio between potential survival and analytical power. As one goes down, so does the other. There is more data to be concluded from this than one would think at first glance. It is a very important ratio.

All the percepts are included in an engram. Two of these percepts are physical pain and painful emotion. A third is organic sensation, which is to say, the condition of the organism during the moment of the engram. And how was the organism when the engram was received? Greater or lesser "unconsciousness" was present. This meant that there was an organic sensation of reduced analytical power, since analytical power derives, evidently, from an organ or organs in the body. If an engram is reactivated by a restimulator or restimulators —that is to say, if the individual with an engram receives something in his environment similar to the perceptions in the engram—the engram puts everything it contains, its percepts such as faucets and words, into greater or lesser operation.

There can be greater or lesser restimulation. An engram can be put into force just a little bit by restimulators in the environment of the individual or, with many restimulators present and the body in an already reduced state, the engram can go into a full-force display (which is covered later). But whether the engram is slightly restimulated or greatly restimulated, everything in it goes into effect one way or another.

There is just one common denominator of all engrams, just one thing which every engram has and which is possessed by every other engram. Each contains the datum that the analyzer is more or less shut down. There is a shut-down datum in every engram. Therefore, every time an engram is restimulated, *even though physical pain has not been received by the body,* some analytical power turns off; the organ or organs which are the analyzer are fused out of circuit in some degree.

This is highly important to an understanding of the mechanics of aberration. It is a scientific fact, susceptible of proof, and it never varies. This always happens: when an engram is received, the analyzer is shut down by the physical pain and emotion; when the engram is restimulated, the analyzer shuts down as part of the commands of the engram. Actually, this is a very mechanical thing. Engram is restimulated, part of the analytical power is shut down. This is as inevitable as turning on and off an electric light. Pull the cord and the light goes off. The reduction of the analyzer is not that sharp—there are grades of light—but it is just as mechanical.

Put a man under ether, hurt him in the chest. He has received an engram because his analytical power was turned off first by ether and then by a chest pain. While he was there on the operating table, the reactive mind recorded the click of instruments, everything said, all sounds and smells. Let us suppose that a nurse was holding one of his feet because he was kicking. This is a complete engram.

The engram will be keyed in by something in the future, a similar incident. After this, in greater or lesser degree, whenever he hears clicks like instrument clicks he gets nervous. If he pays attention to what is happening in his body at that minute, he may find that his foot feels slightly as if it were being held. But he is not likely to give any attention to his foot because if he had any attention to give, the chest pain would be found present in some degree. But his analytical ability has been turned off slightly. As the foot felt it was being held, so does the analyzer have the conception of being shut down by ether and pain. The restimulator (the clicking) tended to bring the whole engram slightly into being and part of the engram command is a reduced analytical power.

This is "push button" in its precision. If one knew another's main restimulators (words, voice tones, music, whatever they are—things which are filed in the reactive mind bank as parts of engrams), one could turn another's analytical power almost completely off, actually render him unconscious.

We all know people who make us feel stupid. There can be two causes for that but both of them are from engrams and one of them is the fact that, no matter what engram is brought into restimulation, part of the analytical power is turned off.

Engrams can, if environment is uniform, be held in chronic restimulation! This means a chronic, partial shutdown of analytical power. The recovery of intelligence by a clear and the rise of that intelligence to such fantastic heights results in part from the relief of word commands in engrams that he is stupid and in a larger part from the relief of this chronic shut-down condition.

This is not theory. This is scientific fact. It is strictly test tube. The engram contains the percept of a shut-down analyzer; when it is restimulated the engram puts that datum back into force in some degree.

Engrams, then, being received in "unconsciousness" cause a partial "unconsciousness" to exist every time they are restimulated. The person who has an engram (any aberree) need not receive new physical pain to have a new moment of partial "unconsciousness" take place. Feeling "dopey" or "sleepy" or "dull" results in part from a partially shut-down analyzer. Being "nervous" or in a rage or frightened also carries with it partially shut off analytical power.

The hypnotist has "success" where he does because he is able, by talking to people about "sleep," to put into restimulation some engram which contains the word *sleep* and shut-down analytical power. This is one of the reasons hypnotism "works."

The whole society, however, is liable to analytical shutdown in greater or lesser degree by the restimulation of engrams.

The number of engrams a person's reactive bank contains may not, however, establish the amount of analytical reduction to which he is subjected. A person may have engrams and they may not have been keyed in. And if they have been keyed in, he might not be in an environment which contains any great number of re-stimulators. Under these conditions his survival zone position may be high even though he is possessed of a great many engrams. And again, he might have educated himself over and above these engrams to some slight degree.

But a person who has keyed-in engrams and does exist in the area of many restimulators is liable to an enormous amount of restimulation and analytical shut-down. This is a normal condition. If a person has a large number of engrams, and they are keyed in, and he lives around many restimulators, his condition can vary from normal to insane. And in a single day—as in the case of a man who experiences moments of rage or a woman who drops into apathies—the condition of a person may vary from normal to insane and back to normal. We take here the word *insane* to mean utter irrationality. So there is temporary or chronic insanity.

The court of law which goes through the lugubrious[5] process of having a man pronounced sane or insane after that man has murdered somebody is itself being irrational. Of course the man was insane *when* he committed the murder. What the court is asking now is whether or not the man is *chronically* insane. This has little bearing on the matter. If a man has gone insane enough to murder once, he will go insane enough in the future to murder again. Chronic, then, means either a chronic cycle or a continuous condition. The law says *sanity* is the "ability to tell right from wrong." When man is subject to a mechanism (and all men are) which lets him be rational one minute and restimulated the next, none in the society, if uncleared, can be considered able to always tell right from wrong. This is completely aside from what the law means by *right* and what it means by *wrong*.

This is an example of the roller-coaster sanity curve of the aberree. All aberrees possess engrams (the normal number is probably in the hundreds per individual). Analytically, people have a wide latitude of choice and they can deal even with philosophic rights and wrongs. But in aberrated persons the engram bank is always susceptible of restimulation. The "sanest" aberree of Tuesday may be a murderer on Wednesday if the exactly right situation occurs to trip the exact engram. A clear is not entirely predictable in any given situation—he has such a wide power of choice. But an aberrated person transcends all predictability for the following reasons: (1) what engrams an aberree has in his reactive engram bank none know including himself; (2) what situation will contain what restimulators is a matter of chance;

---

5. lugubrious: very sad or mournful, especially in a way that seems exaggerated or ridiculous.

and (3) what his power of choice will be with the factors in the engrams on a reactive level cannot be established.

The variety of conduct which one can evolve out of these basic mechanics is so wide that it is no wonder that man was considered to be a rather hopeless case by some philosophies.

The cells, if the engram bank is retained on a cellular level, might be theoretically supposed to have made sure that the analyzer did not get too adventurous in this life-and-death matter of living. They therefore could be considered to have copied down all data contained in every moment of physical pain and emotion resulting in or contained in "unconsciousness." Then when any data similar to this appeared in the environment they could be wary and, with a large number of restimulators in sight, they could be considered to shut down the analyzer and proceed on reaction. This has a crude safety factor. Obviously, if the organism survived through one period of "unconsciousness," it could be theorized by the cells that the placing of the data and action in effect under circumstances which threatened to be similar would result once more in survival. What's good enough for Grandpa is good enough for me. What was good enough in the bus accident is good enough in a bus.

This moronic "thinking" is typical of the reactive mind. It is just the sort of thinking it does. It is the ultimate in conservatism. It misses the point and important data at every turn, it overloads the body with pain, it is a whirlpool of confusion. If there were just one engram per situation, maybe it would get by. But there may be ten engrams with similar data in them (an *engram lock chain*[6]) and yet the data may be so contradictory that when a new emergency arises which contains

6. chain: a series of incidents of similar nature or similar subject matter.

the restimulators of the chain, no proper past conduct can be put forth to meet it.

Obviously the *x* factor is language. The cells, if this is a problem in cells (for recall, this part is theory based on data in an effort to explain what happens, and a theory can be altered without altering the scientific usefulness of the facts), probably do not understand languages very well. If they did they wouldn't evolve such "solutions."

Take two engrams about baseball bats. In the first, the individual is hit on the head and knocked out and somebody yells, "Run! Run! Run!" In the second, the individual is knocked out by the bat in the same environment and somebody yells, "Stay there! You're safe!" Now, what does he do when he hears a baseball bat or smells one or sees one or hears these words? Run or stay there? He has a similar pain for each action. What actually happens? He gets a headache. This is that thing called conflict. This is anxiety. And anxiety can become very acute indeed on a purely mechanical level when one has ninety engrams pulling him south and eighty-nine pulling him north. Does he go north or south? Or does he have a "nervous breakdown"?

The level of brilliance of the reactive mind is about the same as a phonograph. The needle gets put on the record and the record plays. The reactive mind merely puts on the needle. When it tries to select several records out and play them all at once, things happen.

By intentional construction or accident in design or bypass in evolution—where the old, useless organ is still built—the cells managed to hide this engram bank fairly well. Man is conscious in his analytical mind. When he is "unconscious," his analytical mind is unable to monitor the incoming data and the data is not to be found in the thing we call, by analogue, the standard banks. Therefore whatever came in passed by consciousness.

And having passed by, consciousness cannot (without Dianetic process) recall it, since there is no channel for recall.

The engram enters when consciousness is absent. It thereafter operates directly into the organism. Only by Dianetic therapy can the analyzer come into possession of this data (and the removal of it does not depend upon the analyzer contacting it at all, despite an old belief that the "realization" of something cures it: "realize" an engram and one is in quick trouble, without Dianetic technique). The engram is received by the cellular body. The reactive mind could be the very lowest level of analytical power, of course, but this does not alter the scientific fact that the engram acts as if it were a soldered-in connection to the life function regulator and the organic coordination and the basic level of the analytical mind itself. By *soldered-in* is meant "permanent connection." This keying-in is the hookup of the engram as part of the operating machinery of the body. An analytical thought process is not permanently hooked in but can be thrown in and out of circuit at the will of the analyzer. This is not true of the engram. Thus the term, *soldered-in*.

The analytical mind lays down a training pattern; on a stimulus-response basis, this training pattern will work smoothly and well whenever it will do the organism the most good. An engram is a training pattern, all complete in a package, "permanently" hooked into the circuits (without Dianetic therapy) and it goes into operation like a training pattern without any consent whatever from the analyzer.

Influenced itself by the engram in the several ways of reduced analytical power and positive suggestion in the engram, the analytical mind is unable to discover any truly valid reason for the conduct of the organism. It therefore makes up a reason, for its job is to make sure the organism is always right. Just as the young man with the detachable coat gave forth a number of silly explanations as to why he was detaching his coat, so does the analytical mind—observing the body engaged in irrational actions, including speech, for which there seems to be no accounting—justify the actions. The engram can dictate all the various processes incident to living; it can dictate beliefs, opinions, thought processes or lack of them and actions of all kinds, and can establish conditions remarkable for their complexity as well as their stupidity. An engram can dictate anything it contains and engrams can contain all the combinations of words in the entire language. And the analytical mind is forced, in the light of irrational behavior or conviction, to *justify* the acts and conditions of the organism, as well as its own strange blunders. This is *justified thought*.

There are three kinds of thought, then, of which the organism is capable: (a) analytical thought, which is rational as modified by education and viewpoint; (b) justified thought, analytical thought attempting to explain reactions; and (c) reactive thought, which is wholly in terms of everything in an engram equals everything in an engram equals all the restimulators in the environment and all things associated with those restimulators.

We have all seen somebody make a blunder and then give forth an explanation of just why that blunder had been made. This is justified thought. The blunder was made, unless out of education or viewpoint, by an engram. The analytical mind then had to justify the blunder to make sure that the body was right and that its computations were right.

Now, there are two other conditions which can be caused by engrams. One is *dramatization* and the other is *valence*.[7]

---

7. valence: personality. The term is used to denote the borrowing of the personality of another. A preclear "in his father's valence" is acting as if he were his father.

You have seen some child come forth with a tirade, a tantrum. You have seen some man go through a whole rage action. You have seen people go through a whole irrational set of actions. These are *dramatizations*. They come about when an engram is thoroughly restimulated, so thoroughly that its soldered-in aspect takes over the organism. It may come into circuit slightly or wholly, which is to say that there are degrees of dramatization. When it is in full parade, the engram is running off verbatim and the individual is like an actor, puppet-like, playing his dictated part. A person can be given new engrams which will make these old ones take secondary importance. (Society's punishment complex is aimed squarely at giving anti-engram education.)

Dramatization is survival conduct—in the silly, reactive mind way of thinking—based on the premise that the organism, in a "similar" situation, lived through it because these actions were present.

The woman who was knocked down and kicked would dramatize her engram, possibly, by doing and saying exactly the same things done and said to her. Her victim may be her child or another woman. It could or would be the person who gave her the engram if she were strong enough to overcome him. Just because she has this engram does not mean she will use it. She may have a hundred other engrams she can use. But when she dramatizes one it is as if the engram, soldered-in, were taking over a puppet. As much analytical power as she has left may be devoted to altering the pattern. Therefore she can make a similar or an identical dramatization.

This aspect of dramatization is strictly "tooth and claw" survival. This is the sort of thing which made observers think that "tooth and claw" was a primary rule.

In went the engram, bypassing rationality and the standard memory banks. Now it is in the organism but the organism does not know it in the level of consciousness. It is keyed in by a conscious level experience. Then it can be dramatized. And far from becoming milder the more it is used, the more an engram is dramatized the more solid is its hold in the circuits. Muscles, nerves, all must comply.

"Tooth and claw" survival. The cells were making sure. And here we come to *valence*. *Valens* means "powerful" in Latin. It is a good term because it is the second half of *ambivalent* (power in two directions) and exists in any good dictionary. It is a good term because it describes (although the dictionary did not mean it to) the intent of the organism when dramatizing an engram. *Multivalence* would mean "many powerfuls." It would embrace the phenomena of split personality, the strange differences of personality in people in one and then another situation. *Valence, in Dianetics, means the personality of one of the dramatic personnel in an engram.*

In the case of the woman being knocked out and kicked, there were two valences present: herself and her husband. If another person had been present the engram would have contained three valences, providing he took any part: herself, her husband and the third person. In an engram, let us say, of a bus accident where ten people speak or act, there would be, in the "unconscious" person, an engram containing eleven valences: the "unconscious" person and the ten who spoke or acted.

Now, in the case of the woman beaten by her husband, the engram contains just two valences. Who won? Here is the law of "tooth and claw," the aspect of survival in engrams. Who won? The husband. Therefore it is the husband who will be dramatized. She didn't win. She got hurt. Aha! When these restimulators are present, the thing to do is to be the winner, the husband, to talk like him, to say what he did, to do what he did. He survived. "Be like him!" say the cells.

Hence, when the woman is restimulated into this engram by some action, let us say, on the part of her child, she dramatizes the winning valence. She knocks the child down and kicks him, tells him he is a faker, that he is no good, that he is always changing his mind.

What would happen if she dramatized herself? She would have to fall down, knocking over a chair, pass out and believe she was a faker, no good and was always changing her mind, and she would have to feel the pain of all blows!

"Be yourself" is advice which falls on deaf reactive mind ears. Here is the scheme. Every time the organism gets punished by life, the analytical mind, according to the reactive mind, has erred. The reactive mind then cuts the analytical mind out of circuit in ratio to the amount of restimulation present (danger) and makes the body react as if it were the person who won in the earlier, but similar, situation where the organism was hurt.

Now what happens if "society" or the husband or some exterior force told this woman, who is dramatizing this engram, that she must face reality? That's impossible. Reality equals being herself, and herself gets hurt. What if some exterior force *breaks the dramatization?* That is to say, if society objects to the dramatization and refuses to let her kick and yell and shout? The engram is still soldered-in. The reactive mind is forcing her to be the winning valence. Now she can't be. As punishment, the reactive mind, the closer she slides into being herself, approximates the conditions of the other valence in the engram. After all, that valence didn't die. And the pain of the blows turns on and she thinks she is a faker, that she is no good and that she always changes her mind. In other words, she is in the losing valence. Consistent *breaking of dramatization* will make a person ill just as certainly as there are gloomy days.

A person accumulates, with the engrams, half a hundred valences before he is ten. Which were the winning valences? You will find him using them every time an engram is kicked into restimulation. Multiple personality? Two persons? Make it fifty to a hundred. In Dianetics, you can see valences turn on and off in people and change with a rapidity which would be awesome to a quick-change artist.

Observe these complexities of conduct, of behavior. If one set out to resolve the problem of aberration by a system of cataloguing everything he observed, and were unaware of the basic source, he would end up with as many separate insanities, neuroses, psychoses, compulsions, repressions, obsessions and disabilities as there are combinations of words in the English language. Discovery of fundamentals by classification is never good research. And the unlimited complexities possible from the engrams (and the severest, most thoroughly controlled experiments discovered these engrams to be capable of just such behavior as is listed here) are the whole catalogue of aberrated human conduct.

There are a few other basic, fundamental things that engrams do. These will be covered under their own headings: parasite circuits, emotional impaction and psychosomatic ills. With the few fundamentals listed here, the problem of aberration can be resolved. These fundamentals are simple, they have given rise to as much trouble as individuals and societies have experienced. The institutions for the insane, the prisons for the criminals, the armaments accumulated by nations, yes, and even the dust which was a civilization of yesterday exist because these fundamentals were not understood.

The cells evolved into an organism and in the evolution created what was once a necessary condition of mind. Man has grown up to a point where he creates now the means of overcoming that evolutionary blunder. Examination of the clear proves he no longer needs it. He is now in a position where he can take an artificial evolutionary step on his own. The bridge has been built across the canyon.

CHAPTER FOUR

The "Demons"

For a moment let us leave such scientific things as cells and consider some further aspects of the problem of understanding the human mind.

People have been working on problems related to man's behavior for a good many millennia. Hindu, Egyptian, Greek, Roman and our own philosophers and researchers of the past few hundred years have been struggling against a superabundance of complexity.

Dianetics could be evolved only by the philosophic compartmentation of the problem into its elements and the invention of several dozen yardsticks, such as "the introduction of an arbitrary," "the law of affinity," "the dynamic," "the equation of the optimum solution," "the laws of the selection of importances," "the science of organizing sciences," "nullification by comparison of authority to authority," and so forth and so forth. All this is fine matter for a tome on philosophy, but here is Dianetics, which is a science. It should be mentioned, however, that one of the first steps taken was not invented but borrowed and modified: that was the "knowable" and "unknowable" of Herbert Spencer.

Absolutism is a fine road to stagnation and I do not think Spencer meant to be so entirely absolute about his "knowable" and "unknowable." **Survive!** is the demarcation point between those things which can be experienced by the senses (our old friends Hume[1] and Locke[2]) and those things which cannot necessarily be known

1. Hume, David: (1711–76) Scottish philosopher and historian.
2. Locke, John: (1632–1704) English philosopher.

through the senses, but which possibly may be known but which one does not necessarily need to solve the problem.

Amongst those things which one did not necessarily need to know (the Dianetic version of the "unknowable") were the realms of mysticism and metaphysics. Many things, in the evolution of Dianetics, were bypassed solely because they had not yielded solution to anyone else. Therefore mysticism got short shrift[3] despite the fact that the author studied it, not in the little-understood, secondhand sources commonly used as authority by some Western mental cults, but in Asia where a mystic who can't make his "astral self" get out and run errands for him is strictly a second-rate character indeed. Well aware that there were pieces in this jigsaw puzzle which were orange with yellow spots and purple with carmine stripes, one found it necessary to pick up only those pieces which were germane. Someday a large number of pieces—about structure with the rest —will come in and there will be answers to telepathy,[4] prescience[5] and so on and on. Understand that there are a lot of pieces in the construction of a philosophic universe. But none of the mystic pieces were found necessary to the creation of a uniformly applicable and aberration-resolving science of mind. No opinion will be delivered at this stage of Dianetics about ghosts or the Indian rope trick beyond the fact they are seen to be multicolored pieces and the only ones we want are white. We have most of the white pieces and it makes a good, solid whiteness where there was blackness before.

Imagine, then, the consternation one must have felt

---

3. short shrift: unsympathetic treatment.

4. telepathy: communication from one mind to another without the use of speech or writing or gestures, etc.

5. prescience: knowledge of events or actions before they happen.

when "demons" were discovered. Socrates had a demon, you'll remember. It told him not what to do but whether or not he had made the right decision. Here we had been pursuing a course in the finite universe which would have pleased Hume himself for its tenacity to those things which could be sensed. And up popped "demons."

A thorough examination of a number of subjects (fourteen) revealed that every one apparently had a "demon" of some sort. They were randomly selected subjects in various conditions in society. Therefore the "demon" aspect was most alarming. However, unlike some of the cults (or schools, as they call themselves), the temptation to sail off into romantic, inexplicable and confounding labels was resisted. A bridge had to be built across a canyon and demons are darned bad girders.

Out in the Pacific islands—Borneo, the Philippines —I had seen quite a bit of demonology at work. Demonology is fascinating stuff. A demon gets into a person and makes him sick. Or it gets in and talks in lieu of him. Or he goes crazy because he has a demon in him and runs around with the demon shouting. This is demonology in a narrow sense. The shaman, the medicine man, these people deal pretty heavily in demonology (it pays well). But, while not skeptical particularly, it had always seemed to me that demons could be explained a little more easily than in terms of ectoplasm[6] or some such unsensible material.

To find "demons" living in one's civilized fellow countrymen was disturbing. But there they were. At least there were the manifestations which the shaman and medicine man had said were caused by demons. It was found that these "demons" could be catalogued. There were "commanding demons," "critical demons,"

---

6. ectoplasm: the luminous substance believed to emanate from a spiritualistic medium.

ordinary "tell-you-what-to-say demons" and "demons" which stood around and yelled or "demons" which simply occluded things and kept them out of sight. These are not all the classes, but they cover the general field of "demonology."

A few experiments with drugged subjects showed that it was possible to set these "demons" up at will. It was even possible to set up the whole analytical mind as a "demon." So there was something wrong with demonology. Without proper ritual, simply by word of mouth, one could make new demons appear in people. _So there are no real demons in Dianetics_ (that's underscored in case some mystic runs around telling people that a new science of mind believes in demons).

A Dianetic demon is a parasitic circuit. It has an action in the mind which approximates another entity than self. And it is derived entirely from words contained in engrams.

How this demon gets there is not very hard to understand once you've inspected one, close up. Papa, while baby is unconscious, yells at Mama that she's got to listen to him and nobody else, by God. The baby gets an engram. It is keyed in some time between babyhood and death. And then there's the demon circuit at work.

An electronics engineer can set up demons in a radio circuit to his heart's content. In human terms, it is as if one ran a line from the standard banks toward the analyzer but before it got there he put in a speaker and a microphone and then continued the line to the plane of consciousness. Between the speaker and the microphone would be a section of the analyzer which was an ordinary, working section but compartmented off from the remainder of the analyzer. "I" on a conscious plane wants data. It should come straight from the standard bank, compute on a sublevel and arrive just as data. Not spoken data. Just data.

117

With the portion of the analyzer compartmented off and the speaker-microphone installation and the engram containing the above words "got to listen to me, by God" in chronic restimulation, another thing happens. The "I" in the upper level attention units wants data. He starts to scan the standard banks with a sublevel. The data comes to him *spoken*. Like a voice inside his head.

A clear does not have any "mental voices"! He does not think vocally. He thinks without articulation of his thoughts and his thoughts are not in voice terms. This will come as a surprise to many people. The "listen to me" demon is common in the society, which is to say this engram circulates widely. "Stay right there and listen to me" fixes the engram in present time (and fixes the individual in the time of the engram, to some extent). After it is keyed in and from there on, the individual thinks "out loud," which is to say, he puts his thoughts into language. This is very slow. The mind thinks out solutions (in a clear) at such speed that the word stream of consciousness would be left at the post.[7]

Proving this was very easy. In clearing every case, without exception, one or another of these demons was discovered. Some cases had three or four. Some had ten. Some had one. It is a safe assumption that almost every aberree contains a demon circuit.

The type of engram which makes a critical demon is, "You are always criticizing me." There are dozens of such statements contained in engrams, any one of which will make a critical demon, just as any combination of words resulting in a demand to listen and obey orders will make a commanding demon.

All these demons are parasitic. That is to say, they take a part of the analyzer and compartment it off. A demon can think only as well as the person's mind can

---

7. post: the starting gate at a racetrack.

think. There is no extra power. No benefit. All loss.

It is possible to set up the whole computer (analyzer) as a demon circuit and leave "I" on a tiny and forlorn shelf. This, on the surface, is a pretty good stunt. It makes it possible for the whole analytical mind to work out computations undisturbed and relay the answer to the "I." But in practice it is very bad, for "I" is the will, the determining force of the organism, the awareness. And very soon "I" becomes so dependent upon this circuit that the circuit begins to absorb him. Any such circuit, to last, would have to have pain and be chronic. It would have to be, in short, an engram. Therefore, it would have to be reductive of the intellect and would victimize the owner by eventually making him ill one way or another.

Of all the engram demon circuits found and removed, those which contained a seemingly all-powerful exterior entity which would solve all problems and answer every want were the most dangerous. As the engram keyed in further and further and was constantly re-stimulated, it eventually made a spineless puppet out of "I"; because other engrams existed, the sum of the reduction tended toward insanity of a serious sort. If you want a sample, just imagine what you would have to say to a hypnotized person to make him think that he was in the hands of a powerful being who gave him orders and then imagine this as the phrase spoken when an individual had been knocked unconscious one way or another.

There is another full class of demons, the occlusion demons, the demons who shut things off. These are not properly demons because they don't talk. A bona fide demon is one who gives thoughts voice or echoes the spoken word interiorly or who gives all sorts of complicated advice like a real, live voice exteriorly. (People who hear voices have exterior vocal demons—circuits which have tied up their imagination circuits.) The occlusion demon doesn't have anything to say. It is what he doesn't permit to be said or done that makes the mental derangement.

An occlusion demon can exist for a single word. For instance, a child receives an engram by falling off her bicycle and losing consciousness; a policeman tries to assist her; she is still unconscious but moving and mutters that she can't move (an old engram at work); the officer says, cheerfully, "Never say can't!" Some time later she has a conscious level experience such as another fall but without injury. (We keep mentioning this second necessary step, the *lock,* because it is the thing old time mystics thought was causing all the trouble—it is "mental anguish.") Now she has difficulty saying "can't." Dangerous in any event. What if she had that common engram expression, "Never say no!"?

Occlusion demons hide things from "I." It is as easy for one to mask many words. The individual having one will then omit these words or alter them or misspell them and make mistakes with them. The demon is not the only reason words get altered but he is a specific case. An occlusion demon can be of a much higher strength and breadth. He can be created with the phrase, "Don't talk!" or "Never talk back to your elders," or "You can't talk here. Who said you could talk?" Any of these phrases might produce a stammerer.

Other things besides speech can be occluded. Any ability of the mind can be inhibited by a demon specifically designed to obstruct that ability. "You can't see!" will occlude visual recall. "You can't hear!" will occlude audio recall. "You can't feel!" occludes pain and tactile recall (homonymic stuff, English).

Any perception can be occluded in recall. And whenever it is occluded in recall, it affects actual perception and the organ of perception as well. "You can't see!" may reduce not only recall but the actual organic ability of the eyes, as in astigmatism[8] or myopia.

One can imagine, with the entire English language (or in other lands with other tongues, any language) susceptible to inclusion within engrams just how many abilities of the mind's operation can be occluded. An extremely common one is "You can't think!"

So far now, *you* has been used in illustrations and examples in order to keep the similarity to hypnotic or drug tests. Actually sentences which contain *I* are more destructive. "I can't feel anything," "I can't think," "I can't remember." These and their thousands and thousands of variations, when spoken within the hearing of an "unconscious" person, are applicable to himself when he gets the engram keyed into circuit.

You has several effects. The statement, "You are no good," to an awake person makes that person feel very angry perhaps when he has an engram to that effect. Within him he feels, possibly, that people think he is no good. He may have a demon that tells him he is no good. And he will dramatize by telling other people that *they* are no good. It can be sprayed off by being dramatized. A person who has an engram to the effect that he is sexually sterile, for instance, will tell people that they are sexually sterile. ("Don't do as I do, do as I say.") If he has an engram that says, "You are no good, you have to eat with your knife," he may eat with his knife but he gets excited about people eating with their knives, and he would grow very angry if somebody said *he* ate with *his* knife.

Thus, there are "compulsion demons" and "confusion demons" and so forth and so on.

The engram has a command value. There is a power of choice exercised in the reactive mind about which and what engrams will be used. But any engram, strongly

8. astigmatism: a defect in an eye or lens preventing proper focusing.

enough restimulated, will come to the surface to be dramatized. And if dramatization is blocked, it will turn on the individual either temporarily or chronically.

The literalness of this reactive mind, in its interpretation of commands and the literalness of their action within the poor, harassed analytical mind, is a strange thing in itself. "It is too horrible to be borne" might be interpreted to the effect that a baby was in such bad condition that it had better not be born. There are thousands of clichés in any language which, when literally taken, mean quite the opposite from what the speaker intends.

The reactive engram bank takes them, stores them with pain and emotion and "unconsciousness" and with moronic literalness, hands them forth to be **law** and **command** to the analytical mind. And when the happy little moron who runs the engram bank sees it possible to use up some analytical mind circuits with some of these confounded demons, it is done.

The analytical mind, then, can be seen to be subject to yet another form of attrition. Its circuits, ordinarily intended for smooth, rapid computation, become tied up and overloaded with demon lash-ups. The demons are parasites. They are pieces of analytical mind compartmented off and denied to larger computation.

Is it any wonder that, when these demons are deleted, IQ soars, as it can be observed to do in a clear? Add the demon circuits to the shut-down aspect of restimulation, and truth can be seen in the observation that people run on about one-twentieth of their mental power. Research and scientific tabulation indicate that with the "unconsciousness" aspect and the demon circuits deleted from the engram bank, and the data restored into the standard bank as experience where it should be, about forty-nine fiftieths of the mind have been placed at the service of "I" which he never could use as an aberree.

CHAPTER FIVE

Psychosomatic Illness

Psychosomatic illnesses are those which have a mental origin but which are nevertheless organic. Despite the fact that there existed no precise scientific proof of this before Dianetics, an opinion as to their existence has been strong since the days of Greece, and in recent times various drug preparations have been concocted and sold which were supposed to overcome these sicknesses. Some success was experienced, sufficient to warrant a great deal of work on the part of researchers. Peptic ulcers,[1] for instance, have yielded to persuasion and environmental change. A drug called ACTH[2] has had astonishing but wildly unpredictable results. Allergies have been found to yield more or less to things which depressed histamine[3] in the body.

The problem of psychosomatic illness is entirely embraced by Dianetics, and by Dianetic technique such illness has been eradicated entirely in every case.

About 70 percent of the physician's current roster of diseases fall into the category of psychosomatic illness. How many more can be so classified after Dianetics has been in practice for a few years is difficult to predict, but it is certain that more illnesses are psychosomatic than have been so classified to date. That *all* illnesses are psychosomatic is, of course, absurd, for there exist, after

---

1. peptic ulcer: an open sore in the stomach.

2. ACTH: a hormone that was sometimes used to combat symptoms of rheumatoid arthritis; it stimulates the production of other hormones in the body.

3. histamine: a chemical compound in body tissues that causes many allergic reactions.

all, life forms called germs which have survival as *their* goals.

The work of Louis Pasteur formulated the germ theory of disease. With Dianetics is gained the nongerm theory of disease. These two, with biochemistry, complement each other to form the whole field of pathology[4] so far as can be determined at this time, providing of course that the virus is included under the germ theory.

Dianetics adds an additional leaf to the germ theory in that it includes *predisposition*. There are three stages of pathology: *predisposition*, by which is meant the factors which prepared the body for sickness; *precipitation*, by which is meant the factors which cause the sickness to manifest itself; and *perpetuation*, by which is meant the factors which cause the sickness to continue.

There are two kinds of illness: the first could be called *autogenetic*, which means that it originated within the organism and was self-generated; and *exogenetic*, which means that the origin of the illness was exterior. Actually, although this is good medicine, it is not quite as precise as Dianetics could desire. Mental illness itself is actually exterior in origin. But medically, we consider that the body can generate its own sicknesses (autogenetic) or that the sickness can come from an exterior source such as bacteria (exogenetic). The Pasteur germ theory would be the theory of exogenetic—exteriorly generated—illness. Psychosomatic illness would be autogenetic, generated by the body itself.

Treatment for accidental injury, surgery for various things such as malformation inherent in the body on a genetic basis, and orthopedics,[5] which actually can be classed under both, remain properly outside the field of

---

4. pathology: the scientific study of diseases of the body.

5. orthopedics: the branch of medicine dealing with the correction of deformities in bones or muscles.

Dianetics, although it can be remarked in passing that almost all accidents are to be traced to dramatization of engrams and that clears rarely have accidents.

Psycho, of course, refers to mind and *somatic* refers to body; the term *psychosomatic* means the mind making the body ill or illnesses which have been created physically within the body by derangement of the mind. Naturally such diseases, when one has resolved the problem of human aberration, become uniformly susceptible to cure.

Arthritis, dermatitis, allergies, asthma, some coronary difficulties, eye trouble, bursitis, ulcers, sinusitis, etc., form a very small section of the psychosomatic catalogue. Bizarre aches and pains in various portions of the body are generally psychosomatic. Migraine headaches are psychosomatic and, with the others, are uniformly cured by Dianetic therapy. (And the word *cured* is used in its fullest sense.)

Just how many physical errors are psychosomatic depends upon how many conditions the body can generate out of the factors in the engrams. For example, the common cold has been found to be psychosomatic. Clears do not get colds. Just what, if any, part the virus plays in the common cold is not known, but it is known that when engrams about colds are lifted, no further colds appear—which is a laboratory fact not so far contradicted by 270 cases. The common cold comes about, usually, from an engram which suggests it and which is confirmed by actual mucus present in another engram. A number of germ diseases are predisposed and perpetuated by engrams. Tuberculosis[6] is one.

The engram itself, as has been covered, follows a cycle of action. The body is predisposed to the conduct

---

6. tuberculosis: an infectious wasting disease affecting various parts of the body.

and conditions contained in the engram when that engram is first received. Then a conscious level experience keys in the engram, and other experience or the content of the engram itself may make it chronic. This is predisposition, precipitation and perpetuation in the mental plane.

Engrams and inherited disabilities and accidents and germs are the four ways an organism can be reduced physically from the optimum. Many conditions which have been called "inherited disabilities" are actually engramic. Engrams predispose people to accidents. Engrams can predispose and perpetuate bacterial infections. Therefore the catalogue of ills affected by Dianetics is very long. This is not a book listing effects but a book stating causes, and so the reader is asked to call upon his own knowledge or consult a medical text to understand just how many thousands and thousands of conditions result from engrams to disturb or derange the body.

At the present time, Dianetic research is scheduled to include cancer and diabetes.[7] There are a number of reasons to suppose that these may be engramic in cause, particularly malignant cancer. This is remarked so that attention may be given to the possibility; no tests of any kind have been made on cancer or diabetic patients, and the thought is purely theory and is not to be taken as any kind of an avowal about a cancer cure. Those diseases which were catalogued above, however, have been thoroughly tested and have uniformly yielded to Dianetic therapy.

The mechanism by which the mind is able to cause a physical disability or predispose the body to an illness and perpetuate sickness is, in its basic cause, a very

---

7. diabetes: a disease in which sugar and starch are not properly absorbed by the body.

simple thing. The complexity arrives when one begins to combine all the factors possible; then a staggering list of potential illnesses can be written.

A series of simple tests can be made on drugged or hypnotic patients which will prove clinically in other laboratories this basic mechanism. A series of these tests were run in the formulation of Dianetics with uniform success.

Let us take first something which is only mildly psychosomatic and scarcely an illness at all. A patient is hypnotized. He is given the positive suggestion that he will be able to hear much more acutely. This is "extended hearing." Controlling out other means of his gaining data (including safeguards against telepathy between operator and subject) the hearing can be found to be amplifiable many times over. In fact, there exist all around aberrees who have "extended hearing." By suggestion, the power of the hearing can be tuned down or up so that a person is nearly deaf or can hear pins fall at a great distance. When the suggestion is removed, the subject's hearing returns to its previous normal state.

Similarly, experiments can be performed on the eyes, using light sensitivity. The patient's sight is tuned up or down so that his eyes are much more or much less sensitive to light than is normal for him. This is done entirely on the word suggestion basis such as "The light will appear very, very bright to you," or "The light will appear so dim it will be hard for you to see." With the former suggestion the patient can be made to see almost as well as a cat, although other people around might think it impossible to see objects the patient can unerringly point out. In the latter suggestion the patient can be placed under light almost blinding and yet can read through a glare with apparent comfort.

The tactile sense can likewise be tuned up or down by verbal suggestion until touch becomes painfully acute or so dull it scarcely registers.

So with the various senses. Here we have simply the spoken word going into the mind and causing physical function to change.

Let us now address the heart. By deep hypnosis or drugs we take a patient into amnesia trance, a state of being wherein the "I" is not in control but the operator is the "I" (and that's all there is, really, to the function of hypnosis: the transfer of analytical power through the law of affinity from subject to operator, a thing which had a racial development and survival value in animals which ran in packs).

A caution should be observed that a patient who has a very sound heart and no heart trouble history be chosen for this experiment, which, even above any other hypnotic experiment, can make a patient very ill if he has a heart history. And none of these hypnotic tests should be performed until one has finished this book and knows how to get rid of the suggestions; for hypnosis, as practiced, is strictly live-fuse stuff and the hypnotist who is unacquainted with Dianetics has no more idea how to get rid of a suggestion he has made than he has of how to peel an atom. He has *thought* he had the answer, but Dianetics has treated many, many former hypnotic subjects who were thoroughly, as the engineers interested in Dianetics say, "loused up." This is no criticism of hypnosis or hypnotists, who are often very able people, but it is a comment that there is more to be known about it.

The heart, by positive suggestion alone, can be speeded up, slowed down or otherwise excited. Here are *words* spoken into the deep strata of the mind which cause *physical* action. Further, blood flow can be inhibited in some area of the body by suggestion alone. (This experiment, it is warned, particularly overloads the heart.) Blood can be denied to a hand, for instance, so that if you were to cut a vein in that hand it would bleed slightly if at all. A fine swami trick, which most amazed the author in India, was the inhibition of blood flow by the awake individual in himself. On command a cut would bleed or not bleed. It looked fantastic and made very good press-agentry that here was a swami who had so associated himself with nirvana that he was in control of all material matters. Awe faded when the author learned that, via hypnosis, he could make his own body do the same thing and no nirvana involved. The mechanism fades out rapidly and in a few days would have to be renewed: the body has its own optimum operation, and although such a function can be "analytically" handled, it is not an upper-echelon analytical job to keep the blood going in the hand. The point here is that blood flow can be interrupted by verbal suggestion. Words connect up with the physical being.

How this can come about can be shown by an analogic explanation, such as a schematic diagram, but we are not so much interested in structure as in function at this stage of the science of mind—because by knowing function alone we can cure aberrations and psychosomatic ills every time, predict new ills and conditions, and generally "work miracles," as such actions were once called before man knew anything about the mind.

Excreta are among the easiest things to regulate by suggestion. Constipation can be caused or cured by positive suggestion with remarkable speed and facility. The urine can also be so controlled. *And so can the endocrine system.*

It is harder to make tests on some of the more poorly understood functions of the endocrines. Glandular research has not progressed very far at this time. But, by removing engrams and watching the endocrine system rebalance, it has been made obvious that the endocrine system is a part of the control mechanism with which the mind handles the body. The glands are easily influenced. These fluids and secretions—testosterone,[8] estrogen,[9] adrenaline, thyroid,[10] parathyroid,[11] pituitrin,[12] etc.—are the substances the mind uses as one means of controlling the body. They form relay circuits, so to speak. Each one has its own action within the body.

This experiment tends to prove the fallacy of an ancient assumption that the mind was controlled by the glands. An aberree is given a shot of 25 mg of testosterone in oil twice a week. There may be some improvement in his physical status—for a short time his voice may deepen and he may grow more hair on his chest. Now, without suggestion, we simply delete the engrams from his reactive bank so that they can re-form as experience in the standard bank. Before we have completed this task his body begins to use more of the testosterone. The dose can be markedly reduced and still give more benefit than formerly. Finally, the dose can be eliminated. This experiment has also been performed on people who had not been able to receive benefit from glandular substances such as testosterone and estrogen. And upon people who were made ill by the administration of these hormones. The deletion of the engrams from the reactive bank uniformly brought about a condition where they could receive benefit from the hormones but where such artificial administration was not necessary, save in cases of extreme age. What this means

---

8. testosterone: a male sex hormone.

9. estrogen: a sex hormone or other substance capable of developing and maintaining female characteristics of the body.

10. thyroid: a hormone that regulates the body's growth and development.

11. parathyroid: a hormone regulating calcium levels in the body.

12. pituitrin: the various substances secreted by the pituitary gland, located at the base of the brain, which have important influences on growth and bodily functions.

to gerontology (the study of longevity in life) cannot at this time be estimated, but it can be predicted with confidence that the deletion of engrams from the reactive bank has a marked effect upon the extension of life. A hundred years or so from now this data will be available, but no clears have lived that long as yet.

Just now, to our purpose, it is easy to demonstrate the effect of positive suggestion upon the endocrine system and the lack of effect of artificial hormones upon aberrees.

This sort of an engram has a terribly reductive effect upon testosterone manufacture: "Sex is horrible; it is nasty; I hate it."

The autonomic nervous system,[13] which has been supposed to run without much connection to the mind, can be shown to be influenced in its parts by the mind. There is a dwindling spiral effect (note the lines on the survival potential chart) whereby the engram starts malfunction in the life function regulator; this produces malfunction in the mind, which in turn has further effect on the life function regulator; this again reduces physical activity, and the mind, being part of the organ and, so far as we can tell, organic itself, is further reduced in tone. Mental tone makes body tone go down. Body tone, then being down, makes mental tone go down. This is a matter of inverse geometric progression. A man starts to get sick and, having engrams, he gets sicker. Clears are not subject to this dwindling spiral. Indeed, so entirely superficial is this horrible stuff called psychosomatic illness that it is the first thing which surrenders and can be alleviated without clearing.

Now, the reason why various drug preparations

---

13. autonomic nervous system: a system of nerves in the body that functions more or less automatically and regulates the function of the heart, lungs, intestines, glands and other internal organs.

which seek to change psychosomatic illness meet with such uncertain success lies in the fact that the mind, containing these engrams which are "survival" (like a fellow needs a hole in his head), handles the life function regulator to actively produce illnesses. Something comes to take them away (they're "survival," you see, and these confounded cells moronically insist upon it) and the mind has to rapidly reverse the activity and put an illness back in place again. Try to influence the reactive mind by reason or needles and it is not any easier to convince than a drug-crazed man bent on murdering everybody in a bar. He's "surviving," too.

A concoction like ACTH has a slightly different effect. It is too exclusive to have any research done with it, but on reports about it, it seems to affect engrams in the time sense. That is to say, as will be covered under therapy, the individual's reactive location in time is shifted by it. ACTH and perhaps many others in its category move the individual from one chronic engram into another. This is about as reliable as changing dictators in Europe. The next one may be twice as bad. It may even be a manic and that's horrible, despite its apparent "euphoria."

Electric shock treatment, the beatings of Bedlam and other things of their ilk, *including surgical treatment of things psychosomatic in origin,* have another effect, but one not dissimilar to drugs like ACTH, in that they give another shock which transfers the engram pattern to another part of the body (and switches around the aberrations; when these things work it is because the new aberration is less violent than the old one). Shocks, blows, surgery and maybe even things like cobra venom change the effect of the engram bank on the body, not necessarily for the worse, not necessarily for the better; they just change them. Like shooting dice: sometimes one gets a seven.

Then there is the deletion-of-tissue treatment of psychosomatic ills. This simply removes the area which is busy dramatizing in the physical line. This can be the removal of a toe or the removal of a brain. These things are quite commonly used, as this is being written. The removal of the toe is addressed to one part of the engram content, the *somatic,* and the removal of parts of the brain (as in the transorbital leukotomy[14] and the prefrontal lobotomy[15] or anything else more recent) is addressed mistakenly to "the removal of" the psychoaberration. There is a surrender system at work in this as well: the surgeon or the patient has an aberration about "getting rid of it," and so bits of the body are cut up or removed. Some patients surrender anatomy on advice or at their own insistence like old-timers shed blood in a phlebotomy.[16] There is a straight parallel between bleeding the patient to make him well and cutting away parts of him to make him well. Both are based on a surrender (get rid of) engram and neither are effective in any way. Barber basin medicine,[17] it is hoped, will eventually die out, as did its patients.

These are the five classes of psychosomatic ills: (1) those ills resulting from mentally caused derangement in physical fluid flow, which class subdivides into (a) inhibition of fluid flow and (b) magnification of fluid flow;

---

14. transorbital leukotomy: an operation which, while the patient is being electrically shocked, thrusts an ordinary dime store ice pick into each eye and reaches up to rip the analyzer apart.

15. prefrontal lobotomy: an operation in which the white fibers joining the prefrontal and frontal lobes to the interior region of the brain are severed.

16. phlebotomy: the act or practice of bloodletting as a therapeutic measure.

17. barber basin medicine: refers to the practice of surgery by barbers in earlier centuries. Generally untrained in medical procedures, their "treatments" were very painful with severe infections and often death resulting from unsanitary conditions.

(2) those ills resulting from mentally caused derangement of physical growth, which class subdivides into (a) inhibition of growth and (b) magnification of growth; (3) those ills resulting from predisposition to disease resulting from a chronic psychosomatic pain in an area; (4) those ills resulting from perpetuation of a disease on account of chronic pain in an area; and (5) those ills caused by the verbal command content of the engrams.

In Class 1 (a) fall such ordinary things as constipation and such extraordinary things as arthritis. Arthritis is a complex mechanism with a simple cause and a relatively simple cure. Remember that there are two things present in an engram: physical pain and verbal command. In arthritis both must be present (as in the bulk of psychosomatic ills). There must have been an accident to the joint or area affected, and there must have been a command during the "unconsciousness" which attended the injury which would make the engram susceptible to chronic restimulation. (Such commands as "It is always like this" or "It just goes right on hurting" or "I'm stuck" will produce similar results.) Given this engram and given this engram keyed in, there is a chronic pain in the area of the injury. It may be minor, but it is a pain just the same. (It can be a pain but not be felt if the engram contains a command which is anesthetic, such as "He'll never feel this," which produces a similar condition but makes one "unconscious" of the pain there.) This pain in the body probably tells the cells and the blood that this area is dangerous. It is therefore avoided. The command permits the mind to influence, let us say, the parathyroid, which contains the secret of the calcium content in the bloodstream. A mineral deposit then begins to be laid down in the area. The mineral deposit is not necessarily the cause of the pain, but it is an organic restimulator so that the more mineral, the more pain, the more the engram keys in. This is the dwindling spiral. And this is arthritis in action. Understand that the parathyroid and the blood avoidance are theoretical cause; the scientific fact is that when an engram is picked up and deleted about an area containing arthritis, that arthritis vanishes and does not return and this is X-ray plate evidence; it happens every time and does not happen because of any suggestion or medicine; it happens because an engram is picked up and refiled. As the engram goes away, so goes the pain, so vanishes the arthritis. This forms a whole class of ills, of which arthritis is only one. The mechanisms involved vary slightly. All can be headed under "physical derangement caused by reduced body fluid flow."

Class 1 (b) of psychosomatic ills, magnification of fluid flow, contains such things as high blood pressure, diarrhea, sinusitis, priapism (overactivity of the male sex glands) or any other physical condition resulting from a superabundance of fluid.

Class 2 (a) can cause such things as a withered arm, a foreshortened nose, underdeveloped genital organs or any other underdevelopment of a gland having to do with size (which cross-classes this with 1[a]), hairlessness (which also like the rest can be part of the gene pattern and therefore inherent), and, in short, reduction in size of any part of the body.

Class 2 (b) causes such things as oversized hands, a lengthened nose, oversized ears, enlarged organs and other common physical malformations. (Cancer might possibly come under this heading as overhealing.)

Class 3 would include tuberculosis (some cases), liver trouble, kidney trouble, rashes, common colds, etc. (cross-classing with others, as do all of these in one way or another).

Class 4 would include those diseases which, arising without psychosomatic influence, yet fix upon, by accident, a previously injured area and, by restimulation, keep an engram keyed in in that area so that a condition becomes chronic. Tuberculosis could be included here. Conjunctivitis,[18] all running sores and any condition which refuses to heal, etc.

This fourth class would also include all bizarre pains and sicknesses which cannot be found to have actual pathology.

Class 5 includes an enormously wide catalogue of conditions, any one of which may cross-index to other classes or which arise solely out of engrams which dictate the presence or necessity of an illness. "You always have colds," "I have sore feet," etc., announce a psychosomatic illness and the mechanisms of the body can furnish one.

Any disease whatever can be precipitated by engrams. The disease may be of germ origin: the individual possesses an engram to the effect that he may become sick and, on this generalization, becomes sick with whatever is to hand. Further and even more general, the engram reduces the physical resistance of the body to disease, and when an engram goes into restimulation (perhaps because of a domestic quarrel, an accident or some such thing) the ability of the individual to resist sickness is automatically decreased.

Children, as will be explained, have many more engrams than has been supposed. Almost all childhood illnesses are preceded by psychic disturbance and if psychic disturbance is present—keeping an engram restimulated—such illnesses can be far more violent than they should be. Measles, for instance, can be just measles or it can be measles in company with engramic restimulation, in which case it can be nearly or entirely

---

18. conjunctivitis: inflammation of the conjunctiva, the mucous membrane lining the inner eyelid and part of the eye.

fatal. A check of many subjects on this matter of child-hood illness being predisposed by, precipitated by and perpetuated by engrams causes one to wonder just how violent the diseases themselves really are: they have never been observed in a cleared child and there is reason to investigate the possibility that childhood illnesses are in themselves extremely mild and are complicated only by psychic disturbance—which is to say, the restimulation of engrams.

In fact, one could ask this question of the entire field of pathology: What is the actual effect of disease minus the mental equation? How serious are bacteria?

The field of bacteriology has been without dynamic principles until now: the dynamic, survival, is applicable to all life forms, and "life forms" include germs. The purpose of the germ is to survive. Its problems are those of food, protection (offense and defense) and procreation. To accomplish these things the germ survives at its optimum efficiency. It mutates, alters with natural selection and changes dynamically from survival necessity (the missing step of the evolution theory, that last) in order to accomplish the maximum survival possible. It makes errors by killing the hosts, but to have a purpose to survive does not mean that a form necessarily survives.

In pathology, the germ, bent on its purpose, acts as a suppressor to the survival dynamic of the human species. How serious this suppressor is in the absence of engram suppression in the human has not been determined; enough data exists to indicate that a human individual with his potential in the fourth zone is not, apparently, very subject to disease: the common cold, for instance, if it is a virus or not, passes him by; chronic infections are absent. What antibodies have to do with this or what this factor is, is yet another question. But it remains that a clear is not easily made ill. In the aberree illness closely pursues mental depression (depression of the dynamic level).

The aberration of mind and body by engrams leads, then, not only to psychosomatic ills but also to actual pathology, which has hitherto been considered more or less independent of the mental state. As has been proven by clinical research, clearing of engrams does more than remove psychosomatic illness, potential, acute or chronic. The clearing also tends to proof the individual against the receipt of pathology: to what extent, it is not yet known, for such a wide and long-term view is required to establish the actual statistics that the project will require thousands of cases and the observations of medical doctors over a long term.

The amount of aberration which a person manifests, which is to say, the position he would occupy on a sanity scale, has little to do with psychosomatic illness. Such illnesses require only one or two engrams of a specific nature to become manifest. These engrams may not be aberrative in any other way than to predispose the individual to illness. Having a psychosomatic illness is not the same as being "crazy" or having hypochondriacal tendencies. The hypochondriac thinks he has illnesses, a special case of Class 5 above.

Derangement falls sharply into two categories: the first is the mental derangement—any irrational condition —which, in Dianetics, we call *aberration* in order to avoid constant cataloguing of the thousands, the millions of manifestations irrationality can have. The other derangement of the individual is *somatic:* this applies entirely to his physical being and physical ability and health. Both these things are present in every engram: the *aberration* and the *somatic*. But the engram can manifest itself chronically as either a *somatic* (a noun has been made out of an adjective here and it is commonly employed in Dianetics to avoid the use of the word *pain,* which is not embracive and which is restimulative) or as an *aberration* or as both together.

An engram must contain physical pain. When an engram is restimulated in everyday life, that physical pain may appear or it may not. If it does not appear as pain but as aberration, then the individual is in another valence than his own (the "necessity to manifest his hostilities"). If he is sane enough to be in his own valence, the physical pain will be present. In Dianetics, we say the *somatic* has appeared. When any somatic appears, unless the individual is a preclear[19] in therapy, some of the aberration is also appearing. In short, the aberration can appear by itself or the somatic plus some of the aberration can appear. When a person dramatizes another valence than his own, the aberration is present; when the dramatization, running off the engram phonograph-record-wise in one or another valence, is suppressed by some other factor, such as the police or a stronger person or even the individual himself (this has been called *repression*—the term is not used here because it is loaded with other meanings), the somatic most certainly will come into view.

The individual is, then, apparently "better off" (as the cells meant him to be) to occupy the survival role in the engram (the winning valence), for he is, at least, not ill. But how many people have been killed, how many banks have been robbed and how many marital partners have been driven mad by these dramatizations? So the health of the individual would be considered by society, in its effort to protect its members, to be a secondary affair. In fact, "society" has not known about this mechanical aspect. The individual who dramatizes the survival valence in his engrams may do violent things to other people. The individual who will not permit himself

---

19. preclear: from pre- clear, a person not yet clear; generally a person being audited, who is thus on the road to clear; a person who, through Dianetics processing, is finding out more about himself and life.

such a dramatization or who is forced by society away from such dramatization will most certainly become psychosomatically ill. "Heads I win, tails you lose." The answer is in the alleviation or deletion of the engram. For there are many additional aspects to the problem: the man who dramatizes his engrams, society or no society, is not apt to survive; and if he dramatizes them, he is subject to whatever slurs were leveled at the valence he is in by another valence in that same engram.

The combinations of the classes and aspects of psychosomatic illness listed and described here lead to some highly complex situations. It is a scientific fact that no psychosomatic ill exists without an aberration. And it is true that no aberration exists without a potential or actual psychosomatic ill. One of the psychosomatic illnesses one would least expect to find as a psychosomatic affair is the illness of sexual perversion.

The sexual pervert (and by this term Dianetics, to be brief, includes any and all forms of deviation in dynamic two such as homosexuality, lesbianism, sexual sadism, etc., and all down the catalogue of Ellis[20] and Krafft-Ebing[21]) is actually quite ill physically. Perversion, as an illness, has so many manifestations that it must be spread through the entire gamut of classes from 1 to 5 above. Overdevelopment of sexual organs, underdevelopment, seminal inhibition or magnification, etc., are found some in one pervert, some in another. And the sum of it is that the pervert is always a very ill person in one way or another, whether he is conscious of it or not. He is very far from culpable for his condition, but he is also so far from normal and so extremely dangerous to society that the tolerance of perversion is as thoroughly bad for society as punishment for it. Lacking proper

20. Ellis, Henry Havelock: (1859–1939) English criminologist and psychologist. Conducted studies in psychology and sociology of sex.

21. Krafft-Ebing, Baron Richard von: (1840–1902) German neurologist and psychiatrist.

means prior to this time, society has been caught between tolerance and punishment, and the problem of perversion has, of course, not been resolved. A bit off the subject here, but it can be remarked about perversion that the best previous explanation for it was something about girls becoming envious of Papa's penis or boys becoming upset about that terrible thing, the vulva, which Mama was incautious enough to show one day. It takes a great deal more than this utter tripe to make a pervert. It is, rather, something on the order of kicking a baby's head in, running over him with a steamroller, cutting him in half with a rusty knife, boiling him in Lysol, and all the while with crazy people screaming the most horrifying and unprintable things at him. The human being is a very tough character. He is so confoundedly tough that he has whipped the whole animal kingdom and he can shake the stars. And when it comes to throwing his second dynamic out of balance, what that takes is straight out of Dante[22] and Sax Rohmer[23] combined. Hence the pervert, containing hundreds and hundreds of vicious engrams, has had little choice between being dead and being a pervert. But with an effective science to handle the problem, a society which would continue to endure perversion and all its sad and sordid effects doesn't deserve to survive.

Perversion can have other aspects. In one society examined, these aberrations had multiplied so far that a principal mystic cult had sprung up which contended that all mental illness came from sex; this, of course, gave further impetus to aberrations on the second dynamic (sex), as such a cultic belief must have been

---

22. Dante: originally Durante, Alighieri: (1265–1321) Italian poet. Wrote *Divina Commedia*, recounting an imaginary journey by the author through Hell, Purgatory and Paradise.

23. Rohmer, Sax: pseudonym of Arthur Sarsfield Ward: (1883–1959) English author of *Dr. Fu Manchu*.

originated by an individual who had severe aberrations across the second dynamic. This belief that sex was the only source of human aberration and travail naturally attracted as its practitioners individuals who had similar aberrative patterns. And so the cult further enforced existing aberrative factors in the society, since all their activity was leveled at making sex something ogreish and dreadful by labeling it the society's primary source of mental illness. The prophet of this god was Manichaeus, a Persian of the third century, who taught that all things about the body, especially sex, were evil; the cult of Manichaeus carried on well into the Dark Ages and then vanished, to trouble man no more.

Any dynamic can be blocked: the personal dynamic, the sex dynamic, the group dynamic or the mankind dynamic. Each one has been the target at some time of one cult or another seeking to cure all man's ills and save him. Dianetics is not interested in saving man, but it can do much to prevent him from *being* "saved." As an organized body of scientific knowledge, Dianetics can draw only the conclusion which it observes in the laboratory.

It can be observed that the Church is entirely correct in doing all in its power to prevent blasphemy. Blasphemy can very often be uttered during the "unconsciousness" of a person who has been struck. This would enter sacred names and curses into engrams which, reacting within the individual, give him an unnatural terror and compulsion or repulsion toward God. It is not the religion which is at fault, it is the blaspheming of the religion. Such blasphemy makes the insane zealot and the murderous atheist, both of whom the Church would very gladly do without.

In the realm of psychosomatic illness, any combination of the language is as damaging a factor in an engram as any other factor. The moronic reasoning of

142

the reactive mind, which considers everything in an engram equal to everything in an engram, also considers that everything similar to the engram in the exterior world (the restimulators) is sufficient cause to place an engram in effect. Hence aberration and illness can come about.

There is, however, a peculiarity in psychosomatic illnesses which is chronic: the aberree's reactive mind exercises a power of choice to the extent that *only pro-survival engrams become chronic.* It could be said, on a reactive level, that the aberree will not permit himself to suffer illness from his engrams unless that illness has a "survival" value. This is very important in therapy. The chronic psychosomatic illnesses which a patient displays are those which have a sympathy (prosurvival) background.

It is not possible to "spoil" a child with love and affection. Whoever postulated that it was possible was postulating out of bad data and no observation. A child *needs* all the love and affection it can possibly get. A test was run in one hospital which tended to show that babies, when left without attention, ran fevers. When given attention, the fevers immediately abated. The test, while not observed personally by the author, seems to have been conducted with proper controls according to report. If this is true, it postulates a mechanism in the human being which uses illness for affection on a genetic basis. There is no reason why not; there have been enough years of engineering—almost two billion—to build anything into the blueprint. These babies, in several groups, were left in the hospital by their parents for the test; they uniformly became ill when not given affection. Here is the law of affinity at work, if these tests were accurately conducted. Their purpose was not to help Dianetics, but to show that the leaving of a baby in the hospital after his birth because he has a slight illness invariably increases that illness.

A series of severely controlled Dianetic experiments over a much longer period demonstrated that the law of affinity, as applicable to psychosomatic illness, was more powerful than fear and antagonism by a very wide margin. So great is this margin that it could be compared as the strength of a steel girder to a straw. It was found, as above, that chronic psychosomatic ills existed only when they had a sympathy engram behind them. The law of affinity might be interpreted as the law of cohesion; *affinity* might be defined as "love" in both its meanings. Deprivation of or absence of affection could be considered as a violation of the law of affinity. Man must be in affinity with man to survive. The suicide ordinarily commits the act on the computation that the removal of self will some way benefit other selves—this, on the reactive mind level, is a very ordinary computation, deriving exclusively from engrams. The violent industrial chieftain with his merciless mien,[24] when he suffers from a psychosomatic ill, ordinarily derives it out of a sympathy engram.

The sympathy engram pretends to be prosurvival. As one preclear said, a man is not victimized by his enemies but by his friends. An engram comes about always from a greater or lesser moment of "unconsciousness." There is no engram without "unconsciousness." It is only when the analyzer is out of circuit that the exterior world can come interior, unrationalized, and work from within. The second the analyzer identifies one of those engrams as such, that engram loses about 20 percent of its value to aberrate and usually 100 percent of its value to cause a psychosomatic illness. Pain is extremely perishable. Pleasure is recorded in bronze. (Not poetry here, science. Physical pain will

---

24. mien: a person's manner or bearing.

delete with brief attention; a pleasant or even a media-media[25] experience is so solidly fixed in the mind that no treatment known to Dianetics will shake it and a great deal of effort has been leveled at pleasure recordings just to test them for permanence. They are permanent; physical pain is perishable. Too bad, Schopenhauer,[26] but you were a most mistaken man.)

Exposing a lock to the analyzer—a moment of "mental anguish"—once the engram which gave it power is gone causes that lock to blow away like chaff. The analyzer works on the "doctrine of the true datum": it has no truck[27] with anything which it once discovers to be false. Just exposing an engram without relieving it has some therapeutic value—20 percent—and this gave rise to a belief that all one had to do was know about his ills and they would vanish. Nice if it were so.

The most aberrative engram, then, is one which is held down by the reactive mind's—that moron's—concept that it is needed in the survival of the individual. This sympathy engram is the one which comes forward and stays chronic as a psychosomatic illness. There are two reasons for this: one is usually in one's own valence when a sympathy engram is received; and one's reactive mind, knowing well the value of affinity, puts forward the psychosomatic illness to attract affinity. There is no volition here on the part of the individual's "I," analytical self. But there is every "volition" on the part of the reactive mind.

A sympathy engram would go something like this: a small boy, much victimized by his parents, is extremely

---

25. media-media: average.

26. Schopenhauer, Arthur: (1788–1860) German philosopher. Chief expounder of pessimism.

27. truck: dealings; business.

ill. His grandmother attends him and, while he is delirious, soothes him and tells him she will take care of him, that she will stay right there until he is well. This puts a high "survival" value on being sick. He does not feel safe around his parents; he wants his grandmother present (she is a winning valence because she orders the parents around), and he now has an engram. Minus the engram there would be no psychosomatic illness. Sickness, "unconsciousness" and physical pain are essential to the receipt of this engram. But it is not a contra-survival engram. It is a prosurvival engram. It can be dramatized in one's own valence.

The psychosomatic illness, in such a case as this, would be a "precious possession." "I" doesn't even know the computation. The analyzer was out when the engram went in. The analyzer cannot recall that engram with anything short of Dianetic therapy. And the engram will not clear away.

Now, with this engram we have a patient with sinusitis and a predisposition to lung infections. It may be that he was luckless enough to marry a counterpart of his mother or his grandmother. The reactive mind cannot tell the difference between Grandmother or Mother and wife if they are even vaguely similar in speech, voice tone or mannerisms. The wife is not sympathetic. In goes the engram to demand that sympathy. And even if the wife thinks that sinusitis and lung infection are repulsive enough to lead to divorce, the reactive mind keeps that engram keyed in. The more hatred from the wife, the more that engram keys in. You can kill a man that way.

The above is a standard sympathy engram. When a therapist tries to get that engram away from the patient, the reactive mind balks. The "I" doesn't balk. The analyzer doesn't balk. These are hopeful that this engram will spring. But the reactive mind keeps it nailed down until the Dianeticist puts a crowbar under it. Then it is gone. (Enough locks may be lifted, by the way, to alleviate this condition. But the patient will dig up another engram!)

Resistance to past therapies has resulted from these sympathy engrams. Yet they lie right there on the surface, fully exposed as chronic psychosomatic illness.

Feeding a patient with a psychosomatic ill any number of drugs can result in only temporary relief. "I" doesn't want the illness. The analyzer doesn't want it. But the body has it, and if anybody succeeds in curing it short of removing that engram, the body, at the command of the reactive mind, will find something else to substitute for that ill or develop an "allergy" to the drug or annul the effect of the drug entirely.

Of course, one can always rip living tissue out of the skull with knives, ice picks or shock in wholesale quantities. This will cure a psychosomatic ill. It also, unhappily, cures the personality, the intellect and all too often, life itself.

In Dianetics, the application of technique to relieve the engrams causing these ills has brought the uniform relief of all patients treated, without relapse. In short and in brief, psychosomatic ills can now be cured. All of them.

Emotion and the Dynamics

Emotion is a θ^1 quantity, which is to say that it is so involved with life forces that Dianetics, at this stage, handles it with invariable success but does not attempt to give forth more than a descriptive theory. Much research must be done on emotion; but so long as the therapy embraces it and releases it with success, further data can be dispensed with up to a point.

Emotion would have to be divided sharply into minus emotions and plus emotions. The minus emotion would be nonsurvival in character, the plus emotion would be prosurvival. The pleasant and pleasurable emotions are not of any great concern to us here. It is believed that all emotion is the same thing but in its aspects above zone 1 it can be bypassed as unnecessary to explain at this time for the purpose of this book.

In zones 1 and 0, emotion becomes very important to therapy. As has been covered earlier, zones 1 and 0 are the anger and apathy zones respectively. From death up to the border between anger and fear is zone 0. From this borderline to the beginning of boredom is anger, zone 1.

It is as if the survival dynamic, in becoming contracted into zone 1, first began to display hostility, then, on further suppression toward death, anger. On further suppression, rage began to be displayed. Then fear as the next lower level, then terror and finally, just above death, apathy.

And as the dynamic is suppressed, the cells react

---

1. θ: theta, the eighth letter in the Greek alphabet. Greek for thought or life or the spirit.

forcefully to the menace, it could be said, by resisting the menace. The analyzer resists down to the top border of zone 1, but in ever-decreasing control. From here on down the cells, the actual organism, do the resisting in a last-ditch effort. The reactive mind is thoroughly in command from the top border of zone 1 straight on down to death, and it is in ever-increasing command of the organism as the dynamic is suppressed.

Emotion seems to be inextricably connected up with the actual force of life. That there is a life force no engineer could doubt. Man and medicine usually look at the pitcher and forget that the pitcher is only there to hold milk and that the milk is the important quantity. Life force is the helium which fills the free balloon. Out goes the helium, down comes the balloon. When this type of energy is located and isolated as itself—if it *is* just an energy type—then medicine can start moving forward in strides which will make all former steps look like those of a man in a sack race. Medicine doesn't have any spare helium, for one thing.

How high this life force can go on the survival scale is not known. Above zone 3 is the area of question marks. A clear goes up into a level of persistence, vigor, tenacity, rationality and happiness. Perhaps someday a clear will attain the nebulosity the author used to hear about in India which marked the man who was all soul.

How far down it can go is definitely known. A man dies. He doesn't move or think. He dies as an organism, then he dies as cells. There are different periods of "life after death" for the cells, and biologists remark that the hair and nail cells do not die for months. So here is a spectrum of death, first the organism and then, colony by colony, the cells.

That is from the bottom of zone 0 downward. But what we are interested in is the area from zone 1 down to the bottom of zone 0. It could be postulated that the analytical mind has its greatest bounce against the suppressor, its highest ability to care for the organism, when it is in the third zone. As the suppressor thrusts downward against it, the analyzer, within lower zone 3, thrusts heavily back. This is *necessity* at work. *The necessity level can rise, in this action, to a point which keys out[2] all engrams!*

It must be realized that the analyzer considers future suppressors and is continually engaged upon computations which pose problems of the future which the analyzer resolves—this is one of the functions of the imagination. It must further be realized that the analyzer is engaged upon a multitude of computations about the present, for the analytical mind is dealing continually with an enormous number of factors which comprise the suppressor of the present and the suppressor of the future. It computes, for instance, on the alliances with friends and symbiotes and its greatest victories are achieved by taking some of the suppressor and turning it into an alliance factor.

The individual can be visualized, on the survival spectrum, as being at the tip of the survival dynamic. The suppressor thrusts down, or future suppressors threaten a thrust, and the analytical mind thrusts up with solutions. The level of the individual is determined by how well these suppressors are apparently met.

We speak now of the clear, and until further mention we will continue to use the clear. The clear is an unaberrated person. He is rational in that he forms the best possible solutions he can on the data he has and from his viewpoint. He obtains the maximum pleasure for the organism, present and future, as well as for the subjects along the other dynamics. The clear has no engrams which can be restimulated to throw out the

---

2. key out: the engram drops away without being erased.

correctness of computation by entering hidden and false data into it. No aberration. Hence the reason we use him here as an example.

The survival dynamic is high, more than balancing the suppressor. Take this as a first condition. This would place the dynamic in zone 3, tone 3.9. Now increase the suppressor. The dynamic is pushed back to tone 3.2. Necessity surges up. The suppressor is thrust back. The dynamic is once more at tone 3.9. This action could be termed an enthusiastic resurgence. The individual has actually gotten "angry"—that is to say, he has called upon his being to furnish power for thought and action. Mentally, he calls upon whatever constitutes mental energy. Physically, if the suppression was physical, he would call upon his adrenaline. This is proper use of the endocrines, to use them for regaining position in relation to the suppressor. Any and all body function is under analytical (but not necessarily monitored) command.

Now let us suppose that the suppressor surges down against the dynamic and drives the dynamic to 3.0. Necessity level comes up. Action is taken. The full force of the being is thrown against the suppressor. Now let us suppose that a new factor comes into the suppressor and makes it much, much stronger. The individual still attempts to resurge against it. But the suppressor weighs heavier and heavier against him. He is beginning to exhaust his supplies of mental or physical energy (and this suppressor can be on either a mental or physical level). Wearying, the individual drops down to a 2.5. The suppressor again increases. Resurgence is attempted once more. The last supply of available energy or data is thrown out. And another factor comes into the suppressor, increasing its weight. The individual sags down to 2.0.

At exactly this point the analyzer, having failed, finally cuts out. Here is entered the top of zone 1.

Hostility sets in. The suppressor is down, pressing down against actual cellular survival. And it drops lower. The individual goes into anger, recruiting cellularly, but not sentiently, the last forces. Again the suppressor gets new weight. The individual goes into rage. Once more the suppressor drops. The individual goes into fear, tone 0.9. Again the suppressor lowers, recruiting new factors. The individual is thrust down to 0.6 and, here, is in terror. Once more the suppressor drops with new force. The individual slides into fear paralysis, 0.2.

Suppose we parallel this in a very simple, dramatic example so that we do not have to consider a thousand subtle factors. A clear, inexperienced in hunting, determines to shoot a grizzly. He has a fine rifle. The grizzly appears to be easy game. The man is at 3.9 or above. He feels good. He is going to get that grizzly, as the grizzly has been threatening the man's stock. High enthusiasm carries him to the lair. He waits, he finally sees the grizzly. There is a cliff above the man which he could not ordinarily climb. But to get a good shot before the grizzly vanishes, the man has to climb the cliff. Seeing he was in danger of losing the game brought the man down to 3.2. Necessity sends him up the cliff. He fires but in firing falls back down the cliff. The grizzly is wounded. He starts toward the man. Necessity surges up. The man recovers the gun and shoots again. He is at 3.0 the moment he shoots. He misses. He fires again but the miss, with the grizzly charging, brought him down to 2.5. He shoots once more. The grizzly takes the ball and keeps on coming. The man shoots again but he has suddenly realized that his rifle is not going to stop this grizzly. His tone drops to 2.0. He begins to snarl and feverishly work his gun. His bullets go wild. He experiences rage at the gun, the grizzly, the world, and throws the gun away, ready to meet the grizzly, almost upon him, with bare hands. Suddenly the man knows fear. His tone is 1.2. It drops to 0.9 with a smell in his nostrils of the bear. He knows the bear will kill him. He turns and tries to claw up the cliff and get away but his efforts are frenzied. He is at tone 0.6, stark terror. The bear strikes him and knocks him from the cliffside. The man lies still, breathing almost halted, heartbeat slowed to nearly nothing. The bear hits him again and the man lies still. Then the bear decides he is dead and walks away. Shaken, the man eventually comes around, his tone gradually rising up to 2.0, the point where his analyzer shut off. He stirs more and gets up. His tone is back to 2.5: he is analytically afraid and cautious. He recovers his gun. He begins to leave the scene. He feels a great necessity to recoup his own self-esteem and his tone comes to 3.2. He walks away and reaches a safe area. Suddenly it occurs to him that he can borrow a friend's Mauser.[3] He begins to make plans to get that bear. His enthusiasm mounts. But, completely aside from the engram received when the bear knocked him out, he acts on his experience. Three days later he kills the bear and his tone rises to 4.0 for the space of contemplation and telling the tale, and then his mind occupies itself with new matters.

Life is much more complicated than the business of killing grizzlies, usually a lot less dramatic but always full of situations which cause a fluctuation of the suppressor. The gaining of all pleasurable goals—a bear killed, a woman kissed, a seat in the front row at the opera, a friend won, an apple stolen—are sweeps through various levels of tone. And the individual is generally carrying on three or three thousand computations at once and there are thirty or thirty thousand variables in his computations. Too many unknowns, too many entrances of "didn't know the gun was loaded"

---

3. Mauser: a brand of military or hunting rifles.

factors: all these can throw the analyzer from a direct alignment into the scattered dispersal of nonfunction. The analyzer can be considered to cut out when tone 2.0 is reached. From 2.5 down, the computations it makes are not very rational—too many unknowns, too many unexpected factors, too many discoveries of miscalculations.

This is living on a "clear" basis. When our hunter was hit by the bear he received an engram. That engram, when it keyed in, would give him a fear, an apathy attitude, in the presence of certain factors: every perceptic present—the smell of that ground, twigs, bear breath, etc. But he killed the bear. The chances of that engram keying in are remote. Not because he killed the bear but because he was, after all, a grown man. And, if a clear, he could have thought back and cleared the whole thing himself.

This is a complete cycle of *emotion*. Enthusiasm and high pleasure are at the extreme top. Fear and paralysis are at the bottom. Feigned death, in man, is very close to the actual thing on the tone scale. It is a valid mechanism. But it is complete apathy.

So long as the analyzer is operating, the receipt of an engram is impossible. Everything files in the standard banks. As soon as the border 2.0 is passed on the way down, "unconsciousness" can be judged to have set in and anything registered, in company with pain or painful emotion, is an engram. This is not a shift of definition. The analyzer cuts out, with surgical anesthetic, at 2.0. The anesthetic may depress the level of awareness further. Pain may depress it even more. But depressing the level of awareness is not necessarily depressing emotion. How much conceived danger or sympathy is present in the environment? This is what depresses the tone scale. There can be a reactive engram which contains a tone 4.0, or one that contains a 1.0 or another that contains a 0.1.

This is not, then, quite two-dimensional, this emotion.

The level of depth of consciousness can be affected by painful emotion, poisons or other things which depress awareness. After that it is all engram, and the engrams have their own tone scale which runs from 4.0 down to 0.1.

It can be seen now that two things are at work. First is the state of physical being. It is this which tunes down the analyzer. Then there is the mental state of being. This is what tunes down the emotional tone scale.

But remember that in engrams there is another factor present: valence. Once its own analyzer is out, the body will assume the evaluation or emotional condition of any other analyzer present. Here we have affinity at work in earnest. "Unconscious" in the presence of other beings, an individual picks up a valence for every other being present. Some of these valences are incidental. He will pick first that valence which is most sympathetic as a desirable future friend (or some similar person). And he will pick that valence which is the top valence (highest survival, the boss, the winner) for his dramatization. He will also take the valence of the winning entity (winning over himself or others) for emotional tone. If the winning valence is also the sympathetic valence, he has an engram which can be utilized to its fullest extent.

Let us make this an example: a man is under nitrous oxide (the most vicious anesthetic ever invented, as it is actually *not* anesthetic but a hypnotic) undergoing exodontistry.[4] As usual, everybody present around the "unconscious" patient chatters and yaps about the patient, the weather, the most popular movie star or baseball. The exodontist is a tough character, bossy to the nurse, apt to be angry about trifles; he is also very sympathetic toward the patient. The nurse is a blue-eyed

---

4. exodontistry: the extraction of teeth.

blonde who is sexually aberrated. The patient—actually in agony, receiving an engram amongst engrams which may ruin his life (terrible stuff, nitrous oxide; really hands out a fancy engram as any Dianeticist can attest) —is unanalytical. Everything said to him or around him is taken literally. He takes the valence of the exodontist as both the top valence present and the sympathetic valence. But every phrase uttered is aberrative and will be interpreted by that happy little moron, the reactive mind, on the order of Simple Simon who was told he had to be careful how he stepped in the pies, so he stepped in them carefully. These people may be talking about somebody else but every "I" or "he" or "you" uttered is engramic and will be applied to others and himself by the patient in the most literal sense. "He can't remember anything," says the exodontist. All right, when the engram keys in, this patient will have an occlusion on memory in greater or lesser degree. "He can't see or feel it": this means an occlusion on sight, pain and tactile. If the patient has his eyes watering in agony at the moment (though completely "under"), he may get actual bad vision as well as poor visual recall from this experience. Now they put him in the hands of this blonde nurse to let him sleep off the drug and recover. She is an aberree amongst aberrees. She knows patients do weird things when they are still "out" so she pumps him for information about his life. And she knows they are hypnotic (yes, she sure does) so she gives him some positive suggestions. Amusing herself. She says he'll like her. That she'll be good to him. And stay there now for the present.

So the poor patient, who has had two wisdom teeth, impacted, taken out, has a full anger-sympathy dramatization. The general tone he takes is the tone the exodontist showed to the others in the room. The exodontist was angry at the nurse. With his recalls all messed up, the patient a few years later meets a woman similar to this nurse. The nurse has given him compulsions toward her. The silly little moron, the reactive mind, sees in this entirely different person enough similarity to create an identity between the nurse and this new woman. So the patient divorces his wife and marries the pseudonurse. Only now that he has married the pseudonurse, the dental engram begins to key in in earnest. Physically he gets ill: the two molars adjacent to where the wisdom teeth came out develop large cavities and begin to rot (circulation shutdown, pain in the area but can't be felt because there's a pain recall shut-off). His memory goes to pieces. His recalls become worse. He begins to develop eye trouble and a strange conjunctivitis. Further (because the dentist leaned on his chest and stomach with a sharp elbow from time to time), he has chest and stomach pains. The nitrous oxide hurt his lungs and this pain is also in chronic restimulation. But most horrible: he believes that this pseudonurse will take care of him and he stops to some degree taking care of himself in any way; his energy dissipates; and analytically he knows it is all wrong and that he is not himself. For he is now fixed in the valence of the exodontist who is angry with this nurse and so he beats the pseudonurse because he senses that from her all evil flows. The girl he married is not and was not the nurse: she sounds something like her and is a blonde. She has her own engrams and reacts. She attempts suicide.

Then, one day, since this is one engram among many, the mental hospital gets our patient and the doctors there decide that all he needs is a good solid series of electric shocks to tear his brain up, and if that doesn't work, a nice ice pick into each eyeball after and during electric shock, the ice pick sweeping a wide arc to tear the analytical mind to pieces. His wife agrees. Our patient can't defend himself: he's insane and the insane have no rights, you know.

Only the cavalry, in this one case, arrived in the form of Dianetics and cleared the patient and the wife and they are happy today. This is an actual engram and an actual case history. It is a sympathy engram, pro-survival on the moronic reactive mind level.

This is to show the ebb and flow of emotion within this one engram. The physical being is out and in agony. The mental being is given a variety of emotional tones on a contagion principle. The actual emotional tone of the patient, his own, is beaten apathy; hence, he can no longer "be himself."

In passing, it should be mentioned that only absolute silence, utter silence and tomb-like silence should attend an operation or injury of any kind. *There is nothing which can be said or given as a perceptic in any moment of "unconsciousness" which is beneficial to a patient. Nothing!* In the light of these researches and scientific findings (which can be proven in any other laboratory or group of people in very short order), speech or sound in the vicinity of an "unconscious" person should be punished criminally as, to anyone who knows these facts, such an act would be a willful effort to destroy the intellect or mental balance of an individual. If the patient is complimented, as in hypnosis or during an injury or operation, a *manic* is formed which will give him temporary euphoria and eventually plunge him into the *depressive* stage of the cycle.[5]

---

5. The author is well aware that many physicians, in using narcosynthesis [drug hypnotism], have occasionally accidentally entered "unconscious" periods. They have promptly considered, then, that these areas were equivocal, that the patient was probably not unconscious. In Dianetic research, patients have been rendered "unconscious" to the satisfaction of two doctors, both skeptical (since no longer skeptical) and have been given material which the Dianeticist knew nothing about. Along with the complete data of the tests—as muttered by the doctors as they took them to make sure by blood pressure, respiration, etc., that the patient could not be more "unconscious" unless he were

The golden rule could be altered to read: If you love your brother, keep your mouth shut when he is unconscious.

Emotion can be seen then to exist in two planes, the personal plane and the extravalence plane. It is communicable in terms of identical thinking. Rage present when a man is "unconscious" will give him a tone 1 engram: it will contain rage. Apathy present in the vicinity of an "unconscious" person will give him a tone 0 engram. Happiness present during an engram is not very aberrative but will give a tone 4 engram. And so forth. In other words, the emotions of those present around an "unconscious" person are communicated into the person as part of his engram. Any mood can be so communicated.

In dramatizing an engram, the aberree always takes the winning valence and that valence is not, of course, himself. If only one other person is present and the other is talking in terms of apathy, then the apathy is the tone value of the engram. When an apathy engram is restimulated, the individual, unless he wants to be hurt severely, is apathetic and this tone, being the nearest to death, is the most dangerous one to the individual. The rage emotion communicated to an "unconscious" person gives him a rage engram he can dramatize. This is most harmful to the society. A merely hostile tone present around an "unconscious" person gives him a merely hostile engram (covert hostility). With two people present, each having a different mood, the "unconscious" person receives an engram with two valences other than

dead, the data were recovered in full in every case and for every condition of "unconsciousness." Two patients were for a time severely aberrated by the careless comments of the anesthetizing and examining doctors: a note added to warn those attempting this experiment in the future. This is the stuff of which insanity is made. Be careful with it when manhandling patients.

his own. When this happens he will first dramatize the winning valence with its mood and, if forced from this, will dramatize the second valence with its mood. Driven from this in a chronic engram, he goes insane.

Nothing here should be construed to mean that a person only uses or dramatizes sympathy engrams. This is very far from the case. The sympathy engram gives him the chronic psychosomatic illness. He can dramatize any engram he has when it is restimulated.

Emotion, then, is communication *and* a personal condition. The cellular level evaluation of a situation depends upon any other analyzer present, even if that analyzer is thoroughly hostile to it. Lacking such evaluation, the individual takes his own tone for the moment.

There is another condition of emotion which is of extreme and useful interest to the therapist since it is the first thing with which he will have to deal in opening a case. We do not mean here to start discussing therapy but to describe a necessary part of emotion.

Great loss and other swift and severe suppressor action dams up emotion in an engram. Loss itself can be a shock to reduce analytical power. And an engram is received. If it is the loss of a sympathetic person on whom an individual has depended, it seems to the individual as if death itself stalks him. When such a suppressor effect occurs, it is as if a strong steel spring had been compressed within the engram. When it releases, it comes with a terrible rush of emotion (if this discharge is, indeed, emotion, though we hardly know what other name to call it).

Life force apparently gets dammed up at these points in life. There may be enormous quantities of that life force available but some of it becomes suppressed into a loss engram. After that the person does not seem to possess as much fluid vitality as before. This may be not emotion but life force itself. The mind, then, has below it, as in a cyst, a great quantity of sorrow or despair. The more of these charges exist in such an encysted state, the less free are the emotions of the individual. This may be on a basis of suppression to a point from which there is no swift rising. Nothing in the person's future seems to bring him up to any plane like those he occupied before.

The glory and color of childhood vanishes as one progresses into later years. But the strange part of it is that this glamor and beauty and sensitivity to life are not *gone*. They are encysted. One of the most remarkable experiences a clear has is to find, in the process of therapy, that he is recovering appreciation of the beauty in the world.

Persons, as they live forward from childhood, suffer loss after loss, and each loss takes from them a little more of this θ quantity which may be, indeed, life force itself. Bound up within them, that force is denied them and, indeed, reacts against them.

Only this emotional encysting can, for instance, compartment the mind of a person who is multivalent or who cannot see or hear his past. The analytical mind, worked upon by the reactive bank, compartments and divides with loss after loss until there is no free flow left. Then a man dies.

Thus we could say that emotion, or what has been called emotion, is really in two sections: first, there is the endocrine system which, handled either by the analytical mind in the upper two zones or the reactive mind in the lower two zones, brings emotional responses of fear, enthusiasm, apathy, etc.; second, there would be life force itself becoming compartmented by engrams and being sealed up, little by little, in the reactive bank.

It is possible that a therapy could be formulated

which would spring out these various life force charges only and create thereby a full clear. Unfortunately, to date, this has not been possible.

The odd part of emotion is that it is so ordinarily based on the word content of engrams. If an engram says, "I am afraid," then the aberree is afraid. If an engram says, "I am calm," even if the rest of the engram gives him chattering shakes, the aberree still has to be "calm."

The problem of emotion as endocrine balance and life force has another complication in that the physical pain in an engram is often mistaken for a particular emotion named in the engram. For instance, the engram can say with verbal content that the individual is "sexually excited" and have, as a pain content, an ache in the legs and have, as an actual emotional content (the valence that says, "I'm sexually excited"), anger. This, to the aberree dramatizing it, is a complex affair. When he is "sexually excited"—he has an idea what that means as just language—he is also angry and has an ache in the legs. This is actually very amusing in many cases and has led to a standard set of clinical jokes, all of which begin with, "You know, I feel like everybody else."

Dianeticists, having discovered that people evaluate the emotions, beliefs, intelligence and somatics of the world in terms of their own engramic reactions, delight in discovering new concepts of "emotion." "You know how people feel when they're happy. Their ears burn." "I feel just like anybody else when I'm happy; my feet and eyes ache." "Of course I know how people feel when they're happy; just pin prickles going all over them." "I wonder how people can stand to be passionate when it makes their noses hurt so." "Of course I know how people feel when they're excited; they have to go to the toilet."

Probably every person on earth has his own peculiar definition for every emotional state in terms of engram command. The command plus the somatics and perceptics make what they call an "emotional state."

Actually, the problem, then, should be defined in terms of the clear, who can function without engramic orders from the reactive mind. So defined, it breaks down in terms of the endocrine system and the varying level of life force free to resurge against the suppressor.

Laughter, it should be added, is not, strictly speaking, an emotion but a relief from emotion. The early Italians had a very definite idea, as represented by their folk tales, that laughter was of therapeutic value. Melancholy was the only mental illness these tales consider and laughter was its only cure. In Dianetics, we have a great deal to do with laughter. In therapy, patients vary in their laughter reaction from the slight chuckle to hilarious mirth. Any engram which really releases may be expected to begin somewhere between tears and boredom and end with laughter; the nearer the engram's tone is to tears at the first contact, the more certainly laughter will appear as it is relieved.

There is a stage of therapy often reached by the preclear when his entire past life seems to be a subject of uncontrollable mirth. This does not mean he is clear but it means that a large proportion of the encysted charges have been tapped. A preclear has laughed for two days almost without ceasing. Hebephrenia[6] is not the same thing as this laughter, for the relief of the preclear on realizing the shadowy aspect and completely knowable character of his past fears and terrors is hearty.

Laughter plays a definite role in therapy. It is quite amusing to see a preclear, who has been haunted by an

---

6. hebephrenia: a form of aberration characterized by childish or silly behavior.

engram which contained great emotional charge, suddenly relieve it, for the situation, no matter how gruesome it was, when relieved, is in all its aspects a subject of great mirth. The laughter fades away as he becomes disinterested in it and he can be said to be "tone 3" about it.

Laughter is definitely the relief of painful emotion.

The complete tone scale, its use in predicting the behavior of others as well as assisting in auditing, is given in the book *Science of Survival* by L. Ron Hubbard. See page 607 in the back of this book.

CHAPTER SEVEN

Prenatal[1] Experience and Birth

Old women less than a hundred years ago talked wisely about "prenatal influence" and how a woman marked her child. Many such intuitive thoughts are based, actually, on observed data. It can be observed that the child born out of wedlock is often a luckless creature (in a society which frowns upon such bearings). These tenets have been held in the marketplace for a great many millennia. Just because they have been held is no reason they are true, but they make an excellent beginning for a chapter on prenatal experience and birth.

If Dianetics had worked on obscure theories, such as those of the old women or those of the mystics who believe that "childish delusions" are capable of aberrating a child, Dianetics would not be a science of mind. But it was no obscure theory which brought about the discovery of the exact role prenatal experience and birth play in aberration and psychosomatic ills.

Many schools of mental healing from the Aesculapian to the modern hypnotist were studied after the basic philosophy of Dianetics had been postulated. Much data was accumulated, many experiments were made. The fundamentals about engrams had been formulated and "unconsciousness" had been discovered as being a period of actual recording, when the theory began to predict new phenomena not hitherto observed.

There has been, in recent years, a practice called

---

1. prenatal: existing or taking place before birth.

"narcosynthesis."[2] This was actually a branch of "hypnoanalysis"[3] and "deep analysis."[4] It did not produce clears and it did not even produce alleviation in the majority of its cases. But it was discovered to be an aberrative factor in itself. A thing which aberrates may well lead to something which removes aberrations if it is studied scientifically. Narcosynthesis was so studied. Several cases were examined on which narcosynthesis had been employed. Some of these cases had experienced relief from narcosynthesis. Others had become a great deal worse.

Working with hypnoanalysis it was discovered that the technique could be varied until it would actually remove the aberrative charge contained in *locks*. In treating schizophrenics with narcosynthesis it was found that the *locks* (periods of mental anguish not including physical pain or "unconsciousness") would sometimes spring (clear) and sometimes not.

Narcosynthesis is a complicated name for a very ancient process quite well known in Greece and India. It is drug hypnotism. And it is generally employed either by those practitioners who do not know hypnosis or on those patients who will not succumb to ordinary hypnotism. A shot of sodium pentothal is given intravenously to the patient and he is asked to count backwards. Shortly he stops counting at which the injection is also stopped. The patient is now in a state of "deep sleep." That this is not *sleep* seems to have missed both narco-

---

2. narcosynthesis: the practice of inducing sleep with drugs and then talking to the patient to draw out buried thoughts.

3. hypnoanalysis: the use of hypnosis or hypnotic drugs in combination with psychoanalytic techniques.

4. deep analysis: depth therapy, a form of psychotherapy that attempts to work through unconscious conflicts to resolve problems in behavior.

synthesists and hypnotists. It is actually a depressant on the awareness of an individual so that those attention units[5] which remain behind the curtain of his reactive bank can be reached directly. These attention units are up against the standard banks. The bypass circuits (demon circuits) which lie between these banks and "I" have themselves been bypassed. In other words, a section of the analytical mind has been exposed which is not aberrated. It is not very powerful and it is not highly intelligent, but it has the advantage of being hard up against the standard banks. This is *basic personality*.[6] The intent and purpose and persistence of these few attention units have the same quality and direction as the whole analytical mind would have if it were clear. It is a very nice, cooperative group of attention units and it is very useful; for *basic personality* has all recalls—sonic, audio, tactile, smell, pain, etc. It can get at anything that is in the banks—which is everything perceived or thought in a lifetime, minute by minute. These qualities of basic personality have been very poorly described in hypnotism, and it is doubtful even if it was generally known that sonic was part of the recall system disclosed by deep hypnotism or the drug hypnotism called narcosynthesis.

A study of basic personality in a multivalent subject who had poor memory, no good recalls and scant imagination disclosed the information that BP (the attention units called *basic personality*) was more able to select out data than AP (*aberrated personality*, as represented by

---

5. attention unit: a quantity of awareness. Any organism is aware to some degree. A rational or relatively rational organism is aware of being aware. Attention units could be said to exist in the mind in varying quantity from person to person.

6. basic personality: the basic self, the individual himself.

the awake subject). It was further discovered that AP could ordinarily *return* better than BP so far as time-distance went but that when AP arrived at the earliest place it was unable to manage recall. But if AP had gone back and established a vague contact with an incident, drug hypnotism or standard hypnotism used on him when he was in *present time* (no longer *returned*) would then permit BP to return. Drug hypnotism has seldom been able to force back very early into a patient's life. But by making the strength of AP go back and then using BP for the recall, some very early incidents could be reached. This trick was invented to overcome some of the difficulties which had made drug hypnosis relatively uncertain in results.

Then another factor was discovered. All those patients who had been treated by narcosynthesis had become worse every time the people doing the work had crossed over but left (because "everybody knew" an "unconscious" person didn't record) a period of "unconsciousness." When one of these "unconscious" periods was so probed—by the drug hypnosis called narcosynthesis—the patient usually became worse, not better. Doing a little more probing than had been done by the usual practitioners, Dianetic research entered some of the late-life "unconscious" periods and, with much labor, laid them bare.

Now, all drug hypnosis, whether it is called narcosynthesis or a visit from the god Aesculapius, is still hypnosis. Whatever is said to a hypnotized subject remains as a positive suggestion, and these positive suggestions are simply engrams with a somewhat lighter effect and a shorter duration. When a drug is present the hypnotism is complicated by the fact that hypnotic drugs are, after all, poisons; the body is then possessed of a permanent (at least until Dianetics was discovered) somatic to go along with the suggestion. Drug hypnotism invariably creates an engram. Whatever a practitioner says to a drugged subject becomes engramic in some degree. In the course of Dianetic research, it first was supposed, playing back the careless chatter of practitioners out of the minds of patients they had placed under drug hypnosis, that this carelessness in saying so many aberrative things was responsible for some of the failure. But this was found to be true in a very limited sense. Then it was discovered that when the "unconscious" periods were reached by drug hypnosis they refused to *lift* even when the patient recounted them scores of times. This was blamed on the drug character of the hypnosis.

Straight hypnotism was then used to reach these late "unconscious" periods and these periods still failed to *lift*. Therefore it was adjudged safe to continue drug use on those patients who refused hypnosis. And the AP-BP alternate trick began to be employed.

It was discovered by drug hypnosis, where it was necessary, and straight hypnosis, where that was possible, that the "schizophrenic" (the *multivalent* aberree) could be made to reach very early periods in every case. And it was further found that an *early* period of "unconsciousness" would often lift. Experimentation brought about a scientific axiom: *The earlier the period of "unconsciousness" the more likely it is to lift.* That is a fundamental axiom of Dianetic therapy.

Manic-depressives who had sonic recall were worked upon, most of them by straight hypnosis, and it was discovered that they also followed this rule. But it was most dramatic in the multivalent aberree: for when the engram did not lift, it impinged against his analytical mind when he was awakened and created a variation in his psychoses and brought with it psychosomatic illnesses as well.

This brought about an understanding of why the

multivalent aberree, under narcosynthesis, was made worse whenever some practitioner had glided over (but not entered, of course) a late-life period of "unconsciousness." Now came the problem of applying the axiom. It was postulated that the primary engram must in some way suppress later engrams. In view of other data and postulates, this was an entirely reasonable assumption. The earlier a person went in the life of a multivalent aberree the less likelihood there was of restimulating him artificially. Often an engram at around two or three years of age would lift entirely and give him a great deal of relief.

The problem of this research was very far from the same problem of those who, not knowing about the reactive mind and "unconsciousness," tried merely to find computing factors on a rational level or incidents of everyday life as aberrative factors in a patient.

When an engram is touched, it is very resistive, particularly above the age of two years. Further, the whole reactive bank was buried deeply under foggy layers of "unconsciousness," and was further safeguarded by a mechanism of the analytical mind which tended to prohibit it from touching pain or painful emotion. The reactive bank was protecting itself all the way through the research but it was obviously the answer. The problem was how to achieve its relief, if it could be relieved.

Having made several multivalent personalities intensely uncomfortable, a new necessity level was reached whereby something had to be done about the problem. But there was this shining hope, the above axiom. A bridge between insanity and sanity had to be built and there, in the axiom, one had at least a glimmer of a plan. The earlier one had experienced this fog and pain, the lighter these engrams seemed to be.

Then, one day, a multivalent patient, under drugs, went back to his birth. He suffered the pain—and it was very painful with this crude technique, for Dianetics had not yet smoothed down to a well-oiled piece of machinery—and he floundered through the "unconsciousness" of the period and he fought the doctor who had tried to put drops in his eyes and he generally resented the entire proceedings. AP had been sent down first, then later, under drugs, BP had contacted the incident.

This seemed a remarkable day for Dianetics. After twenty runs through birth, the patient experienced a recession of all somatics and "unconsciousness" and aberrative content. He had had asthma. It seemed that this asthma had been caused by the doctor's enthusiasm in yanking him off the table just when he was fighting for his first breath. He had had conjunctivitis. That came from the eye drops. He had had sinusitis. That had come from the nose swabs used by the pretty nurse.

Rejoicing was held, for he seemed to be a new man. A primary psychosis about being "pushed around" had vanished. The subjective reality of this incident was intense. Objective reality did not matter, but this patient had a mother near at hand and objective reality was established simply by returning her in therapy to *his* birth. They had not communicated about it in detail. The recording of her sequence compared word for word with his sequence, detail for detail, name for name. Possibility, even if they had communicated, of such duplication, outside the Dianetic situation, was mathematically impossible. And she had been "unconscious" during his birth and had always supposed that the affair had been quite different and the *return* data collapsed her awake description of it as being so much fable.

In order to make sure that this was no freak (for it is a very poor research man who will base conclusions on a series of one), two manic-depressives were returned to their births and both completed the experience. *But one of these two birth engrams would not lift!*

The postulated axiom was called into play again. If one could find the earliest engram, then the others would lift each in turn. That was the hope.

The manic-depressive whose birth had not lifted was returned to a period before birth in an effort to find an earlier engram.

Structural theories, as fondly held for ages, had thoroughly collapsed already when "unconscious" fog and pain had been penetrated to discover the engram as an aberrative unit. Tests had held up the discovery that all data, awake, asleep and "unconscious," from the moment of conception on, was always recorded somewhere in the mind or body. The little matter of myelin sheathing,[7] since it had already been disproven by laboratory research which included the reaching of birth, was discarded. The theory that no recordings can take place in the mind until the nerves are sheathed depends upon a theoretical postulate, has never been subjected to scientific research and depends for its existence upon authority alone—and a "science" which depends on authority alone is a breath in the wind of truth and is therefore no science at all. That babies cannot record until the myelin sheathing is formed has about as much truth, on investigation, as the fact that penis envy is the cause of female homosexuality. Neither theory, when applied, works. For the baby, after all, is composed of cells and it is evidenced now by much research that the cell, not an organ, records the engram.

Thus there was no inhibition about looking earlier than birth for what Dianetics had begun to call *basic-basic* (the first engram of the first chain of engrams). And an earlier engram was reached.

It has since been discovered that a great deal of

---

7. myelin sheathing: the fatty layer of tissues coating the nerves.

recording is done by the child in the womb which is not engramic. For a time it was thought that the child in the womb records on the proposition of "extended hearing," where hearing tunes up in the presence of danger and particularly during "unconsciousness." But the first research discovered prenatal engrams to be most easily reached when they contained a great deal of pain. *Cells, not the individual, are evidenced to record pain. And the reactive engram bank is composed only of cells.*

Recourse to nature rather than recourse to authority is the very building block of modern science. So long as Galen[8] remained an authority on blood, none but "madmen" like da Vinci, Shakespeare and William Harvey[9] even thought to experiment to find out what truly was the action of blood! So long as Aristotle[10] remained the authority for all, the Dark Ages reigned. Advance comes from asking free-minded questions of nature, not from quoting the works and thinking the thoughts of bygone years. Recourse to precedent is an assertion that yesterday's mentors were better informed than today's: an assertion which fades before the truth that knowledge is compounded of the experience of yesterdays, of which we have more, most certainly, than the best-informed mentor of yesterday itself.

In that Dianetics was based on a philosophy that used the cell as the basic building block, the fact that recording of engrams was done by cells came with less surprise than it otherwise might have. The engram is not a memory; *it is a cellular trace of recordings impinged deeply into the very structure of the body itself.*

---

8. Galen: second-century A.D. physician.

9. Harvey, William: (1578–1657) English physician and anatomist, discoverer of the mechanics of blood circulation.

10. Aristotle: (384–322 B.C.) Greek philosopher.

The experience of which cells themselves were capable had already been tested. It had been found that a monocell divided not only its substance but gave its total experience, as a master disc will make duplicates, to its offspring. Now, this is a peculiarity of monocells: they survive as identities. Each is personally its forebear. Cell A divides to a first generation; this generation is also Cell A; the second generation, the second division, creates an entity which is still Cell A. Lacking the necessity of such laborious processes as construction and birth and growth before reproduction, the monocell simply splits. And everything it has learned could be postulated to be contained in the new generation. Cell A dies but through generations from it, the latest generation is still Cell A. Man's belief that *he* is to live in his progeny might possibly derive from this cellular identity of procreation. Another interesting possibility lies in the fact that even neurons exist in embryo[11] in the zygote, and neurons do not themselves divide but are like organisms (and may have the virus as their basic building block).

Dianetics, as a study of function and the science of mind, does not need any postulate concerning structure, however. The only test is whether or not a fact works. If it does work and can be used, it is a scientific fact. And the prenatal engram is a scientific fact. Tested and checked for objective reality, it still stands firm. And as for subjective reality, *the acceptance of the prenatal engram as a working fact alone makes possible the clear*.

At the end of a series of 270 clears and alleviations, a short series of five cases was taken to finally settle the argument. These five cases were not permitted to admit anything before birth. They were treated with everything Dianetics, hypnotism and other therapeutics could offer, and no clear was obtained. This ruled out the

---

11. embryo: an early or undeveloped stage of something.

"personality of the operator" or "suggestion" or "faith" as factors in Dianetics. These five cases had never been informed of prenatal engrams. Each swerved in toward them but was restrained without informing him that engrams existed that early. The five were alleviated as to some variety of psychosomatic ills but the ills were only alleviated, not completely cured. The aberrations remained but little changed. They were extremely disappointed since each had heard something of "the miracles Dianetics could perform." Before them, 270 cases had been worked and 270 cases had reached prenatal engrams. And 270 cases had been cleared or alleviated as the Dianeticist chose and time permitted. All could have been cleared with an additional average of 100 or so hours for each of the persons who were alleviated. In short, on random cases—and selected cases, so that at least two of each classification of neurosis or psychosis were included in the clearing—when prenatal engrams and birth were taken into account and used in therapy, results were obtained. When these factors were not taken into account, results were no more favorable than those attained in the best successes of past schools—which is not nearly good enough for a science of mind.

Dianetics had prenatal and birth engrams wished off on it as facts existing in the nature of things. That past schools have been passing over these engrams and into the prenatal area without success does not mean that prenatals could not be found any more than it means that these past schools found much value in prenatal experience when they considered it at all. The problem is slightly more complex: the difficulty lay in finding the reactive bank which was occluded by "unconsciousness" which had never before been penetrated wittingly as "unconsciousness." The discovery of this reactive bank led to the discovery of *prenatal engrams*, which are quite different from "prenatal memory."

After a few cases had been examined as to objective and subjective reality, Dianetics was forced to accept, if it wished a clear, the fact that the cells of the fetus[12] record. A few more cases and a little more experience discovered that the embryo cells record. And suddenly it was discovered that recording begins in the cells of the zygote—which is to say, with conception. That the body recalls conception, which is a high-level survival activity, has little to do with engrams. Most patients to date sooner or later startle themselves by finding themselves swimming up a channel or waiting to be connected with. The recording is there. And there's little use arguing with a preclear that he cannot recall being a sperm, engramic or not as the case may be. It must be remarked because any Dianeticist will encounter this.

Anyone postulating that "return to the womb" was an ambition should have examined life in the womb a little more carefully. Even a poor scientist would have at least tried to find out if anybody could recall it before he made a statement that there was a memory of it. But life in the womb does not seem to be the paradise it has been poetically, if not scientifically, represented. Actuality discloses that three men and a horse in a telephone booth would have but little less room than an unborn baby. The womb is wet, uncomfortable and unprotected.

Mama sneezes, baby gets knocked "unconscious." Mama runs lightly and blithely into a table and baby gets its head staved in. Mama has constipation and baby, in the anxious effort, gets squashed. Papa becomes passionate and baby has the sensation of being put into a running washing machine. Mama gets hysterical, baby gets an engram. Papa hits Mama, baby gets

---

12. fetus: in man, the offspring in the womb from the end of the third month of pregnancy until birth.

an engram. Junior bounces on Mama's lap, baby gets an engram. And so it goes.

People have scores of prenatal engrams when they are normal. They can have more than two hundred. And each one is aberrative. Each contains pain and "unconsciousness."

Engrams received as a zygote are potentially the most aberrative, being wholly reactive. Those received as an embryo are intensely aberrative. Those received as the fetus are enough to send people to institutions all by themselves.

Zygote, embryo, fetus, infant, child, adult: these are all the same person. Time has been considered the great healer. That can be filed with the things "everybody knew." On a conscious level it may be true. But on a reactive level time is nothing. The engram, whenever received, is strong in proportion to the degree it is restimulated.

The mechanism of an engram has an interesting feature. It is not "reasoned" or analyzed, nor does it have any meaning until it has been keyed in. A baby, before speech, could have an engram in restimulation, but that engram must have been keyed in by the analytical data the baby has.

The reactive mind steals meaning from the analytical mind. An engram is just so many wave recordings until it is keyed in, and those recordings, by such restimulation, become effective upon the analytical mind. It may be that the engram never has any reason or meaning in itself but only thrusts its waves forward as unreasoned things at the body and analyzer, and the body and analyzer, through mechanisms, give them meaning. In other words, the engram is not a sentient recording containing meanings. It is merely a series of impressions such as a needle might make on wax. These impressions are meaningless to the body until the engram keys in, at which time aberrations and psychosomatics occur.

Thus, it can be understood that the prenatal child has no remotest idea of what is being said in terms of words. It does learn, being an organism, that certain things may mean certain dangers. But this is every bit as far as it goes with recording. The mind must become more or less fully formed before the engram can impinge into the analytical level.

The prenatal child can, of course, experience terror. When the parents or the professional abortionist start after it and thrust it full of holes, it knows fear and pain.

It has, however, this prenatal child, an advantage in its situation. Being surrounded by amniotic fluid[13] and dependent for nutrition on its mother, being in a state of growth and easily re-formed physically, it can repair an enormous amount of damage and does. The recovery qualities of the human body are never higher than before birth. Damage which would maim an infant for life or would kill a grown man can be taken in stride by the prenatal child. Not that this damage does not make an engram—it certainly does, complete with all data and speech and emotion—but that this damage does not easily kill it is the point here.

Why people try to abort children is a problem which has its answer only in aberration, for it is very difficult to abort a child. One can say that in the attempt the mother herself is in more danger of dying than the child, *no matter what method is used.*

A society which suppresses sex as evil and which is so aberrated that any member of it will attempt an abortion is a society which is dooming itself to ever-rising insanity. For it is a scientific fact that abortion attempts are the most important factor in aberration. The child on whom the abortion is attempted is condemned to live with *murderers* whom he reactively knows

---

13. amniotic fluid: the fluid surrounding the embryo or fetus.

to be murderers through all his weak and helpless youth! He forms unreasonable attachments to grandparents, has terrified reactions to all punishments, grows ill easily and suffers long. And there is no such thing as a guaranteed way to abort a child. Use contraceptives, not a knitting needle or the douche bag, to hold down population. Once the child is conceived, no matter how "shameful" the circumstances, no matter the *mores*, no matter the income, that man or woman who would attempt an abortion on an unborn child is attempting a murder which will seldom succeed and is laying the foundation of a childhood of illness and heartache. Anyone attempting an abortion is committing an act against the whole society and the future; any judge or doctor recommending an abortion should be instantly deprived of position and practice, whatever his "reason."

If a person knows he has committed this crime against a child who has been born, he should do all possible to have that child "cleared" as soon as possible after the age of eight and in the meantime should treat that child with all the decency and courtesy possible in order to keep the engram out of restimulation. Otherwise he may send that child to an institution for the insane.

A large proportion of allegedly feebleminded children are actually attempted-abortion cases whose engrams place them in fear paralysis or regressive palsy[14] and which command them not to grow but to be where they are forever.

However many billions America spends yearly on institutions for the insane and jails for the criminals are spent primarily because of attempted abortions done by some sex-blocked mother to whom children are a curse, not a blessing of God.

---

14. palsy: paralysis, especially with involuntary tremors.

Antipathy toward children means a blocked second dynamic. Physiological examination of anyone with such blockage will demonstrate a physical derangement of the genitalia or glands. Dianetic therapy would demonstrate attempted abortion or an equally foul prenatal existence and would clear the individual.

The case of the child who, as this is read, is not yet born but upon whom abortion has been attempted, is not hopeless. If he is treated with decency after he is born and if he is not restimulated by witnessing quarrels, he will wax and grow fat until he is eight and can be cleared, at which time he will probably be much startled to learn the truth. But that startlement and any antagonism included in it will vanish with the finishing of the clear, and his love of his parents will be greater than before.

All these things are scientific facts, tested and rechecked and tested again. And with them can be produced a clear, on whom our racial future depends.

CHAPTER EIGHT

Contagion of Aberration

Disease is contagious. Germs, traveling from one individual to another, wander through an entire society, respecting none until stopped by such things as sulfa[1] or penicillin.

Aberrations are contagious. Like germs they respect none and carry forward from individual to individual, from parents to child, respecting none until they are stopped by Dianetics.

The people of yesterday supposed that genetic insanity must exist, for it could be observed that the children of aberrated parents were often themselves aberrated. There is genetic insanity but it is limited to the case of actually missing parts. A very small percentage of insanity falls into such a category and its manifestation is mental dullness or failure to coordinate and beyond these has no aberrative quality whatever (such people receive engrams which complicate their cases).

The contagion of aberration is too simple in principle to be much labored here. In Dianetics, we learn that only moments of "unconsciousness," short or long and of greater or lesser depth, can contain engrams. When a person is rendered "unconscious," people in his vicinity react more or less at the dictates of their engrams: in fact, the "unconsciousness" is quite ordinarily caused by somebody's dramatization. A clear, then, could be rendered unconscious by an aberree who is dramatizing and the aberree's dramatization of his engram would

---

1. sulfa: any of a group of chemical compounds with antibacterial properties.

enter as an engram into the clear.

The mechanics are simple. People under stress, if aberrated, dramatize engrams. Such dramatization may involve the injury of another person and render him more or less "unconscious." The unconscious person then receives as an engram the dramatization.

This is not the only way contagion of aberration gets about. People on operating tables, under anesthetic, are subjected to the more or less aberrated conversation of those present. This conversation enters into the "unconscious" person as an engram. Similarly, at the scene of accidents, the emergency nature of the experience may excite people into dramatizations, and if a person is "unconscious" because of the accident, an engram is received.

Aberrated parents are certain to infect their children with engrams. The father and mother, in dramatizing their own engrams around sick or injured children, pass them along just as certainly as if those engrams were bacteria. This does not mean that the total reactive bank of a child is composed solely of the parents' engrams, for there are many exterior influences to the home which can enter into the child when it is "unconscious." And it does not mean that the child is going to react to the same engrams the way either parent might react, for the child, after all, is an individual with an inherent personality, a power of choice and a different experience pattern. But it does mean that it is utterly inevitable that aberrated parents will in some way aberrate their children.

Misconceptions and poor data in a society's culture become engrams because not all the conduct around an "unconscious" person is dramatization. If some society believed that fish-eating brought on leprosy, it is quite certain that this false datum would find its way into engrams and sooner or later someone would develop a leprosy-like disease after having eaten fish.

Primitive societies, being subject to much mauling by the elements, have many more occasions for injury than civilized societies. Further, such primitive societies are alive with false data. Further, their practice of medicine and mental healing is on a very aberrative level by itself. The number of engrams in a Zulu would be astonishing. Moved out of his restimulative area and taught English he would escape the penalty of much of his reactive data; but in his native habitat the Zulu is only outside the bars of a madhouse because there are no madhouses provided by his tribe. It is a safe estimate, and one based on better experience than is generally available to those who base conclusions on "modern man" by studying primitive races, that primitives are far more aberrated than civilized peoples. Their savageness, their unprogressiveness, their incidence of illness: all stem from their reactive patterns, not from their inherent personalities. Measuring one set of aberrees by another set of aberrees is not likely to lead to much data. And the contagion of aberration, being much greater in a primitive tribe, and the falsity of the superstitious data in the engrams of such a tribe both lead to a conclusion which, observed on the scene, is carried out by actuality.

Contagion of aberration is very easily studied in the process of clearing any aberree whose parents fought. Mother, for instance, might be relatively unaberrated at the beginning of the marriage. If she is beaten by her husband who is, after all, dramatizing, she will begin to pick up his aberrations as part of her own reactive pattern. This is particularly noticeable when one is clearing a person who was conceived shortly after his parents' marriage or before it. Papa may begin with a certain dramatization which includes beating a wife. Whatever he says in such a dramatization will sooner or later begin to affect the wife and she may—unless extraordinarily well-balanced—begin to dramatize these things on her own. Eventually, when the child is born, she will begin to dramatize on the child, thus putting him into a continual state of restimulation.

Birth is one of the most remarkable engrams in terms of contagion. Here the mother and child both receive the same engram which differs only in the location of pain and the depths of "unconsciousness." Whatever the doctors, nurses and other people associated with the delivery say to the mother during labor and birth and immediately afterwards before the child is taken away is recorded in the reactive bank, making an identical engram in both mother and child.

This engram is remarkably destructive in several ways. The mother's voice can restimulate the birth engram in the child and the presence of the child can restimulate the giving-birth engram in the mother. Thus they are mutually restimulative. In view of the fact that they have all the other restimulators also in common, a later life situation can cause them each to suffer simultaneously from the engram. If birth included a slammed window, a slammed window may trigger birth dramatization in both, simultaneously, with resultant hostilities or apathies.

Should a doctor become angry or despairing, the emotional tone of birth can be severe. And if the doctor talks at all, the conversation takes on its full, reactive, literal meaning to both mother and child.

Many cases were cleared where both mother and child were available. One such case found the mother (as heard by the child in Dianetic clearing) moaning, "I'm so ashamed, I'm so ashamed," over and over. The child had a neurosis about shame. When the mother was cleared, it was found that *her* mother at birth was moaning, "I'm so ashamed, I'm so ashamed." One can presume that this has been going along, by contagion, since Cheops[2] built his tomb.

In the larger sphere of society, contagion of aberration is extremely dangerous and cannot but be considered as a vital factor in undermining the health of that society.

The social body behaves similarly to an organism in that there are social aberrations which exist within the society. The society grows and may fade like an organism which has people, not cells, for its parts. Where pain is leveled by the head of the society at any member in that society, a source of aberration is begun which will be contagious. The reasons against corporal punishment are not "humanitarian," they are practical. A society which practices punishment of any kind against any of its members is carrying on a contagion of aberration. The society has a social engram, society size, which says punishment is necessary. Punishment is meted. The jails and institutions fill. And then one day some portion of the society, depressed into zone 1 by a government's freedom with government engrams, jumps up and wipes the government out. And a new set of aberrations is formed from the violence attending the destruction. Violent revolutions never win because they begin this cycle of aberration.

A society filled with aberrees may feel it necessary to punish. There has been no remedy other than punishment. The provision of a remedy for unsocial conduct by members of the group is of more than passing interest to a government for a continuance of its own corporal practices; adding these to the continuing aberrations of the past seriously depresses the survival potential of that government and will someday cause that government to

---

2. Cheops: first king of Fourth Dynasty of Egypt (reigned circa 2900–2877 B.C.).

fall. After many governments so fall, its people, too, perish from this earth.

Contagion of aberration is never more apparent than in that social insanity called war. Wars never solve the need of wars. Fight to save the world for democracy or save it from Confucianism[3] and the fight is inevitably lost by all. War has become associated in the past with competition, and it has been believed, therefore, by shifty logic, that wars were necessary. A society which advances into a war as a solution of its problems cannot but depress its own survival potential. No government was ever permitted to enter a war without costing its people some of their liberties. The end product is the apathy of a ruling priesthood, where mystery and superstition alone can band the insane remnants of a people together. This is too easily observed in past histories to need much amplification. A democracy engaging in war has always lost some of its democratic rights. As it engages in more and more wars, it eventually comes under the command of a dictator (rule by a single engram). The dictator, forcing his rule, increases the aberrations by his activity against minorities. Revolt begins to follow revolt. Priesthoods flourish. Apathy awaits. And after apathy comes death. So went Greece, so went Rome. So goes England. So goes Russia. And so goes the United States and with it goes mankind.

Rule by force is a violation of the law of affinity, for force begets force. Rule by force reduces the self-determinism of the individuals in a society and therefore the self-determinism of the society itself. Contagion of aberration sweeps along like a forest fire. Engrams beget engrams. And unless the dwindling spiral is interrupted by new lands and mongrel races which escape their

3. Confucianism: the system of morality taught by Confucius, a Chinese philosopher (551?–479? B.C.).

aberrative environments, or by the arrival of a means to break the contagion of aberration by clearing individuals, a race will reach downward to the end of the cycle—zone 0.

A race is as great as its individual members are self-determined.

In the smaller sphere of the family, as in the national scenes, contagion of aberration produces an interruption of optimum survival.

Self-determinism is the only possible way a computer can be built to give rational answers. Holding down seven in an adding machine causes it to give wrong answers. Entering fixed and not-to-be-rationalized answers into any human being will cause him to compute wrong answers. Survival depends on right answers. Engrams enter from the exterior world into the hidden recesses below rational thinking and prevent rational answers being reached. This is exterior-determinism. Any interference with self-determinism cannot but lead to wrong computations.

In that a clear is cooperative, a society of clears would cooperate. This may be an idyllic, utopian[4] dream and it may not be. In a family of clears there is observable harmony and cooperation. A clear can recognize a superior computation when he sees one. He does not have to be slugged and held down and made to *obey* to make him put a shoulder to the wheel. If he *is* made to obey, independent of his thinking, his self-determinism is interrupted to a point where he cannot get right answers; the society which holds him has penalized, itself, his ability to think and act rationally. The only way a clear could so be forced would be to give him engrams or turn a neurosurgeon loose upon his brain.

---

4. utopian: of or like a utopia, any idealized place, state or situation of perfection.

But a clear does not need to be forced for, if the job is important enough to do in terms of general need, he will most certainly do it according to his intelligence and do it as well as possible. One never observes the *forced* individual doing a job well, just as one never observes a *forced* society winning against an equally prosperous free society.

A family which runs on the godhead plan, where somebody must be obeyed without question, is never a happy family. Its prosperity may be present in some material aspects but its apparent survival as a unit is superficial.

Forced groups are invariably less efficient than free groups working for the common good. But any group which contains aberrated members is likely to become entirely aberrated as a group through contagion. The effort to restrain aberrated members of a group inevitably restrains the group as a whole and leads to further and further restraint.

Clearing one member of a family of aberrees is seldom enough to resolve the problems of that family. If the husband has been aberrated, he will have aberrated or restimulated his wife and children in one way or another, even when he used no physical violence upon them. The parents implant their mutual aberrations in the children and the children, being potentially self-determined units, revolt back to stir up the aberrations of the parents. In that so many of these aberrations, by contagion, have become mutual and held in common with the whole family, the happiness of the family is severely undermined.

The corporal punishment of children is just another facet of the problem of the forced group. If anyone cares to argue over the necessity of punishing children, let him examine the source of the misbehavior of the children.

The child who is aberrated may not have his engrams entirely keyed in. He may have to wait until he himself is married and has children or a pregnant wife to have restimulators enough to cause him to become, suddenly, one of these things they call a "mature adult," blind to the beauty of the world and burdened by all its griefs. But the child is nevertheless aberrated and has many dramatizations. The child is in a very unlucky situation in that he has with him his two most powerful restimulators—his mother and father. These assume the power of physical punishment over him. And they are giants to him. He is a pygmy. And he has to depend upon them for food, clothing and shelter. One can speak very grandly about the "delusions of childhood" until he knows the engram background of most children.

The child is on the unkind receiving end of all the dramatizations of his parents. A cleared child is a most remarkable thing to observe: he is human! Affinity alone can pull him through. The spoiled child is the child whose decisions have been interrupted continuously and who is robbed of his independence. Affection could no more spoil a child than the sun could be put out by a bucket of gasoline.

The beginning and end of "child psychology" is that a child is a human being, that he is entitled to his dignity and self-determinism. The child of aberrated parents is a problem because of the contagion of aberration and because he is denied any right to dramatize or counter. The wonder is not that children are a problem but that they are sane in any action, for—by contagion, punishment and denial of self-determinism—the children of today have been denied all the things required to make a rational life. And these are the future family and the future race.

This is not a dissertation on children or politics, however, but a chapter on contagion of aberration.

Dianetics covers human thought, and human thought is wide ground. When one gazes at the potentialities inherent in the mechanism of contagion, respect for the inherent stability of man cannot but arise. No "wild animal" reacting with inherent "asocial tendencies" could have built Nineveh[5] or Boulder Dam. Carrying the contagion mechanism like some Old Man of the Sea,[6] we have yet come far. Now that we know it, perhaps we shall truly reach the stars.

---

5. Nineveh: capital of the ancient empire of Assyria, situated on the east bank of the Tigris River, opposite modern Mosul, Iraq.

6. Old Man of the Sea: character in the story of "Sindbad the Sailor" in the *Arabian Nights*. A seemingly harmless old man, he climbs onto the shoulders of the obliging Sindbad and refuses to get off. He clings there for many days and nights until Sindbad escapes by getting him drunk.

CHAPTER NINE

Keying In the Engram

The single source of inorganic mental illness and organic psychosomatic illness is the reactive engram bank. The reactive mind impinges these engrams upon the analytical mind and the organism whenever they are restimulated after being keyed in.

There are many known incidents in a lifetime which apparently have a profound influence upon the happiness and mental condition of the individual. The individual remembers these and to them attributes his troubles. In a measure he is right: he is at least looking back at incidents which are held in place by engrams. He does not see the engrams. In fact, unless he is acquainted with Dianetics, he does not know the engrams are there. And even then he will not know their contents until he has undergone therapy.

It can be demonstrated with ease that any moment of "conscious level" unhappiness which contained great stress or emotion was not guilty of the charge of causing aberration and psychosomatic illness. These moments, of course, played a role in the matter: they were the *key-ins*.

The process of keying in an engram is not very complex. Engram 105, let us say, was a moment of "unconsciousness" when the prenatal child was struck, via Mother, by Father. The father, aware or not of the child, uttered the words "Goddamn you, you filthy whore: you're no good!" This engram lay where it was impressed, in the reactive bank. Now, it could lie there for seventy years and never become keyed in. It contains

191

a headache and a falling body and the grating of teeth and the intestinal sounds of the mother. And any of these sounds, postbirth, may be present in large quantities without *keying in* this engram.

One day, however, the father becomes exasperated at the child. The child is tired and feverish, which is to say that his analytical mind may not be at its highest level of activity. And the father has a certain set of engrams which he dramatizes and one of these engrams is the above incident. And the father reaches out and slaps the child and says, "Goddamn you: you're no good!" The child cries. That night he has a headache and is much worse physically. And he feels both an intense hatred and a fear of his father. The engram has *keyed in*. Now the sound of a falling body or grating teeth or any trace of anger of any kind in the father's voice will make the child nervous. His physical health will suffer. He will begin to have headaches.

If we take this child who has now become an adult and rake back over his past, we shall discover (though it may be occluded) a lock like the above key-in. And now not only the key-in; we may discover half a hundred, half a thousand, such locks just on this one subject. One would say, unless he knew Dianetics, that this child was ruined postnatally by being beaten by the father, and one might attempt to bring the patient's mind back into better condition by removing these locks.

There are literally thousands, tens of thousands, of locks in the average life. To take all of these locks away would be a task for Hercules. Every engram a person has, if it has been keyed in, may have its hundreds of locks.

If conditioning existed as a mechanism of pain and stress, mankind would be in very bad condition. Fortunately, conditioning does not so exist. It appears to exist but the appearance is not the fact. One would think that if a child were daily thrust around and reviled[1] he would eventually become conditioned into a belief that this was the way life was and that he had better turn against it.

Conditioning does not, however, exist. Pavlov[2] may have been able to drive dogs mad by repeated experiments: this was simply bad observation on the part of the observer. The dogs might be trained to do this or that. But it was not conditioning. The dogs went mad because they were given engrams—if and when they did go mad. A series of such experiments, properly conducted and observed, proves this contention.

The boy who was daily told he was no good and who apparently went into a decline solely because of that, declined only because of the engram. This is a happy fact. The engram may take a while to locate—a few hours—but when it is alleviated or refiled in the standard memory banks, everything which had locked on to it also refiles.

People trying to help others with their aberrations who did not know about engrams were, of course, operating with 2.9 strikes against any success. In the first place, the locks themselves may vanish down into the reactive bank. Thus we get a patient who says, "Oh, my father wasn't so bad. He was a pretty good guy." And we discovered, and the patient discovers, when an engram is sprung, that Father was customarily to be found dramatizing. What the patient knows about his past before engrams are sprung is not worth cataloguing. In another case we may find a patient saying, "Oh, I had a terrible childhood, a terrible childhood. I was beaten seriously." And we discover, when we get the engrams refiled, that the parents of this patient never laid

---

1. revile: to criticize angrily in abusive language.

2. Pavlov, Ivan Petrovich: (1849–1936) Russian physiologist; noted for behavioral experiments on dogs.

a hand on him in punishment or wrath in his entire life.

An engram may coast along without being keyed in for decades. One of the most remarkable types of case is one which spent an entire youth without displaying any aberration. Then suddenly, at the age of twenty-six, we discover him to be so aberrated, so suddenly, that it appears he must have been hexed. Perhaps most of his engrams were concerned with the action of getting married and having children. He has never been married before. The first time he is weary or ill and realizes he has a wife on his hands, the first engram keys in. Then the dwindling spiral begins to go to work. This one shuts down the analyzer enough so that others can be keyed in. And finally we may discover him in an institution.

The young girl who has been happy and carefree to the age of thirteen and then suddenly goes into a decline has not, that moment, received an engram. She has had an engram key in, which let another key in. Fission reaction. This key-in may have required nothing more than the discovery that she was bleeding from the vagina. She has an emotional engram about this; she becomes frantic. The other engrams, as the days follow, may swing into position to impinge upon her. And so she becomes ill.

The first sexual experience may be one which keys in an engram. This is so standard that sex has gotten a rather bad name for itself here and there as being an aberrative factor all by itself. Sex is not and never has been aberrative. Physical pain and emotion which incidentally contain sex as a subject are the aberrative factors.

It may be that a patient is urgent in her insistence that her father raped her when she was nine and that this is the cause of all her misery. Large numbers of insane patients claim this. And it is perfectly true. Father did rape her, but it happened she was only nine days beyond conception at the time. The pressure and upset of coitus is very uncomfortable to the child and normally can be expected to give the child an engram which will have as its content the sexual act and everything that was said.

Drug hypnosis is dangerous when one is trying to treat psychotics, as has been mentioned. And there are other reasons it is dangerous. Any operation under anesthetic or any drugging of a patient may bring about the keying in of engrams. Here is the analyzer shutdown, there is the reactive bank open to be stirred by any comment made by the people around the drugged subject. Hypnotism itself is a condition in which engrams may be keyed in which have never before been restimulated: the glassy-eyed stare of the person who has been "too often hypnotized," the lack of will seen in people too often hypnotized, the dependence of the subject upon the hypnotic operator: all these things stem from the keying in of engrams. *Any* time the body is rendered "unconscious" without physical pain, no matter how light the degree of "unconsciousness" is, even if it is only the lightness of weariness, an engram may be keyed in. And when "unconsciousness" is complicated by new physical pain, a new engram is formed which may gather up with it an entire bundle of old engrams not hitherto keyed in. Such a late engram would be a *cross engram* in that it crosses chains of engrams. And if such an engram resulted in a loss of sanity, it would be called a *break engram*.

There are some aspects to various drug "unconsciousnesses" which have been very perplexing in the past. Psychotic women often maintain, after they are awakened from a drugged sleep (and sometimes a hypnotic sleep), that they have been raped. Men occasionally maintain that the operator has tried to perform a homosexual act upon them while they were drugged. Although it occasionally occurs that people *are* raped after being drugged, the largest number of such assertions are merely an aspect of the key-in mechanism. Almost any child has been put through the prenatal discomfort of coitus. Often there was violent emotion other than passion present. Such an engram may stay out of circuit for years until drugged "unconsciousness" or some such thing keys it in. The patient goes to sleep without a keyed-in engram; he wakes up with one. He tries to justify the strange sensations he has (and engrams are timeless things unless they are arranged properly on the time track[3]) and comes out with the "solution" that he must have been raped.

Childhood rapes are very seldom the responsible cause in sexual aberration. They are the key-in.

One looks at the conscious level locks and sees sadness, mental anguish and misfortune. Some of the experience there seems to be so terrible that it must certainly cause aberration. But it does not. Man is a tough, resilient creature. These conscious level experiences are at best only guideposts leading toward the actual seat of trouble, and that is not known in any detailed way to the individual.

The engram is never "computed." An example of this, on a lightly aberrative level, can be found in a child's punishment. If one examines a childhood where punishment has been corporal and frequent, he begins to understand the utter futility of the pain-drive theory. Punishment actually and literally and emphatically does no good of any kind whatsoever but accomplishes quite the reverse, since it occasions a reactive revolt against the punishment source, and is likely to cause not only a disintegration of a mind but also a continual bedevilment of the punishment source. Man reacts to fight

_____

3. time track: the time span of the individual from conception to present time on which lies the sequence of events of his life.

sources of pain. When he stops fighting them he is mentally broken and of little use to anyone, much less himself.

We take a case of a boy who was beaten with a hairbrush every time he was "bad." In researching this case, the most searching inquiry fails to reveal any vivid recall of *why* he was punished but only *that* he was punished. The progress of the event would go something like this: activity more or less rational, fright at threatened punishment, punishment, sorrow over punishment, renewed activity. The mechanics of the case showed the person to have been engaged on some activity which, whether others would consider it so or not, was nevertheless survival activity to him, giving him either pleasure or actual gains or even the assertion that he could and would survive. The moment punishment is threatened old punishments go into restimulation as minor engrams, resting usually on major engrams: this shuts down the analytical power to some extent and the recording is now being done on a reactive level; the punishment takes place, submerging analytical awareness so that the punishment records in the engram bank only; the sorrow following is still in the period of analytical shutdown; the analyzer gradually turns on; full awareness returns, and then activity on an analytical plane can be resumed. All corporal punishment runs this gamut and all other punishments are, at best, locks, following this same pattern with only the complete shutdown resulting from pain missing.

If the analyzer wants this data for computation, it is not available. There is a reaction in the reactive mind when the matter is approached. *But there are five courses the reactive mind can take with this data!* And there is no guarantee and no method between land and sky of knowing what course the reactive mind will take with the data except knowing the full engram bank—and if that is known, the person could be cleared with a few more hours' work and would need no punishment.

These five ways of handling data make corporal punishment an unstable and unreliable thing. A ratio exists which can be tested and proven in any man's experience: *A man is evil in the direct ratio that destructiveness has been leveled against him.* An individual (including those individuals society is liable to forget as individuals: children) reacts *against* the punishment source whether that source be parents or government. Anything which sets itself forward against an individual as a punishment source will be considered in greater or lesser degree (as it is in proportion to benefits) as a target for the reactions of the individual.

The little accidental milk glass upsets of children, that noise which just accidentally occurs on the porch where the children are playing, that little accidental ruination of Papa's hat or Mama's rug: these are often cold, calculated, reactive mind actions against pain sources. The analytical mind may temporize[4] about love and affection and the need of three square meals. The reactive mind runs off the lessons it has learned and devil take the meals.

If one turned an idiot loose on an adding machine to let him audit the company books and let him prevent the auditor[5] from touching equipment and data which has to be his if any answers will be right, one would get very little in the way of correct answers. And if one kept feeding the idiot and made him fat and powerful, the firm would sooner or later go to ruin. The reactive mind is the idiot, the auditor is "I" and the firm is the organism. Punishment feeds the idiot.

---

4. temporize: to effect a compromise; negotiate.

5. auditor: a person who is authorized to audit [to check or examine] accounts.

The helpless amazement of police about the "confirmed criminal" (and the police belief in the "criminal type" and the "criminal mind") comes about through this cycle. Police, for some reason or other, like governments, have become identified with society. Take any one of these "criminals" and clear him and the society regains a rational being of which it can use all it can get. Keep up the punishment cycle and the prisons will get more numerous and more full.

The problem of the child lashing back at his parents by "negation" and the problem of Jimmie the Cob blowing a bank guard apart in an armed robbery stem both from the same mechanism. The child, examined on the "conscious level," is not aware of his causes but will put forth various justifications for his conduct. Jimmie the Cob, waiting for this oh-so-very-sentient society to tie him down with straps in an electric chair and give him an electric shock therapy which will cause him to cease and desist forever, examined for his causes, will pour forth justifications to explain his life and conduct. The human mind is a pretty wonderful computing machine. The reasons it can evolve for unreasonable acts have staggered one and all and particularly social workers. Without knowing the cause and the mechanism, the chances of drawing a correct conclusion by comparing all conducts available are as remote as winning at fan-tan[6] from a Chinese. Hence, the punishments have continued as the muddled answer to a very muddled society.

There are five ways in which a human being reacts toward a source of danger. These are also the five courses he can take on any given problem. And it might be said that this is five-valued action.

---

6. fan-tan: a Chinese betting game in which the players lay wagers on the number of pieces that will remain when a hidden pile of them has been divided by four.

The parable of the black panther[7] is appropriate here. Let us suppose that a particularly black-tempered black panther is sitting on the stairs and that a man named Gus is sitting in the living room. Gus wants to go to bed. But there is the black panther. The problem is to get upstairs. There are five things that Gus can do about this panther: (1) he can go *attack* the black panther; (2) he can run out of the house and *flee* the black panther; (3) he can use the back stairs and *avoid* the black panther; (4) he can *neglect* the black panther; and (5) he can *succumb* to the black panther.

These are the five mechanisms: *attack, flee, avoid, neglect* or *succumb*.

All actions can be seen to fall within these courses. And all actions are visible in life. In the case of a punishment source, the reactive mind can succumb, neglect, avoid, flee or attack it. The action is dictated by a complexity of engrams and depends upon which one comes into restimulation. This maelstrom[8] of reaction generally resolves itself, however, in one of the five courses.

If a child is punished and thereafter obeys, he can be considered to have succumbed. And the value of a child who will succumb to punishment is so slight that the Spartans[9] would long since have drowned him, for it means he has sunk into an apathy unless it so happens that he himself has computed the idea, bypassing all reaction, that the thing for which he was punished was

---

7. In Dianetics considerable slang has been developed by patients and Dianeticists and they call a neglect of the problem the "black panther mechanism." One supposes this stems from the ridiculousness of biting black panthers.

8. maelstrom: an agitated or tumultuous state of affairs.

9. Spartans: the citizens of Sparta, a city in ancient Greece, who would permit a child to live only if he showed potential of becoming an asset to the state.

not bright (he can't be assisted in this computation if punishment is entered into the reactive mind by the source trying to assist him). He can flee the punishment source, which at least is not apathy but merely cowardice by popular judgment. He can neglect the matter entirely and ignore the punishment source—and would have been called a stoic by the ancients, but might be called merely dull-witted by his friends. He can avoid the punishment source, which might give him the doubtful compliment of being sly or cunning or pandering.[10] Or he can attack the punishment source either by direct action or by upsetting or fouling the person or the possessions of the source—in which instance he would be called, on direct action, a valiant fool, taking parental size into account, or in a less direct fashion he could be called "covertly hostile" or could be said to be "negating." As long as a human being will attack as a response to a valid threat, he can be said to be in fair mental condition—"normal"—and a child is said to be "just acting like any normal child."

Enter punishment into the computation and it no longer computes. It is entirely different in the case of "experience." Life has plenty of painful experience waiting for any human being without other human beings complicating the score. A person who is still unblocked in his dynamics or who has been unblocked by Dianetics can absorb the most amazing amount of hammering in the business of living. Here, even when the reactive mind receives engrams as a result of some of this experience, the analytical mind can continue to cope with the situation without becoming aberrated in any way. Man is a tough, resilient, competent character. But when the law of affinity begins to be broken and such a breaking of affinity gets into the reactive bank, *human beings,* as

---

10. pander: to minister to others' passions or prejudices for selfish ends.

antagonistic sources of nonsurvival, become a punishment source. If no contrasurvival engrams involving human beings are in the earlier (before five years) content of the engram bank, prosurvival engrams are taken as a matter of course and are not severely aberrative. In other words, it is the breaking of affinity with his fellows on an engramic level which most solidly blocks the dynamics. Man's affinity with man is far more a scientific fact than it is a poetic and idyllic idea.

The cycle, then, of life which will be "normal" (current average state) or psychotic is an easy thing to draw. It begins with a large number of engrams before birth, it gathers more in the dependent and rather helpless condition postbirth. Punishment of various kinds, entering now as locks, key in the engrams. New engrams which will involve the earlier ones enter. New locks accumulate. Illness and aberrated action set in most certainly by the age of forty or fifty. And death ensues sometime afterwards.

Short of the optimum solution of clearing the engrams, there are several things which can be done about aberration and psychosomatic ills. That these methods are uncertain and of only limited value does not mean that they will not occasionally meet with some astonishingly beneficial responses.

Such methods can be classified under the headings of environmental change, education and physical treatment. Taking factors out of the environment of an aberree or taking the aberree out of the environment in which he is unhappy or ineffective can bring about some astonishingly swift recoveries: this is valid therapy. It removes the restimulators from the individual or takes the individual away from the restimulators. It is ordinarily quite hit-or-miss (and more miss than hit) and it will not remove *all* the restimulators by nine-tenths, since the individual himself carries the bulk of these around with him or is compelled to contact them. One is reminded of a case which had severe asthma. He had received it in a very severe birth engram; his frantic parents carried him to every mountain asthma resort suggested and spent tens of thousands of dollars in these jauntings. When this patient was cleared and the engram refiled, it was discovered that the restimulator for his asthma was clean, cold air! The only certainty in the environment approach is that a sickly child will recover when removed from restimulative parents and taken where he is loved and feels safe—for his sickness is the inevitable result of restimulation of prenatal engrams by one or the other or both his parents. Somewhere along the line there is probably a husband or a wife who has descended chronically into the first two zones after marriage, after having married pseudomother or pseudofather or pseudoabortionist.

In the educational field, new data or enthusiasms may very well key out engrams by overbalancing the reactive mind in the light of a new analytical surge. If a man can simply be convinced he has been fighting shadows or if he can be persuaded to hang his fears on some indicated cause, whether that cause is true or not, he can be benefited. Sometimes he can be "educated" into a strong faith in some deity or cult which will cause him to feel so invulnerable that he rises above his engrams. Raising his survival potential in any way will raise his general tone to a point where it is no longer on a par with the reactive bank. Giving him an education in engineering or music, where he can receive a higher level of respect, will often defend him from his restimulators. A rise to a position of esteem is actually a change of environment, but it is also educational since he is now taught he is valuable. If a man can be made busy at a hobby or work by personal or exterior education that it is good for him, another mechanism comes into being:

the analytical mind becomes so engrossed that it takes to itself more and more energy for its activity and begins to align with a new purpose.

Physical treatment resulting in improved physical condition will bring about hope or change a man's reactions by shifting him on his time track. It may key out engrams.

These methods are valid therapy: they are also, in reverse, the things which cause aberrations to manifest themselves. There are wrong ways to act and wrong things to do and wrong ways to treat men which, in the light of what we know now, are criminal.

Thrusting a man into an environment which restimulates him and making him stay there is a slice of murder. Making him keep an associate who is restimulative is bad; making a man or a woman stay with a marriage partner who is restimulative is unworkable *mores* unless Dianetic therapy is used; making a child stay in a home where he is restimulated is most certainly inhibitive, not only of his happiness but of his mental and physical development—a child should have many more rights about such things, more places to go.

On the physical therapy level, anything as violent as surgery or exodontistry in the psychosomatic plane is utter barbarism in the light of Dianetics. "Toothache" is normally psychosomatic. Organic illnesses enough to fill several catalogues are psychosomatic. No recourse to surgery of any kind should be had until it is certain that the ailment is not psychosomatic or that the illness will not diminish by itself if the potency of the reactive mind is reduced. Mental-physical therapy is too ridiculous, with the source of aberration now a science, to be seriously mentioned. For no thinking doctor or psychiatrist possessed of this information would touch another electrode for electric shock therapy or even glance at a scalpel or ice pick to perform an operation on the prefrontal lobes of the brain unless that doctor or psychiatrist is himself so thoroughly aberrated that the act springs, not from any desire to heal, but from the most utter and craven[11] sadism[12] to which engrams can bring a man.[13]

---

11. craven: cowardly.

12. sadism: enjoyment of inflicting or watching cruelty.

13. Many persons investigating the treatment of the mentally ill by psychiatrists and others in charge of mental institutions are prompted —when they discover just what the prefrontal lobotomy, the transorbital leukotomy and electric shock actually do to patients—to revile the psychiatrist as unworthy of trust and accuse him of using it to conduct vivisection experiments on human beings. That any possible hope of recovery via Dianetics may be gone for these unfortunate patients in the majority of cases should not be blamed upon the psychiatrist and neurosurgeon. These people have only followed their teachings in various universities and have practiced such actions merely because they believed the problem of the mind could not be solved by anyone. A witch-burning attitude toward these people is very far from the one adopted by Dianetics. Pointing to the fact that they have murdered minds which would otherwise have recovered, labeling them "mind snatchers," and making a horror story out of their actions is far from rational conduct. On the whole, these people have been entirely sincere in their efforts to help the insane. By contagion of aberration such people have been subjected to enormous stresses in this work, having had their own engrams in continual restimulation. They can be cleared and their experience is valuable. Legislation against them such as that recently mentioned by a senator who was familiar with Dianetics, horror stories about them in newspapers and a general public antipathy, as well as the medical doctors' traditional distrust of them, cannot but bring about a disorderly condition. Dianetics is a newly discovered science and is nonpartisan.

CHAPTER TEN

Preventive Dianetics

There are many branches in Dianetics. It is actually a family of sciences covered by a single set of axioms. There is, for instance, *Educational Dianetics,* which contains the body of organized knowledge necessary to train minds to their optimum efficiency and to an optimum of skill and knowledge in the various branches of the works of man. And there is *Political Dianetics,* which embraces the field of group activity and organization to establish the optimum conditions and processes of leadership and intergroup relations. And again there is *Medical Dianetics.* And there is *Social Dianetics.* There are many such subdivisions which are sciences within themselves guided by their own axioms.

We are dealing in this volume, actually, with basic Dianetics and Dianetic therapy as applied to the individual. This is the most immediately important and the most valuable to the individual.

But no book on Dianetic therapy would be complete without a mention of a branch of Dianetics which, some say, is even more important to the race than the therapy. This is *Preventive Dianetics.*

If one knows the cause of something, he can usually prevent the cause from going into effect. The discovery and proof of Ronald Ross[1] that the malaria germ was carried by the mosquito makes it possible to prevent the disease from committing the ravages it once enjoyed at the expense of mankind. Similarly, when one knows the cause of aberration and psychosomatic illness, he

---

1. Ross, Ronald: (1857–1932) British physician.

can do a great deal toward preventing them.

While Preventive Dianetics is a large subject, infiltrating the fields of industry and agriculture and other specialized activities of man, its basic principle is the scientific fact that engrams can be held to minimal content or prevented entirely with large gains in favor of mental health and physical well-being as well as social adjustment.

The engram is actually a very simple thing: it is a moment when the analytical mind is shut down by physical pain, drugs or other means, and the reactive bank is open to the receipt of a recording. When that recording has verbal content, it becomes most severely aberrative. When it contains antagonism on an emotional level, it becomes very destructive. When it is intensely prosurvival in content, it is most certainly capable of thoroughly deranging a life.

The engram, amongst other things, determines fate. The engram says that a man has to fail to survive, and so he contrives numerous ways to fail. The engram commands that he can only experience pleasure amongst the members of another race and so he goes amongst them and abandons his own. It commands that he must kill to live and so he kills. And far more subtly, the engram weaves its way from incident to incident to cause the catastrophe which it dictates.

A recent case was plotted out to have actually gone to enormous lengths to break his arm, for with a broken arm he received the sympathy without which the engram said he could not live. The plot covered three years and half a hundred apparently innocent incidents which, when netted together, told the story.

The accident-prone person is a case where the reactive mind commands accidents. He is a serious menace in any society for his accidents are reactively intentional and they include the destruction of other people who are innocent.

Drivers with several accidents on their records are generally accident-prone. They have engrams which command them to have accidents. When you have run a case, just one, you will see how thoroughly and maliciously disposed this moronic thing, the reactive mind, can be about such things. Cleared drivers could have accidents only through two sources: (a) mechanical failure and, more important, (b) because of accident-prone people. The terrible and awesome death toll taken by our automotive transport is almost all attributable to reactive mind driving rather than learned response driving. The apathy of this society is measured by the fact that it does not act severely to prevent *all* automotive accidents; just one broken windshield is one too many. Now that an answer is to hand, action can take place.

The aberree, in thousands of ways, complicates the lives of others. Preventive Dianetics makes it possible to sort out the aberree who is accident-prone and bar him from activities which will menace others. This is one general aspect of Preventive Dianetics. That the aberrees so isolated can be cleared is another type of problem.

The other general aspect of Preventive Dianetics, and the more important, is the prevention of engrams and modification of content both on the social and the individual scale. On the social scale one would delete from the society the causes of aberration in that society as if he were deleting engrams from the individual. In the same way, one can prevent the social causes from occurring in the first place.

In the individual, the prevention of engrams is a very easy matter. Once the source of aberration and illness is known, one can prevent the source from entering a life. If the source has been known to enter, one can prevent the next step, the key-in. Of course, the final answer in all this is therapy to a clearing, but there is one aspect of the source which is not so answered.

The child cannot be safely cleared until he is at least five years of age and current practice is to place this figure at about eight years. Improved address to the problem may reduce this figure, but it cannot be reduced below the age of speech unless someone in the future invents a catalyst which simply clears out the reactive mind without further treatment (not as wild as it may sound). But just now, and probably for a long time to come, the child will remain a problem to Dianetics.

Childhood illness is chiefly derived from engrams. It is most likely to be severe before the age of speech and the number of deaths within the first year of life, while medicine may reduce them, is yet a serious thing.

Preventive Dianetics addresses this problem in two phases: first, the prevention of engrams; and second, the prevention of the key-in.

Taking the key-in first, there are two things which can be done to prevent it. The child can be given a calm and harmonious atmosphere which is not restimulative or, if the child appears to be restimulated despite kindly treatment, he can be removed to another environment which will be minus the two most certain sources—his father and mother—and which will contain a source of affection. The test of whether or not a child is restimulated, prespeech or postspeech, is very simple. Is he susceptible to illness? Does he eat well? Is he nervous? There can be actual physical things wrong with the child, of course, but these are quickly established by a doctor and they lie in the category of physical derangement.

Quarrels within the hearing of a child, loud noises, frantic conduct, drooling sympathy when he is sick or hurt: these things are some of the key-in catalogue. These make a child *ill* physically and aberrated mentally by keying in his engrams. And nobody can say how many he has!

The primary source of prevention lies in the field, oddly enough, of the regard in which another person is held—his mother.

It is not "biological love" which makes Mother play such an enormous role in the life of a human being. It is the simple mechanical truth that Mother is a common denominator to all the child's prenatals. The prenatal engram is far more serious than the postnatal. Any such engram a person has contains his mother or his mother and another person, but always his mother. Therefore her voice, the things she says, the things she does, have an enormous and vast effect upon the unborn child.

It is not true that emotion gets into a child through the umbilical cord, as people always suppose the moment they hear of prenatals. Emotion comes on another (more electrical than physical) type of wave—what type is a problem for structure. Therefore, anyone who is emotional around a pregnant woman is communicating that emotion straight into the child. And Mother's emotion is, in the same manner, so conducted to his reactive mind.

Whether or not the unborn child is "unanalytical" has no bearing on his susceptibility to engrams. The prenatal engram is just another engram. Only when the child is actually struck or hurt by high blood pressure or orgasms or other sources of injury does he become "unconscious." When he becomes "unconscious" he receives all the percepts and words in the area of the mother as engrams. Analytical power has nothing to do with engrams. If the child is "unanalytical," this does not predispose him to engrams. If the child is "unconscious" or hurt, it does. The presence or absence of "analytical power" has nothing to do with whether or not engrams are received.

Morning sickness, coughing, all monologuing

(Mother talking to herself), street noises, household noises, etc., are all communicated to the "unconscious" child when he is injured. And the child is very easily injured. He is not protected by formed bones and he has no mobility. He is there: when something strikes him or presses him, his cells and organs are injured. A simple experiment to demonstrate how mobility influences this is to lie down in bed and place one's head on a pillow. Then have somebody lean a hand on one's forehead. As there is no mobility, the pressure of the hand is far stronger than it would be if a hand were laid on the forehead when one was standing. The tissue and the water around the child form very slight buffers. In an injury, amniotic fluid, as an incompressible medium, presses him, for it cannot compress itself. The child's situation is far from armored. Mother's act of tying her shoes, in the later stages of pregnancy, even may be severe on the child. Mother's strain when lifting heavy objects is particularly injurious. And Mother's collision with objects like a table edge might well crush a baby's head. The repair facilities of the unborn child, as mentioned elsewhere, are far above anything ever before discovered. The child may have its head crushed but the blueprint is still there and the building materials and repair can be made. So it is not a case of the child being "all right" just because it can live through almost anything. It is a case of whether or not these injuries are going to have high aberrative value as engrams.

Attempted abortion is very common. And remarkably lacking in success. The mother, every time she injures the child in such a fiendish fashion, is actually penalizing herself. Morning sickness is entirely engramic, so far as can be discovered, since clears have not so far experienced it during their own pregnancies. And the act of vomiting because of pregnancy is via contagion of aberration. Actual illness generally results only when

Mother has been interfering with the child either by douches or knitting needles or some such thing. Such interference causes the mother to become ill and, from an actual physical standpoint, is much harder on the mother than on the child. Morning sickness evidently gets into a society because of these interferences such as attempted abortion and, of course, injury.

The cells know when pregnancy occurs. The reactive mind is acquainted with the fact before the analyzer by process of organic sensation, since the endocrine system is altered. Hence, the mother's discovery of pregnancy has little to do with whether or not she was sick before the discovery.

This entire field has been a subject of considerable research in Dianetics. Much more research must be done. These conclusions are tentative. But the conclusion that the engram is received and that it is as violent as its content, rather than its actual pain, is a scientific fact and not in any way a theory. It is as real a discovery as gravity.

Preventing these engrams is the first consideration. Preventing them from having any content is the second. Women who lead peasant lives, doing heavy labor, are subject to all manner of accident. Perhaps such accidents cannot be prevented because of the purpose these women serve in the society. But when it is known that any injury to the mother can create an engram in the unborn child, it should be the concern of all those present during such an injury, including the mother, to maintain a complete and utter silence. *Any remark is aberrative* in an engram. Even such a statement as "You can remember this when in Dianetic therapy," made toward an unborn child, installs an engram so that every word in this statement means a physical pain just where he received it at the time, and in the future "Dianetic therapy" will be restimulative to him.

The doctor, punching around to find out if Mother is pregnant, may say, "Well, it's hard to tell this early." The patient in Dianetic therapy years later will *return* into the vicinity of this incident only to draw a blank until the Dianeticist suddenly guesses the content from how the patient describes his reactions. If the doctor is very tough and says, "You had better take good care of yourself, Mrs. Jones. If you don't, you'll be mighty sick!" the child, "unconscious" from the examination no matter how mild it is, will get a mild hypochondria when the engram keys in and be very concerned over his health.

If the husband uses language during coitus, every word of it is going to be engramic. If the mother is beaten by him, that beating and everything he says and that *she* says will become part of the engram.

If she does not want the child and he does, the child will later react toward him as an ally[2] and perhaps have a nervous breakdown when the father dies. If she wants the child and he doesn't, the ally computation[3] is reversed. This is true when abortion is threatened or attempted providing the threat is contained in an engram.

Should the mother be injured and the father be highly solicitous,[4] the engram has this for content and the child has a sympathy engram. The way to survive,

2. ally: in Dianetics it basically means someone who protects a person who is in a weak state and becomes a very strong influence over the person. The weaker person, such as a child, even partakes the characteristics of the ally so that one may find that a person who has, for instance, a bad leg, has it because a protector or ally in his youth had a bad leg. The word is from French and Latin and means to bind together.

3. ally computation: little more than a mere idiot calculation that anyone who is a friend can be kept a friend only by approximating the conditions wherein the friendship was realized. It is a *computation* on the basis that one can only be safe in the vicinity of certain people and that one can only be in the vicinity of certain people by being sick or crazy or poor and generally disabled.

4. solicitous: anxious and concerned about a person's welfare or comfort.

then, is to be pathetic when injured, and even see to it that one is injured.

A woman who is pregnant should be given every consideration by a society which has any feeling for its future generations. If she falls, she should be helped—but *silently*. She must not be expected to carry heavy things. And she should not have coitus forced upon her. *For every coital experience is an engram in the child during pregnancy.*

An astonishing number of pregnancies must take place which are never realized. The violence of coitus, the use of douches and jellies (used because the woman is still contracepting and does not know she is already pregnant), straining bowel movements, falls and accidents must account for a large number of miscarriages which come about sometime around the first period after conception. For the zygote and embryo forms of the child have a rather frail grip on existence and are very severely injured by things the mother would consider nothing. Once past the first missed period, the chances of miscarriage rapidly grow less and only when the child is a genetic monstrosity or when abortion attempts are made can a miscarriage be expected to take place. The monstrosities are so small a percentage that they are negligible as a possibility.

The amniotic sac[5] can be pierced many times and repeatedly and emptied of all water after the first missed period and the child can still survive. Twenty or thirty abortion attempts are not uncommon in the aberree and in every attempt the child could have been pierced through the body or brain.

The child before birth does not depend upon the standard senses for its perceptions. Engrams are not

5. amniotic sac: the membrane sac enclosing the developing fetus and amniotic fluid.

memories but cellular level recordings. Therefore, the child needs no eardrums to record an engram. Cases are on hand where whatever hearing mechanism the unborn child had must have been temporarily destroyed by an abortion attempt. And the engram was still recorded. The cells rebuilt the apparatus which was to be the source of sound in the standard banks and stored their own data in the reactive bank.

Release of such engrams means a restoration of rationality to the individual far above the current norm and a stability and well-being greater than man ever thought man possessed. These engrams have been confirmed by taking the data from a child, from the mother and the father, and all data checked. So we are dealing here with scientific facts which, no matter how startling, are nevertheless true.

The mother, then, should be extremely gentle on herself during pregnancy and those around her should be entirely informed of the necessity for silence after any jar or injury. And in view of the fact that it is not possible to tell when a woman has become pregnant and in view also of the high potentiality of aberration in the zygote and embryo engrams, it is obvious that society must better its ways toward women if the future health of the child is to be preserved.

The woman has, to some degree, become considered less valuable in this society than in other societies and times. She is expected to be in competition with men. Such a thing is nonsense. A woman has as high a plane of activity as man. He cannot compete with her any more than she can compete with him in the fields of structure and vigorous activity. Much of the social maelstrom now in existence has as its hub the failure to recognize the important role of the woman as a woman and the separation of the fields of women and men.

The changes which will come about in the next

twenty years need no urging here. But with the recent discoveries in photosynthesis which should secure enough food to feed man better and at less cost, the importance of birth control dwindles. The morality standards have already changed, no matter what moralists do to try to block the change. And woman, therefore, can be freed of many of her undesirable chains.

In the custody of man is the current world and its activity and structure. In the charge of woman is the care of the person of the human being and his children. Almost sole custodian of tomorrow's generation, she is entitled to much more respect than her chattel[6]-period of the past gave her.

It is not, then, any wild utopian thought that woman can be placed above the level hitherto occupied. And so she must be placed if the childhood of tomorrow's generation is to reach any high standard, if homes are to be peaceful and unharassed and if society is to advance.

Preventive Dianetics, in the sphere of the home, must place emphasis on the woman in order to safeguard the child.

As any first step, a mother should be cleared, for any mother who attempts an abortion is blocked across the second dynamic and any block menaces her health as well as her happiness. An antipathy for children has been found to accompany sexual aberration.

Preventive Dianetics, then, on the level of the individual, asks for cleared parents and then precaution against the aberrating of the child, and further precaution against the keying in of any aberration the child might have received.

To do this is very easy. Maintain silence in the presence of injury. Do what has to be done for the injured or ill and do it in silence. Maintain silence in the

---

6. chattel: a movable possession (as opposed to a house or land).

presence of birth to save both the sanity of the mother *and* the child and safeguard the home to which they will go. And the maintaining of silence does not mean a volley of "Sh's," for those make stammerers.

In a wider field, the maintenance of silence around any "unconscious" or injured person is second in importance only to preventing the "unconsciousness" in the first place.

Say nothing and make no sound around an "unconscious" or injured person. To speak, no matter what is said, is to threaten his sanity. Say nothing while a person is being operated upon. Say nothing when there is a street accident. Don't talk!

Say nothing around a sick child or an injured child. Smile, appear calm, but say nothing. Actions do not speak louder than words but actions are all that can be done around the sick and injured, unless one has an active desire to drive them into neurosis or insanity or, at best, to give them a future illness.

And above all, say nothing around a woman who has been struck or jarred in any way. Help her. If she speaks, don't answer. Just help her. You have no idea of whether she is pregnant or not.

And it is a remarkable fact, a scientific fact, that the healthiest children come from the happiest mothers. Birth, for one thing, in a cleared mother, is a very mild affair. Only birth engrams in the mother made it hard. A cleared mother needs no anesthetic. And that is well because the anesthetic makes a dazed child and the engram, when it reacts, makes him appear a dull child. A happy woman has very little trouble. And even a few engrams, which arrive despite all precautions, are nothing if the general tone of the mother is happy.

Woman, you have a right and a reason to demand good treatment.

Book Three

Therapy

CHAPTER ONE

The Mind's Protection

The mind is a self-protecting mechanism. Short of the use of drugs as in narcosynthesis, shock, hypnotism or surgery, no mistake can be made by an auditor[1] which cannot be remedied either by himself or by another auditor. Those things which are stressed, then, in this book, are ways to accomplish therapy as swiftly as possible with minimal errors; for errors take time. Auditors are going to make errors, that is inevitable. If they make the same error repeatedly, they had better get someone to guide *them* through therapy.

There are probably thousands of ways to get into trouble with mental healing, but all these ways can be classed in these groups: (1) use of shock or surgery on the brain; (2) use of strong drugs; (3) use of hypnosis as such; and (4) trying to crossbreed Dianetics with older forms of therapy.

The mind will not permit itself to be seriously overloaded so long as it can retain partial awareness of itself; it can only be overloaded when its awareness is reduced to a point where it cannot evaluate anything: it can then be thoroughly upset. Dianetic *reverie*[2] leaves a patient

---

1. auditor: the term *auditor* is used in Dianetics to designate anyone skilled in the practice of Dianetics therapy. To *audit* is both to listen and to compute.

2. reverie: the state of reverie is actually just a name. It is a label introduced to make the patient feel that his state has altered and that he has gone into a state where his memory is very good or where he can do something he couldn't ordinarily do before. The actuality is that he is able to do it all the time anyway. It is not a strange state. The person is wide awake, but merely by asking him to close his eyes he is technically in reverie.

fully aware of everything which is taking place and with full recall of everything which has happened. Types of therapy which do not do this are possible and useful but they must be approached with the full knowledge that they are not foolproof. Dianetics, then, uses the reverie for the majority of its work, and, using the reverie, an auditor cannot possibly get himself into any trouble from which he cannot extricate himself and the patient. He is working with an almost foolproof mechanism as long as the mind retains some awareness: a radio or a clock or an electric motor are far more susceptible to injury in the hands of a workman than the human mind. The mind was built to be as tough as possible. It will be found that it is difficult to get it into situations which make it uncomfortable and impossible, with the reverie, to embroil it enough to cause neurosis or insanity.

In the U.S. infantry manual there is a line about decision: "Any plan, no matter how poorly conceived, if boldly executed, is better than inaction."

In Dianetics, any case,[3] no matter how serious, no matter how unskilled the auditor, is better opened than left closed. It is better to start therapy if it is to be interrupted after two hours of work than not to start therapy at all. It is better to contact an engram than to leave an engram uncontacted even if the result is physical discomfort for the patient—for that engram will not thereafter possess as much power and the discomfort will gradually abate.

This is scientific fact. The mechanism Dianetics uses is an ability of the brain which man as a whole did not know he had. It is a process of thought which everyone possesses inherently and which was evidently meant to be used in the overall process of thinking but which, by some strange oversight, man has never before dis-

---

3. case: all the content of the reactive mind.

covered. Once a person has learned that he possesses just this one new faculty, he is better able to think than he was before, and he can learn this faculty in ten minutes. Further, when one approaches an engram with this faculty (which, when intensified, is the reverie), some of that engram's sublevel connections are broken and the aberrative factors no longer have as much force either in the physical or mental spheres. Further, the knowledge that there is a solution to mental ills is a stabilizing factor.

Approaching an engram with the reverie is very far from the same as restimulating the engram exteriorly as is done in life. The engram is a powerful and vicious character only so long as it is untapped. In place and active, it can be restimulated to cause innumerable mental and physical ills. But approaching it with reverie is approaching it on a new circuit, one that disarms it. The power of the engram is partly the fear of the unknown—knowing brings stability by itself.

Do not think that you will not make patients uncomfortable. That is not true. The auditor's work, when it taps engrams which cannot be lifted, may cause the patient to have headaches, various aches and pains and even mild physical illness, even when the work is carefully done. But life has been doing this to the patient on a much grander scale for years and, no matter how badly the case is mauled around, no matter how many aberrations spring into view to plague the patient for a day or two, none are as serious as those which can be occasioned by the environment acting upon the untapped engram.

The auditor can do everything backwards, upside down and utterly wrong and the patient will still be better, provided only that he does not try to use drugs before he has worked a few cases, that he does not use hypnotism as hypnotism and he does not try to cross Dianetics with some older therapy. He can use drugs in

Dianetics if he knows his Dianetics and if he has medical concurrence. He can use all the techniques of hypnotism so long as he is thoroughly experienced with *Dianetics*. And once he has used Dianetics, he will not fall back to mystic efforts to heal minds. In short, the point which is offered here is that so long as the auditor takes a relatively simple case at first to see how the mechanisms of the mind work and uses only the reverie, he cannot get into trouble. There will be those, certainly, who believe they are so vastly experienced in tom-tom beating or gourd rattling that they won't give Dianetics a chance to work as Dianetics but will sail in and begin to plague the patient about "penis envy" or make him repent his sins; but the patient who starts to get this will be smart to simply change positions from the couch to the auditor's chair and clear up some of the aberrations of the auditor before work proceeds.

Anybody who has read this book once through and procured a patient with sonic recall for a trial effort will know more about the mind, in those actions, than he has ever known before, and he will be more skilled and able to treat the mind than anyone attempting to do so, regardless of reputation, a very short while ago. This does not mean that men who have had experience with mental patients will not, knowing Dianetics *(knowing Dianetics)* have an edge on those who do not realize some of the foibles[4] of which man in an aberrated state is capable. And on the other hand it does not mean that some engineer or lawyer or cook with a few Dianetic cases under his belt will not be more skilled than all other practitioners of whatever background or kind. In this case, the sky is no limit.

One could not say, offhand, that an able hypnotist or an able psychologist, ready and willing to jettison and

4. foible: a harmless peculiarity in a person's character.

unlearn yesterday's mistakes, is not better prepared to practice Dianetics. In the field of psychosomatic medicine, the medical doctor, with a vast fund of experience in healing, might very well be far and above other auditors in Dianetic work. But it is not necessarily the case, for in research it has been proven that men and women with most unlikely professional backgrounds have suddenly become auditors superior in skill to those in fields you might suspect were more closely allied. Engineers particularly are excellent material and make excellent auditors. Again, Dianetics is not being released to a profession, for no profession could encompass it. It is insufficiently complicated to warrant years of study in some university. It belongs to man and it is doubtful if anyone could manage to gain a corner on it for it does not fall within any legislation of any kind in any place and if Dianetics were legislated into a licensed profession, then it is to be feared that listening to stories and jokes and personal experience would also have to be legislated into a profession. Such laws would put all men of good will who lend a sympathetic ear to a friend's troubles inside the barbed wire. Dianetics is *not* psychiatry. It is *not* psychoanalysis. It is *not* psychology. It is *not* personal relations. It is *not* hypnotism. It is a science of mind and needs about as much licensing and regulation as the application of the science of physics. Those things which are legislated against are a matter of law because they may in some way injure individuals or society. Legislation exists about psychoanalysis in some three states in the Union, legislation against or about psychiatry exists everywhere. If an auditor wishes to constitute himself a psychiatrist with the power of vivisecting[5] human brains, if he wants to constitute himself a doctor and administer drugs and medicines, if he wants to

---

5. vivisect: to perform surgical experiments on living animals.

practice hypnotism and pour suggestions into a patient, then he must square it with psychiatry, medicine and the local laws about hypnotism, for he has entered other fields than Dianetics. In Dianetics, hypnotism is not used, no brains are operated upon and no drugs are given unless the local medico is part of the staff. Dianetics is not in any way covered by legislation anywhere, for no law can prevent one man sitting down and telling another man his troubles, and if anyone wants a monopoly on Dianetics, be assured that he wants it for reasons which have to do not with Dianetics but with profit. There are not enough psychiatrists in the country to begin to staff the mental institutions. Surely this generation, particularly with all the iatrogenic[6] work which has been done, will continue to need those institutions and will need psychiatrists: their field is the treatment of the insane by definition and that has nothing to do with thee and me. In psychology, Dianetics drops into line without disturbing anything concerned with staffs or research or teaching posts, for psychology is simply the study of the psyche and now that there exists a science of the psyche it can go ahead with a will. Thus, Dianetics is the enemy of none, and Dianetics falls utterly outside all existing legislation, none of which anticipated or made any provision for a science of mind.

---

6. *Iatrogenic* means illness generated by doctors. An operation during which the doctor's knife slipped and accidentally harmed the patient might cause an iatrogenic illness or injury since the fault would have been with the surgeons.

CHAPTER TWO

Release or Clear

The object of Dianetic therapy is to bring about a *release* or a *clear*.

A *release* (noun) is an individual from whom major stress and anxiety have been removed by Dianetic therapy.

A *clear* (noun) is an individual who, as a result of Dianetic therapy, has neither active nor potential psychosomatic illness or aberration.

To *clear* (verb) is to release all the physical pain and painful emotion from the life of an individual or, as in Political Dianetics, a society. The result of this will bring about persistence in the four dynamics, optimum analytical ability for the individual and, with that, all recall. The experience of his entire life is available to the *clear* and he has all his inherent mental ability and imagination free to use it. His physical vitality and health are markedly improved and all psychosomatic illnesses have vanished and will not return. He has greater resistance to actual disease. And he is adaptable to and able to change his environment. He is not "adjusted"; he is dynamic. His ethical and moral standards are high, his ability to seek and experience pleasure is great. His personality is heightened and he is creative and constructive. It is not yet known how much longevity is added to a life in the process of clearing, but in view of the automatic rebalancing of the endocrine system, the lowered incidence of accident and the improvement of general physical tone, it is most certainly raised.

A *release* is an individual from whom have been released the current or chronic mental and physical difficulties and painful emotion. The value of a release, when compared to a clear, may not at first thought be considered great, but when one understands that a release is usually in excess of the contemporary norm in mental stability, it can be seen that the condition is not without great value.

As a standard of comparison, a clear is to the contemporary norm as the contemporary norm is to a contemporary institutional case. The margin is wide and it would be difficult to exaggerate it. A clear, for instance, has complete recall of everything which has ever happened to him or anything he has ever studied. He does mental computations, such as those of chess, for example, which a normal would do in half an hour, in ten or fifteen seconds. He does not think "vocally" but spontaneously. There are no demon circuits in his mind except those which it might amuse him to set up—and break down again—to care for various approaches to living. He is entirely self-determined. And his creative imagination is high. He can do a swift study of anything within his intellectual capacity, which is inherent, and the study would be the equivalent to him of a year or two of training when he was "normal." His vigor, persistence and tenacity to life are very much higher than anyone has thought possible.

The objection that it is dangerous to create too many clears in a society is a thoughtless one. The clear is rational. The acts which damage a society are irrational. That a handful of clears could probably handle any number of "normals" is within reason, but that the clear would handle them to their detriment is unreasonable. The more clears a society possessed, the more chance that society would have to prosper. That a clear is unambitious is not proven out by scientific observation, for the curve of dwindling ambition follows the curve of reducing rationality; and those who have been cleared have proven the matter by reactivating all their skills toward goals they had once desired but had begun to consider unattainable when "norms."[1] That a clear is in some degree separated from the "norm" is attributable to the gulf between their respective mental abilities, for he has achieved solutions and conclusions before the "norm" has begun to form an idea of what to conclude. This does not make a clear intolerable to the "norm," for the clear has none of that superiority attitude which is actually a product of engrams. This is a quick glance at the state of being clear, but the state cannot be described; it has to be experienced to be appreciated.

A *release* is a somewhat variable quantity. Anyone well advanced on the road to clear is a *release*. There is no comparison between a *clear* and anything man has before believed obtainable, and there is no comparison between clearing and any therapy hitherto practiced. In the case of the *release* only is there a basis of comparison between Dianetics and past therapies such as "psychoanalysis" and any other. A *release* can be effected in a few weeks. The resulting condition will be at least equivalent to that following two years of "psychoanalysis" with the difference that the release has a guarantee of permanent results and no guarantee of success has ever been made by "psychoanalysis." A release does not relapse into any pattern which has been relieved.

These are the two goals of the Dianetic auditor: *clear* and *release*. It is not known at this writing how long is the average time to raise the institutionally insane into the neurotic level: it has been done in two hours, it

---

1. *Norm* is a term in psychology denoting the normal individual, which is to say, an average person. The IQ and behavior of a "norm" would be an averaging out of the current population. There is nothing desirable about being a "norm," for he is badly aberrated.

has been done in ten and in some cases it has required two hundred.[2]

The Dianetic *auditor* should determine beforehand in any case whether he wishes to attempt a *release* or a *clear*. He can achieve either with anyone not organically insane (missing or seared portions of the brain bringing about insanity, mainly genetic or iatrogenic and relatively rare except in institutions). But he should make an estimate of the amount of time he can invest in any one person and regulate his intention accordingly and announce it to his patient. The two goals are slightly different. In a *release*, one does not attempt entrance into phases of the case which will or may bring about a necessity of long work and gives his attention to the location and release of emotional charge. In clearing, the auditor gives his attention to the location of the *basic-basic* engram, the discharge of emotion and the entire engram bank.

There is a third goal which could be considered a subhead of a release. This is an *assist:* it is done after injury, or illness following the injury, or illness just sustained, in order to promote more rapid recovery; to *assist* the body in its rehabilitation after injury or illness. This is specialized therapy which will probably be practiced commonly enough but is of primary benefit to the medical doctor who, with it, can save lives and speed healing by releasing the engram of that particular illness or injury, thus removing the various engram conceptions which the furtherance of the injury restimulates.

---

2. The Dianetic *auditor* who practices with the institutionally insane exclusively should provide himself with the text now in preparation on that subject. The techniques are similar to those described here but incline more toward heroic measures. This present volume is addressed to treatment of the normal person or the neurotic patient not sufficiently violent to be institutionalized. However, with intelligence and imagination, these same techniques can be applied with success to any mental state or physical illness. Institutional Dianetics is primarily the reduction of an insanity to a neurosis.

Any Dianetic auditor can practice this. The *assist* has about the same level of usefulness as a faith-healing miracle which would work every time.

Estimations of the amount of time the case will require are difficult to attain with any accuracy greater than 50 percent and it should be understood by the patient that the time in therapy is variable. It depends in a measure upon the skill of the auditor, the number of unsuspected engrams never hitherto reactivated, and the amount of restimulation to which the patient is subject during therapy. Therefore, the auditor should not be optimistic in estimating time but should make his patient understand that greater or lesser time may be consumed in the therapy.

Any person who is intelligent and possessed of average persistency and who is willing to read this book thoroughly should be able to become a Dianetic auditor. When he has cleared two or three cases he will have learned far more and understood far more than is contained in this book, for there is nothing which develops an understanding of a machine like handling it in action. This is the instruction book, the machine in question is ready to hand wherever there are men. Contrary to superstition about the mind, it is almost impossible to permanently injure the mechanism. It can be done with an electric shock or a scalpel or an ice pick, but it is almost impossible to do it with Dianetic therapy.

CHAPTER THREE

The Auditor's Role

The purpose of therapy and its sole target is the removal of the content of the reactive engram bank. In a *release*, the majority of emotional stress is deleted from this bank. In a *clear*, the entire content is removed.[1]

The application of a science is an art. That is true of any science. The efficacy of its application depends upon the understanding, skill and ability of whoever applies it. The chemist has a science of chemistry and yet the profession of being a chemist is an art. The engineer may have behind him the precision of all the physical sciences and yet the practice of engineering is an art.

Certain rules of procedure can be laid down after the basic axioms of a science are understood. Beyond those rules of procedure is the understanding, skill and ability necessary to application.

Dianetics is extremely simple. This does not mean that cases cannot be extremely complicated. To cover one case for each kind of case in this book would necessitate two billion cases and that would only encompass the current population. For each man is a great deal different from every other man. His inherent personality is different. His composite of experience is different. And his dynamics are of different strengths. The only constant is the mechanism of the reactive engram bank and that alone does not vary. The content of that bank is different from man to man both in quantity and intensity

---

1. The content of the engram bank is actually *shifted* rather than *removed*, for it refiles under the heading of experience in the standard banks. The material, however, appears to vanish in therapy because the therapy is addressed to the engram bank, not the standard banks.

but the mechanism of operation of the bank and therefore the basic mechanisms of Dianetics are constant from man to man, and were in every age and will be in every future age until man evolves into another organism.

The target is the engram. It is also the target of the patient's analytical mind and the patient's dynamics as he tries to live his life: it is the target of the auditor's analytical mind and the auditor's dynamics. So bracketed[2] and salvoed,[3] it gives up its store of engrams.

This should be extremely plain to any auditor: the amount he relaxes from the position of auditor and forgets the target, he garners trouble which will consume his time. The moment he makes the error of thinking that the *person*, the *analytical mind* or the *dynamics* of the patient are resisting, trying to stop therapy or giving up, the auditor has made the fundamental and primary error in the practice of Dianetics. Almost anything that goes wrong can be traced back to this error. It cannot be too emphatically stated that the analytical mind and the dynamics of the patient never, never, never resist the auditor. The auditor is not there to be resisted. He has no concern with resistance from anything except the patient's (and sometimes his own) engrams.

The auditor is not there as the patient's driver or adviser. He is not there to be intimidated by the patient's engrams or be frightened by their aspects. He is there to audit and only to audit. If he feels that he is called upon to be lordly to the patient, then the auditor had better change chair for couch because he has a case of authoritarianism coming into view. The word *auditor* is used, not *operator* or *therapist*, because it is a cooperative

---

2. bracket: to place shots both short of the target and beyond it in order to find the range.

3. salvo: fire at with a number of guns or artillery pieces at one time.

effort between the auditor and the patient, and the law of affinity is at work.

The patient cannot see his own aberrations. That is one of the reasons why the auditor is there. The patient needs to be bolstered to face the unknowns of his life. That is another reason the auditor is there. The patient would not dare address the world which has gotten inside him and turn his back upon the world that is outside him unless he has a sentry. That is another reason the auditor is there.

The auditor's job is to safeguard the person of the patient during therapy, to compute the reasons why the patient's mind cannot reach into the engram bank, to strengthen the patient's nerve and *to get those engrams*.

There is a three-way case of affinity at work this moment. I am in affinity with the auditor: I am telling him all that has been discovered and is in practice in Dianetics and I want him to succeed. The auditor is in affinity with the patient: he wants the patient to attack engrams. The patient is in affinity with the auditor because, with minimal work, that patient is going to get better and—with persistence lent him by the auditor, plus his own—will become a *release* or a *clear*. There are even more affinities at work, a vast network of them. This is a cooperative endeavor.

The engram bank is the target, not the patient. If the patient swears and moans and weeps and pleads, those are engrams talking. After a while the engrams that make him swear and moan and weep and plead will be discharged and refiled. The patient, in whatever state, knows full well that the action taken is necessary. If the auditor is so short of rationality that he mistakes this swearing or moaning as something directed at him personally, that auditor had better change places with the patient and undergo therapy.

The only thing which resists is the engram! When it

is being restimulated it impinges against the patient's analyzer, tends to reduce analytical power, and the patient exhibits a modified dramatization. Any auditor with two brain cells to click together will never be in any slightest danger of his person at the hands of the *prerelease* or *preclear*.[4] If the auditor wants to use hypnotism and try to run late physically painful engrams, such as operations, when early ones are available, he may find himself targeted. But then he has done something very wrong. If the auditor suddenly gets supermoral and lectures the patient, he may get involved, but again he has done something very wrong. If the auditor snarls and snaps at the patient, he may get targeted, but once more a fundamental error has been made.

The target is the engram bank. It is the auditor's job to attack the preclear's engram bank. It is the preclear's job to attack that bank. To attack the preclear is to permit his engram bank to attack the preclear.

We know that there are five methods of handling an engram. Four of them are wrong. To succumb to an engram is apathy, to neglect one is carelessness, but to avoid or flee from one is cowardice. *Attack,* and only *attack,* resolves the problem. It is the duty of the auditor to make very sure that the preclear keeps attacking engrams, not the auditor or the exterior world. If the auditor attacks the preclear, that's bad gunnery and very poor logic.

The engram bank is best attacked primarily by discharging its emotional charge anywhere it can be contacted. After that it is best attacked by finding out what the preclear, in reverie, thinks would happen to him if he got well, got better, found out, etc. And then it is most

---

4. The terms *prerelease* and *preclear* are used to designate an individual entered into and undergoing Dianetic therapy. The term *preclear* is used most commonly. The word *patient* is less descriptive because it implies illness, but it is used interchangeably.

and always most important, in any way possible, to contact the primary moment of pain or unconsciousness in the patient's life. This is *basic-basic*. Once an auditor has *basic-basic*, the case will swiftly resolve. If the preclear's reactive mind is suppressing *basic-basic*, then the auditor should discharge more reactive emotion, discover the computation now in force, and try again. He will eventually get *basic-basic*. That's important. And that is all that is important in a preclear.

In the prerelease (patient working toward release only), the task is to discharge emotion and as many early engrams as will present themselves easily. The reduction of locks may be included in prerelease; but only when they lead to basic-basic should locks be touched in a preclear.

There are three levels of healing. The first is getting the job done efficiently. Below that is making the patient comfortable. Below that is sympathy. In short, if you can do nothing for a man with a broken back, you can make him comfortable. If you can't even make him comfortable, you can sympathize with him.

The second and third echelons above are entirely unwarranted in Dianetics. The job can be done efficiently. Making the patient comfortable is a waste of time. Giving him sympathy may snarl up the entire case, for his worst engrams will be sympathy engrams and sympathy may restimulate them out of place. The auditor who indulges in "hand-patting," no matter how much it seems to be indicated, is wasting time and slowing down the case. Undue roughness is not indicated. A friendly, cheerful, optimistic attitude will take care of everything. A preclear sometimes needs a grin. But he has already had more "hand-patting" than the analyzer has been able to compute. *His chronic psychosomatic illness contains sympathy in its engram.*

The next thing the auditor should know and live is

the Auditor's Code.[5] This may sound like something from "When Knighthood Was in Flower" or the "Thirteen Rituals for Heavenly Bliss and Nirvana," but unless it is employed by the auditor on his patients, the auditor will have some heavy slogging. This code is not for the comfort of the preclear; it is exclusively for the protection of the auditor.

The Auditor's Code should *never* be violated. Practice in Dianetics has demonstrated that violation of the Auditor's Code alone can interrupt cases.

The auditor should be *courteous* in his treatment of all preclears.

The auditor should be *kind,* not giving way to any indulgence of cruelty toward preclears, nor surrendering to any desire to punish.

The auditor should be *quiet* during therapy, not given to talk beyond the absolute essentials of Dianetics during an actual session.

The auditor should be *trustworthy,* keeping his word when given, keeping his appointments in schedules and his commitments to work, and never giving forth any commitment of any kind which he has any slightest reason to believe he cannot keep.

The auditor should be *courageous,* never giving ground or violating the fundamentals of therapy because a preclear thinks he should.

The auditor should be *patient* in his working, never becoming restless or annoyed by the preclear, no matter

---

5. Auditor's Code: a collection of rules (do's and don'ts) that an auditor follows while auditing someone, which assures that the preclear will get the greatest possible gain out of the processing he is having.

It is interesting that the Auditor's Code outlines, save for its last clause, the *survival conduct pattern* of man. The clear operates more or less automatically on this code. Dianetics is a parallel to thought, since it follows the natural laws of thought. What works in Dianetics works as well in life.

what the preclear is doing or saying.

The auditor should be *thorough,* never permitting his plan of work to be swayed or a charge to be avoided.

The auditor should be *persistent,* never giving up until he has achieved results.

The auditor should be *uncommunicative,* never giving the patient any information whatsoever about his case, including evaluations of data or further estimates of time in therapy.

Various conditions ensue when any of the above are violated. All violations slow therapy and cause the auditor more work. All violations come back to the detriment of the auditor.

For instance, in the last, it is not part of the auditor's work to inform the preclear of anything. As soon as he starts doing so, the preclear promptly hooks the auditor into the circuit as the source of information and so avoids engrams.

The auditor will see in progress the most violent and disturbing human emotions. He may be moved to sympathy, but if he is, he has overlooked something and hindered therapy: whenever an emotion shows, it is an emotion which will shortly be history. Whatever gyrations the preclear may go through, however much he may move or wrestle around, the auditor must keep firmly in mind that every moan or gyration is one step closer to the goal. For why be frightened or waste sympathy about something which, when it has been recounted a few times, will leave a preclear happier?

If the auditor becomes frightened and pulls that error of all errors when a preclear begins to shake, "Come up to present time!" he can be sure that the preclear will have a couple of bad days and that the next time the auditor wants to enter that engram it will be blocked.

If an auditor assumes the state of mind that he can

sit and whistle while Rome burns before him and be prepared to grin about it, then he will do an optimum job. The things at which he gazes, no matter how they look, no matter how they sound, are solid gains. It's the quiet, orderly patient who is making few gains. This does not mean that the auditor is trying for nothing but violence, but it does mean that when he gets it he can be cheerful and content that one more engram has lost its charge.

The task of auditing is rather much a shepherd's task, herding the little sheep, the engrams, into the pen for slaughter. The preclear isn't under the auditor's orders but the preclear, if the case runs well, will do whatever the auditor wants with these engrams because *the analytical mind and the dynamics of the preclear want that job done. The mind knows how the mind operates.*

CHAPTER FOUR

Diagnosis

One of the most important contributions of Dianetics is the resolution of the problem of diagnosis in the field of aberration. Hitherto there have been almost unlimited classifications; further, there has been no optimum standard.[1] As one researches in the field of psychiatric texts, he finds wide disagreement in classification and continual complaint that classification is very complex and lacking in usefulness. Without an optimum goal of conduct or mental state and without knowledge of the cause of aberration, catalogues of descriptions alone were possible and these were so involved and contradictory that it was nearly impossible to sharply assign to a psychotic or neurotic any classification which would lead to an understanding of his case.[2] The main disability in this classification system was that the classification did not lead to a cure, for there was no standard treatment and there was no optimum state to indicate when treatment was at end; and as there was no cure for aberration or psychosomatic illness, there could be no classification which would indicate the direction which was to be taken or what could uniformly be expected of a case.

---

1. "Psychology has . . . no mental standards to set up. . . . The psychologist does not occupy himself with the establishment of norms." *The Psychology of Abnormal People,* by John J. B. Morgan, Longmans, Green & Co., New York, 1928.

2. "The work of the psychiatrist was taken up mainly with describing and classifying symptoms. This procedure has been strongly criticized by some students on the ground that it leads nowhere and encourages a false pretense of understanding where there is none. Giving a name to something does not increase our understanding of it." *Ibid.,* Intro.

This is no criticism of past efforts surely, but it is a source of relief to know that the classification of aberration is unnecessary along such complicated lines as have been used and that the cataloguing of psychosomatic ills, while necessary to the physician, is unimportant to the auditor. In the evolution of the science of Dianetics there were several stages of classification until it finally became clear that the label on a pathological condition should only be whatever the auditor had to overcome to achieve cure. This system, as now evolved through practice, makes it possible for the auditor to "diagnose" without any more knowledge than is contained in this chapter and his own future experience.

The number of aberrations possible is the number of combinations of words possible in a language as contained in engrams. In other words, if a psychotic thinks he is God, he has an engram which says he is God. If he is worried about poison in his hash, he has an engram which tells him he may get poison in his hash. If he is certain he may be "fired" from his job any moment, even though he is competent and well-liked, he has an engram which tells him he is about to be "fired." If he thinks he is ugly, he has an engram about being ugly. If he is afraid of snakes or cats, he has engrams which tell him to fear snakes and cats. If he is sure he has to buy everything he sees, despite his income, he has an engram which tells him to buy everything he sees. And in view of the fact that anyone not released or cleared has upwards of two or three hundred engrams and as these engrams contain a most remarkable assortment of language and as he may choose one of five ways of handling any one of these engrams, the problem of aberration is of no importance *to the auditor* except where it slows therapy.

Most aberrated people talk in a large measure out

of their engrams. Whatever the chronic patter[3] of the individual may be, his rage patter, his apathy patter, his general attitude toward life, this patter is contained in engrams wherever it departs even in the slightest degree from complete rationality. The man who "cannot be sure," who "does not know" and who is skeptical of everything, is talking out of engrams. The man who is certain "it cannot be true," that "it isn't possible," that "authority must be contacted," is talking out of engrams. The woman who is so certain she needs a divorce or that her husband is going to murder her some night is talking out of either her own or his engrams. The man who comes in and says he has a bad pain in his stomach that feels "just like a #12 gauge[4] copper wire going straight through me," has quite possibly had a #12 gauge copper wire through him in an attempted abortion or talk of such a thing while he was in pain. The man who says *it* "has to be cut out" is talking straight out of an engram, either from some operation of his own or his mother's or from an attempted abortion. The man who "has to get rid of it" is again possibly talking out of an attempted-abortion engram. The man who "can't get rid of it" may be talking from the same source but from another valence. People, in short, especially when talking about Dianetics and engrams, give forth with engram talk in steady streams. They have no awareness, ordinarily, that the things they are saying are minor dramatizations of their engrams and suppose that they have concluded these things themselves or think these things: the supposition and explanation is only justified thought—the analyzer performing its duty in guaranteeing that the organism is right no matter how foolishly it is acting.

---

3. patter: the jargon of a particular group.
4. gauge: thickness or diameter, as of sheet metal or wire.

The auditor can be assured, particularly when he is talking about Dianetics, that he is going to hear in return a lot of engram content; for discussion of the reactive mind generally takes place in language which it itself holds.

Recall that the reactive mind can think only on this equation—$A = A = A$, where the three A's may be respectively a horse, a swear word and the verb *to spit*. Spitting is the same as horses is the same as God. The reactive mind is a very zealous Simple Simon, carefully stepping in each pie. Thus, when a man is told he has to delete the content of the reactive bank, he may say that if he did, he is sure he would lose all his ambition. Be assured—and how easily this proves up on therapy and how red-eared some preclears become—that he has an engram which may run something like this:

(Blow or bump, prenatal)

Father: Damn it, Agnes, you've got to get rid of that goddamned baby. If you don't, we'll starve to death. I can't afford it.

Mother: Oh, no, no, no. I can't get rid of it, I can't, I can't, I can't! Honest, I will take care of it. I'll work and slave and support it. Please don't make me get rid of it. If I did I'd just die. I'd lose my mind! I wouldn't have anything to hope for. I'd lose all my interest in life. I'd lose my ambition. Please let me keep it!

What a common one that engram is: and how sincere and "rational" and earnest an aberree can be in supporting his conclusion that he has just "thought up" the "computation" that if he "gets rid of it," he'll lose his mind and ambition, maybe even die!

As this work is written, most of the engrams that will be found in adults come from the first quarter of the twentieth century. This was the period of "Aha, Jack Dalton,[5] at last I have you in my possession!" It was the period of *Blood and Sand*[6] and Theda Bara.[7] It was the period of bootleg whiskey and woman suffrage. It covered the days of "flaming youth" and "The Yanks Are Coming," and bits of such color will be demanding action in the engram banks. Dianetic auditors have picked up whole passages of the great play *Drunkard*[8] out of prenatal engrams, not as a piece of funny "corn" but as Mama's sincere and passionate effort to reform Papa. Superdrama, mellerdrammer. And not only that but also tragedy. The hangover of the Gay Nineties,[9] when the "business girl" had just begun to be "free" and Carry Nation[10] was saving the world at the expense of bartenders, will be common fare in engrams found in today's adults. Yesterday's clichés and absurdities become, tragically enough, today's engramic commands. One very, very morose young man, for instance, was found to have as the central motif of his reactive mind Hamlet's[11] historic vacillations[12] about whether "to be or not to be, that is the question." Mama (who was what these colloquially minded auditors call a "loop") had gotten it by contagion from an actor-father whose

---

5. Dalton, Jack: member of an outlaw gang in the nineteenth-century American West; also a character in early westerns.

6. *Blood and Sand:* title of a silent movie featuring Rudolph Valentino.

7. Bara, Theda: stage name of Theodosia Goodman (1890–1955) U.S. actress.

8. *Drunkard:* a play written by William H. Smith and "A Gentleman" in the late 1800s, a moral domestic drama of American life.

9. Gay Nineties: the 1890s, a period of sudden affluence in the U.S. brought on by the industrial revolution.

10. Nation, Carry: (1846–1911) American temperance agitator.

11. Hamlet: hero of a play of the same name by William Shakespeare.

12. vacillate: to waver, to keep changing one's mind.

failure to be a Barrymore[13] had driven him to drink and wife beating; and our young man would sit for hours in a morose apathy wondering about life. To classify his psychosis required nothing more than "apathetic young fellow."

Most of engram content is merely clichés and commonplaces and emotional crash dives by Mama or Papa. But the auditor will have his moments. And when he suddenly learns about them, the preclear will have his laughs.

In other words, aberration can be any combination of words contained in an engram. Thus, to classify by aberration is not only utterly impossible but completely unnecessary. After an auditor has run one case, he will be far more able to appreciate this.

As for psychosomatic ills, as classified in an earlier chapter, these depend also upon accidental or intentional word combinations and all the variety of injury and unbalanced fluid and growth possible. It is very well to call an obscure pain "tendonitis," but more probably and more accurately it is a fall or injury before birth. Asthma comes fairly constantly from birth, as do conjunctivitis and sinusitis, but when these can occur in birth, there is generally prenatal background. Thus it can be said that wherever a man or woman aches is of minor importance to the auditor beyond using the patient's chronic illness to locate the chain of sympathy engrams, and all the auditor needs to know of that illness is that some area of the body hurts the patient. That, for the auditor, is enough for psychosomatic diagnosis.

It happens that the extent of aberration and the extent of psychosomatic illness are not the regulating factors which establish how long a case may take. A

---

13. Barrymore: famous family of stage and motion-picture actors: Maurice Barrymore and children Lionel, Ethyl and John.

patient may be a screaming lunatic and yet require only a hundred hours to clear. Another may be a "well-balanced" and moderately successful person and yet take five hundred hours to clear. Therefore, in the light of the fact that the extent of aberration and illness has only a minor influence on what the auditor is interested in—therapy—classification by these is so much wasted time.

Oh, there are such things as a man being too sick from heart trouble to be worked very hard, and such things as a patient worrying so continuously as a manifestation of his usual life that the auditor finds his work difficult, but these are rarities and again have little bearing on the classification of a case.

The rule in diagnosis is that whatever the individual offers the auditor as a detrimental reaction to therapy is engramic and will prove so in the process. Whatever impedes the auditor in his work is identical to whatever is impeding the patient in his thinking and living. Think of it this way: the auditor is an analytical mind (his own) confronted with a reactive mind (the preclear's). Therapy is a process of thinking. Whatever troubles the patient will also trouble the auditor; whatever troubles the auditor has also troubled the patient's analytical mind. The patient is not a whole analytical mind. The auditor will find himself occasionally with a patient who does nothing but swear at him and yet when the appointment time arrives, there that patient is, anxious to continue therapy; or the auditor may find a patient who tells him how useless the entire procedure is and how she hates to be worked upon and yet if he were to tell her, "All right, we'll stop work," she would go into a prompt decline. The analytical mind of the patient wants to do the same thing the auditor is trying to do: fight down into the reactive bank. Therefore, the auditor, when he encounters opposition, adverse theory about Dianetics, personal criticism, etc., is not listening to analytical data but reactive engrams and he should calmly proceed, secure in that knowledge; for the patient's dynamics, all that can be brought to bear, will help him so long as the auditor is an ally against the preclear's reactive mind, rather than a critic or attacker of the preclear's analytical mind.

This is an example:

(In reverie—prenatal basic area)

Preclear: (Believing he means Dianetics) I don't know. I don't know. I just can't remember. It won't work. I know it won't work.

Auditor: (Repeater technique,[14] described later) Go over that. Say, "It won't work."

Preclear: "It won't work. It won't work. It won't work . . ." etc., etc. Ouch, my stomach hurts! "It won't work. It won't work. It won't work. . . ." (Laughter of relief) That's my mother. Talking to herself.

Auditor: All right, let's pick up the entire engram. Begin at the beginning.

Preclear: (Quoting recall with somatics [pains]) "I don't know how to do it. I just can't remember what Becky told me. I just can't remember it. Oh, I am so discouraged. It won't work this way. It just won't work. I wish I knew what Becky told me but I can't remember. Oh, I wish . . ." Hey, what's she got in here? Why, goddamn her, that's beginning to burn! It's a douche. Say! Let me out of here. Bring me up to present time! That really burns!

Auditor: Go back to the beginning and go over it again.

---

14. repeater technique: after the auditor has placed the patient in reverie, if he discovers the patient, for instance, insists he "can't go anyplace," the auditor makes him repeat the phrase. Repetition of such a phrase, over and over, sucks the patient back down the track and into contact with an engram which contains it.

Pick up whatever additional data you can contact.

Preclear: Repeats engram, finding all the old phrases and some new ones, plus some sounds. Recounts four more times, "reexperiencing" everything. Begins to yawn, almost falls asleep (unconsciousness coming off), revives and repeats engram twice more. Then begins to chuckle over it. Somatic is gone. Suddenly engram is "gone" (refiled and he cannot discover it again). He is much pleased.

Auditor: Go to the next earliest moment of pain or discomfort.

Preclear: Uh. Mmmmm. I can't get in there. Say, I can't get in there! I mean it. I wonder where . . .

Auditor: Go over the line, "Can't get in there."

Preclear: "Can't get in there. Can't . . ." My legs feel funny. There's a sharp pain. Say, what the hell is she doing? Why, damn her. Boy, I'd like to get my hands on her just once. Just once!

Auditor: Begin at the beginning and recount it.

Preclear: (Recounts engram several times, yawns off "unconsciousness," chuckles when he can't find the engram anymore. Feels better.) Oh, well, I guess she had her troubles.

Auditor: (Carefully refraining from agreeing that Mama had her troubles, since that would make him an ally of Mama) Go to the next moment of pain or discomfort.

Preclear: (Uncomfortable) I can't. I'm not moving on the time track. I'm stuck. Oh, all right. "I'm stuck, I'm stuck." No. "It's stuck. It's stuck that time." No. "I stuck it that time." Why damn her! That's my coronary trouble! That's it! That's the sharp pain I get!

Auditor: Begin at the beginning of the engram and recount, etc.

Each time, it can be seen in this example, that the patient in reverie encountered analytically the engram in near proximity, the engram command impinged itself upon the patient himself, who gave it forth as an analytical opinion to the auditor. A preclear in reverie is close up against the source material of his aberrations. An aberree wide awake may be giving forth highly complex opinions which he will battle to the death to defend as his own but which are, in reality, only his aberrations impinging against his analytical mind. Patients will go right on declaring that they know the auditor is dangerous, that he shouldn't ever have started them in therapy, etc., and still keep working well and efficiently. That's one of the reasons why the Auditor's Code is so important: the patient is just as eager to relieve himself of his engrams as could be wished, but the engrams give the appearance of being a long way from anxious to be relieved.

It will also be seen in the above example that the auditor is not making any positive suggestion. If the phrase is not engramic, the patient will very rapidly tell him so in no uncertain terms and although it still may be, the auditor has no great influence over the preclear in reverie beyond helping him to attack engrams. If the preclear contradicted any of the above, it means that the engram containing the words suggested is not ready to be relieved and another paraphrase is in order.

Diagnosis, then, is something which takes care of itself on the aberration and psychosomatic plane. The auditor could have guessed—and kept it to himself—that a series of attempted abortions were coming up in the above example before he entered the area. He might have guessed that the indecisiveness of the patient was from his mother. The auditor, however, does not communicate his guesses. This would be suggestion and might be seized upon by the patient. It is up to the preclear to find out. The auditor, for instance, could not have known where on the time track the preclear's "coronary pain" was nor the nature of the injury. Chasing up and down looking for a specific pain would be just so much wasted time. All such things will surrender in the course of therapy. The only interest in them is whether or not the aberrations and illnesses go, to return no more. At the end of therapy they will be gone. At the beginning they are only complication.

Diagnosis of aberration and psychosomatic illness, then, is not an essential part of Dianetic diagnosis.

What we are interested in is the mechanical operation of the mind. *That* is the sphere of diagnosis. What are the working mechanics of the analytical mind?

1. Perception: Sight, hearing, tactile and pain, etc.
2. Recall: Visio-color, tone-sonic,[15] tactile, etc.
3. Imagination: Visio-color, tone-sonic, tactile, etc.

These are the mechanical processes. Diagnosis deals primarily with these factors and with these factors can establish the length of time a case should take, how difficult the case will be, etc. And we need only a few of these.

This further simplifies into a code:

1. Perception (over or under optimum):
   a. Sight
   b. Sound
2. Recall (under):
   a. Sonic
   b. Visio
3. Imagination (over):
   a. Sonic
   b. Visio

In other words, when we examine a patient before we make him a preclear (by starting him into therapy),

---

15. *Visio* means sight *recall* in Dianetics. *Sonic* means sound *recall*. *Somatic* means pain *recall*. A patient who can *see, hear* and *feel pain* stores them. "I," remembering, recalls them as *visio, sonic* and *somatic*.

we are interested in three things only: too much or too little perception, too little recall, too much imagination.

In perception, we mean how well or how poorly he can hear, see and feel.

In recall, we want to know if he can recall by sonic (hearing), visio (seeing) and somatic (feeling).

In imagination, we want to know if he "recalls" sonics, visios or somatics too much.

Let us make this extremely clear: it is very simple, it is not complex, and it requires no great examination. But it is important and establishes the length of time in therapy.

There is nothing wrong with an active imagination so long as the person *knows* he is imagining. The kind of imagination we are interested in is that used for unknowing "dub-in"[16] and in that kind only. An active imagination which the patient knows to be imagination is an extremely valuable asset to him. An imagination which substitutes itself for recall is very trying in therapy.

"Hysterical" blindness and deafness or extended sight or hearing are useful in diagnosis. The first, "hysterical" blindness, means the patient is afraid to see; "hysterical" deafness means he is afraid to hear. These will require considerable therapy. Likewise, extended sight and extended hearing, while not as bad as blindness and deafness, are an index of *how frightened* the patient really is and is often a straight index of the prenatal content in terms of violence.

If the patient is afraid to see with his eyes or hear with his ears in present time, be assured there is much in his background to make him afraid, for these actual perceptions do not "turn off" easily.

If the patient jumps at sounds and is startled by sights or is very disturbed by these things, his perceptions

---

16. dub-in: *noun,* imaginary recall.

can be said to be extended, which means the reactive bank has a great deal in it labeled "death."

The recalls in which we are interested in diagnosis are those which are less than optimum only. When they are "*over*optimum," they are actually imagination "dubbed in" for recall. Recall (under) and imagination (over) are actually, then, one group, but for simplicity and clarity we keep them apart.

If the patient cannot "hear" sounds or voices in past incidents he does not have sonic. If he does not "see" scenes of past experiences in motion-color pictures, he does not have visio.

If the patient hears voices which have not existed or sees scenes which have not existed and yet supposes that these voices really spoke and these scenes were real, we have "*over*imagination." In Dianetics, imaginary sound recall would be *hyper-sonic*, sight recall, *hyper-visio* (hyper=over).

Let us take specific examples of each one of these three classes and demonstrate how they become fundamental in therapy and how their presence or absence can make a case difficult.

A patient with a mild case of "hysterical" deafness is one who has difficulty in hearing. The deafness can be organic but, if organic, it will not vary from time to time. This patient has something he is afraid to hear. He plays the radio very loudly, makes people repeat continually and misses pieces of the conversation. Do not go to an institution to find this degree of "hysterical" deafness. Men and women are "hysterically" deaf without any conscious knowledge of it. Their "hearing just isn't so good." In Dianetics, this is being called *hypo-hearing* (hypo=under).

The patient who is always losing something when it lies in fair view before him, who misses signposts, theater bills and people who are in plain sight, is "hysterically" blind to some degree. He is afraid he will see something. In Dianetics, this is being called, since the word *hysterical* is a very inadequate and overly dramatic one, *hypo-sight*.

Then there is the case of *over*perception. This is not necessarily imagination, but it can go to the length of seeing and hearing things which are not there at all, which happens to be a common insanity. We are interested in a less dramatic grade in standard operation.

A girl, for instance, who sees something or thinks she sees something but knows she doesn't and is very startled, who jumps in fright when anyone silently comes into a room, and can be so startled rather habitually, is suffering from extended sight. She is afraid she will encounter something. But instead of being blind to it, she is too alive to it. This is *hyper-sight*.

A person who is much alarmed by noises, by sounds in general, by certain voices, who gets a headache or gets angry when the people around are "noisy" or the door slams or the dishes rattle, is a victim of extended hearing. She hears sounds far louder than they actually are. This is *hyper-hearing*.

The actual quality of the seeing and hearing does not need to be good. The actual organs of sight and sound can be in poor condition. The only fact of importance is the "nervousness" about reception.

This disposes of the two perceptions in which we are interested in Dianetics. As the auditor talks to people around him and gets their reactions to sights and sounds, he will find wide variety in quality of response.

Recall is the most directly important to therapy, for it is not a symptom, it is an actual tool of work. There are many ways to use recall. The clear has vivid and accurate recall for every one of the senses. Few aberrees have. The auditor is not interested in other senses than sight and sound because the others will be cared for in the usual course of therapy. But if he has a patient who has no sonic, watch out. And if he has a patient with neither sonic nor visio, beware! This is the multivalent personality, the schizophrenic, the paranoid of psychiatry with symptoms not acute enough to be so classified in normal life. This does not mean—emphatically does not mean—that people without sight and sound recall are insane, but it does mean an above-average case and it means a case which will take some time. It does not mean the case is "incurable," for nothing can be further from the truth: but such cases sometimes take five hundred hours. It simply means that such a case isn't any stroll through the park: there is drammer back there in that reactive mind, drammer which says, "Don't see! Don't hear!" Some of the engrams in this case demand reduced or no recall. The organs of sight and sound may be highly extended in their reception. This does not mean that anything need be wrong with the way this person perceives sound or light waves and records them. But it does mean that after he has recorded them, he cannot easily get them back out of the standard bank because the reactive engram bank has set up circuits (occlusion demon circuits) to keep him from finding out about his past. There are, of course, greater or lesser degrees of recall.

The test is simple. Tell the patient, wide awake, to "go back" to the time he was entering the room. Ask him what was being said. If he can "hear" it wide awake, he has sonic recall. The auditor knows very well what was said, for if he means to use this test, he utters a certain set of words and notes the actual sounds present. Therefore, if the patient falls into the following category, the "dub-in," the auditor will be apprised of that.

The sight recall test is equally simple. Show the patient a book with an illustration. After a time interval, ask him to "go back" while he is wide awake and look at that book "in his mind" and see if he can see it. If he can't, this is *hypo-visio*.

More tests similar to this will clearly establish whether or not our patient is recall blind and deaf or whether he falls into the next group.

The overactive imagination which enthusiastically "dubs in" sight and sound for the patient without knowledge is something which is definitely a hindrance to fast therapy. There are many demon circuits which snarl up thinking, but these particular "dub-in" demons mean that the operator is going to get a most awful cargo of what the auditors colloquially call "garbage."[17] There is—as they further use some of the doubtlessly disgraceful terminology which, despite anything one can do, keeps rising up in this field—something at work in the brain which is a "lie factory."[18]

The patient, asked to recount the conversation as he entered the door by "hearing it" again, may confidently start in to give forth all manner of speech which was entirely paraphrase or utterly fictitious. Asked to tell about the picture and page he is shown, he will "see" vividly a lot more than was there or something entirely different. If he is doubtful about it, that is a healthy sign. If he is certain, beware, for it is a demon circuit "dubbing in" without his analytical knowledge, and the auditor will have to listen to more incidents which never happened than he could begin to catalogue and will have to sort out and pick his way through this "garbage" continually to get his preclear to a point where the data is reliable. (And it isn't a matter of grading "garbage" by its improbability—truth is always stranger than fiction

---

17. *Garbage* was technically called *delusion* in the philosophic work of Dianetics, but the term is too harsh and critical, for who has not *some* misconception of a past incident?

18. *Lie factory* is, technically, a phrase contained in an engram demanding prevarication [the telling of lies]—it was originally called a *fabricator*.

—it is a matter of trying to reduce[19] engrams which are not present or bypass engrams which are present and so on in a tangled hash.)

The optimum preclear would be one who had average response to noises and sights, who had accurate sonic and visio and who could imagine and know that he was imagining, in color-visio and tone-sonic. This person, understand clearly, may have aberrations which make him climb every chimney in town, drink every drop in every bar every night (or try it anyway), beat his wife, drown his children and suppose himself to be a jub-jub bird.[20] In the psychosomatic line he may have arthritis, gallbladder trouble, dermatitis,[21] migraine headaches and flat feet. Or he may have that much more horrible aberration—pride in being average and "adjusted." He is still a relatively easy case to clear.

In the case which has sonic and visio shut-off without "dub-in," we are dealing with engrams which have shut down some of the primary working mechanisms of the mind. The auditor will have to slog through hours and hours and hours of trying to contact engrams when the patient cannot hear them or see them. A case which merely has a shut-down sonic recall still means that the auditor is going to do a lot more work than on an average case. This case is very, very far from impossible to resolve. That is not the idea here, to frighten off any attempt on such a case. But this case will only be resolved after a great deal of persistent effort. Such a

---

19. reduce: to take all the charge or pain out of an incident. This means to have the preclear recount the incident from beginning to end (while returned to it in reverie) over and over again, picking up all the somatics and perceptions present just as though the incident were happening at that moment. To *reduce* means, technically, to render free of aberrative material as far as possible to make the case progress.

20. jub-jub bird: imaginary creature from the poem "Jabberwocky" by Lewis Carroll.

21. dermatitis: inflammation of the skin.

person may be apparently very successful. He may be enormously intelligent. He may have few or no psychosomatic ills. Yet he will prove to have a crammed engram bank, any part of which may come into restimulation at any time and swamp him. Usually, however, this type of case is quite worried and anxious about many things, and such worry and anxiety may put a little more time on the worksheet.

In the case of the "dub-in" who doesn't know it, where circuits are giving him back altered recall, we have a case which may very likely prove to be very long and require artful treatment. For there is a "lie factory" somewhere in that engram bank. This case may be the soul of truthfulness in his everyday life. But when he starts tackling his engrams, they have content which makes him give out material which is not there.

Sharply and clearly, then, without further reservation or condition, this is Dianetic diagnosis: The aberration *is* the engram content; the psychosomatic illness *is* the former injury. The perceptions of sight and sound, underoptimum recall, overoptimum imagination regulate the length of the case.

If the auditor wants to be fancy, he can list the general tone scale position of the individual mentally and physically. The woman who is dull and apathetic is, of course, around tone 0.5 in the zone 0 part of the dynamic scale earlier in the book. If the man is angry or hostile, the auditor can mark him down as a 1.5 or somewhere generally in the zone 1 range of the survival scale. These markings would apply to the probable average tone of the aggregate engrams in the reactive mind. This is interesting because it means that a zone 0 person is far more likely to be ill and is a slightly harder case than a zone 1 person. And, as therapy raises tone to zone 4, the 1.5 is closer to the goal.

It is difficult to estimate time in therapy. As mentioned before, it has several variables such as auditor skill, restimulative elements in the patient's environment and sheer volume of engrams.

The auditor is advised, in his first case, to seek out some member of the family or a friend who is as close as possible to the optimum preclear, which is to say, a person with visio and sonic recall and average perceptions. In clearing this one case he will learn at first hand much of what can be expected in the engram banks of any mind, and he will see clearly how engrams behave. If the auditor himself falls into one of the harder brackets and if he means to work with somebody in one of these brackets, that poses no great difficulty; either case can be *released* in a hundredth the time of any former mental healing technique and they can be cleared, if any skill at all is used, in five hundred hours of work per case. But if two cases are particularly difficult, before they work on each other, each would be wise to find and clear a nearly optimum preclear. That way each will be a competent operator when the rougher cases are approached.

Thus, diagnosis. The other perceptions, recalls and imaginations are interesting but not vital in measuring case time. IQ, unless it falls down into the feebleminded level, is no great factor. And even then the IQ of any patient goes up like a skyrocket with clearing and rises all the while during the work.

There are organic insanities. Iatrogenic psychoses (caused by doctors) are equivocal in Dianetics, for a part of the machinery may have been wrecked. Nevertheless, with many organic psychoses a case can be improved by Dianetics, even if an optimum cannot be reached. And so all an auditor can do is try. Insanities caused by missing parts of the nervous system have not been extensively investigated by auditors at this time: the reviving of corpses is not the end of Dianetics; the bringing about an optimum mind in the normal or merely neurotic person has had the main emphasis. Dianetics can be otherwise used, is being and will be. But with so many potentially valuable people who can be made highly valuable to themselves and society, emphasis has been placed on inorganic aberrations and organic psychosomatic illnesses. Cases which have been subjected to prefrontal lobotomy (which saws a section out of the analytical mind), the topectomy (which removes pieces of brain somewhat as an apple corer cores apples), the transorbital leukotomy (which, while the patient is being electrically shocked, thrusts an ordinary dime-store ice pick into each eye and reaches up to rip the analyzer apart), and electric shock "therapy" (which sears the brain with 110 volts), as well as insulin shock[22] and other treatments, are considered by Dianetics to be equivocal. There are ordinary organic insanities such as paresis,[23] but most of these, even so, can be benefited by Dianetics.

---

22. insulin shock: a state of collapse caused by a decrease in blood sugar resulting from the administration of excessive insulin.

23. paresis: partial paralysis, affecting muscular movement but not sensation, caused by degenerative disease of the brain.

CHAPTER FIVE

Returning, the File Clerk[1] and the Time Track

There is a method of "thinking" which man did not know he had.

If you would like an illustration of this, ask a small child if she would like to go sleigh riding in memory. She will try to remember the last time she rode her sleigh. She will frown and pucker her brows perhaps. Now tell her to *go back* to the last time she was sleigh riding. Coaxed, she will suddenly come forth with a complete experience and, unless she is badly aberrated, will be able to tell you about the snow getting down her collar and so forth. She is right back there sleigh riding, swimming or whatever you choose.

Man, when and if he thought about this at all, must have mistaken it for imagination. But it is not imagination. Anyone, unless he is very severely aberrated indeed, can be "sent back," wide-awake, to an experience of the past. In initial tests one should use experiences not long gone and experiences which are pleasant.

This is not *memory* in the way one "remembers something." It is *returning*. *Remembering* is a far more complicated process than returning. Just why people go around seeking to *remember* some specific or complex datum when they can *return* is something of a mystery when one considers lost articles, things read, conversations had and so forth. *Remembering*, of course, has a very definite role and is an automatic process which

---

1. file clerk: Dianetics auditor's slang for the mechanism of the mind which acts as a data monitor. Auditors can get instant or "flash" answers direct from the file clerk to aid in contacting incidents.

provides "I" with conclusions and data in a never-ending stream. But when one wishes a very precise, specific bit of information or when one seeks a past pleasure to contemplate it, *returning* is more to the point.

The hypnotist, with much mumbo-jumbo and hand passes, *et al.,* has something which he calls "regression." This is a very complicated business which requires being hypnotized. True enough, regression has research value since, by hypnosis, it bypasses occlusions which are not otherwise easy to get around. And regression served Dianetics well when the author was checking his data on memory banks. But it evidently had occurred to none that regression is an artificial use of a natural process.

Undoubtedly some people use *returning* for some of their mental work, and these people probably think that "everybody else" does likewise, which is far from true. But even those people who *return* naturally seldom understand that this is a distinct process, much different from *remembering*.

People also *relive* without being hypnotized or drugged; this is a rarer thing. If a person sits in contemplation of some past glory for a while he will begin to relive instead of simply return.

In Dianetics, we have had much to do with "spectrums." The spectrum of gradations is a much better mechanism for philosophy than Aristotle's pendulum which swung from one extreme to the other. We have the spectrum of the dynamics. We call them four dynamics, through which the command **Survive!** is expressed, and the four are actually a great number of gradations from the cells of "I," through "I," through family and children, through club and city and state, through nation and race and hemisphere and finally all mankind. That is a spectrum: gradations of something which are really the same thing but which have wider and wider scope or range.

In much the same way as the spectrum of **Survive!**
we have a spectrum of memory at work. First there is
memory in its most precise, present-time sense. Then
there is memory of the past. Then there is more memory
of the past. And so we move into a part of the spectrum
which has been overlooked: part of the "I" returns into
the past, then a greater part of "I" returns into the past
(at which point we have *return*) and finally, at the extreme, all of "I" is back in the past. First there is
remembering. This is the furthest from exact data (except in a clear). Then there is *returning*, in which part of
the "I" is actually in the past and records appear to be
perceptions he is actually experiencing. Then there is
reliving, where a man is so thoroughly in the past for the
moment that, while he was recalling an infant experience, if startled he would react just as he would have
when a baby.

There is a lot of aberrated notion in this present
society about the evils of living in the past. These stem
partially from an unwillingness of aberrated people to
face and understand yesterday.

One of the prime sources of "bad memory" is
Mother. Often enough, Mother has been sufficiently
panic-stricken at the thought of Junior's recalling just
what she did to Junior that a mankind-wide aberration
seems to have sprung up. The standard attempted abortion case nearly always has an infanthood and childhood
full of Mama assuring him that he cannot remember
anything when he was a baby. She doesn't want him to
recall how handy she was, if unsuccessful, in her efforts
with various instruments. Possibly prenatal memory itself would be just ordinary memory and in full recall to
the whole race if this guilty conscience in Mother had
not been rolling along lo! these millennia. In the normal
course of work, the auditor will have his hands full of
Mama screaming objections about her grown son's or

daughter's entering into therapy because of what they might find out: Mama has been known, by auditors, to go into a complete nervous collapse at the thought of her child's recalling prenatal incidents. Not all of this, by the way, is based on attempted abortion. Mama often has had a couple of more men than Papa that Papa never knew about; and Mama would very often rather condemn her child to illness or insanity or merely unhappiness than let a child pursue the course of the preclear even though Mother avowedly has no recollection whatever of anything bad ever happening to the child. Under therapy herself, she usually volunteers the truth. Here is the source of why good memory is discouraged in a society and infant and prenatal memory overlooked, to say nothing of the ability to *return* and *relive*.

The index system of the standard bank is a wonderful thing to behold. Everything is there, filed by subject, filed by time and filed by conclusions. All perceptions are present.

With the time-file system we have what is called in Dianetics a *time track*. Going back along this track with part of "I" is *returning*. It is definitely present for both conscious and "unconscious" data. The *time track* is of vast and interesting concern to the auditor.

The mind is a well-built computer and it has various services. Auditors, backing off from Latin and complexity, call the source of one of these services the *file clerk*.[2] This is not a very dignified name and it is certainly anthropomorphic. There is no small man or woman in there with a green eyeshade. But the action which takes place is a close approximation to what would happen if such an entity did dwell within the mind.

The *file clerk* is the bank monitor. "He" monitors

---

2. Technically, the name of the *file clerk* might be "bank monitor units" but the phrase is too unwieldy.

for both the reactive engram bank and the standard banks. When he is asked for a datum by the auditor or "I," he will hand out a datum to the auditor via "I." He is a trifle moronic when he handles the reactive engram bank, a contagion from the reactive mind, and he will at times hand out puns and crazy dreams when he should be delivering serious data.

The file clerk, if the auditor asks the preclear for the last time he saw a movie, will hand out the movie, the date it was seen, the age and physical being of the person, all perceptics, the plot of the movie, the weather —in short, he hands out everything that was present and connected with the movie.

In ordinary living the file clerk feeds memory to "I" at a rapid rate. A good memory gets its data in split seconds. If the file clerk has to shove the memory around various reactive occlusions, it may take minutes or days for the data to arrive.

If we had a big computing machine of the most modern design, it would have a "memory bank" of punched cards or some such thing and it would have to have a selector and feeder device to thrust out the data the machine wants. The brain has one of these—it could not operate without it. This is the bank monitor—the file clerk.

Keep in mind these two parts of the mind: the *time track* and the *file clerk* and keep in memory this mechanism of *returning*. These are the three things we use, with the reactive and standard banks, in the Dianetic *reverie*.

The file clerk is a very obliging fellow. If he has been having trouble getting to the "I" around the reactive occlusions and circuits in general, he is particularly obliging. He cooperates with the auditor.

The monitor system could be considered on the basis of attention units, where a man could be supposed to have a thousand. Thus a thousand possible attention units would be available to a clear's "I." In the aberree, probably fifty are available to "I," five or six hundred absorbed in the reactive engrams, and the remainder variously used besides composing this mechanism we call the bank monitor, the file clerk.

It seems as if the file clerk in an aberree would rather work with the auditor than with the aberree. That may appear an astonishing fact, but it is a scientific fact. The file clerk works best, then, when he is selecting data out of a preclear's banks to present to the auditor. This is an aspect of the law of affinity. "I's" file clerk and the auditor are a team, and they work very often in close harmony without enough consent from the preclear's analyzer to notice.

The *return* is most easily effected, in the aberree, by the auditor's addressing the file clerk, not the patient. This can actually be done with the patient wide-awake. The auditor asks him for information, tells him to go back to it. "I" is suddenly in possession of the whole file. Something inside the mind, then, works in close harmony with the auditor and works better for the auditor than it does for the person in whose mind it is. That is the file clerk.

The object of the auditor is to take what the file clerk hands forth and to keep the file clerk from getting swamped by reactive data. Once the data has been given out by the file clerk, it is the business of the auditor to see that the preclear goes over it enough times to take the charge out of it. The mechanism of doing this is extremely simple. In order to help matters and keep the preclear from being distracted, the auditor goes through a routine with every session which disposes the patient to let the file clerk work.

The patient sits in a comfortable chair, with arms, or lies on a couch in a quiet room where perceptic distractions are minimal. The auditor tells him to look at the ceiling. The auditor says: "When I count from one to seven your eyes will close." The auditor then counts from one to seven and keeps counting quietly and pleasantly until the patient closes his eyes. A tremble of the lashes will be noticed in optimum *reverie*.

This is the entire routine. Consider it more a signal that proceedings are to begin and a means of concentrating the patient on his own concerns and the auditor than anything else. *This is not hypnotism.* It is vastly different. In the first place, the patient knows everything which is going on around him. He is not "asleep," and can bring himself out of it any time he likes. He is free to move about, but, because it distracts the patient, the auditor does not usually permit him to smoke.

The auditor makes very sure that the patient is not hypnotized by telling him, before he begins to count, "You will know everything which goes on. You will be able to remember everything that happens. You can exercise your own control. If you do not like what is happening, you can instantly pull out of it. Now, one, two, three, four," etc.

To make doubly sure, for we want no hypnotism, even by accident, the auditor installs a *canceler*. This is an extremely important step and should not be omitted even when you may be entirely certain that he is in no way influenced by your words. The auditor may inadvertently use restimulative language which will key in an engram: he may, when he is especially new in Dianetics, use such a thing as a *holder*[3] or a *denyer*,[4] telling the preclear to "stay there," when he is returned on the track or telling him, worst of all things, to "forget it," one of a class of phrases of the forgetter mechanism which is

3. holder: any engram command which makes an individual remain in an engram knowingly or unknowingly.

4. denyer: a species of command which, literally translated, means that the engram doesn't exist.

most severe in its aberrative effect, denying the data entirely to the analyzer. To prevent such things from happening, the *canceler* is vital. It is a contract with the patient that whatever the auditor says will not become literally interpreted by the patient or used by him in any way. It is installed immediately after the condition of reverie is established. A *canceler* is worded more or less as follows: "In the future, when I utter the word *canceled*, everything which I have said to you while you are in a therapy session will be canceled and will have no force with you. Any suggestion I have made to you will be without force when I say the word *canceled*. Do you understand?"

The word *canceled* is then said to the patient immediately before he is permitted to open his eyes at the end of the session. It is not further amplified. The single word is used.

The canceler is vital. It prevents accidental positive suggestion. The patient may be suggestible or even in a permanent, light hypnotic trance (many people go through life in such a trance). An engram is actually a hypnotic suggestion. It could be said that the purpose of therapy is to awaken a person in every period of his life when he has been forced into "unconsciousness." Dianetics wakes people up. It is not hypnotism, which puts people to sleep. Dianetic therapy wakes them up. Hypnotism puts them to sleep. Can you ask for a wider difference in polarity? Dianetic therapy removes engrams. Hypnotism installs engrams. Further, Dianetics is a science, an organized body of knowledge—hypnotism is a tool and an art and is such a wild variable that man has suspected it as a dangerous thing for centuries and centuries, use it though he did.[5]

---

5. An additional difference is that a patient can be *returned* with *no* counting whatever.

The auditor will inevitably get cases into his hands which will drop into a hypnotic sleep for all he can do to prevent it. Such cases have engrams which make them do this, just as others have engrams which make them stay awake. The auditor then mentions neither "sleep" nor "wake." He takes his cases wherever they drop into their own inversion[6] level and works them from there. Patients will plead to be drugged or put into a trance. *Let them plead!* The reverie has a clear at its end—drugs and hypnotism have dependency on the auditor and many other undesirable aspects. A case takes longer in amnesia trance than in reverie. The gains in reverie are certain. The patient gets more and more well. When amnesia trance or hypnotism are used instead of reverie, no matter how easily the data seems to come up, the usual run of cases so treated experience little relief until the case is nearly completed, when the patient so long uncomfortable gets suddenly well. Hypnotism carries with it transference,[7] enormous operator responsibility and other impedimenta[8] with which Dianetics, in long practice, has done without. Hypnotism was used for research, then abandoned.

Hence, install the canceler every time. Never neglect to install it in every session. The patient may be trancing, which is something we don't want, but something which we cannot always avoid, and which we cannot always detect. Just install the canceler at the beginning of the session, then after you bring the patient to present time, use the canceler word.

This is a rehearsal, then, of the entire routine:

---

6. inversion: acute awareness of self.

7. transference: the process in and by which a person's feelings, thoughts and wishes shift from one person to another, especially this process in psychoanalysis with the analyst made the object of the shift.

8. impedimenta: encumberances, baggage.

Auditor: Look at the ceiling. When I count from one to seven your eyes will close. You will remain aware of everything which goes on. You will be able to remember everything that happens here. You can pull yourself out of anything which you get into if you don't like it. All right (slowly, soothingly): One, two, three, four, five, six, seven.[9] One, two, three, four, five, six, seven. One, two, three (patient's eyes close and eyelids flicker), four, five, six, seven. (Auditor pauses; installs canceler.) All right, let us go back to your fifth birthday . . . (work continues until the auditor has worked the patient enough for the period) . . . Come to present time. Are you in present time? (Yes.) (Use canceler word.) When I count from five to one and snap my fingers you will feel alert. Five, four, three, two, one. *(Snap!)*

As it can be seen in this example, when work for the day is concluded, the preclear, who may have been *returned* into his past for two hours, *must* be brought back to present time and startled with a finger snap to restore his awareness of his age and condition. Sometimes he is unable easily to come back to present, for which there is quick remedy which we will cover later, so the auditor must always assure himself that the patient feels he actually is in present time.

This is the reverie. This is all one needs to know about its actual mechanics. Experience will show him a great deal. But these are the basic processes:

1. Assure patient he will know everything that happens.
2. Count until he closes his eyes.
3. Install canceler.
4. Return him to a period in the past.

---

9. If the patient objects to numbers, use letters of the alphabet. He may have been counted down in some past surgical operation so that numbers make him nervous.

5. Work with file clerk to get data.
6. Reduce all engrams contacted so that no charge remains.
7. Bring patient to present time.
8. Be sure he is in present time.
9. Give him canceler word.
10. Restore full awareness of his surroundings.

The patient's time track, in the lowest level of attention units, is always in excellent condition. It can be depended upon to reach any date and hour of his life and all the data in it. In the higher levels of awareness, this time track may appear to be in very foul condition. The reactive mind engram circuits stand between these lower levels—right up against the banks—and the higher levels which contain "I." The lower levels contain only a shadow of the force of "I" and appear to be another "I" in a case of multivalent personality.

You can draw this on a piece of scratch paper and it would be helpful if you would do so. Draw a tall rectangle (the standard banks) to the left of the page. Draw half a dozen circles up against the right side of this rectangle for a representation of the file clerk—the bank monitor units. Now draw, about the center of the sheet, a large rectangle. Black it in. This is the area of the reactive engram circuits. It is *not* the reactive bank. It is the circuit pattern from the reactive engram bank, which borrows from the analyzer to make demons, vocal thinking, etc. Now, to the right of the page, draw a white rectangle. This is the portion of the analyzer which is "consciousness" and "I."

The whole task of therapy is to get that black rectangle, the reactive engram bank circuits, deleted so that from the standard bank to the left of the sheet to the analyzer portion to the right of the sheet is *all* analyzer. It can't be done with a knife as some people have supposed, evaluating the situation from their own engrams, for that black area you have drawn is *all* analyzer rendered useless by engrams, and when therapy is done, it will all be available for thinking. This increases IQ to an enormous extent.

Now suppose that the bottom of your picture is conception and the top is present time. The vertical route up and down, then, is the time track. In this graph it can be supposed that present time just keeps adding up higher and higher, further and further from conception in the form of new construction (an analogy). For "I" to get data from the standard banks to the left, "I" would have to work through this black rectangle, the reactive mind circuits. To a large extent "I" manages to get data from around this black area. But to a much larger extent it doesn't.

Now suppose that we draw a vertical line at the right of the picture. This line is "awareness." Consider that it can be moved, still vertical, to the left. As the line passes toward the left, we get deeper and deeper "trance." As the line moves into the reactive mind area, it becomes hypnotic trance. Now, as it moves even further left and into the circles we are calling "file clerk," it becomes the amnesia trance of hypnotism. Thus, anywhere we place this line we establish a "depth of trance." We want to work over to the right of the reactive bank, nearest the awake level, so that we can keep "I" in contact with his surroundings and keep unwanted data from coming through which will make the patient chronically uncomfortable. If the patient instantly slides from the right all the way to the left so that the attention units, the circles, of the file clerk itself are present, and does so the instant you count from one to seven, he is a hypnotic subject. He may not be aware, when he wakens, of what has taken place, for "I" was out of contact. Work him there, for he will have full sonic, etc., but be very, very careful to work very early in his prenatal area. He might not be able to recall what has taken place, and a late engram (which, if tapped, will not reduce) may have its full force opened up on "I" when the patient regains possession of himself. Further, you might give him a positive suggestion by accident. Work by preference with trance depth well to the right of the reactive bank.

The characteristics of the units we label "file clerk" are similar in desires to those of the basic individual when he is cleared. Thus, in any patient, the *basic personality* can be reached, for here is a sample of it. But the auditor should be content to know it is there; as the clearing goes forward, he will see more and more of it. The individual is himself, his personality does not alter, it simply becomes what he wanted it to be all the time at his optimum moments.

The units up against the standard banks can be considered the file clerk. But the file clerk has more than just the standard bank which he can tap. He also has the entire engram bank from which he can pull forth data.

The time track may have several aspects to the preclear. There is actually no track there except time and time is invisible, but the awareness, the "I," can return along it. The track is always there, stretched out. But aberrated ideas of it continually occur and recur in the same patient. It may get all bunched up. It may be very long. It may be that he cannot get on it at all (here's the schizophrenic—he is *off* his time track). But it is there. It is the filing system by *time* and "I" can be returned back along time by the simple request that he do so. If he does not, he is stuck in the present or an engram, which is easy to resolve. And so forth.

Now let us consider the engram bank. It was drawn as a black rectangle in the above sketch. Let us alter that a trifle and draw all this again, with the rectangles represented as triangles with all their points downwards and together but all else as before—the standard banks, the analyzer (consciousness) and "I." This is a working model now, an analogy, of what the auditor is trying to contact. It is as if the engram bank itself existed in that black triangle. Actually it doesn't, only its circuits, but all we need to visualize is that it does. Therefore, there is a thin point at the bottom. "I" and the file clerk can get together here. This is the bottom of the time track. This is immediately after conception. A little higher up, let's say two and one-half months after conception, it is a little harder for "I" and the file clerk to achieve contact. There is more reactive circuit between them. At seven months after conception, it is more difficult. And at twenty years of age, it has approached impossibility in most cases without Dianetic technique.

Hence, the auditor will find it expedient to work in the prenatal area and as early in that as possible. If he can clear the time from conception to birth, including birth, his task is nine-tenths complete. To clear the entire reactive bank is his goal.

The reactive bank is like a pyramid which is fairly well armored everywhere but just under the point, and which becomes unarmored when the point is contacted. This is taking the reactive bank in an exposed sector. The effort is to get into the *basic area*, contact early engrams, erase the basic-basic engram by recountings and then progress upwards, erasing engrams. These engrams apparently vanish. Actually, it takes a hard search to discover them once they are really gone. They exist as memory in the standard bank, but that memory is so unimportant, having been integrated now as experience, that it cannot aberrate. *Nothing in the standard bank can aberrate.* Only the contents of the reactive bank can aberrate—moments of "unconsciousness" and what was recorded within them—and locks. The auditor, in his work, considers an engram erased when it vanishes, when the preclear can no longer contact any part of it, but only after the preclear has thoroughly reexperienced it, complete with somatics.[10]

This inverted pyramid, in its upper reaches, is effect. In the lower reaches, it is the primary cause of aberration. The cement that holds this inverted pyramid together is physical pain and painful emotion. All the physical pain ever recorded by the organism and all the painful emotion are parts of this inverted pyramid.

The auditor first *discharges* the painful emotion from later life as it was displayed in "conscious moments." He runs these periods as true engrams until the preclear is no longer affected by them. Then he tries to contact *basic-basic,* that first engram. He reduces all engrams he contacts en route to that primary goal. *In every session he tries to reach basic-basic until he is certain he has it.*

Basic-basic is the bottom point. Once it has been gained, an erasure is begun during which engram after engram is "reexperienced" with all somatics until it is gone. Before *basic-basic* had been reached, the auditor may have had to run engrams twenty times before they reduced. Later he may have found they reduced in five runs. Then he contacts and erases *basic-basic.* If the patient has sonic by this time—or if he has had it all along—the engrams start erasing with one or two recountings.

The file clerk is smart. The auditor who does not

---

10. You can contact the file clerk by drugs or hypnotism and gather and reduce engrams. But this is an oversimplified solution. What we are doing in Dianetic therapy is more than this—we are trying to get "I" in contact with the file clerk, not just work the file clerk alone. Hypnoanalysis and narcosynthesis failed because they knew nothing of the engram bank and because they tried, without knowing what it was, to work only the file clerk. The desire of the patient to be worked in amnesia trance or any drugged state is an effort to spare "I" and throw the burden on the file clerk.

credit the ability of these attention units will involve the case beyond necessity and will lengthen it. The file clerk may hand things out *by phrases, by somatics, by time.* Whatever he hands out ordinarily will reduce on recountings. By *working with,* not trying to *command* the file clerk, the auditor will find the case steadily improving until it is released or fully cleared. The only time the auditor disregards this is when he uses the repeater system, which will be described.

We have "I" in a *reverie;* we *return* him to a period in his life along his *time track;* the *file clerk* gives incidents forth which the preclear reexperiences; the auditor makes the preclear recount the *engram* until it is relieved or has "vanished"[11] (all engrams will eventually "vanish" after *basic-basic* is erased); anything new the file clerk offers, even during the recounting, is addressed by the auditor to make the preclear reexperience it. That is the total sum of activity in Dianetics. There are, as accessories, the repeater technique and a few shortcuts. This is therapy. Amplification is needed, of course, and will be found in the ensuing pages to give the auditor all the data he needs. But this is the entire outline of Dianetic therapy.

---

11. The words *vanished* or *erased,* when applied to an engram which has been treated, mean that the engram has disappeared from the engram bank. It cannot be found afterwards except by search of the standard memory.

CHAPTER SIX

The Laws of Returning

The engram has the aspect of—and is not—a live entity which protects itself in various ways. Any and all phrases in it can be considered commands. These commands react on the analytical mind in such a way as to cause the analytical mind to behave erratically.

Dianetic therapy is parallel to the methods of thought and thinking itself. Anything which reacts against Dianetics and the auditor can uniformly and without exception be found to react in just that way on the patient's analytical mind. Conversely, the patient's problems of thinking in his usual activities are the auditor's problems in therapy.

The bulk of these "commands" the engrams contain are not computable in any way, since they are contradictory or demand unreasonable acts. It is the impossibility of computing them and reconciling them to thought and existence which makes the patient aberrated.

Let us take an engram which comes from one of Mother's bowel movements. She is straining, which causes compression, which brings about "unconsciousness" in the unborn child. Then, if she habitually talks to herself (a monologuist), as an enormous number of aberrated women do, she may say, "Oh, this is hell. I am all jammed up inside. I feel so stuffy I can't think. This is too terrible to be borne."

This may be in the basic area. The dream mechanism of the mind (which thinks in puns mostly, symbologists to the contrary) may bring forth a dream about hellfire as the engram is approached. The preclear may be sure that he is going to descend into fire if he goes on his time track toward this engram. Further, he may think his time track is all jammed up. This will mean, perhaps, that the incidents are all in one place on it. So much for "This is hell," and "all jammed up inside." Now let us take a look at what happens with "I'm so stuffy I can't think." The preclear sniffles because he thinks this means a cold in his nose. And as for "This is too terrible to be borne," he is filled with an emotion of terror at the thought of touching the engram, for this command says it is too painful to bear. Additionally, engrams being literal in their action, he may think that *he* was too terrible to be *born*.

The emotional reaction to hell, from some other place on the track—as contained in some other engram—may say that "going to hell" is loud sobbing. Hence, he does not "want" to recount this engram. Further, he is terrified of it because it is "too terrible to be borne." That Mother was only discussing with her ambivalent[1] self the necessity of laxatives is never entered into the computation. *For the reactive mind does not reason, it thinks in identities, seeking to command the analytical mind.*

There is only as much data as is in the engram and the analytical reaction to this unthinking thing is utterly literal.

Let us look at another. This is a coitus experience. It has, as its somatic, varying pressure. It is not painful—and by the way, no matter how painful these engrams may be in present time when restimulated, no matter how forceful, when they are actually contacted, their reexperienced pain is very mild, no matter what it was when received. So this is a shaking up of the unborn

---

1. ambivalent: also called multivalence: *valens* means "powerful" in Latin. It is the second half of *ambivalent* "power in two directions" (*ambi-* is Latin for both"). *Multivalence* means "many powerfuls." It embraces the phenomena of split personality, the strange differences of personality in people in one and then another situation.

child, that is all. But it *says,* "Oh, darling, I'm afraid you'll come in me. I'll just die if you come in me. Oh, please, don't come in me!"

What does the analytical mind do with this? Does it think about coitus? Does it worry about pregnancy? No, emphatically not. The engram that would make one think about coitus would say, "Think about coitus!" and the engram that contained a worry about pregnancy would say, "I am worried about pregnancy." The pain is not severe in this coitus experience but it specifically states that the engram is not to be entered: "Do not come in me!" He would die if he did, wouldn't he? It says so right there. And the patient finds himself wandering around the track until the auditor uses repeater technique (as will be covered).

How about another type of engram? Let us suppose that our poor patient has been unlucky enough to get a Junior tagged on him. Let us suppose his name is Ralph and his father's name is Ralph. (Be careful of these Junior cases, they are unusually complex sometimes.) Mother (see the Kinsey[2] report, if you've any doubts) is having a quiet affair on the side with Jim. This coitus somatic is no more painful than being gently sat upon, but the patient has a terrible time with it. Mother: "Oh, honey, you are so wonderful. I wish Ralph were more like you but he isn't. He just doesn't seem to be able to excite a girl at all." Lover: "Oh, Ralph isn't so bad. I like him." Mother: "You don't know his pride. If Ralph found out about this, it would kill him. He would just die, I know." Lover: "Don't worry, Ralph'll never hear."

This little gem of an engram is more common than one would suppose before he begins to get an embryo-eye view of Mother. This won't compute in the analyzer

---

2. Kinsey, Alfred C.: U.S. zoologist, studied human sexual behavior in the U.S.

as data. Therefore it is a worry. (A worry is contradictory engram commands which cannot be computed.) Ralph, Junior, finds that he is very shy sexually. That is the aberrative pattern. Approaching it in therapy, we find we have a sympathy computation with the lover. After all, he said Ralph wasn't so bad, that he liked Ralph. Well, the only Ralph is, of course, to the reactive mind, Junior. This keeps our patient from approaching this engram because he thinks he will lose a friend if he touches it. Further, on the aberrative side, Junior has always worried about people's pride. As we contact this in therapy, he shies violently from it. After all, if he found out about it it would "kill him dead right where he lies." And there is another thing here, a sonic shut-off. It says right there that Ralph will never hear. This is survival stuff. That is what the cells believe. Therefore Ralph never hears *in recall*. There will be more sonic shut-offs. Mother is promiscuous[3] and that generally means blockage on the second dynamic. Blockage on the second dynamic often means she dislikes children. In short, this would be an attempted-abortion case which stabbed Junior full of enough holes to supply a cheese factory for some time. Junior, now a man, may have extended hearing because he is frightened in general of "life." But his sonic recall is zero. This engram, then, would have to be sorted out through the demon circuits as "impressions" which come to the mind. The auditor, taking what the patient says about this, may very soon guess its content and explode it by repeater technique.

Now take the case of the mother who, a soul of propriety (if a little on the whiny side), discovers she is pregnant and goes to the doctor. Mother: "I think I'm pregnant. I'm afraid I am." Doctor punches her around for a while, knocking the unborn child, who is our

---

3. promiscuous: having sexual relations with many people.

preclear thirty years later, into an "unconscious" state. Doctor: "I don't think so." Mother: "I'm really afraid I am. I'm sure I'm caught. I just know it." Doctor (more punching): "Well, it's hard to tell this early."

It says right there that this man patient of ours is pregnant. If we look, we'll see he has a paunch. That's good survival, that is. And in therapy we find he is afraid he exists: "I am afraid I *am*." And suddenly he isn't moving on the time track. Why? He's caught. That doesn't mean he's pregnant, that means he is *caught*. Further, he won't be able to recount it. Why? Because it is "hard to *tell* this early." Consequently, he doesn't speak about it. We free him on the track with repeater technique.

Oh, this language of ours which says everything it doesn't mean! Put into the hands of the moronic reactive mind, what havoc it wreaks! Literal interpretation of everything! Part of the aberrative pattern of the person who had the above engram was great cautiousness about advancing any opinion. After all, it was hard to tell, this early.

Now let us take an engram from a girl patient whose father was badly aberrated. He strikes Mother because he is afraid Mother is pregnant and Father is blocked on dynamics one, two, three and four. Father: "Get out! Get out! I know you haven't been true to me! You were no virgin when I married you. I should have killed you long ago! Now you're pregnant. Get out!"

The girl, some five weeks after conception, is knocked "unconscious" by the blow to Mother's abdomen. She has a severe engram here because it has painful emotional value which she will never be able to dramatize satisfactorily. The aberrative pattern here demonstrates itself in hysterics whenever a man might accuse her of not being true. She was a virgin when she was married twenty-one years after this engram was received, but she was sure she was not. She has had a "childhood delusion" that her father was likely to kill her. And she is always afraid of being pregnant because it says *now* she is pregnant, which means always, since time is a march of "nows." In therapy, we try to get near this engram. We return the patient to basic area and suddenly find her talking about something which happened when she was five years of age. We return her again and now she is talking about something which happened when she was ten years of age. The auditor, observing any such reaction as this, knows he is handling a *bouncer*.[4] It says, "Get out!" and the patient gets out. The auditor recognizes what is wrong, uses repeater technique and reduces or erases the engram.

Always and invariably, the analytical mind reacts to these engrams as though commanded. It performs on the track as these engrams state. And it computes about the case or about life as these engrams dictate. Healthy things to have around, engrams! Real, good survival! Survival good enough to lay any man in his grave.

The auditor is not much worried by the phrases which assist therapy. An engram received from Father beating Mother which says: "Take that! Take it, I tell you. You've got to take it!" means that our patient has possibly had tendencies as a kleptomaniac.[5] (Such things are the whole source of the impulses of a thief, the test being that when an auditor erases all such engrams in a patient, the patient no longer steals.) The auditor will find it eagerly recounted because its content offers it to the analytical mind.

The whole species of engrams which say, "Come

---

4. bouncer: an engramic command (such as "Can't stay here," "Get out!") which sends the preclear up the track toward present time.

5. kleptomaniac: a person suffering from an uncontrollable tendency to steal things, with no desire to use or profit by them.

back here! Now stay here!" as fathers are so fond of saying, accounts for a snap back to an engram when therapy is entered. The patient goes straight back to it the moment it is exposed. When recounted the command is no longer effective. But while that engram existed, unentered, it was fully capable of sending people to an institution to lie in a fetal position. Anyone left in institutions who has not been given shocks or prefrontal lobotomy and who suffers from this type of insanity can be released from such an engram and restored to present time simply by use of repeater technique. It sometimes takes only half an hour.

Traveling on the track, then, and wandering through the computations the analyzer is compelled by these engrams to attempt is something like playing a child's game which has a number of squares, along which one is supposed to move a "man." A game could actually be composed on the basis of this time track and engram commands. It would be similar to Parcheesi.[6] Move so many squares, land on one which says, "Get out!" which means one would go back to present time or toward it. Move so many squares and then lose a move because this square on which we now land says, "Stay here!" and the "man" would stay until the auditor let him out by technique (but because this is struck by therapy, it would have no power to hold long). Then move so many squares to one which said, "Go to sleep," at which the "man" would have to go to sleep. Move so many squares until one was hit which said, "Nobody must find out," and so there would be no square. Move so many until one was reached which said, "I'm afraid," at which the "man" would be afraid. Move again to a square which said, "I must go away," so the "man"

---

6. Parcheesi: a trademark for a board game based on the game of pachisi (ancient game of India similar to backgammon).

would go away. Move once more to a square which says, "I'm not here," and the square would be missing. And so forth and so forth.

The classes of commands which particularly trouble the auditor are only a few. Because the mind actually does some part of its thinking, especially when remembering, by return, even when the individual is not returning, all these commands also impede the thought processes of the mind. In therapy they are particularly irksome and are the constant target of attention of the auditor.

First is the *patient-ejector* species of command. These are colloquially called *bouncers*. They include such things as "Get out!" "Don't ever come back," "I've got to stay away," etc., etc., including any combination of words which *literally* mean ejection.

Second is the *patient-holder* species of command. These include such things as "Stay here," "Sit right there and think about it," "Come back and sit down," "I can't go," "I mustn't leave," etc.

Third is the *engram-denyer* species of command which, literally translated, means that the engram doesn't exist: "I'm not here," "This is getting nowhere," "I must not talk about it," "I can't remember," etc.

Fourth is the *engram-grouper* species of command which, literally translated, means that all incidents are in one place on the time track: "I'm jammed up," "Everything happens at once," "Everything comes in on me at once," "I'll get even with you," etc.

Fifth is the *patient-misdirector* which sends the preclear in the wrong direction, makes him go earlier when he should be going later, go later when he should go earlier, etc. "You can't go back at this point," "You're turned around," etc.

The *bouncer* sends the preclear soaring back toward present time. The *holder* keeps him right where he is.

The *denyer* makes him feel that there is no incident present. The fourth, the *grouper,* foreshortens his time track so that there is no time track. The *misdirector* reverses the necessary direction of travel.

Contacting any engram causes the preclear to react "analytically." Just as in the case of an engram being restimulated, the commands are impinged upon his analyzer, and although the analyzer may firmly believe it has just computed the reaction all of its own accord, it is actually speaking straight out of the content of an engram or engrams.

This is the method of *repeater technique.*

As he goes back along the track contacting engrams, the preclear runs into areas of "unconsciousness" which are occluded by "unconsciousness" or emotion. In most early engrams the preclear can be expected to yawn and yawn. It is not the command "to sleep" which is responsible for this: the "unconsciousness" is releasing (boiling off, the auditors call it). A preclear may, for a space of two hours, fumble around, drop off into "unconsciousness," appear doped, start to go to sleep, without any such command being present.

Part of the engram bundle of data is the analyzer shut-off. When he is returned and an engram is contacted, the preclear then experiences an analyzer attenuation, which means he is much less able to think in the area. Boiling off "unconsciousness" is a process very necessary to therapy, for this "unconsciousness" could be restimulated in the everyday life of the individual and, when restimulated, make his wits shut off just a little or a very great deal, slowing down his thought processes.

The aspect of "unconsciousness," then, reduces the preclear's awareness whenever it is contacted. He has dreams, he mumbles foolish things, he flounders. His analyzer is penetrating the veil which kept him from the engram. But it is also highly susceptible, when in this state, to an engram command.

When urged by the auditor to go through the engram and recount it (although the auditor knows it may take minutes for this "unconsciousness" to boil off enough to let the patient through), the preclear may complain that "I can't go back at this point." The auditor promptly takes note of this. It is an engram command coming through. He does not apprise the patient of this knowledge; the patient usually doesn't know what he's saying. If the patient then continues to have trouble, the auditor tells him, "Say, 'I can't go back at this point.'" The patient then repeats this, the auditor making him go over it and over it. Suddenly the somatic turns on and the engram is contacted.

In interviewing a patient, the auditor notes carefully, without appearing to do so, what phrases the patient chooses and repeats about his ills or about Dianetics. After he has placed the patient in reverie, if he discovers the patient, for instance, insists he "can't go anyplace," the auditor makes him repeat the phrase.

Repetition of such a phrase, over and over, sucks the patient back down the track and into contact with an engram which contains it. It may happen that this engram will not release—having too many before it—but it will not release only in case it has that same phrase in an earlier engram. So the repeater technique is continued with the auditor making the patient go earlier and earlier for it. If all goes on schedule the patient will very often let out a chuckle or a laugh of relief. The phrase has been sprung. The engram has not been erased, but that much of it will not thereafter influence therapy.

Anything the patient does about engrams and any words he uses to describe the action are contained, usually, in those engrams. Repeater technique takes the charge off the phrases so that the engrams can be approached.

This technique, of course, can very occasionally land the patient in trouble, but the kind of trouble into which one can get in Dianetics is not very severe. The engram, restimulated in everyday life, can be and is violent. Murders, rapes and arsons, attempted abortions, backwardness in school—any aberrated aspect of life—stem from these engrams. But the act of approaching them in Dianetic therapy goes on another channel, a channel closer to the source of the engram. Ordinarily, acting on an unsuspecting individual, the engram has enormous motor and speech power, ties up great numbers of circuits in the mind which should be used for rationality, and generally effects havoc: its contacts are "soldered in" and cannot be thrown out by the analyzer. In therapy, the patient is headed toward the engram: that act alone begins to disconnect some of its "permanent leads."[7] A patient can be gotten into an engram which, unless approached on the therapy route, might have made him curl up like a fetus and get shipped off to the nearest institution. On the therapy route, which is a return down the time track, the most powerful holder has its force limited: a patient can get into a holder which in normal life might be a psychosis: his only manifestation, perhaps, is that when he is told to "Come up to present time," he simply opens his eyes without actually traversing the interval up the track to present time. He does not suspect he is in a holder until the auditor, watchful for such a manifestation, feeds him repeater technique.

Auditor: Are you in present time?
Preclear: Sure.
Auditor: How do you feel?

---

7. lead: an electrical conductor (usually a wire) conveying current from a source to a place of use.

Preclear: Oh, I've got a slight headache.

Auditor: Close your eyes. Now say, "Stay here."

Preclear: All right. "Stay here. Stay here. Stay here." (Several times)

Auditor: Are you moving?

Preclear: No.

Auditor: Say, "I'm caught. I'm caught."

Preclear: "I'm caught." (Several times)

Auditor: Are you moving on the track?

Preclear: Nope.

Auditor: Say, "I'm trapped."

Preclear: "I'm trapped. I——" Ouch, my head!

Auditor: Keep going over it.

Preclear: "I'm trapped. I'm trapped. I'm trapped." Ouch! That's worse! (His somatic is getting stronger as he approaches the engram holding him on the other side of the "unconsciousness" veil.)

Auditor: Keep going over it.

Preclear: "I'm trapped—oh, God, I'm trapped. I'll never get out of this place. I'll never get out. I'm trapped!"

Auditor: Contact it closely. Make sure there is nothing more in it. (A trick to keep the preclear from replaying what he himself has just said and keep running the engram.)

Preclear: My head hurts! Let me come up to present time!

Auditor: Go through it again. (If the preclear comes up with this much charge, he'll be unhappy and the incident may be hard to enter next time.)

Preclear: "Oh, God, I'm trapped. I'm afraid I'm trapped." (New word showed up.) "I'll never get out of this place as long as I live. I'm trapped. I'll never get out. I'm trapped." (aside) She's crying. "Oh, why did I ever have to marry such a man!"

Auditor: How's your head?

Preclear: Hurts less. Say, that's a dirty trick. She's pounding herself on the stomach. That's mean! Why, confound her!

Auditor: Reexperience it again. Let's make sure there isn't more in it. (Same mechanism to keep the preclear from replaying what he said before rather than what he now gets from the engram. If he *replays* rather than *reexperiences,* the engram won't lift.)

Preclear: (Does so, getting some new words and several sounds including the thud of the blows on her abdomen and an auto horn [bulb type] in the street outside.) Don't tell me I have to run this thing again.

Auditor: Recount it, please.

Preclear: Well, so this dame tries to bust my head in and get rid of me. And so I jumped out and beat hell out of her.

Auditor: Please reexperience the engram.

Preclear: (Starts to do so, suddenly finds out that, like a piece of string with a loop in it, this engram has straightened out and contains more data where the loops were.) "I've got to think of something to tell Harry. He'll jump all over me." (This was the source of his joking—"jumped out," etc.)

Auditor: Please go over it again. There may be more in it.

Preclear: (Does so, old parts of it reduce, two new sounds appear, her footsteps and running water. Then he is happy and laughs at it. This engram is *released* because it may not have entirely vanished. Such an engram is in this shape only when it is contacted prior to basic-basic.)

This is both repeater technique and an engram talked into *recession.* This engram may appear again with a very faint additional charge after basic-basic is contacted, but it has lost all power to aberrate or give out a psychosomatic headache or other illness. Yet this engram, not contacted by therapy, was quite enough to make this patient, when a boy, scream with terror every time he found he could not get out of some closed space (claustrophobia).

The repeater technique is the one particular phase of Dianetics which requires cleverness from the auditor. Given persistency and patience, any auditor can succeed in the other phases of the science with minimal intelligence. In the repeater technique he must learn how to think—for therapy purposes—like an engram. And he will have to observe how the subject is conducting himself along the time track. And he will have to observe the type of reaction the subject has and draw from this the conclusion as to what sort of command is troubling the subject when the subject himself either does not cooperate or does not know.

This is not to say that the repeater technique is hard: it is not. But the ability of the auditor to use it is the principal reason why a case takes longer with one auditor than another. It is a definite ability. It is playing the game mentioned earlier with cleverness. Where is the preclear stuck and with what command? Why has the preclear suddenly stopped cooperating? Where is the emotional charge which is holding up the case? With the repeater technique the auditor can resolve all these problems and a clever auditor resolves them much faster than an unclever one.

How does one think like an engram? Ronald Ross, discovering that insects carried germs, considered it necessary to think like a mosquito. Here is a similar menace, the engram. One has to learn to think, for therapy purposes, like an engram.

The auditor could not and does not have to be able to look into a patient's eyes and guess why the patient won't eat anything but cauliflower on Wednesdays. That is an aberration and the auditor does not have to guess at either aberrations or psychosomatic illness sources: they all come out in time and he will learn much about them as he goes. But the auditor must be able to keep his patient straightened out on the track, moving earlier into the basic area, moving upwards from there for a reduction. The current answer to this is the *repeater technique*. Understand that a whole new art of practice, or many arts of practice, could be evolved for Dianetics: one would be unhappy with his fellow man if such evolution and betterment did not take place. Just now, the best that has come forward—and the criterion of best is that it works uniformly in all cases—is the repeater technique. The auditor must be able to use it if he expects anything like results from a case at this time. When the auditor—or some auditor—has run a few cases and knows the nature of this beast, the engram, he may—and better had—come forward with improved techniques of his own. The real drawback which repeater technique has is that it requires the auditor to be clever.

Being clever does not mean talking a lot. In Dianetics, when one is auditing, that is being very unclever. Indeed, auditors, when they begin to work cases, almost invariably so love the sound of their own voices and the feel of their skill that the poor preclear hardly gets a chance to get a word in reactivewise—and it is the preclear who is to be cleared, who has the only accurate information, who can make the only evaluations.

Being clever in the sense of the repeater technique is being able to pick out, from the subject's conversation or action, just what the engrams contain which will prevent his reaching them, progressing through them and so forth. The repeater technique is addressed only to *action*, not to aberration.

Here is a case, for instance, which was so "sealed in"

that thirty hours of almost continual repeater technique were necessary to break the walls between the analytical mind and the engrams. *It is important to know that an engram would not be an engram if the preclear could contact it easily.* Any engram which can be easily contacted and has no emotional charge is about as aberrative as a glass of soda water.

A young girl, with sonic recall, but with extended hearing and such a complete imbalance of the endocrine system that she had become an old woman at twenty-two, was worked for seventy-five hours before she contacted anything in the basic area. This is almost incredible but it happened. In a patient with sonic shut-off and off his time track, seventy-five hours of work would just about get the wheels greased. But this girl, having sonic recall, should have been well on the road to being clear and she had yet to touch basic-basic.

By repeater technique and repeater alone the case was finally resolved. It contained practically no holders or bouncers. It simply appeared that the whole prenatal area was a blank.

Now, it happens that an engram, being not a memory with reason in it, is just a set of waves or some other type of recording which impinges itself on the analytical mind and the somatic mind and runs the voice and muscles and other parts of the body. The analytical mind, to justify what it finds going forward, and cut down by the engram in dramatization, may be interjecting data to make this action seem reasonable—to justify it. But this does not make an engram sentient. When an engram is first approached in therapy it appears to be absent entirely. It may be that three sessions will be required to "develop" this engram. As many are worked, this does not mean three blank sessions, but it means that the "I," in returning, must pass over an engram a few times for the engram to "develop." This is important to know. Just as you ask the mind for a datum one week and don't find it (in an aberree) and ask it again the next week and find it, so with engrams. A cardinal principle in therapy is that *if you keep asking for it, you will eventually get the engram.* Returning over and over the prenatal area will, of itself alone, eventually develop the engrams in it so that the analytical mind can attack them and reduce them. This is slow freight. The repeater technique—although the engram is still in need of development by several sessions—speeds the process immensely.

In the case of this young girl it probably would have taken another fifty or sixty hours of work to contact the engrams unless a technique like repeater had been used. Repeater technique resolved it when the auditor noted that she kept saying, "I'm sure there's a good reason why I feel bad up in my childhood. After all, my brother raped me when I was five. I'm sure it's up in my childhood, much later. My mother was terribly jealous of me. I'm sure it's later."

This young lady, as might be imagined, had studied some school of mental healing in college which thought sex or eating vitamins caused aberrations of the mind and she had often held forth on the fact that, while she was not averse[8] to what she called "analysis," she did think it dull to expect a fetus to hear anything. She would go into the area before birth and declare she was quite comfortable. *But birth was not in sight.* That is important. The basic engram or engrams in the basic area—around the embryo period—cannot vanish and will not vanish short of therapy, and when birth cannot even be contacted by so much as one somatic, it is certain that something lies before it. If birth were the first engram, everybody could be cleared in five hours.

---

8. averse: not willing or inclined; reluctant; opposed (*to*).

Birth can even be in sight and there may still remain half a hundred severe prenatal experiences. In her case, nothing was in sight. Her educational pattern had slowed the case: she was always trying to sit in present time and "remember" with a memory so full of occlusions that she couldn't have recalled her mother's right name. (She had acquired this from being in the hands of mental practitioners for ten years who had asked her to do nothing but "remember.") As has been said, she was quite comfortable before birth, sensed the amniotic fluid and was certain that life in the womb was a joyous life for all. The incongruity that she could experience the sensations of this amniotic fluid and floating comfort and warmth and a continued belief that there was no prenatal memory escaped her utterly. The auditor made no slightest effort to convince her. Knowing his business, he merely kept sending her back and forth, trying this mechanism or that.

She finally wanted to know if there *had* to be prenatal experience and was told that what was there was there, that if there was no prenatal memory then she wouldn't recall any but that if there was, she might. This is a good, equivocal attitude for an auditor. Dianetics, after all, as one auditor put it, "just shows the yard goods" and makes no sales effort at all.

The auditor had been using repeater technique on varieties of phrases. She was moving on the track so there must be a denyer present. And he had utterly run out of ideas when he realized, suddenly, that she was very handy with that phrase, "much later."

Auditor: Say "much later" and return into the prenatal area.

Girl: "Much later. Much later," etc. (very bored and uncooperative).

Auditor: Continue please. (Never say "Go ahead," for

that means to do just that. Say "Continue" when you want them to keep on progressing along an engram or repeating, and "Return over it" when rerunning an engram already run once.)

Girl: "Much later. Much . . ." I have a somatic in my face! It feels like I am being pushed. (This was good news for the auditor knew she had a midprenatal pain shut-off which prevented later somatics from appearing.)

Auditor: Contact it more closely and continue to repeat.

Girl: "Much later. Much later." It's getting stronger. (Naturally. On repeater technique, the somatic gets stronger until the phrase appears, exactly right. On a nonsonic case it impinges itself indirectly on "I"; in a sonic, the sound comes through as sound.)

Auditor: Continue.

Girl: "Much . . ." I hear a voice! There. That's it. Why, that's my father's voice!

Auditor: Listen to the words and repeat them, please.

Girl: He's talking to my mother. Say, this face pressure is uncomfortable. It keeps going up and down on me. It hurts!

Auditor: Repeat his words, please.

Girl: He's saying, "Oh honey, I won't come in you now. It's better to wait until much later to have one." And there's my mother's voice. Say, this pressure is hurting me. No, it's eased up considerably. Funny, the minute I contacted his voice, it got less.

Auditor: What is your mother saying, please, if you hear her?

Girl: She's saying, "I don't want you in there at all then!" She's mad! Say, the somatic stopped. (Coitus had ended at this point.)

Auditor: Please return to the start of this and recount.

Girl: (Regains the beginning, somatic returns) I wonder

what they're doing? (then a pause) I hear a squish-
ing sound! (then a pause and embarrassment) Oh!

Auditor: Recount the engram, please.

Girl: There's a sort of faint rhythm at first and then it
gets faster. I can hear breathing. Now it's beginning
to bear down harder but a lot less than it did the
first time. Then it eases up and I hear my father's
voice: "Oh, honey, I won't come in you now. It's
better to wait until much later to have one. I'm
not too sure I like children that well. Besides, my
job . . ." And my mother must shove at him because
there's a sharper somatic here. "I don't want you in
there at all then. You cold fish!"

Auditor: Return to the beginning and recount it again,
please.

Girl: (Recounts it several times, somatic finally vanishes.
She feels quite cheerful about it but doesn't think
to mention that she doubted prenatals existed.)

This is *repeater technique* at work. This particular
case had had about two hundred phrases thrown at her
for repeater technique without finding one of them that
would fit. In the first place, there were only a few lower
engrams which the file clerk was willing to give out and
the auditor was guessing at the whole gamut of denyers.
A later incident might have contained—and did, but no
somatic appeared—numbers of the phrases he used. But
the file clerk was willing to settle for this one for it was
early and could be erased.

The file clerk rarely hands out something in a badly
occluded case which cannot be reduced to recession. And
an auditor *never* leaves an engram so offered until he has
made every effort with many recountings to reduce it. The
file clerk, in this case, by the by, would have let down the
auditor by putting forth such an engram as birth, which
would not have lifted and which would have caused a lot

of lost work and given the patient a headache for a few days. The auditor would have let the file clerk down if he had not reduced the engram offered by making the girl go over it several times until the somatic was gone and the voice faded out.

The reason this engram stayed hidden was because its content said so. Actually it was a coitus. As an engram it seemed to say that the incidents would be found later on in life. Further, as an engram, it said that it was not to be entered.

Repeater technique will sometimes embroil a patient in trouble of a minor sort by getting him "sucked into" incidents which will not lift. This is not common but the file clerk occasionally hands out a late incident, rather than an early one. However, this is not an error on the part of the file clerk. Remember, he has these engrams filed by subject, somatic and time, and the auditor can use any one of these. When the file clerk responds and hands out a somatic on a repeater phrase the auditor has gleaned from the preclear's chatter or has guessed himself and yet that somatic will not lift or no voice appears with it (in a sonic case, or merely won't lift with a nonsonic), the file clerk had to unstack a pile of material. Therefore, the auditor, realizing this, finding that a voice does not appear or that the somatic will not lift, has the preclear repeat the same phrase and tells him to go earlier and earlier. Another somatic may turn up in a different place in the body. The file clerk has gotten an even earlier one loose, now that a small amount of trouble has been taken from what he could first get. Now this earlier one is addressed similarly. It may get mediumly strong as a somatic, the preclear repeating the phrase all the while, and still no voice may appear. The auditor then sends the preclear earlier. The file clerk again has managed to get out an even earlier one, now that something has been taken from the second. This time again, an even earlier somatic turns on, probably down around the basic area in a case which has not previously contacted this area; and this time a voice can be heard. The engram reduces. The file clerk, in short, was willing to risk trouble in order to get several somatics unstacked and let the auditor get a basic incident.

There are variations on this sort of thing. As the filing system is by subject, somatic and time, the auditor can use other things than phrases. He can send a preclear to the "highest intensity of a somatic," and often results may be obtained, though this is not as reliable as by subject nor as foolproof. The preclear, incidentally, does not mind going to any "highest intensity" of somatic because somatics are about a thousandth part as strong as the original agony, though they are quite strong enough. In present time with the preclear not in therapy, the intensity of one of these somatics can be a drastic affair, as witness the migraine headache. Taking the migraine, a preclear can be returned to the very moment of its reception when one would think its intensity would be the highest and yet find a mild, dull ache such as one would get with a hangover. This is part of the principle that any entrance of a case is better than a case not entered at all. For, by return with standard reverie technique, the source is approached, and if the source is contacted at all, the power of the engram to aberrate has become reduced in strength no matter how many mistakes the auditor makes.

Returning to "maximum intensity" of a somatic, then, is nothing very painful. *Actual* maximum intensity is when the preclear is awake before the contact with the incident is made. But in returning to "maximum intensity" the incident may often be contacted and reduced. If "maximum intensity" however, contains in its engram the phrases, "I can't stand it!" "It's killing me," or "I'm terrified," then expect our preclear to respond to it in some such way. If he does not respond, then he has an emotional shut-off, which is another problem which will be taken up later.

Similarly, the auditor can handle his preclear in time. There exists a very accurate clock in the mind. The file clerk is very well acquainted with this clock and wherever possible will comply. The auditor who wants the patient to go "six minutes before this phrase is uttered" will generally find that his preclear is now six minutes before it, even though the incident is prenatal. The auditor can bring his preclear forward, then, minute by minute as he desires. He can take a preclear straight through an incident by announcing, "It is one minute later. It is two minutes later. Three minutes have gone by," and so forth. The auditor does not have to wait for those minutes to elapse; he just announces them. He can make a preclear go through time at five-minute intervals or hour intervals or day intervals, and unless there is engramic material which holds him or otherwise affects the operation, the auditor can move the preclear on the time track at will. It would be very nice if the auditor could send the preclear to conception and then tell him it is one hour later, two hours later and so forth, to pick up the first engram. However, there are more factors involved than time, and the plan, though pretty, is not feasible. The time shift is generally used when the auditor is trying to get the preclear ahead of an incident to make sure that he really has a beginning. By returning the preclear by five- or ten-minute intervals, the auditor may sometimes discover that he is running backwards into a very long and complicated incident and that the headache he has been seeking to alleviate on the preclear was received, actually, hours before the period in which he thought it had initially been received. In such a case there is a second engram appended to an earlier engram and the auditor cannot lift the second one until he has the first one.

Actually, time shift is of limited use. The auditor who tries to go chasing backwards through time will find that he will have on his hands an artificially restimulated case and that the work is much impeded. Repeater technique works best and is most easily handled by the file clerk. The auditor uses a time shift to get the preclear as close to basic area (early prenatal) as possible and then generally, if the file clerk doesn't simply go to work handing out engrams which can be washed, one after the other, the auditor uses repeater technique. Time shift and "running down a somatic" have some limited use. Some experimentation will show about how much use they have.

The laws of returning are these:

1. A returned patient reacts more, theoretically, to those commands which are earlier than he is on the time track and less to those commands which are later than his point in time.

2. A preclear reacts to those engramic commands which are: (a) in chronic restimulation, or (b) to which he is nearest on the time track. Thus, if an engram says, "I'm afraid," he is. If it says, "I'd rather die than face this," he would. If the command to which he is near says, "I'm sleepy," he will be. If it says, "Forget it," he will. Commands in chronic restimulation give a false color to the personality: "I can never be sure of anything," "I don't know," "I can't hear anything" are all possibly in chronic restimulation. If the file clerk won't give them up, then keep working the case anyway around these. They will give up after a while.

3. The action of the preclear on the time track and the condition of the track are regulated exclusively by engramic commands classifiable as *bouncers, holders, denyers* and *groupers* and *misdirectors*. (These conditions,

it is repeated, are quite variable, as variable as language: "I don't know whether I am coming or going," for instance, in an engram makes it very confusing. "I can't go back at this point" makes the preclear keep progressing later and later.)

4. The engramic command manifests itself either in the awake speech of the preclear before a session of therapy or is inadvertently announced as a supposedly "analytical" thought when he nears the vicinity of the command.

5. The engram is not a sentient, rationalized memory, but a collection of unanalyzed perceptions, and it will develop into contact simply by the process of returning through it, to it, over it or asking for it.

6. The file clerk will give the auditor whatever can be extracted from the engram bank. The auditor must aid the file clerk by reducing in charge or severity everything the file clerk offers. This is done by making the patient recount it. (Otherwise the file clerk gets so much material piled around that, with this in restimulation, he can no longer get at the files. The auditor who bucks the file clerk is not rare. The file clerk who will buck an auditor, except by withholding data which will not reduce, has yet to be found.)

The techniques available to the auditor are as follows:

1. *Returning,* in which the preclear is sent as early as possible on his track before therapy itself is engaged upon.

2. *Repeater technique,* by which the file clerk is asked for data on certain subjects, particularly those affecting the return and travel on the time track, and which aid the ability of the preclear to contact engrams.

3. *Time shift,* by which a preclear can be moved short or long distances on the track by specific announcement of the amount of time forward the preclear is to go or time backwards, or return or progression

through intervals of time. (It is also useful to find out if the preclear is moving or which direction he is moving on the time track in order to discover the action some engram may be having upon him.)

4. *Somatic location,* by which the moment of reception of the somatic is located, in an effort to discover whether it is received in this engram or to find an engram containing it.

CHAPTER SEVEN

Emotion and the Life Force

One of the largest roles in therapy is played by emotion. In the second book we covered this subject and divided it tentatively as a theory only into three divisions: (a) the emotions contained in the command of engrams whereby physical pain became confused with emotions; (b) the emotions contained as endocrine reactions subject to the analytical mind of the clear and the analytical mind and reactive mind of the aberree; and (c) the emotions contained in engrams which bound up free units of life force.

Further work and research on emotion will undoubtedly bring about an even closer understanding of it. But we have a workable knowledge of emotion now. We can use what we know and produce results with it. When we know more, we shall be able to produce much better results but just now we can produce the release and the clear. If we treat emotion as bound-up life force and if we follow these general precepts to release it, we shall obtain a very large gain in any preclear; indeed, we shall produce our largest single gains by so releasing emotion.

In an engineering science like Dianetics, we can work on a push-button basis. We know that throwing a switch will stop a motor, that closing it again will start it and that no matter how many times we open or close that switch our motor will stop or start. We are using here a force which is still as mysterious to us as electricity was to James Clerk Maxwell. Much earlier Benjamin Franklin had observed that electricity existed and had done some interesting things with it: but he had not used it much and he could not control it. A philosopher like Bergson[1] selected out a thing he called *élan vital,* a life force. Man is alive, there must be a force or flow of something which keeps him alive; when man is dead there is no force or flow. This is life force in the Benjamin Franklin stage. As he considered electricity, so did Bergson consider life force. Now we are up, in Dianetics, to the James Clerk Maxwell stage, or very nearly. We know that certain equations can be made about life force and we can use those equations. And we can theorize that "life force" and what has been called a certain kind of "emotion" are either similar or the same thing. We may have the wrong theory, but so might James Clerk Maxwell. Indeed, Maxwell's theories may still be wrong: at least we have electric lights. In Dianetics, we are pretty certain that the majority of tenets are parallels of natural law: these are the big computations. We are not certain that we have emotion properly bracketed, but then we shall not be sure until we have actually taken a dead man and pumped him up with life force again. Short of this extreme, we are on solid ground with emotion as life force.

We can, for instance, take a girl, examine something of her background with, let us say, an electroencephalograph (an instrument for measuring nervous impulses and reactions)[2] and then proceed on the basis of the

---

1. Bergson, Henri: (1859–1941) French philosopher. Awarded Nobel Prize for literature (1927).

2. The electroencephalograph, hypnoscopes, intelligence charts, tests for various dynamics and so forth are all mechanical aids to Dianetics. They are primarily used in research. They can be used in practice where available and the skill of the auditor permits, but they have not been generally in such practical use and at this time and with this therapy are not needed. Some chemist, one of these days, is going to invent a perfect "trance gas," I hope, which will speed the clearing of a schizophrenic; and some engineer, I trust, will make something to measure nerve impulses cheap enough to be used in general practice. Right now, we can get along without them, no matter how desirable they may be to the future.

information so obtained to do one of two things. The first is inhuman and would not be done, of course, but she could be made sick or insane merely by using this data, so obtained. (If the data is obtained in therapy, it is obtained by actual contact with engrams and an engram contacted in reverie has lost its power to aberrate: Dianetic therapy thus makes such an eventuality utterly impossible.) The second and far more important fact to us is that she can be made to recover, with this same data, all the force, interest, persistence and tenacity to life and all the physical and mental well-being possible. If it could not be made to work both ways, we would not have the answer, at least in workable form. (Some fiction writer, by the way, if tempted to horrorize on the first fact, must please recall that the data was obtained with apparatus which would have staggered Doctor Frankenstein for intricacy and skill in use and that Dianetic therapy contacts the data at source; the apparatus is necessary to keep from touching the source, for the instant the source is touched by therapy its power vanishes like yesterday's headlines. So let's have no *Gaslight*[3] plays about Dianetics, please; they'd be technically inaccurate.)

This is not as simple as electricity in that the switch cannot be turned off and on. So far as Dianetics is concerned, it can only be turned on. We have a rheostat,[4] then, which will not drop back but which, when pressed forward, releases more and more dynamic force into the individual and gives him more and more control over its use.

Man is intended to be a self-determined organism. That is to say that as long as he can make evaluations of

---

3. *Gaslight:* a play by Patrick Hamilton (later called *Angel Street*) in which a man tries to drive his wife insane.

4. rheostat: an electrical instrument used to control current by varying resistance.

his data without artificial compulsions or repressions (held-down sevens in an adding machine) he can operate to maximum efficiency. When man becomes exteriorly determined, which is to say compelled to do or repressed from doing without his own rational consent, he becomes a push-button animal. This push-button factor is so sharply defined that an auditor, in therapy, who discovers a key phrase in an engram (and does not release it) can use that phrase for a little while to make a patient cough or laugh or stop coughing or stop laughing at the auditor's will. In the case of the auditor, because he got the data at source—contacted the engram itself, which robbed it of some power—the push button will not last very long, certainly less than two or three hundred pushes. The whole pain-drive effort at handling human beings, and most of the data accumulated in the past by various schools, has been, unwittingly, this push-button material. If the engram is not touched at source it is good for endless use, its power never diminishing. Touched at source, however, the original recording has been reached and so it loses its power. The "handling of human beings" and what people have been calling, roughly, "psychology" have been actually push-button handling of a person's aberrational phrases and sounds. Children discover them in their parents and use them with a vengeance. The clerk discovers that his boss can't stand a full wastebasket and so always has one full. The bosun[5] on a ship finds out one of his sailors cringes every time he hears the phrase, "fancy pants" and so uses the words to intimidate the man. This is push-button warfare amongst aberrees. Wives may find that certain words make the husband wince or make him angry or make him refrain from doing something and so they use these "push buttons." And husbands find their

---

5. bosun: a ship's petty officer in charge of rigging, boats, anchors, etc.

wives' push buttons and keep them from buying clothes or using the car. This defensive and offensive dueling amongst aberrees is occasioned by push buttons reacting against push buttons. Whole populaces are handled by their push-button responses. Advertising learns about push buttons and uses them in such things as "body odor" or constipation. And in the entertainment field and the songwriting field push buttons are pushed in whole racks and batteries to produce aberrated responses. Pornography appeals to people who have pornographic push buttons. Corn-and-games[6] government appeals to people who have "care for me" push buttons and others. It might be said that there is no necessity to appeal to reason when there are so many push buttons around.

These same push buttons, because they are sevens held down by pain and emotion (false data forced into the computer by engrams—and every society has its own special patterns of engrams), also happen to drive people insane, make them ill and generally raise havoc. The only push button the clear has is whatever his own computer, evaluating on his experience which itself has been evaluated by the computer, tells him is survival conduct along his four dynamics. And so, being no marionette in the hands of careless or designing[7] people, he remains well and sane.

It is not true, however, that a clear is not emotional, that his reason is cold, and that he is a self-conscious puppet to his own computations. His computer works so rapidly and on so many levels with so many of his computations going on simultaneously but out of the sight of "I" (though "I" can examine any one of them he

---

6. corn-and-games: late in Roman history, the leaders of the Roman government and commerce gave away free food and staged free games (circuses) for the populace of Rome.

7. designing: crafty, conniving.

chooses) that his *inversion* or acute awareness of self is minimal. *Inversion* is the condition of the aberree whose poor computer is wrestling with heavy imponderables and held-down sevens in his engrams such as "I must do it. I just have to do it. But no, I'd better change my mind."

The computational difference between the clear and the aberree is very wide. But there is a much grander difference: life force. The dynamics have, evidently, so much potential force. This force manifests itself as tenacity to life, persistence in endeavor, vigor of thought and act and ability to experience pleasure. The dynamics in a man's cells may be no stronger than those in a cat's cells. But the dynamics in the whole man are easily greater than those in any other animal. Assign this as one will, the man is basically *more alive* in that he has a more volatile response. By *more alive* is meant that his sentient, emotional urge to live is greater than those found in other life forms. If this were not true, he would not now command the other kingdoms. Regardless of what a shark or a beaver does when threatened with final extinction, the shark and the beaver get short shrift when they encounter the dynamics of man: the shark gets worn as leather or eaten as vitamins and the beaver decks[8] a lady's back.

The fundamental aspect of this is seen in a single reaction. Animals are content to survive in their environments and seek to adjust themselves to those environments. That very dangerous animal—or god—man has a slightly different idea. Ancient schools were fond of telling the poor demented aberree that he *must* face reality. This was optimum conduct: facing reality. Only it isn't man's optimum conduct. Just as these schools

---

8. deck: to decorate, to dress up.

made the fundamental error of supposing that the aber-ree was *unwilling* to face his environment when he was actually, because of engrams, *unable* to face it, they supposed that the mere facing of reality would lead to sanity. Perhaps it does, but it does not lead to a victory of man over the elements and other forms. Man has something more: some people call it creative imagination, some call it this or some call it that; but whatever it is called, it adds up to the interesting fact that man is not content merely to "face reality" as most other life forms are. *Man makes reality face him.* Propaganda about "the necessity of facing reality," like propaganda to the effect that a man could be driven mad by a "childhood delusion" (whatever that is), does not face the reality that where the beaver down his ages of evolution built mud dams and keeps on building mud dams, man graduates in half a century from a stone and wood dam to make a mill wheel pond to structures like Grand Coulee Dam,[9] and changes the whole and entire aspect of a respectable portion of nature's real estate from a desert to productive soil, from a flow of water to lightning bolts. It may not be as poetic as Rousseau desired, it may not be as pretty as some "nature lover" would desire, but it's a new reality. Two thousand years ago the Chinese built a wall which would have been visible from the moon had anybody been up there to look; three thousand years ago he had North Africa green and fertile; ten thousand years ago he was engaged upon some other project; but always he has been shaping things up pretty well to suit man.

There's an extra quality at work or perhaps just more of it, so much more of it that it looks like a new thing entirely.

---

9. Grand Coulee Dam: a large, concrete dam located on the Columbia River in central Washington.

Now, all this is not any great digression from therapy; it is stated here as an aspect of life force. Where the individual finds himself "possessed of less and less life force," he is losing some of the free units somewhere. And the free units of this life force, in a society or an individual, are the extra surge that is needed to tame North Africa, divide an atom or reach the stars.

The mechanical theory here—and recall it is but theory and Dianetics can stand without it—is that there are so many units of force per individual. These units may be held in common by a group and may build to higher and higher numbers as "enthusiasm" increases; but for our purposes, we can consider that man, as an individual or a society—both are organisms—has a ready number to hand for use in any given hour or day. He may manufacture these life units as required and he may simply have a given supply: that is beside the point. What is to the point is that he can be considered, at any hour or day, as just so much *alive*. Consider this as his dynamic potential as we can see on our descriptic earlier.

What happens, then, to this dynamic potential in the aberree? He has a large quantity of engrams in his bank. We know that these engrams *can* sleep for his entire life without being "keyed in," and we know that any or all of them can be keyed in and thereafter wait for restimulators in the environment to set them into action. We know that his necessity level can suddenly rise and surmount all these keyed-in engrams, and we know that a high survival activity can bring him such a chance of pleasure that the engrams can stay unrestimulated, though keyed in. And we can suppose that these engrams, from one period of life to another, can actually key out again and stay out because of some vast change of environment or survival chances.

The usual case, however, is that a few engrams stay

keyed in continually and are restimulated rather chronically by the environment of the individual, and that if he changes environment the old may key out but eventually new ones will key in.

Most aberrees are in a state of chronic restimulation which, on the average, starts the spiral dwindling down rather rapidly.

As this pertains to life force, the mechanical action of an engram, on being keyed in, is to capture so many of these units of life force. Sudden and sweeping restimulation of the engram permits it to capture a great many more units of life force. In the average case, every restimulation captures a greater residue of life force and holds it. When enthusiasm or impetus aligns the purpose of the individual toward a true survival goal (as opposed to a pseudogoal in the engrams) he recaptures some of these units. But the spiral is dwindling: he cannot capture back, except in very unusual circumstances, as many as he has lost into the engram bank.

Thus it can be said, for purposes of this theory of life force action, that more and more life force units out of an individual's supply are captured and held in the engram bank. Here they are perverted in use to counterfeit themselves as dynamic (as in the manic and the high euphoria case) and force action upon the somatic and analytical mind. In this engram bank, the life force units are not available as free feeling or for free action but are used against the individual from within.

An observation here tends to demonstrate this action: the more restimulated an aberree is, the less free feeling he may possess. If caught in a manic (highly complimentary prosurvival engram), his life force is channeling straight through the engram and his behavior, no matter how enthusiastic or euphoric, is actually very aberrated: if he has this much life force to be so channeled, then he can be shown to have even more life force, sentiently directed, when clear. (This has been done.)

We have demonstrated the parasitic quality of the "demon circuits" which use pieces of the analytical mind and its processes. This parasitic quality is common to engrams in other ways. If a man has, arbitrarily, 1,000 units of life force, he has an ability to channel them, when clear, into highly zestful existence: in a manic state, with a prosurvival engram in full restimulation, the life force is directed through an aberrated command and gives him, let us say, 500 units of pseudodynamic thrust.

In other words, the power is out of the same battery: such an engram has, at best, less power than the whole organism, cleared, would have. (This aspect of the manic or superpersonality neurotic has misled some of the old schools of mental healing into the thoroughly aberrated and poorly observed belief that insanities alone were responsible for man's ability to survive, a concept which can be disproven in the laboratory simply by clearing one of these manics or any other aberree.)

The engram uses the same current but perverts it, just as it uses the same analytical mind but usurps it. Not only does the engram have no life of its own, but it is wasteful, as are so many parasites, of the life force of the host. It is thoroughly inefficient. If a comparable device were fitted into an electronic circuit, it would merely lead off and make "unalterable" some of the functions of the equipment which should be left variable and would, in addition, consume, simply by lengthened leads and bad condensers[10] and tubes, power supply vital to the machine.

In the human mind, the engram assumes its most forceful "assist" aspect in the manic, channeling and

---

10. condenser: a device storing a charge of electricity.

commanding the organism into some activity of wild violence and monomanic[11] concentration. The "super-salesman," the violently buoyant[12] "glad-hander,"[13] the fanatical and apparently unkillable religious zealot are classifiable as manics. The abundance of "power" in these people, even when it is as grim as Torquemada's[14] or as destructive as Genghis Khan's, is an object of admiration in many quarters. The manic, as will be later covered, is a "prosurvival," "assist" command in an engram which yet fixes the individual on some certain course. But an engram is capable only of as much "power" as is present in the host, just as it is capable of tying up only as much analyzer as is present.

Let us take a forceful manic who is displaying and functioning on 500 arbitrary units of life force. Let us assume that the entire being is possessed of 1,000 arbitrary units of life force. Suppose we have here an Alexander.[15] The dynamics of the average person are unassisted by manics in most cases but are dispersed as a stream of electrons might be dispersed by a block before them. Here are scattered activity, scattered thoughts, uncomputable problems, lack of alignment. In such a person, with 1,000 units present, 950 of those units could be so captured in the engram banks and yet so thoroughly counteractive that the person displays a functioning capacity of only 50 units. In the case of

---

11. monomanic: one who suffers from an obsession with one idea or interest.

12. buoyant: lighthearted, cheerful.

13. glad-hand: a hearty welcome, especially when insincere.

14. Torquemada, Tomás de: (1420?–98) Spanish Dominican monk. Organized the Inquisition in Spain, became notorious for the severity of his judgments and the cruelty of his punishments.

15. Alexander: Alexander III, known as Alexander the Great: (356–323 B.C.) king of Macedonia (ancient kingdom located in what is now Greece and Yugoslavia).

Alexander, it could be assumed, the manic must have been an alignment in a general direction of his own basic purposes. His *basic purpose* is a strong regulator: the manic happens to align with it: a person of great ability and personal prowess becomes possessed of 500 units *via* a manic engram, believes he is a god and goes out and conquers the known world. He was educated to believe he was a god, his manic engram said he was a god and had a holder in it. Alexander conquered the world and died at thirty-three. He could hold in his manic only so long as it could be obeyed: when it could no longer be obeyed, it changed his valence, became no more a manic and drove him, with pain, into dispersed activities. The engram, received from his mother, Olympias, can almost be read even at this late date. It must have said he would be a joyous god who would conquer all the world and must keep on conquering, that he must always strive to rise higher and higher. It was probably a ritual chant of some sort from his mother, who was a high priestess of Lesbos[16] and who must have received some injury just before the ritual. She hated her husband, Philip.[17] A son who would conquer all was the answer. Alexander may well have had fifty or a hundred such "assist" engrams, the violent praying of a woman aberrated enough to murder. Thus, he could be assumed to have conquered until he could no longer stretch a line of supply for conquering, at which time he, of course, would no longer be able to obey the engram and its force of pain would turn on him. The engrams dictated attack *to conquer,* and they enforced the command with pain:

16. Lesbos: Greek island in the Aegean Sea. The word *lesbian* derives from the ancient Greek name of this island, from the eroticism and homosexuality attributed to Sappho (ancient Greek poetess) and her followers.

17. Philip: Philip II: (382–336 B.C.) king of Macedonia, father of Alexander.

313

once *conquering* could no longer be accomplished, the pain attacked Alexander. He realized one day he was dying: within the week he was dead, and at the height of his power. Such, on a very large scale, is a manic phrase in an engram at work.

Now let us suppose that Alexander, with only education to turn him against his father, with only prayers to ask him to conquer the world, not engrams, had been cleared. Answer: given a sufficient and rational reason, he would most certainly have been able to conquer the world and at eighty might well have been alive to enjoy it. How can we assume this?

The manic with 500 units of directed purpose has been cleared. He now has 1,000 units of *sentiently* directed purpose. He is exactly twice as forceful as he was when he was in a forceful manic and his basic purpose may be similar but now can be realized and will not turn on him the moment he has reached a goal or failed.

This is clinical, the theory behind life force. It was formulated in an effort to explain observed phenomena. The theory may be wrong, the observed data is not. But the theory must be somewhere close to right because with it could be predicted considerable phenomena which had not been known to exist before: in other words, it is a profitable theory. It followed after Dianetics was well formulated, for a strange fact, vital to the therapist, turned up: *the preclear advanced in therapy in exact ratio to the amount of emotional charge released from his reactive bank.*

The purpose and persistency of the aberree was hindered in ratio to the amount of emotional charge within his engram bank. His recovery of survival potential increased in ratio to the amount of energy freed from the engram bank. His health increased in ratio to the amount of energy freed from the engram bank.

The engrams which contained the greatest discharge were those which centered around loss of imagined survival factors.

Hence, this theory of life force was formulated. Any manic, cleared, seemed to demonstrate far more actual power and energy than before he was cleared. And any "normal," cleared, increased in accessible life force units to compare with any manic cleared.

Undoubtedly further work and observation will refine this theory. At the present moment, however, it serves. It is one of those "scientific theories" thrown in to explain an operation or a long series of observations. In this case, it happens to be squarely aligned with the basic tenets of Dianetics, for it predicts data which can then be found and does not throw out former data predicted by the basic mathematics and philosophy of Dianetics.

Here we are speaking, actually, not of this slippery term, *emotion,* but, we believe, life force. This life force is considerably enhanced by success and pleasure in general and is, according to this theory, augmented, in terms of arbitrary units, by pleasure. In other words, pleasure is a thing which recharges the batteries or permits them to be recharged; and in a clear, far from leading to softness, leads to renewed activity since indolence is engramic.

Pleasure is a vitally important factor: creative and constructive endeavor, the overcoming of not unknowable obstacles toward some goal, the contemplation of past goals reached: all combine to recharge life force. The person, for instance, who has been an enormous success and then loses that success and so becomes ill is following no rational cycle but an engramic command cycle. In a way, he has disobeyed an engramic command and having disobeyed, suffers pain. The "child wonder" who early "burns out" is actually, via therapy, about as burned out as a banked furnace. Any "child wonder" is a forced affair: think of the dreams Mama must have poured through his engrams. She's hurt: "Oh, I'll never forgive myself! If I have ruined my child, I will never forgive myself. My child, that's to be the world's greatest violinist!" or "Oh, you brute! You have struck me! You have injured our child. I'll show you. I'll make him the greatest child pianist in all Brooklyn! He's to be a beautiful child, a wonder child! And you've struck him, you brute. Oh, I am going to sit right here until you go away!" (Actual engrams.) The last computes that the way to get even with Papa is to be the greatest pianist in all Brooklyn. The child is a great success—musical ear, practice and great "purpose." He gets this engram restimulated constantly by his mother. But then, one day he loses a contest, he knows suddenly he is no longer a child, that he has failed. His purpose wavers. He gets headaches (Papa's blow) and is at last "neurotic" and "burned out." Cleared, he went back to being a pianist, not as an "adjusted" person but one of the best-paid concert pianists in Hollywood. Music aligned with basic purpose.

Again, in another manic example, a patient who had been some time in therapy—not the first to do this by far—raved that he had been "turned on" by Dianetics. He was walking about a foot off the earth, chest punched out and so forth. His glasses suddenly would not fit him; his eyes were too good. He was a beaming, powerful case of euphoria. Artificial restimulation had touched a manic engram, had brought it into key for the first time in his life. He felt wonderful. The auditor knew that he was due for a complete comedown within thirty-six hours to three days (the usual time) because an artificial restimulation, by therapy, had tapped the engram. It happened that his grandmother had told her daughter that she must not abort the child because someday it might become a "fine upstanding man or beautiful woman." He was upstanding all right: it almost strained his back muscles. Another glance at the engram in therapy and the manic phase was gone.

This manic, then, as in the case of the boy wonder, can be assumed to have gathered up available life force and suddenly channeled it along basic purpose lines, making a high level of concentration of life force. In the case of the pianist, his cleared force was well above the manic force. In the other case, currently in process, a level has been reached which is approaching the former level and will surpass it by far.

In the same way, an enthusiasm for a project will channel life force along some purpose line and necessity will suddenly rob back from engrams enough power to carry an individual far, although he has no active manics whatever.

Now we come to the heart of this matter: the pro-survival engram. It is pseudosurvival like all engramic "assists," a mirage which dissolves and leaves burning sands.

Formerly, we spoke mainly of contrasurvival engrams. These lie across the dynamics of the individual and his basic purpose.[18]

The contrasurvival engram is to the dynamics like a log jam which dams a necessary river. The dynamic is blocked in some degree. Any blockage to any one of the

_____

18. It happens that there is an additional specialization of the dynamics in everyone, a sort of built-in personal dynamic. It is a clinical fact that the basic purpose is apparently known to the individual before he is two years of age: talent and inherent personality and basic purpose go together as a package. They seem to be part of the genetic pattern. Anyone, by Dianetic reliving, can be sent to the age of two years and consulted about his purpose in life, and he will come forth with a very specific desire as to what he wishes to accomplish in life (and two-year-old activity as reviewed confirmed it). It will be discovered that his later life has followed this general pattern wherever he succeeded. Of fifteen persons examined, the basic purpose was found formed at two years of age, and when cleared these persons used and pursued that basic purpose.

four dynamics (or any section of that spectrum) causes a dispersal of the flow. It does not make less dynamic, particularly, but it does misdirect it in the same order that the river, blocked in its natural flow, might become five streams going in various directions or flood a fertile pasture it should merely have watered.

The prosurvival engram alleges to assist (but does not actually assist) the dynamic on its way. It pretends it *is* the dynamic. In the analogy of the river, the prosurvival engram would be a canal which took the river's force and sent it off in some unintended direction. The prosurvival engram is not a manic; it can and does contain at times manic phrases.

A contrasurvival engram says, "He's worthless, damn him, let's kill him."

The prosurvival engram says, "I am saving him." If it added, "He is a darling and a very wonder with the ladies," it would then be a prosurvival *with* a manic.

In terms of the descriptic which defines the survival dynamic and the suppressor earlier in this book, the contrasurvival engram would be part of the suppressor (an aberrated part) and the prosurvival engram would be part of the dynamic thrust (an aberrated part).

Neither one of these things is actually a sentient and computable portion of survival dynamic or suppressor.

The engram (delirium from illness, perhaps) which says, "I will stay with you, darling, so long as you are sick" is an apparent but wholly shadow-stuff part of the survival dynamic. But the reactive mind has no sense of time when restimulated, and this engram, keyed in and constantly restimulated by some concept in it such as an odor or a person's voice who may or may not be the original person, demands that the person who has it be ill just as he was ill when it was said. This way, according to our moron, the reactive mind, lies survival: "I had someone taking care of me when I was ill. I need someone to take care of me. I must be ill." Here is the basic pattern of all sympathy engrams. Here is the basic pattern of the engram which will contain the chronic psychosomatic illness in any patient. The variety is, of course, very large but all insist that the individual who has them be ill in order to survive.

The suppressor-type engram, always contrasurvival, can be cut into restimulation in exactly the same way as the prosurvival engram. An engram is an engram and all the mechanics are the same. The fact that the analytical mind cannot time the engram can make any engram seem omnipresent.[19] Time can "heal" the experiences of the analytical mind, perhaps, but not the reactive mind, which has no time; a fact which makes time not the great healer but the great charlatan.[20] There may be no actuality at all in this suppressor data. It is false data. Such engrams let an individual, for instance, see a butterfly and then tell him it is dangerous: he then comes to detest spring because that is the time he sees butterflies. This engram may say, "You're all against me. You're against everything I do," which was actually Mama making a stand against her husband and mother-in-law. It contains a concept, a recording of the sound of a sewing machine as well. The individual possessing this engram hears a sewing machine (if this engram has at some time been keyed in) at a moment when he is weary and dull and, looking toward the machine (he never identifies the actual sound: these engrams protect themselves), sees his wife. She is the *associative restimulator,* something his analytical mind, told to scent danger, picks up as the cause. So he searches around and finds something he is angry about (something almost "rational") and begins

---

19. omnipresent: present everywhere at the same time, widely or constantly met with.

20. charlatan: a person who falsely claims to be an expert.

to tell her she is against him. Or it can be an engram of such low emotional tone that it is an apathy, and so he sits down and weeps and moans that she is against him. If, during "unconsciousness" at birth, the doctor said he'd have to spank him, the individual possessing this engram howls and gets headaches when he is spanked and, when grown, spanks his children as the strongest suppressor he can think of.

There is a difference, then, between the pro- and contra-engrams, particularly the real sympathy pro-engram and the contra-engram. And it is a difference, even if we have been long on the road in this chapter, which is of vital interest to the auditor.

All the real reluctance he will see in preclears during therapy will come from these sympathy prosurvival engrams. These add up into some very weird computations. They tell the patient that he had better not "get rid of it" and so the patient struggles to retain his engrams. Such an engram is very common. A typical case is Mama pushing off Papa, who insists he cannot afford a child. The struggle injures the child and in the "unconsciousness" he receives, of course, an engram: Mama is refusing to get rid of it, Mama is on baby's side, therefore baby had better do exactly as Mama says and "not get rid of it." This aligns with purpose, the deepest purpose, to survive. If he gets rid of his engrams, he will die because getting rid of it means death, for Mama said she would die if she got rid of it. Further, on up through life, Mama may have the nasty habit of telling him when he is ill that she will "take care of her baby and protect him from his father," and this makes a new force in the old computation.

Thus we come to the *ally computation*. This will be the chief and number one struggle of the auditor, the thing which will most elusively resist him, the thing which lies down close to the core of a person.

The *ally computation* is severe enough that an auditor once said that a man is not victimized by his enemies, he is murdered by his friends. Engramically speaking, that is quite true.

The only aberration and psychosomatic ill the patient will continually hold to is a prosurvival engram which is part of an ally computation. That could be written fifty times here without being stressed enough. It is most important, it is the first thing which the auditor is going to buck when he enters a case, the first thing he must discharge if he wishes therapy to go swiftly. He may have to touch and reduce many contrasurvival engrams, for they come swiftly enough when called, before he can even get an idea of what the ally computation is. But when he gets an ally computation he had better run it out and discharge all its emotion or the case will hang fire.

The ally computation is the reactive mind level moronism that survival depends on Grandma or Aunt Sue or some serving maid thirty years dead. The attendants of the individual when he was ill, the people who begged his pregnant mother to stop trying to abort him, or fed him or otherwise tried to keep him from being hurt: these are the allies.

The reactive mind operates wholly on two-valued logic. Things are life or they are death, they are right or they are wrong, just as the engram wording states. And the personnel of engrams are friends or enemies. The friends, the allies, mean life! The enemies mean death! There is no middle ground. Any restimulator or associated restimulator for the prosurvival engram means life: and any restimulator or associated restimulator for a contrasurvival engram means death!

The auditor, of course, may be a really restimulative person (one who is a pseudofather, a pseudolover of Mother before birth, etc.) but he is always an associative restimulator, the person who may take away these terribly, horribly vital things, the prosurvival engrams. The contrasurvival engrams outbalance this factor and, of course, the analytical mind of the preclear is always all for the auditor and the therapy.

The trouble comes when the analytical mind is shut down by restimulation and the auditor is seeking the ally computation. Then the preclear's reactive mind dodges and avoids.

The ally computation, however, is simple to trace. And it is very vital to trace it, for this computation may contain the bulk of all the emotional discharge of the case. Freeing the complete ally computation wholly before basic-basic is reached is wholly impossible. But as much life force as possible must be restored to the preclear to make the case work well.

For the ally computation, above all things, encysts the life force of the individual. Here is caught and held the *free feeling,* the very heartbeat of life itself. A preclear is only placed in apathy by ally computations. The body can be almost dead in the presence of antagonism and still rally and fight. But it cannot fight its friends. The law of affinity has been aberrated into an entrance into the reactive engram bank. And that law, even when twisted with the murky shadows of unreason in the reactive mind, still works. It is a good law. It is too good when the auditor is trying to find and reduce engrams which are making the preclear ache with arthritis or bleed internally with stomach ulcers. Why can't he "get rid of" his arthritis? Mama said, when she gracefully fell over a pig, "Oh, I can't get up! Oh, my poor, poor baby. Oh, my baby! I wonder if I hurt my poor, poor baby. Oh, I hope my baby is still alive! Please, God, let him live. Please, God, let me keep my baby. Please!" Only the God to which she prayed was the reactive mind, which makes one of its idiot computations on the basis of everything is equal to everything. A holder, a prayer for life, a thoroughly bruised baby's spine, Mama's sympathy, a pig grunt, a prayer to God: all these things are equal to the reactive mind and so we have a fine case of arthritis, particularly since our patient sought "survival" by marrying a girl with a voice just like Mama's sounded when he was in the womb. Ask him to get rid of his arthritis? The reactive mind says "NO!" Arthritis is a baby is a pig grunt is a prayer to God is wife's sympathy is being poor is Mama's voice and all these things are desirable. He's kept himself poor and he's kept his arthritis and he married a wife who would make a harlot[21] blush and this is prosurvival: wonderful stuff, survival, when the reactive mind computes it! And in the case of the ulcers, here was baby poked full of holes (Mama is having a terrible time trying to abort him so she can pretend a miscarriage, and she uses assorted household instruments thrust into the cervix[22] to do it) and some of the holes are through and through this baby's abdomen and stomach: he will live because he is surrounded by protein and has a food supply and because the sac is like one of these puncture-proof inner tubes that seals up every hole. (Nature has been smart about attempted abortion for a long, long time.) It so happens that Mama in this case was not a monologuist, although most of Mama's activity on this line is a dramatization and has conversation with it; but it also so happens that Grandma lives next door and she comes over unexpectedly, shortly after the latest effort to make baby meet oblivion. Grandma may have been an attempted abortionist in her day but now she is old and highly

---

21. harlot: a prostitute.

22. cervix: a neck-shaped, anatomical structure, as the narrow outer end of the uterus.

moral and besides, this baby is not giving her any morning sickness; she therefore finds much to censure[23] when she sees a bloody orangewood stick in the bathroom. Baby is still "unconscious." Grandma berates Mama: "Any daughter of mine who would do such a horrible thing should be punished by the vengeance of God," (the principle of, "don't do as I do, do as I say," for who gave Mama this dramatization in the first place?) "and driven through the streets. Your baby has a perfect right to live: if you don't think you can take care of him, *I* certainly will. Now you go right on through with your pregnancy, Eloisia, and when that baby is born, if you don't want him, you bring him to me! The idea of trying to hurt that poor thing!" And so, when our bleeding ulcer case gets born, there is Grandma and there is security and safety. Grandma is here the ally (and she can become an ally in a thousand different ways, any of them based on the principle that she talks sympathetically to baby when he is out like a flounder, and fights Mama in his favor when he is "unconscious"), and when he grows to boyhood he can be found placing a large dependency on Grandma, much to the parental wonder (for *they* never did anything to little Roger, not *they*). And Roger will, when Grandma is dead, develop bleeding ulcers to get her back.

Whoever is a friend is to be clasped to the bosom with bonds of steel, says this great genius, the reactive mind, even though it kills the organism.

The ally computation is a little more than the mere idiot calculation that anyone who is a friend can be kept a friend only by approximating the conditions wherein the friendship was realized. It is a computation on the basis that one can only be safe in the vicinity of certain

---

23. censure: to criticize severely.

people and that one can only be in the vicinity of certain people by being sick or crazy or poor and generally disabled.

Show an auditor a child who was easily frightened by punishment, who was not at ease around home and who had allies who seemed more important to him than the parents (grandparents, aunts, boarders, doctors, nurses, etc.) and who was sickly, and the auditor can usually spring into view an attempted abortion background because, more often than not, it is there. Show an auditor a child who showed enormous attachment for one parent and detestation for the other and the auditor can bring out a background wherein one person wanted to get rid of or hurt the child and the other parent did not.

The ally computation, then, is important. And it is also very secret. Trying to get the real allies in a case is often a great struggle. It may be that a patient had eight or ten of these allies in some cases and tried desperately to hold to them, and when he could not, searched and found mates and friends who were approximations of his allies. A wife, around whom A is continually ill but whom he will not leave under any circumstances, is usually a pseudoally, which is to say she approximates some mannerism of the actual ally, has a similar voice or even a similar first name. B, who will not leave a job and yet who is working far below his ability level in life, may be there because his boss is a pseudoally; further, he may be working at this job because an ally had a similar station in life and he is being the ally.

Anything which can so far corrupt a person's life is naturally going to be difficult to some degree in therapy, for when he is asked to get rid of his ally computation, it is as likely that he will give any clue to it as it is that he would have spit in his ally's face.

These prosurvival engrams containing the ally computation can be described as those which contain personnel who defended the patient's existence in moments when the patient conceived that his existence was under attack. This need not be an actual, rational defense: it may only be that the content of the engram seems to indicate it; but it can safely be assumed that the worst ally computations are those when the life of the patient was defended against attackers by the ally. Most ally computations have their genesis in the prenatal area.

The ally computation is sought as the first action in any case and new ally computations are sought throughout a case.

These sympathy prosurvival engrams, which make up the ally computations, vary only in intensity from the standard prosurvival engram. A standard prosurvival engram is bad only because someone has expressed friendship for the patient or another person when he was "unconscious": it is difficult to discover and clear even when it actually has been entirely misread—which is to say that the prosurvival content was intended for another person than the patient but is only misconstrued by the patient. If the patient is "unconscious" and somebody says "he is a good guy," actually meaning another person entirely, the egocentric[24] reactive mind takes the phrase to have been meant for oneself. In the sympathy prosurvival engram (the ally computation is composed only of these) there is an actual defense of the person from danger by some ally: this can vary from a dramatic scene wherein somebody has been bent on killing the patient and the ally has arrived, like the cavalry, in the nick of time, to the incident wherein the patient was simply saved (or assumed he was being saved) from destruction such as drowning, being run over, etc. And

---

24. egocentric: self-centered.

the sympathy prosurvival engram is only as good as its content in words, for it does not rationalize the action. Engrams have been discovered where the patient was actually being murdered but the content was such that he was convinced he was being saved: such a case would include what auditors call a "mutual AA"—a father and mother together attempting an abortion, *AA* meaning "attempted abortion"—wherein Mama was in utter agreement and disposed herself for the operation but became frightened and began to scream about "her precious baby" in an effort to save herself from being injured: patients with this sort of sympathy prosurvival engram can get pretty confused about Mother.

The insidious[25] aspects of the sympathy prosurvival engrams are several: (1) They are aligned with the fundamental dynamic of survival in the most literal sense and are therefore aligned with the purpose of the individual; (2) they are like cysts round which contrasurvival engrams serve as the outer shell; (3) they most sharply affect the health of the individual and are always the basic factor beneath the psychosomatic illness which the individual displays; (4) they cause the reactive mind (but not the analytical mind) to resist therapy; and (5) they are the largest drain upon the life force units.

In (3) above, the prosurvival sympathy engram does more than just carry forward the injury which becomes the psychosomatic illness. Any engram is a bundle of data which includes not only all perceptics and speech present but also metering for emotion and state of physical being. The last, the state of physical being, would be serious enough. This metering says that *structure* was so and such at the moment this sympathy prosurvival engram was received. In the case of an embryo engram,

---

25. insidious: spreading or developing or acting inconspicuously but with harmful effect.

then, the reactive mind, in forcing the engram back into action, may also force the structural pattern back upon the body: this occasionally results in retarded development, embryo-like skin, embryo-type back curvature, and so forth. The glands themselves, being physical organs, are also sometimes so suppressed in the reactive mind's effort to approximate all conditions. The underdeveloped gonads,[26] the sublevel thyroid, the wasted limb: all these things often come from sympathy prosurvival engrams. This is so observably the case that when an individual is being cleared, growth process begins to bring the body up to genetic blueprint even before the case is completed: the change which takes place in the physical being of the patient is sometimes so remarkable and so marked that it is far more startling than the mere disappearance of a catalogue of psychosomatic ills such as coronary, ulcers, arthritis, allergies, and so on.

It would be supposed that anything powerful enough to twist the physical blueprint and keep the body from developing or make it keep on growing where it should have stopped would resist any therapy. This is true only in a most limited sense. Once one is aware of what suppresses a case, one can go about vanquishing the suppressors, because a prosurvival engram, unlike a contrasurvival engram, has an Achilles' heel.

The most workable answer now known to Dianetics lies in the principle of life force units and a technique for throwing them back into circulation. The prosurvival engram collects and holds such units, according to this theory, and collapses when its power to hold units is broken.

Entering a case, then, where one has a chronic psychosomatic illness (and what case doesn't have, even

---

26. gonad: a bodily organ that produces gametes (mature sperm or eggs capable of participating in fertilization).

though it is as slight as an occasional fit of sneezing or hiccoughs), the auditor first scouts it, going through a returning routine to find out how early he can get for material, how the state of the sonic recall is, how occluded is the youth of the person and so forth. When he has made this survey, he begins to make his computation on the case: first, was the child happy with both Father and Mother, and if not, where was the child happiest? (There will be where the allies live.) Was either parent an unreasonably powerful factor in shaping the thinking powers of the child? Here again may be an ally, even if a poor one. Did the patient have grandparents or other relatives; how did he feel toward them? All this data will be more or less occluded and warped by demon circuits and is about as reliable as the data this patient will inevitably try to get from "loopy" parents or relatives, who not only do not know what happened to him but might be most anxious not to have anything discovered.

What really did happen? Don't let patients ask relatives or parents anything if you can help it, for these are restimulators in the extreme and never have any data you can use; the patient is just trying to use them as bypass circuits to avoid the pain of recalling things himself. When the case is finished he will no longer want to hound these people, and if you want a check for research reasons, get one of the relatives to put him through therapy.

The auditor now has some slight idea of who the allies may be. And here comes the Achilles' heel of the ally computation:

Any ally computation may have included the loss of the ally. And the *loss of the ally* may be the trigger which will start chain fission. For what we are going to try to do is blow off or discharge as many life force units as possible from the reactive engram bank and weaken it. Every charge we get from the bank will reinforce the ability of the patient to carry on in existence and will aid his analytical mind to get into the engram bank. Hence, discharging these frozen units is a vital and important part of therapy and the condition of the case will improve in direct ratio to the number of these units so discharged.

Consider these life units as free life energy: an engram capturing them can set itself up, for all intent, as a life force. It is then an entity and only then. The demon circuits, the valence walls[27] (which compartment the analyzer, so to speak, and bring about multivalence), the force and power of the engram itself are all dependent, according to theory and as observed in practice, upon usurped life units.

To free these units is the primary task of therapy; to relieve pain from the engrams is the secondary task; to make the patient comfortable during therapy does not even rank, though there is no need he should be uncomfortable. The dual character of therapy, then, is actually two sections of the same thing: relieving engrams. There is this dual nature in engrams, however, that they have painful emotion (where that means usurped life force) and physical pain (where that means pain of injury, illness, etc.).

To get as early as possible as fast as possible and find basic-basic is the direction and intent of therapy in its first stages: to accomplish this (when it cannot be done immediately merely by returning and finding basic-basic which can and always should be tried) one relieves the case and robs the engram bank by releasing life units (painful emotion captured them) from the ally computations.

---

27. valence wall: a sort of protective mechanism by which the charge of the case is compartmented to permit the individual to work at least some of the time.

In brief, the entire intent and act of therapy is to find the earliest engram and erase it and then proceed to erase all other engrams as engrams so they can no longer be discovered (they refile in the standard bank but it takes a genius to find them there and a search of hours and hours: hence, to the auditor they can be said to have "erased," for they are no longer engrams and are now experience). The first, last and only job of the auditor is to find the earliest engrams available and erase them. That cannot be said too often or too strongly.

The various ways to accomplish this are the techniques and arts of therapy. Anything which brings about this erasure of engrams in place and their refiling as experience is useful and legitimate *whatever it includes*. An engineer intends to remove a mountain which is in the way of a river: his intent and all his effort is directed toward moving that mountain. The ways and means employed by him to move that mountain—by steam shovel, hydraulic rams or dynamite—are the art and techniques applied to do the job.

There are three degrees of knowledge in our task: (1) In Dianetics, we know the goal: we know the results which come about when that goal is attained; (2) we know the character of the obstructions between us and the goal, but of the *exact character* of the obstruction we can never learn too much; (3) the art and technique of removing the obstruction between us and the goal are legitimate only by the test of whether or not they remove the obstruction.

The method of attack on the problem can always be improved by learning more about the character of the factors in the problem, and by learning new arts and techniques which can be applied to the problem, and by studying to improve our skill in practicing existing arts and techniques. The currently existing art and technique is not to be considered optimum merely because it does the job. The time and ease of work could be shortened by new techniques or advancing skills for old techniques.

All this is interjected so that Dianetics, unlike Aristotelian logic and natural history, will be recognized as an advancing, changing science. It is interjected at this place because no auditor should just sit back with this routine and never try to improve the routine.

Very well. This is the routine. *It works* but it can never be made to work too quickly or too well.

1. Place the patient in reverie and scout into the prenatal area to see if engrams are available for lifting without further work. If they are there and can be found, take the charge out of them and erase them if possible. Do not try to erase anything as remote from basic-basic as birth unless the file clerk insists on presenting birth. In other words, get the subject into the prenatal area and look for the earliest engrams. Do not ask for specific instances, particularly for something like birth; just take whatever is presented. If you can't get back early, take step 2.

2. Scout the patient's life while he is in reverie (do this in any event sooner or later if the case slows down but only if it slows down to a point where early engrams are either not reducing or are without any emotion). Establish in this scout whoever may have been depended upon by the patient, and be suspicious always that he has not told you the really important allies, but do not tell him you are suspicious.

3. Find out when the patient lost any ally through death or departure. Approach this moment and one way or another, by getting earlier material and this incident or getting just this incident, discharge the sorrow of loss out of the incidents. Treat any incident in which the ally departs or the patient is separated from the ally as an engram and erase it accordingly or run it until it has no "charge" of sorrow on it. If the "charge" holds, suspect

332

an early moment of sorrow about this ally and find that and treat it as an engram.

4. First, last and always, the job is to get basic-basic and then ever afterwards the currently existing earliest moment of pain or sorrow, and to erase every incident as it is advanced by the file clerk or found by repeater technique.

5. Any incident that hangs fire always has a similar incident earlier, and the patient should be taken earlier for the prior incident when an engram will not "reduce" on recounting.

6. At any time the engrams start to become emotionless in tone, even though they reduce, suspect another ally computation and, early or late in the patient's life, get it and reduce it at least until the emotional discharge is gone. Do not get everything in a case restimulated by changing from an unreduced incident to something which looks more fruitful, but reduce everything in view before you go looking for a new sorrow charge.

7. It is better to reduce an emotionless early engram than it is to upset the case by hounding him for an ally computation when a cunning search fails to reveal one in sight. Erasing early emotionless engrams will eventually bring a new ally computation into sight if you occasionally look for it.

8. Consider that any holdup on a case, any unwillingness to cooperate, stems from ally computation.

9. Treat all demon circuits as things held in place by life force units absorbed into the bank and address the problem of demon circuits by releasing charges of sorrow.

10. Consider that loss by death or departure of an ally is identical with a death of some part of the patient and that the reduction of a death or departure of an ally will restore that much life back to the patient. And remember that great sorrow charges are not always

death or departure but merely may be a sudden reversal of stand by the ally.

Always keep in mind that that person who most nearly identifies himself with the person of the patient, such as a sympathetic mother or father or grandparent or relative or friend, is considered by the reactive mind to be a part of the person himself and that anything happening to this sympathetic character can be considered to have happened to the patient. In such a case, where an ally has been found to have died of cancer, you may occasionally find the patient to have a sore or scaly place where he supposed the ally's cancer to have been.

The reactive mind thinks in identities only. The sympathetic prosurvival engram identifies the patient with another individual. The death or loss (by departure or denial) of the other individual is therefore a reactive mind conviction that the patient has suffered some portion of death.

Emotional charges may be contained in any engram: the emotion communicates, in the same tone level, from the personnel around the "unconscious" person into his reactive mind. Anger goes into an engram as anger, apathy as apathy, shame as shame. Whatever people have felt emotionally around an "unconscious" person should be found in the engram which resulted from the incident. When the emotional tone of personnel in an engram is obviously angry or apathetic from the word content and yet the patient, recounting, does not feel it, there is something somewhere which has a *valence wall* between the patient and the emotional tone, and that valence wall is nearly always broken down by the discovery of an engram with a sorrow charge some time earlier or later in a patient's life.

The only legitimate reason for entering later portions of a person's life before the prenatal area has been well exhausted is to search for sorrow discharges occasioned by the death, loss or denial by an ally. And by "denial," we mean that the ally turned into an active enemy (real or imaginary) of the patient. The counterpart of the ally, the pseudoally, is a person whom the reactive mind has confused with the real ally. The death, loss or denial by a pseudoally can contain a sorrow charge.

According to theory, the only thing which can lock up life units is this emotion of loss. If some method existed of doing nothing but freeing all life units, the physical pain could be neglected.

A *release* is brought about, one way or another, by freeing as many life units as possible from periods of loss with minimal address to actual engrams.

The loss of an ally or pseudoally need contain no other physical pain or "unconsciousness" than the loss itself occasions. This is serious enough. It makes an engram.

Any person who is suddenly discovered to be occluded in a patient's life can, with some reliability, be considered an ally or pseudoally. If, either while *remembering* or *returning,* large sections of a patient's association with another person are missing, that person can be called an occluded person. It is a better guarantee of ally status if the occlusion surrounds the death of the person or a departure from or a denial by that person. It is possible for occlusion to take place, also, for punishment reasons; which is to say, the occluded person may also be an archenemy. In such a case, however, any memory present will concern the death or defeat or illness of the occluded person. Occlusion of a person's funeral in the memory of a patient would theoretically label that person an ally or pseudoally. Recollection of the funeral of a person but occlusion of pleasant association might tend to mean that the person was an enemy.

Such rules are tentative. But it is certain that any occlusion means that a person had a vast and unrevealed significance in a patient's life which should be explained.

It may be remarked at this point that the recovery of the patient will depend in large measure on the life units freed from his reactive bank. This is a discharge of sorrow and may be quite violent. The usual practice is to "forget" such things and the "sooner forgotten, the sooner healed." Unfortunately this does not work: it would be a happy thing if it did. Anything forgotten is a festering sore when it has despair connected with it. The auditor will find that every time he locates that archdenyer, "forget it," he will get the engram it suppressed; when he can't locate the engram and yet has found a somatic, a "forget it" or "don't think about it" or "can't remember it" or "don't remember it" or some other denyer will be sitting there in the context of the engram. Forgetting is such unhealthy business that when a thing has been "put out of mind," it has been put straight into the reactive engram bank and in there it can absorb life units. This "loopy" computation, that forgetting things makes them bearable, is incredible in view of the fact that the hypnotist, for instance, gets results with a positive suggestion when he puts one of these *denyers* on the end of it. That has been known now for a great many eons: it was one of the first things the author was taught when he studied Asiatic practices. From India it long ago filtered to Greece and Rome and it has come to us via Anton Mesmer;[28] it is a fundamental principle in several mystic arts; its mechanics were known even to the Sioux medicine man. Yet people at large, hitherto unguided about it, and perhaps because they lacked any real remedy, believed that the thing to do with sorrow

---

28. Mesmer, Franz Anton: (1734–1815) Austrian physician who developed the practice of mesmerism—hypnotism.

was to "forget it." Even Hippocrates[29] remarks that the whole of an operation is not finished until the patient has recounted the incident to all of his friends in turn, and while this is inadequate therapy, it has been, like the confessional, a part of popular knowledge for lo, these many ages; yet people persist in suppressing sorrow.

The auditor will many times in his activity be begged by a patient "not to talk to me about so-and-so's death." If he is foolish enough to heed this tearful plea when the patient is in reverie, then the auditor is actively blocking a release. *That* is the first incident he should get!

Perhaps it would be bad, without Dianetic technique, to approach such things; but with our art it is easy not only to enter the actual moment of the incident but to then recount it until the tears and wailings are but echoes in the case book. Treating that loss like an engram, recounting it until it is no longer painful emotionally, is to give back to the patient vitality he has not had since the incident took place. And if the incident does not ease on a dozen recountings, slide back down its sorrow track, just as you would with any other engram, and find earlier and earlier moments. A patient starting to discharge sorrow at the age of fifty may find himself, two hours later, down in the basic area recounting the primary moment of sorrow, at the moment when the lost ally first became an ally. If the auditor can get the whole chain on any one ally, exhausting sorrow from it from later to earlier, taking all the sorrow he can get from every incident and stripping the entire series of engrams of their charge, he may, in a few hours' work, rid the case of enough emotional charge to then begin an orderly erasure.

Please observe this difference: the Achilles' heel of

29. Hippocrates: (460?–370? B.C.) Greek physician, known as "the father of medicine."

the ally computation can be considered late on the chain of incidents which concern that ally, which is to say that we have a funnel here, upright in time, which can be entered late and followed early: the Achilles' heel of the contrasurvival engram chain is in the earliest incidents, exactly the reverse of the emotionally painful engrams.

To regain, out of the engram bank, life units so that enough free emotion is available to release or clear a case, start with late ally or pseudoally losses and work back earlier.

To release the physical pain of the individual from the engram bank, start early (as close to conception as you can get) and work through to late.

Physical pain in the contrasurvival chain can suppress painful emotion in the prosurvival chain.

Painful emotion in the prosurvival chain can suppress physical pain in the contrasurvival engrams.

If you were to draw a picture of the prenatal area of the reactive engram bank, it would appear somewhat as follows: a long line drawn horizontally, representing time, would have dark blots on it representing engrams; one end of the line would represent conception, the other end birth. Above this line would lie a dark area, like a heavy mist, extending from one end of the line to the other and dropping down almost to it. Above this dark mist would lie another horizontal line, the *apparent* time track along which the patient returns. The first long line is the actual time track; the mist is painful emotion; the uppermost dark line is what the patient mistakes and uses for his time track.

The painful emotion is, of course, occasionally tapped in the prenatal area itself, and the opportunity of dispersing it by so discovering prenatal emotional charges should never be overlooked by the auditor: indeed, once much of the later life painful emotion is discharged, a great deal of painful emotion can be found amongst the early engrams. The better part of this mist, and the first part the auditor often contacts, is in late life: although it originates, as charge, in late life, it can be said to lie on this prenatal area.

Moments of loss, the loss by death or departure of any of the patient's allies, and the loss of an ally because he turns against the patient, trap these emotional charges and intervene them between the patient and actuality. Although the moment of loss was postbirth, in infanthood, childhood, adolescence, adulthood, it was retroactive in suppressing early engrams.

This aspect of painful emotion is a key-in of the early incidents by the moment of loss. In other words, a moment of great loss suppresses the individual on the tone scale to a point where he approximates the level of early engrams and these, keyed in, hold the units of charge thereafter.

Life units so seized are held and are the life of engrams. As in electricity, a positive charge glances away from a positive charge: like charges repel each other. The analyzer, operating, it can be said for analogy, on the same kind of charge as that contained in the engram, glances away from the engram, which remains thereby unknown and intact.

As the individual returns into the area of the early engrams—which are held keyed in by virtue of the seized charges from late incidents—he can quite comfortably pass by enormous quantities of aberrative material without even suspecting it is present. However, when the late moments of painful emotion are released, the auditor can go immediately into the early area and find engrams of physical pain which he had not hitherto been able to uncover.

Actually the late moments and the early moments are both engrams: the news or observation of loss shuts down the analyzer, and everything which then enters it is engramic and is filed in the reactive mind. Because of sight and a memory of activity which is connected to the present, all of which serves to keep an individual oriented, a person can often recall the moment of loss, whereas he cannot recall prenatal material, for he lacked in that area any connection with orienting factors which would impinge themselves on the analyzer. While the prenatal infant definitely, especially in the late stages, has an analyzer, experience and memory are not coordinated and the existence of engrams is not then suspected by the analytical mind. This is not true of the later periods of life, particularly those after speech has been learned and is being used. The fact of the matter is that this later-life ability to recall surrounding circumstances without feeling any extremity of pain also serves to hide here the existence of an actual engram: a person feels that he knows all about such a moment of loss analytically: actually he has no contact with the engram itself, which contains a moment of "unconsciousness" of a lesser depth than that, for instance, of the anesthetic variety. *Childhood losses of allies, however, can be so entirely occluded that the allies themselves are not remembered.*

The auditor will find very late engrams easy to contact. And he will also discover something else. The patient may not be, as he is returning to such a moment of loss, occupying his own body. This "phenomenon" has been known for several thousand years and even the latest mention of it merely said that it was "interesting" without making any further effort to find out *why* a person, returned to an area in hypnotic regression, sometimes could be found within himself (which is to say, seeing things as though he were himself) and sometimes saw things there and himself included as part of the scenery (as though he had a detached view). Because we have discovered that a natural function of the mind is to return in an awake state to past incidents does not alter the fact that we encounter aspects hitherto known as mysterious "phenomena" of drug dreams and hypnotism. We are not by any means practicing hypnotism. So, this means that hypnotism and Dianetics use similar abilities of the mind—it does not mean that such abilities belong in the field of hypnotism. And one of the various aspects of the *return* is that it occasionally—or, in some patients, continually—encounters areas where the patient is "outside" his body. These exteriorized views of self have two explanations. One of them is *valence,* whereby the patient has taken unto himself the identity of another person and sees the scene through that other person's eyes; the other is *exteriorization,* in which painful emotion is present in such quantity that the patient cannot occupy himself. That painful emotion may stem from past or future incidents to the moment when the patient is witnessing a scene to which he has been Dianetically returned. On several recountings of the scene, the patient will come nearer and nearer to an occupation of his body until at last he sees the scene from within his body. At times no emotional discharge (tears, etc.) takes place until the patient has gone over the incident several times and until he is within his own body. It is as though, returned, he had to scout the ground to find out if it was safe to occupy himself. If, after a few recountings, no discharge such as tears takes place, then the emotion is suspended elsewhere, earlier or later but usually much later. *Exteriorization* because of emotion is the same as exteriorization because of physical pain to all intents and purposes of the auditor. When he encounters a case which, all the way up and down the track, is continually exterior, he should address his skill to the release of moments of painful emotion.

All patients seem to have the idea that time heals and that some incident of ten or twenty years ago no longer has any effect upon them. Time is a great charlatan, not a great healer, as has been remarked. Time, by the processes of growth and decay, alters, and environment introduces new faces and activities and thus alters the restimulators: a moment of painful emotion in the past has, like any other engram, its own restimulators and is, in addition, holding keyed in all the early engrams which relate to it so that their restimulators also work: every restimulator has a set of restimulators which are associated to it by the analytical mind, which cannot see the real restimulator. All this makes a complex pattern, but complex in therapy only if one does not know the source of aberration. If the auditor returns the patient to any moment of painful emotion in the past and runs it as an engram, he will discover that all its original charge is present and will discharge.

He will usually find the patient shying away from any thought of going into the actual engram: the preclear may attempt to detail all manner of bric-a-brac, his own thoughts, the reasons why it no longer is painful to him, and so forth. These thoughts and data before the fact or after it are about as much use in running an engram as a dissertation about "childhood illusions" was to the problem of removing aberrations from the human mind. The auditor who will listen to these "reasons" and "I remembers" in lieu of running the engram itself will not get his patient well and will waste valuable hours of therapy. An auditor who will do this belongs to the hand-patting school of thought which believes sympathy has value. He does not belong in an auditor's chair. It is wasted time, wasted valuable time, to listen to anything the patient thought or said or did or believed when the patient should be going into the engram and running it as an engram. Certainly there is a necessity to find out, from the patient's talk, where that engram is, but once it is located, all else is dross.[30]

Take a moment when a child is notified of his parents' deaths. The auditor learns that the parents died when the child was two years of age. He can then deduce, without further trouble or questions, that somebody must have told his patient about the death of the parents, that there was a precise moment when the patient, then an infant, learned about that death. Recounting the matter in present time—without being returned—the patient is using all the intervening years as buffers against the painful emotion. The auditor returns the patient, without further preamble than the usual routine of putting the patient into reverie, to the moment when the patient learned of the death of the parents. The patient may do a little fumbling to orient himself in the past, but shortly he will have a contact with the instant somebody informed him. Be assured, if that child loved his parents at all, that an engram exists here. The engram starts at the first moment the child is informed, when the analyzer can be expected to have shut down. The end of the engram is a moment, an hour, a day or even a week later when the analyzer again turned on. Between the first moment of analytical attenuation and a regain of analytical power is the engram. The first minutes of it are the most severe. Running an hour of it (an hour of incident, not of therapy) should be more than ample. Most auditors run only the first few minutes several times to get a test of whether or not there is going to be any emotional discharge. Run such a period of loss which must contain painful emotion exactly as you would run a period of physical pain and "unconsciousness" with another source. For the period of painful emotion is an "unconscious" period just as certainly as if the patient had been struck with a club. If

---

30. dross: inferior, trivial or worthless matter.

the emotion in this period can be contacted with four or five recountings (each time starting at the beginning, making sure the patient is returned and in contact with *all* perceptics of the incident, and running it for what it is, an engram), then the engram should be recounted until the emotion in it is *gone*, until the patient is bored with it or even cheerful about it. If, after four or five recountings the patient is still well exteriorized, still has not contacted any emotion, then the charge is suspended elsewhere, either earlier or later, and tries should be made in terms of other losses, no matter how many years from the unyielding incident, to get a discharge. After a discharge is blown off elsewhere, the incident first addressed, as in the case of the two-year-old who lost his parents, may discharge. It is certain that sooner or later such an incident will discharge and it is also certain that the case will not make much progress in getting any bulk of physically painful engrams until such a severe incident *is* well discharged.

Discharges are contacted, often, in very unlikely places. Somewhere they contact the surface enough so that a touch by the returned patient will permit the units to free, permit engrams to key out and come into view on the time track in their proper places.

The engram bank becomes severely distorted by painful emotion and the areas of painful emotion become severely distorted by physical pain elsewhere. The filing system of the reactive mind is bad. The file clerk is able to recover and deliver to the auditor only so many painful emotion engrams or physical pain engrams at a time. They may be disordered in their positions on the track, which is to say, the auditor may contact an early physically painful engram (always his most important job) then contact one in midprenatal, then one postbirth, and thereafter no other engrams of the physical pain variety seem to be present (engrams of the physical variety which contain knockouts by accidents, illnesses, surgery or injury). This does not mean that the case is stalemated or that the patient is cleared. It more likely means that there are incidents of the other engram variety (painful emotion, stemming from loss by death, departure or reversal of allies) which can now be contacted. The auditor then looks for and exhausts the emotional discharge from the loss engrams, usually later in life. These, with the units freed back in circulation, allow earlier physical pain engrams to appear and the auditor reduces each one of these he can contact. As soon as he can no longer find physically painful engrams, he goes back to a search for painful emotion engrams and so forth alternately as necessary. The mind, being a self-protecting mechanism, will sooner or later block the patient from physical pain engrams if painful emotion engrams are ready; and it will block him from painful emotion engrams as soon as physical pain engrams are ready.

Start late to get painful emotion and work back early. Start early to get physical pain engrams and work toward late. And whenever any engram is contacted, run it until it is no longer troublesome in any way to the patient or is entirely gone (refiled, but gone for all the auditor and patient will be able to tell at the moment). If an incident, after many recountings, shows no signs of lightening (somatic decreasing or emotion either not expressed or not decreasing), only then should the auditor seek another incident. In a painful emotion engram the charge is often later. In a physical pain engram the suspension is invariably caused by the existence of the same phrase in an earlier physical pain engram which can be contacted, and in such case the auditor should go back over the phrases which brought him to the somatic until he finds a contact and a lift of the engram.

It should be extremely clear by this time that rationalization[31] about action or conduct or conditions does not advance therapy and is of no use beyond occasional aid in locating engrams. It should be equally clear that no amount of explanation or hand-patting or evaluation by the auditor is going to advance the erasure of the engrams themselves. It should be plain that what a person thought at the time of the incident was not aberrative. It should be clear that painful emotion puts the compartments and demon circuits into the mind and that the physical engrams hold the aberration and physical pain in the body.

This entire operation is mechanical. It has nothing to do with justified thought or shame or reasons. It has only to do with exhausting the engram bank. When the bulk of painful emotion is gone, the person is *released;* when the engram bank is exhausted of content, the person is *cleared.*

The mind is like a fine piece of equipment: as itself and as a mechanism it is almost impossible to destroy except by removing some of its parts: engrams do not remove parts of the mind, they add unnecessary things to it. Envision a beautiful, streamlined machine, operating perfectly—that would be the mind without the additions of pain and painful emotion. Now envision this beautiful machine in the hands of a crew of moronic mechanics: they start to work around it and do not know that what they do affects the machine at all. Now they see that something is wrong with the machine and are all unwitting that they have placed various assorted monkey wrenches, hatpins, old cigar butts and yesterday's garbage into it and around it. Their first thought is to put something new on or in the machine to correct

---

31. rationalization: justified thought—the excuses one makes to explain his irrational behavior.

its operation and they add arbitrary gadgets to it in order to patch up the machine's operation. Some of these gadgets appear to help the machine (sympathy engrams) and can be used, in the presence of the remaining bric-a-brac, by the machine itself to help its stability. The morons interrupt the fuel supply (painful emotional engrams) or, like the Japanese captain who beat the car with a switch when it would not go, try to goad the machine (punishment drive) and so add more trouble. At last this machine appears to be a hopeless wreck, being almost hidden beneath everything added to it and thrust into it, and the moron mechanics shake their heads and say, "Let's put something else on it or it will stop!" They do and the machine appears to stop (goes insane).

In Dianetics, a workmanlike job of clearing away the debris in and around the machine is performed. It is not done by adding any more debris. The moron mechanics (the content of the reactive mind) seem dismayed at this action, but the machine itself, suddenly aware that something is being done for it which will actually bring it into good running operation again, begins to help. The more debris which is cleared, the better it runs and the less force the moron mechanics have. The course of improvement should be, and is, rapid. We can stop when the machine is running at least as well as the "normal" machine (a release) or we can stop when we have all the debris out of the machine (a clear). When we have effected a clear, we behold something which has never been beheld before because it never before existed in a debris-free state: a perfect machine, streamlined, powerful, shining, able to adjust and care for all its own operations without further therapeutic assistance of any kind.

CHAPTER EIGHT

Some Types of Engrams

Two examples of each kind of engram are given so that the auditor can clearly understand their differences:

Contrasurvival Engram

This is any kind of engram which lies across the dynamics and has no alignment with purpose: fight between Mother and Father shortly after conception. Father strikes Mother in stomach. She screams (first percepts are pain, pressure, sound of blow and scream) and he says, "Goddamn you, I hate you! You are no good. I'm going to kill you!" Mother says, "Please don't hit me again. Please don't. I'm hurt. I'm hurt. I'm frantic with pain!" Father says, "Lie there and rot, damn you! Goodbye!"

In this engram we have a severe aberrative situation: first, because it is early; second, because its content says the person who has it is hurt and frantic; third, because it has a holder and is therefore apt to become chronic ("Lie there"); fourth, because it can produce disease ("and rot"); fifth, because it has religious connotation about God and being damned; sixth, because it gives the individual a feeling other people are no good ("you" applies to other people, ordinarily); seventh, because it has an emotional tone, by content, of hostility ("I hate you"); and eighth, because the individual, postbirth, has to live with these restimulative persons, his father and mother. It has other additional effects, giving, like all engrams, two additional and unnecessary valences to the individual, one of which, the mother's, is a coward valence and the other, the father's, a bully valence. The individual may dramatize this in several ways: if he does not dramatize it, he feels the pain (as he would then be in his own valence) whenever it is restimulated; if he dramatizes the mother, he will feel the pain *she* received, which is a blow in the stomach (whereas his own was on his head and heart); if he dramatizes the father, he will be in trouble with society, to say nothing of his own wife and children. There is no winning with any engram of any kind, but so long as a person has engrams, some kinds, the sympathy engram particularly, serve to hold away antagonistic engrams.

The second contrasurvival example is a morning sickness engram where the mother is vomiting so violently that the compression on the child is severe and renders it "unconscious." The mother is vomiting and gasping and saying to herself between spasms, "Oh, why was I ever born! I knew I shouldn't have let him come in me. I knew it, I knew it. It was wrong but he had to do it anyway. Ugh, how nasty. Sex is nasty. It's horrible. I hate sex. I hate men. I hate them. Oh, ugh, it won't come up, it won't come up. I am so sick at my stomach and it won't come up."

In this engram we have something a woman might dramatize if she were pregnant but which a man could never dramatize as pregnancy but only by being sick at his stomach. Much morning sickness seems to be an aberration stemming from engrams: somewhere back in time some mother may have vomited from food poisoning and started the whole thing—perhaps in the days when man was still in trees. Now note that the mother *is* throwing up, that the content of her stomach *is* being regurgitated: the engram, however, says that it *won't* come up: when this is dramatized with the individual in his own valence, he experiences pressure on him and "unconsciousness" and thus such a dramatization is impossible; when this is dramatized it must be dramatized as the mother, but the *action* is not dramatized so much as the command and we get a condition where the individual with such an engram, when he is sick, cannot vomit. The *command* of the engram is more important than the action people take in it. On a reactive level there is no rationality. If this were on a conscious level, where it would not be aberrative, of course, the action could be mimicked and then would contain actual vomiting, the action on the conscious level being more important than the word content.

In therapy, when we encounter this engram, we may have difficulty entering it because it says that "I shouldn't have let him come in me," which is a *denyer*. We also find, with the "It won't come up," a *holder*. The engram will most certainly lift the moment these words and the somatic lift, and these words could not interrupt the engram. If the engram does not lift, it is because there is a previous engram with much the same content (the aberree has a pattern of dramatization which he repeats over and over and over, giving people around him many incidents which are more or less alike except in their point in time). This could be restimulated in the environment (but not in therapy) to a point where it would cause madness, for "it" may also refer to the child, who, identifying himself with the word "it," then cannot rise to present time. In therapy the engram is somewhat drained of power just by being touched with the returned analytical mind; further, the auditor discovers the patient is not moving on the track and a scout of the situation soon discovers the holder, for the patient will sooner or later say he "can't come up" even if the auditor has not guessed it.

In the aberrative sphere, this engram would probably put a heavy block across the second dynamic and we would find the person in whose reactive mind it was being frigid, prudish and sharp with children (all of which go together in various combinations). Further, we would find an apprehension that "he" was going to have to do something when he found out it was wrong. In the psychosomatic sphere it might cause headaches during or because of coitus or a tendency to nausea whenever coitus was performed. Any of the phrases of this engram, like any other phrases in any other engram, would tend to give him both the somatic and the aberration, providing, of course, the individual was in a state of low analytical power as found in weariness or slight illness. Thus, this one is waiting until somebody says during a future "unconsciousness" period, preferably in a voice like the mother's would sound through the walls of the abdomen and womb, "Ugh, how nasty!" or some other phrase to key it in. "Nastier," by the way, would not key it in: "ugly," despite a similar syllable to "Ugh," would not key it in. The sound of vomiting itself probably would key it in.

Prosurvival Engram

This could be any engram which, by content only, not by any real aid to the individual containing it, pretended to assist survival. Let us take a coitus engram: Mother and Father are engaged in intercourse which, by pressure, is painful to the unborn child and which renders him "unconscious" (common occurrence, like morning sickness, usually present in any engram bank). Mother is saying, "Oh, I can't live without it. It's wonderful. It's wonderful. Oh, how nice. Oh, do it again!" and Father is saying, "Come! Come! Oh, you're so good. You're so wonderful! Ahhhh!" Mother's orgasm puts the finishing touch on the "unconsciousness" in the child. Mother says, "It's beautiful." Father, finished now, says, "Get up," meaning she should take a douche (they do not know she is pregnant) and then begins to snore.

Obviously, this is a valuable incident because one "cannot live without it." Furthermore, "it's beautiful," also, "it's wonderful." But it is also extremely painful. It cannot be followed because it has first something which beckons part of the mind back, "Come!" and then, later, tells it to "Get up." Things that are "beautiful" and "wonderful" can cause our patient, not in therapy, to have an orgasm when she looks at beautiful and wonderful things, providing they have been so labeled.

Dramatization of this can be in either the father valence or the mother valence: to dramatize it in the personal valence would mean physical pain. Thus, the individual holding this will be found, varied only by his other coitus engrams, to be, as Father, disgusted after the act and telling his partner to "Get up." The emotion is contained in *how* the words "Get up" were spoken: this is a telegraphed emotion out of voice tones, not word content: engrams always contain both.

In therapy, we find the reactive mind very chary[1] of letting this one come to view because, after all, one "cannot live without it." There are whole classes of these *favorable evaluation* phrases in engrams, and wherever he comes upon one, the auditor will find the preclear's reactive mind holding out on him. "I don't want to lose you," "Hold on to this," "I can't let go of this, I'd fall," and so forth. But this is, after all, just another engram and "pleasant" or not is aberrative.

Masochistic and sadistic impulses often stem from coital engrams which contain those specific things, so the auditor is not to infer that merely because this coitus

---

1. chary: cautious, wary.

is painful to the child, it will make the child a masochist or a sadist. If masochism or sadism is present in the patient, it is caused by engrams which contain rapes, beating for sexual gratification, enjoyment of pain, etc., and engrams which homonymically seem to state that sex and pain are alike, such as a "normal" coitus which says, "It hurts so good! Hurt me again, Bill. Hurt me again! Oh, shove it in me, way up! Make it hurt so I can come." Dramatized by a boy, this might very well bring about sodomy because the engram is not an observed action but a series of commands, literally taken.

Thus, our prosurvival coitus engram, as the first example of one here, is relatively innocent in a person's aberrative pattern. But by an accident of words, it could be very different in its aberrative effect.

The second prosurvival example concerns another prenatal engram. (One auditor commented, while he was being cleared, that he "had thought of my life B.D.—before Dianetics—as a graph of years, in which the time from conception to birth occupied one-fiftieth of the linear distance between conception and present time, but now think of the prenatal period as occupying two-thirds of the distance between the beginning and now." The prenatal area, cleared, at last went back to being one-fiftieth.)

The mother, subject to high blood pressure, continually brought about a condition of great pain in the unborn infant, particularly when she was agitated. (This is a prime source of migraine headache.) Whatever it was which agitated her into high blood pressure at the moment this engram was received was unknown—and much of the "plot" of prenatal life may remain unknown for the explanatory data may come before the pain and the engram, and a complete recording only happens after the instant of pain when some degree of "unconsciousness" comes about. The mother, at the beginning of the engram, when pressure began to build up and stiffen out the unborn child, was weeping. She was by herself. "Oh, how am I ever going to get out of it? Everything looks so drab and colorless to me. Oh, why did I ever start it; I can't possibly go through with it. But I have to, I have to. I would be sick if I didn't. Oh, Lord, everything comes in on me at once. I am utterly trapped. But there, I will go through with it, I'll feel better. I'll be brave and do it. I've got to be brave. I am brave. I am the bravest person in the world. I have to be and I am." The pressure receded.

Exactly what this was about will remain a mystery to the auditor who reduced it, the patient who had it, the author and the reader: such is often the case with an engram. They are conceived in misunderstanding and they aren't to be understood, save mechanically, and only deleted from the engram bank.

This is a particularly dangerous engram to have for it contains a manic in the words, "bravest person in the world." "I," of course, is ordinarily used by the unborn child to be himself when the engram is at last able to affect an analyzer in which there is speech. Before that moment, of course, there is just a recording without word meaning, although even before the words are given meaning, the engram can be aberrative. This is further dangerous because it says, "I'm trapped," and because it says, "Everything comes in on me at once." "Trapped" is our enemy, the *holder*. But "Everything comes in on me at once" is a *grouper*. Further, the remainder of the content, as an engram, will not compute in the analyzer. It says one "must go through with it," but that one "cannot go through with it," that one "would get sick if I didn't go through with it" but that "it is impossible." Everything being equal to everything, as our moronic enemy, the reactive mind, computes, this engram both repels and attracts therapy: it brings about a condition of indecision in the analytical mind which is insufferable.

The individual holding this engram might find himself—as it acted as aberration—first in the manic portion of being the bravest person in the world and then, regressed a trifle by a slight change of restimulators such as his migraine headache getting bad, find himself utterly undecided about any course of action and with the telegraphed emotion, contained in the tears, of being very depressed. But this is prosurvival because it apparently dictates a way out of a situation. As an additional factor, it brings, with its phrase about "everything being drab and colorless," colorblindness, at least in recall, so that the recalled images of the past are "seen" in the mind as having no color. It can bring about, if added to by enough subsequent dramatizations, actual perceptic colorblindness. The whole engram is very likely, when combined with other factors, to place the individual in an institution with all of his somatic turned on (migraine) and, because of the grouper, all other pain he felt in his life turned on as well. This grouper bunches the track of the engram bank all into one place and then puts the individual squarely in that place.

In therapy, when this was contacted, a case which had been classified as "insane" came into a *release* state of "normal." The patient had been institutionalized, was in the fetal position and had regressed physically. That she kept screaming these exact words and weeping had been placed on her record as the manifestation of a childhood delusion. The case was opened by repeater technique, using the words she kept screaming, after she had had her attention fixed upon the auditor by loud, monotonous noise. There were some former incidents containing these words which had to be reached before the incident in dramatization would ease. However, engrams like this are commonly contacted in more or less "normal" people and are relieved as routine. A very high degree of restimulation had been experienced by this patient and several severe "loss" engrams had occurred which had kept earlier content keyed in.

It might also be remarked *in re*[2] all these "trapped," "caught," "can't get out of it" cases (which is to say, where there are several holders and also a high quantity of painful emotion) that certain fetal aspects are visible even when the case is "normal." A shiny skin, a spinal curvature, only partial development of the gonads: all are common and one or many such signs may be present.

Sympathy Engram

The first example is an illness suffered by a patient when he was a small boy. At two years and a half, he was taken ill with pneumonia. He had a considerable background of attempted abortion and the usual engram cargo received from aberrated parents. He was extremely worried about the quarrels and upsets of his own home; numbers of his engrams had been keyed in and amongst them was his pneumonia. His grandmother came and took him to her home because, whenever he was ill, his mother would go away and leave him. The incident was extremely occluded and was only reached after several late-life painful emotion engrams had been discharged and after almost a hundred prenatal physical pain engrams had been released. The grandmother, when he was crying in delirium, mistook his activity as demonstrating that he was "conscious," which he was not, and she sought to reason with him. She said, "Those people don't really mean to be so bad to you, honey. I know they have good hearts really. You just do what they say and believe what they tell you and you'll be all

2. in re: in regard to.

right. Now promise you'll do that, won't you, honey." The child, in the last depths of reaction, responded and promised her he would believe them and do what they said. "I love you very much," the grandmother continued, "and I will take care of you. Now, don't worry, honey. Forget it now. Just get a little rest."

The phrases contained in this engram, because they were on a trance level and because they could be held in place by his fever and pain, produced a very profound effect on the child. He had to believe whatever was said. This means *literal* belief and cost him, for one thing, much of his sense of humor. Because he wanted to be all right, he had to believe what his parents said; the things they had said, prenatally, contained every kind of a bad datum possible about who was the boss and how much fun it was to beat the mother and so forth. All this, then, was made into "true data" which, because his sympathy engram said so, he had to *believe*. No more horrible curse could ever be laid on anyone than those in sympathy engrams which say "Believe what is said," "Believe what is read," "Believe people," because that engram means literally that the poor old analyzer will now never be able to evaluate its own data unless, by utter rebellion, the individual negates against the whole world, which can occasionally be done. Let this individual, however, as this one did, marry a woman who has characteristics similar to his grandmother's (a pseudograndmother) and he becomes prey to (a) the pain and illness, chronic, which he experienced in his grandmother sympathy engrams (necessary to get and keep her sympathy); and (b) all his prenatals, since the pseudograndmother throws him into his own valence: This makes him quarrel, which makes his wife fight back, and suddenly this woman is not pseudograndmother but pseudomother. Exit sanity.

In therapy, when we encounter this sympathy engram at last, it is discovered to have been buried in two ways: (a) it was aligned with purpose; and (b) it had a *forgetter mechanism* on it.

Because of (a), the self-protection of the mind permitted it to give up the engram only when enough tension was taken off the case to permit the mind to get along without this engram.

In (b) we have a device which is common in engrams. Whenever we try to run an engram which has somatics enough even to make the preclear roll around on the couch but which contains no word content, we suspect a *forgetter mechanism*. There are evidently people in this world who think that the panacea[3] for all mental discomfort is to forget. "Put it out of my mind," "If I remembered it I would go mad," "Junior, you never remember a thing I tell you," "Nobody can remember anything," "Can't remember," and just plain "I don't know," as well as the master of the family of phrases, "Forget it!": all bar information from the analyzer. A whole case, freshly opened, may keep answering everything with one of these *denyers* (there are many other kinds of *denyers,* if you recall). Repeater technique will eventually begin to release the phrase from various engrams and begin to show up incidents. To have a grandmother who says, "Forget it" continually every time a child gets hurt is to be cursed beyond Macbeth.[4] A forgetter, used by an ally, all by itself and with practically no pain or emotion present will submerge data which, in recall, would not be aberrative but which, so buried—by a forgetter—makes things said just before it aberrative and literal.

---

3. panacea: a remedy for all kinds of diseases or troubles.

4. Macbeth: title character of a play by Shakespeare, tortured by his guilt for murders he committed rising to power in Scotland.

Hence, this engram remained utterly out of sight until the case was almost finished and as soon as it was contacted, the already deintensified reactive bank collapsed and the patient was cleared.

The second example of the sympathy engram concerns a childhood experience of a patient who, at the beginning of therapy, was a remarkably confused individual. Here is an example of sympathy engram which is not uncommon. (It will not be primary in any ally computation but, because it is often repeated in the same case, becomes aberrative.) This incident occurred when the child had been badly hurt in an accident. He had received a fractured skull and concussion and was for many days in a coma. He had never learned that such an incident happened to him although examination afterwards disclosed evidence of the fracture and disclosed also that while he had known there was a ridge in his skull he had never wondered about it for an instant. His father and mother were, at the time, on the verge of divorce and, in the presence of the only partly conscious child, quarreled several times in these few days, evidently upset by his accident and recriminative[5] as to whose fault it was. The first part of the series of engrams within this one large engram are unimportant as an example save that they brought about a condition where the mother put herself forward as a defender of the child who was *not* under attack by the father. The mother's conversation aberratively indicated that the father was attacking the child, and the words in an engram rather than the action are important as aberrative factors. Finally the father left the house and home. The mother sat down by the boy's trundle bed and, weeping, told him she would keep him from dying, that she would "work and slave and wear her fingers to the bone" to keep him

5. recriminate: to accuse in return.

alive and "I am the only reason you are alive. I have defended you against that beast and monster. If it were not for me, you would have died long ago and I am going to care for you and protect you. So don't pay any attention to anything people tell you. I am a good mother. I have always been a good mother. Don't listen to them. Please, baby, stay here and get well, please!"

This remarkable piece of nonsense came, of course, straight out of her reactive mind. She did not feel guilty about the way she was taking care of the baby, though she had done her cyclic worst for this child since conception. (There is no such thing as guilt nor a guilt complex that is not straight out of an engram that says, "I am guilty" or some such similar phrase.)

Here is *ambivalence* at work. By *ambivalent* is meant power on two sides. It had better be called *multivalence*, for it is demonstrable that people have many valences, twenty or thirty not being unusual for a "normal." This mother, with her wild pleas and her mawkish[6] sentimentality, shifted around in valences like a whirling dervish.[7] She was capable of being viciously cruel, torturing her child with, as the Navy calls them, "capricious[8] and unusual punishments": yet one of these valences which, unfortunately for the patient, only turned on when he was ill, was one of savage protection for the child and assurances to him that she loved him and would never leave him to starve, etc. She formed, in this child, because of her own reactive pattern and her inabilities,

---

6. mawkish: sentimental in a sickly way.

7. dervish: a member of any various Moslem orders of ascetics (ones who lead a life of austere self-discipline, especially as an act of religious devotion or penance), some of which employ whirling dances and the chanting of religious formulas to produce a collective ecstasy.

8. capricious: characterized by or subject to whim; impulsive and unpredictable.

close to a thousand engrams before he was ten. This particular specimen given was fairly standard.

The aberrative aspect of this engram was a "conviction" that if one's mother were not around and if one were not on good terms with her, one would starve, die or suffer generally. Also, it meant, because of the time it was given, having a bad headache if one wanted to live. The whole series of these engrams made a highly complex pattern of psychosomatic ills including sinusitis, a chronic rash, allergies and numerous other actual physical ills, despite the fact that the patient had always tried to be as forthright in his physical being as possible and was not in any way a hypochondriac.

In therapy, the entire chain of fights in this area, much of the prenatal area and most late-life painful emotion engrams were relieved before this sympathy engram displayed itself.

As a note on the subject of sympathy engrams, these are in no wise exclusively found in childhood: they exist prenatally and postnatally—and sometimes late in life. Any persons who defend the child against further abortion attempts become part of the sympathy engram chains and, of course, they are allies whose loss is something to be dreaded. Late sympathy engrams have been discovered at fifty years of age. One, discovered at thirty, consisted of a nymphomaniac nurse who, during the period when the patient was still under ether and still in pain, talked to him obscenely, played with his genitals and still managed, by the content of her remarks, to plant a sympathy engram which produced a very serious psychic condition in the patient. (It is in no wise true that many cases of sexual play exist while the patient is under anesthetic or drugged, but because this is a standard psychotic reaction of delusion is no reason to rule that the incident cannot occasionally happen.)

The sympathy engram only has to sound like a sympathy engram to become one: there is no evaluation of actual intent by the reactive mind.

Painful Emotion Engram

Three of these are given to illustrate a type of each. They can happen at any period, including prenatally, but are most easily tapped in more recent life, when they will then lead back to early incidents of physical pain, sympathy engrams and the like. The first example is a case of loss by death of an ally. A girl, at the age of eighteen, was given a painful emotion engram by being told by her parents that her aunt was dead. The aunt was a prime ally. The patient, treated at the age of thirty-one, recalled the death of her aunt but attributed her sorrow to other things such as a restimulation of what she called her own "death instinct" (which was, in reality, engramic chatter by Mother about wanting to die and get it all over with). Actually, the aunt had been a large factor in dissuading the mother from "getting rid of" the child and had made the mother promise that she would not. The aunt had also tended the child, postnatally, through illnesses and was, in fact, the only refuge for the girl when a termagant[9] mother and a religiously bigoted father would converge on her, for neither had wanted her and there had been a number of efforts to terminate the pregnancy preterm.

Her father communicated the information to the girl with a sonorous[10] voice and appropriately long face. "I want you to be very respectful at the funeral, Agatha."

---

9. termagant: a shrewish, bullying woman.
10. sonorous: resonant, giving a deep, powerful sound.

("What funeral?") "Your aunt just passed to the great beyond." ("She's dead?") "Yes, death must come to us all and we must all be prepared someday to meet the fate which waits for us at the end of the road. For it is a long path, life, and God and flaming hell wait at its other end and someday we all must die. Be sure you are very respectful at the funeral." She had begun to pale at the word "funeral," she was to all purposes "unconscious" when she heard the first mention of "death" and she remained "unconscious," if moving about, for two whole days.

The case had been very slow until this engram was discovered and run. An enormous discharge of grief took place, which had never before manifested itself. It was reduced to boredom in eight recountings, at which the first moment of the aunt's intervention in the abortion attempts was automatically contacted and *released*. Thereafter the case made progress in the prenatal area, prohibition against "getting rid of it" having been removed; and, according to theory, free units being available, the charge had come off the prenatal area. There were five other allies in this case, the girl, with parents who had been so wicked to her, having attached herself to anyone who would show her interest and refuge. As lower physical pain came into view, more allies showed up and more painful emotion engrams were discharged, permitting new physically painful engrams to display themselves.

The next example is an engram from a patient who had all his life been reared and cared for by "moneyed parents." He had a very severe prenatal area which yet would not lift to view. It was discovered at length that his nurses had been his only source of love and affection and that his mother, being a woman who liked to unsettle the household as often as possible, would discharge a nurse every time she found the child had grown fond of her, even though the mother herself made it plain that she considered the child "nasty." The engram: the boy sees his nurse coming out of the house with her suitcase in her hand: he stops playing in the yard and runs to her to "scare her": she is quite angry from the scene she has just had—an Irish girl—and yet she smooths her face and kneels down beside him. "I am leaving, Buddy. I can't stay here anymore. No, I can't be your nurse now. But there, there, you'll have another one. Don't cry. It's not good for little boys to cry. Goodbye, Buddy. I love you." And she goes off out of sight.

He was stunned from the first instant she said she was leaving. The prohibition against crying was from an ally: whatever an ally says must be good and must be believed because allies are survival and one must survive: allies therefore must be believed. He had not cried except on rare occasions of enormous sorrow in all the years thereafter. Eight of these departures were touched without result but with this one they all loosened and discharged, one after the other.

Any departure of or from an ally contains an emotional charge which, if it will not display itself, is elsewhere suppressed.

The third example of the painful emotion engram is the third type: loss of an ally by reversal. A wife loved her husband very dearly. They had gotten along well together until his parents came into the vicinity and began to malign his wife. He was furious with them for it and quarreled with them. His wife was a pseudoally, and unfortunately that ally had told the child to believe his parents. (This is fairly chronic with allies—if they would give the child correct data when he is emotionally disturbed or ill, there would be less trouble. A remark such as, "Well, you'll grow up someday and be able to care for yourself," is much better than a hat full of Emersonian[11] platitudes.[12]) This brought about a tragic reversal. The reactive mind, restimulated at the sight of his wife (the husband was emotionally disturbed, very restimulated already by his parents) threw in the data that one must believe one's parents. This made his wife no good, as per their aberrative chatter. He went into his father's valence to escape this imponderable situation and that valence beat women. He struck his wife repeatedly, dramatizing one of his father's engrams: "I hate you. You are no good. I should have listened to them sooner. You're no good."

The wife was in therapy. This charge suppressed itself, not out of shame for her husband's actions but for the mechanical reason that the early area had to be relieved before this one would discharge (smart file clerk). Her case had slowed down to a point where the board looked entirely clear although somatics (which she attributed to natural causes) and aberrations (which she said were reasonable reactions) still manifested themselves. Suddenly this incident appeared when repeater technique was used on the auditor's random guess, "I hate you," for it was known that she said this now and then to her husband. Three recountings discharged this painful emotion despite its violence (it made her weep until she almost choked). Immediately twelve prenatals, all fights between her mother and father (an ally, of which her husband was the pseudoally) wherein the mother beat her abdomen and cursed the child, appeared and were erased and the case progressed to clear.

Loss of dogs, dolls, money, position, even the threat

---

11. Emersonian: of Ralph Waldo Emerson: (1803–82) American essayist and poet.

12. platitude: a commonplace remark, especially if uttered solemnly as if it were new.

of a loss: anything may bring about a painful emotion engram so long as it is loss. It may be loss by death, loss by departure, loss by reversal. Anything connected with the life of the patient and associated by him with his own survival seems to be capable of locking up life units when lost. A condition of such painful emotion is that it has early physically painful engrams upon which to append. The physically painful engram is still the villain but it has an accomplice in the painful emotion engram.

Mechanisms and Aspects of Therapy—Part One

The Case Entrance

Every case presents a new problem of entrance. No two human beings are exactly alike and no two cases will follow the exact pattern. However, this presents no problem to Dianetics since the mechanics are always the same.

There are three case classifications: the sonic recall, the nonsonic recall and the imaginary recall (what auditors call a "dub-in" recall).

In the sonic recall case, the entrance is very easy. But in all cases the basic procedure is the same. Put the patient in reverie (and don't worry too much if he doesn't go into a very deep reverie because reverie only serves to fix his attention on himself and the auditor and you can at least accomplish that). Install a canceler. Return him to childhood to pick up a pleasant incident and then find a minor pain incident such as a slap in the face. Run him through this a few times just to let him get the idea. If he doesn't respond well, put him into yesterday and let him ride to work and ask him about sounds and sights, then send him to childhood again.

The object of finding a minor incident such as a slapped face is to find out if the patient has a pain shut-off. A pain shut-off is not particularly difficult in Dianetics. You can get back before the command which installed the anesthesia, but it is interesting to know about it because you want to look for it early in the case. See then if the patient has an emotional shut-off. This again is not particularly embarrassing but again is data you want to find eventually.

Test now to find out if the patient is within himself or if he is outside himself, watching himself. If he is exteriorized, you are working a case which has considerable walled-up emotion in it which must be discharged.

Now make a try to get basic-basic. You might surprise yourself and get it. And you might work fifty hours for it, releasing the case the while. Get whatever the file clerk will give you in the prenatal area and what you get, *reduce.*

Whether basic-basic is contacted or not, locate as many prenatals as will present themselves without much coaxing and reduce each one.

If you find no prenatals, bring the patient up to present time but remind him to keep his eyes closed. Now ask him a few questions about his family, his grandparents, his wife or, if the preclear is a woman, her husband. Ask about any former husbands or wives. Ask about children. And ask particularly about death. You are looking for a painful emotion engram, an instant of loss which will discharge.

Finding out about one, even if it is just the death of a favorite dog, return the preclear to it and run it from the first moment he hears the news of it and for the ensuing few minutes of it. Then start it again. Reduce the moment as an engram. You want an emotional discharge. Run it several times. If you don't get a discharge, find some other moment of loss, some failure, something, anything which will discharge: but do it all quietly as if with sympathy. Lacking any success, start in repeater technique, never for a moment giving any intelligence that you are anything but calmly concerned for his welfare (even if some of his gyrations worry you). Try such phrases as "Poor little _____," using his or her childhood name.

When the preclear has repeated this several times

(the auditor at the same time stating that somatic strip[1] will return to any incident containing the phrase to assist the "suck down"), he may find himself in a high-tension incident which will discharge. If nothing discharges yet, keep calm (all this work will pay dividends in the next session or the next or next), keep searching, keep observing. There is emotional charge here somewhere which will discharge. Try other combinations of words such as those which would be said to a sick and worried child, make the preclear repeat them.

If you have had no success as yet, make another test, without saying it is a test, to see if the preclear is actually leaving present time. Don't let him "try to remember"—you want him to *return* and that is another process, although it is just as natural to the brain. If he is stuck in present time, start him on repeater technique again, suggesting bouncers: "Get out and never come back!" "You can't ever return!" etc., which would account for his being still in present time. If he is not returning after some of this, start in with holder phrases: "I'm stuck!" "Don't move!" and so forth.

Stay calm, never appear anxious. If you get neither a discharge nor an engram with repeater technique in this first session and if you get no motion on the track, read this manual again and try your patient not later than three days after this first session. At that time some of the data you have asked for may be available.

Ordinarily, however, you will receive either a prenatal or a discharge and if you get a discharge, then ask the somatic strip to go back for the prenatal it was sitting on. Reduce everything you can find. If birth turns up and seems to be in full recall, try to reduce that but do so

---

1. somatic strip: so called because it seems to be a physical indicator mechanism which has to do with time. The auditor orders the somatic strip. The somatic strip can be sent back to the beginning of an engram and it will go there.

in the knowledge that it probably will not lift very far and in the knowledge that you had better run it over and over and over to deintensify it all you can.

Sometimes the preclear will go into a deeper reverie than you wish. But do not try to wake him into a higher level. Work him where he is. But if he seems to be in something approaching hypnotic trance, be very careful of your language. Never tell him, for instance, to go back there and stay there until he finds something. That's a holder. Don't use holders and bouncers and groupers, *et al.*, on anyone in Dianetics. "Will you please return to the prenatal area?" "Let's see if the somatic strip can locate an early moment of pain or discomfort." "Please pick up the somatic at the beginning and roll the engram." "What do you hear, please?" "Continue" (when you want him to keep on going from the point of the engram where he is to the later end of the engram). "Recount that again, please."

There's nothing to be nervous about. If you get nervous, then he'll get nervous.

Sometimes you run into a pain shut-off. This has a tendency to put the pain into the muscles and the muscles will jump and quiver and the patient may sense this and still feel nothing more. Once in a great while a patient will have such a thorough pain shut-off that he bounces about, all unconscious of the action, and almost falls from couch to floor. If you run into this, do not be alarmed: the pain is locked in somehow. Get early enough and you'll locate a somatic he can feel, or go late and find an emotional charge.

Don't be misled if he tells you, with regard to emotion, that he has worked it all out in psychoanalysis or some such thing. He may have walled in the death of his wife or sweetheart or child, but the whole engram is still there, crammed with captured units, ready to be run exactly as an engram.

If you run into a heavy emotional charge, simply let the patient weep, keep him at the business of running the engram in a soft, sympathetic voice, have it recounted until there is no charge left in any of it and then run him early into the prenatal area or early childhood to get a physical pain engram that must have been below that emotional charge and held it in place.

The extravagance of emotional discharge is nothing to be alarmed about. Bringing the patient out of it and to present time suddenly would cause him unhappiness about it. Running the painful emotion engram will discharge, in a few recountings, sorrow which society has believed could never be countered or relieved except by repression. Get the moment he first heard the news or observed the thing which made him feel so bad. Run it far enough from its beginning to make sure that you have the initial shock—a few minutes of engram time will do—and then get him to recount it again. He may observe himself to be far outside himself when you start. The moment may not discharge until you have run it several times. Remember, he is *returned* to the incident, he is not running it as a memory, a thing which would do no good whatever.

Do not let him replay anything, ever. *Replay* is a bad habit some preclears have of playing over what they remember they said the last time instead of progressing through the engram freshly on each recounting and contacting what is contained in the engram itself. Tell the preclear there may be some more in it, ask him what color the bed in the room he is returned to is, keep his attention, by any quiet mechanism, upon the scene. And do not let him replay ever, not on any engram at any time: he could replay forever without therapeutic value, each time saying what he remembered he said the last time. There is a difference between this and the repeated reexperiencing of the engram to gather additional data and to get rid of the charge.

Discharge emotion, reduce incidents of physical pain as early prenatally as possible. If you can't get into the prenatal area at first, it has many bouncers in it and repeater technique will take you there.

If the patient keeps saying such a thing as "I can't remember," be patient—always follow the code. Have him start running that phrase as repeater technique. If he gets a somatic but contacts nothing else, send him earlier. If he gets another and still can't contact on "I can't remember," send him earlier, his whole engram bank must be strewn with them—poor fellow. Somebody really didn't want him to know what had happened to him. Eventually you will get back to an engram which will release a phrase. When he has gone over the phrase a few more times, he will smile or chuckle or perhaps merely feel relieved. Now you can either run the engram in which you found the earliest phrase, which is best, or you can come back toward present time, lifting the phrase as it later appeared. Or you can start on something else, which may block the case.

The goal, and the whole goal, is to place the standard bank in entire conscious reach of the individual by deleting (a) early and subsequently all physical pain engrams; (b) all demon circuits (which are merely contained in engrams and come up more or less automatically); and (c) all painful emotion engrams.

The process of work is to get as early as you can, preferably prenatal and very early in that, and try to find and reduce an engram, complete with all somatics (pain) and perceptics (words and other sensations). If you fail in this, you go late, any time from birth forward to present time, and find a moment of loss or threatened loss from which you can get an emotional charge. Then you go back early, early, early and find the engram on which it rested. You try always, until you are certain

372

you have it, to get basic-basic, the earliest engram. You reduce as many early engrams as you can find, using the file clerk and repeater system, and when you seem to run out of material, you go later into life and try to find another emotional charge.

The physically painful engrams cover up later emotional charges. Emotional charges cover up physically painful engrams. Back and forth, back and forth. Run as much as you can get early: when it seems to be running out or getting too unemotional, get some later material.

This is the way you work a case. No matter what kind of a case it is, no matter what the state of its recall, no matter if the case is normal, psychotic or neurotic or what, this is the way.

These are the tools:

1. Reverie, or fixed attention if you cannot get reverie;
2. Return;
3. Repeater technique;
4. A knowledge of bouncers, holders, groupers, misdirectors, denyers;
5. A knowledge of the painful emotion engram;
6. The reduction or the erasure;
7. The flash answer;[2]
8. The valence shift.[3]

This is all you need to do:

1. Keep the patient mobile, able to move on the track.
2. Reduce or erase everything you get your hands on.

---

2. flash answer: the first thing which comes into a person's head when a question is asked of him.

3. valence shift: getting the preclear moving around from one valence to the other.

3. Deduce from the remarks of the patient, in or out of therapy, what must be his bouncers, holders, groupers, misdirectors, denyers.

4. Keep it solidly in mind that the number one goal is basic-basic, the earliest moment of pain and "unconsciousness."

5. Keep in mind that the patient may have "computations" which make his illness or his aberrated state "valuable" to him and discover whence those "computations" come by flash answer to your questions.

6. Keep the case progressing, gaining, work only for progress and gain, not for sudden, soaring results. Worry only when the case remains static and worry then in terms of finding the engram which is balking everything. Its content will be a close approximation to the way the patient says he feels about it and will contain the same or similar words.

7. Get the patient back to present time each time you work and feed him the canceler. Test him with an *age flash*, get his first reply to how old he is, find the holder at that age if he is not at present time.

8. Keep your temper no matter what the patient says.

9. Never try to tell him what his data means: he knows and he alone knows what it means.

10. Keep your nerve and run Dianetics; like Farragut[4] said, "Damn the torpedoes! Go ahead."

11. Wife, son, whatever you may be to the preclear, *you* are the auditor when you are auditing. He cannot compute his own engrams to find them—if he could they would not be engrams. You can compute them. Do what you think a good auditor would do, never what the patient says, save only when he accidentally concurs in his opinion that a good auditor

---

4. Farragut, David Glasgow: (1801–70) American admiral.

would do that. Be the auditor, not the recording device. You and the file clerk in his mind are running the case: what his engrams and his analytical mind believe should have no force in any of your computations. You and his file clerk know. He, as "I," doesn't know.

12. Be surprised at nothing. Audit.

These are the things you must not do:

1. Dilute Dianetics with some practice or belief of yesteryear: you will only slow or sidetrack a case. Analyzing data received on any other basis than getting more engrams leads to delay and confusion for the preclear. It is a temptation to use this material for other reasons than getting engrams if one has been trained in another field than Dianetics. Yielding to that temptation before one knows how Dianetics works is a very unfair test of Dianetics, completely aside from the way it snarls a case. The temptation is great because with Dianetics you get such a wealth of data.

2. Do not bully the patient. If the case is not progressing, then the fault lies with the auditor. Do not surrender to an old practice of getting mad at a patient just because he doesn't get well. *You* may be *sure* the engram you have just reduced out of his reactive engram bank is the reason he won't take baths, but if he still refuses to bathe, be certain there is an earlier reason.

3. Don't assume grandly that you have a "different" case just because it doesn't resolve swiftly. They are all "different" cases.

4. Don't run for help to somebody who does not know Dianetics if your nerve fails you. The reason the case did not progress or became involved is right there—your nerve failed you. Only Dianetics can work a problem in Dianetics.

5. Do not listen to a patient's complaints as complaints; use them as data to get engrams.

6. Do not suppose that just because you cannot reach prenatal engrams in a case that they are not there. There are scores and scores of them in every case. Remember that an engram isn't a memory, it has to be developed to become within recall. There is no human being walking on earth today who does not have a plenitude of prenatals.

7. Do not allow the patient to use his mother or his memory of what he had been told as a bypass of prenatals. *Every time you find a patient talking in past tense instead of present tense he is not returned to an incident.* Unless he is returned, the engram will not lift.

8. Do not suppose that because a patient does not feel bad today about a sorrow of yesterday that a despair charge is not located back on his track when he received the impact of that despair. Time may encyst, it does not heal.

9. Do not think in terms of "guilt complexes" or "shame" unless you think of them as engram content, for there they will be found. Never suggest to a patient that he may be at fault in an engram.

10. Any departure from optimum behavior or conduct or rationality on the part of the patient is engramic: don't make "allowances for human nature" any more than you, as a mathematician, would make allowances for an adding machine which brought up wrong answers. Sexual fears, repressions, defenses are not "natural" as they have been regarded in the past.

11. Don't worry about the patient's aberrations. Work to contact and reduce and erase engrams. You will find, in any patient, enough aberrations to fill a dictionary.

12. Don't fret if your patient does not become a clear in an evening or a month. Just keep working. You'll have him above normal so quickly you won't realize when you passed it. Above that you are shooting for a very high goal.

"Stuck in Present Time"

Cases, when they are entered, are found in various positions and situations on the time track; sometimes they are off the time track entirely, and sometimes the time track is all snarled up in a ball. Now and then the time track is found to be in good condition and the engrams available, but this is not ordinary.

No case can be said to be more difficult than another except in the matter of recalls, "dub-ins" and shut-offs. But the case which seems to be "stuck in present time" and on whom no repeater phrase works is very often quite puzzling to an auditor. The preclear will not return to engrams. Ordinarily there may be pain and emotional shut-offs and the painful emotion cannot be quickly discharged. Sometimes somatics will turn on but no content can be gained. Sometimes there is no somatic but content. The situations are quite various.

There are several things an auditor can do. The first of them is to use his wits. The next is to indoctrinate the patient into returning. This indoctrination is quite simple. The auditor takes the patient back a few hours and has the patient tell what he sees. The sonic and visio may be occluded but the patient may have some idea of what is taking place. The auditor then takes him back a few days, then a few months and finally several years, each time getting the patient to describe his "surroundings" as best he can. The patient now has the idea of returning. He can travel at least along portions of his life which are not occluded by engrams.

When the patient is returned to some early moment in his life, begin to use repeater technique on him, aiming toward obvious things such as feeling shut-offs (going over the word "feel") or forgetter mechanisms (such as "forget"). An engram may then be contacted and reduced.

If repeater technique still does not work and still does not get data, diagnose by his behavior in therapy and his statements what must be troubling him or occluding his recalls and again use these guesses as repeater. For instance, he may have no recollection of some member of his family. Have him repeat the familiar name. Or have him repeat his own childhood nickname until an incident is contacted.

Should this still fail, then find some light locks, incidents which contain minimal pain, and run those. Such things as falls from a tricycle, getting sent from the table, getting spanked or scolded, being kept after school and so forth will serve. After he has reduced several locks, again try to find an engram.

The running of locks will not bring about any great recovery, and there are thousands and thousands of locks in any case, most of which will vanish without assistance from the auditor once the severe engrams are located. But locks may be used to indoctrinate the patient into returning and therapy in general and may even bring about an improved condition in him by demonstrating to him that he *can* face his past.

The foremost things to do in any case at the beginning are to (1) attempt to locate and erase basic-basic, and (2) discharge painful emotion. The sooner emotion can be released, the better, and there is always emotion on a case, just as there is always a plenty of prenatal incidents.

But when a case is stuck in present time either when

it is opened or during progress, it is highly charged with occluded emotion and it is obeying a restimulated engram to the effect that it must go all the way to now and stay there. The wording of this engram will generally be expressed by the patient himself in complaining of his trouble. Repeater technique is used with this clue. That failing, indoctrinate the patient by taking him back to what he can contact and when indoctrination is done, as above, start using repeater technique again.

There is one motto which applies to all therapy, "If you keep asking for it, you'll get it." Any and all engrams surrender on the basis of returning the patient to the area time and again, session after session. The engram bank may be balky but enough asking will bring forth any data in it sooner or later. Just keep asking, keep the routine of therapy running. Even a "stuck in present time" case will eventually begin to return on the sole principle of repeater technique.

There are certain things that the auditor may be doing which are wrong. He may be trying to work the case on data taken from parents or relatives, which is usually fruitless in view of the fact that it undermines the preclear's faith in his own data (all the data will check with the relatives; just don't worry about checking it until the case is finished). Or he may be trying to work the case in the presence of other people. Or he may be violating the Auditor's Code. A list of these deterrents to progress is to be found elsewhere in this volume.

Basic-Basic

The first goal of the auditor is basic-basic and after that always the earliest moment of pain or discomfort which he can reach. He may have to go late for emotional charges and these themselves may be physically painful. Emotion may bar the patient from basic-basic. But always that first turn-off of the analyzer is important and when it is gained, subsequent engrams are much more easily reduced.

Basic-basic is the vital target for two reasons: (1) It contains an analyzer shut-off which itself is restimulated every time a new engram is received. The common denominator of all engrams is analyzer shut-off. Turn it on the first time it was shut off and a vast improvement takes place in the case, for thereafter analyzer shut-off is not as deep. (2) An "erasure" (which is to say, an apparent removal of the engram from the files of the engram bank and refiling in the standard bank as memory) of basic-basic widens the track beyond it markedly and brings many new engrams into view.

Basic-basic is occasionally found weeks before Mother's first missed period, which would place it much earlier than any examination for pregnancy or an attempted abortion. Sometimes in a nonsonic case sonic is discoverable in basic-basic but far from always.

Considerable material may be "erased" before basic-basic appears.

Sometimes basic-basic gets "erased" without either the auditor or the preclear knowing that it has been reached, basic-basic being merely another engram in the basic area. Sometimes much painful emotion must be discharged in the later life areas before basic-basic discloses itself.

Always, however, basic-basic is the target, and until he has a good idea that he has reached it, the auditor, once every session, makes an effort to get it. Thereafter he tries to get the earliest moment of pain or discomfort he can reach *every session*. If he can reach nothing early, he seeks to discharge a late emotional engram. When it is completely discharged, "reduced" or "erased" as an engram, then he goes down into the earliest material the file clerk will give him.

Whatever comes up, the auditor seeks to take all the charge out of it, whether that charge is pain or emotion, before he proceeds on his way to new material. This is done merely by returning the patient back over the incident many times until it no longer affects him either painfully or emotionally, or until it seems to vanish.

The Reduction and the Erasure

These two terms are highly colloquial. Serious effort has been made to deter their use and substitute for them something sonorous and wonderfully Latin, but no progress has been made to date. Auditors insist on using colloquial terms such as *AA* for attempted abortion, *louse up* for engrams which seriously aberrate, *aberree* for a person not released or cleared, *zombie* for an electric shock or neurosurgical case and so forth. It is feared that a tendency exists in them to be disrespectful to the hallowed and sacred tomes of yesteryear, to the dignity of past authorities which labeled much and did little. However this may be, *reduction* and *erasure* are in such common use that to change them is hardly necessary.

To *reduce* means to take all the charge or pain out of an incident. This means to have the preclear recount the incident from beginning to end (while returned to it in reverie) over and over again, picking up all the somatics and perceptions present just as though the incident were happening at that moment. To *reduce* means, technically, to render free of aberrative material as far as possible to make the case progress.

To *erase* an engram means to recount it until it has vanished entirely. There is a distinct difference between a reduction and an "erasure." The difference depends more upon what the engram is going to do than upon what the auditor wants it to do. If the engram is early, if it has no material earlier which will suspend it, that engram will "erase." The patient, trying to find it again for a second or sixth recounting, will suddenly find out he has no faintest idea what was in it. He may ask the auditor who, of course, will give him no information whatever. (The auditor who prompts is slowing down therapy by making himself the patient's memory.) Going through it and trying to find it may cause the patient some amusement when he cannot. Or it may make him puzzled, for here was something which had, on first contact, a painful somatic and a highly aberrative content which now no longer seems to exist. That is an "erasure." Technically the engram is not erased. If the auditor cares to spend some time, solely for purposes of research, he will find that engram in the standard banks now, labeled "formerly aberrative: rather amusing: information which may be useful analytically." Such a search is not germane to therapy. If the incident had a somatic, was recounted a few times and then, when its last new material was found, vanished, it is *erased* so far as the engram bank is concerned. It will no longer be "soldered" into the motor circuits, will no longer be dramatized, it no longer blocks a dynamic and is no longer an engram but a memory.

The "reduction" has some interesting aspects. Let us take a childhood incident (age of four, let us say) which had to do with a scalding. This is contacted while much data remains in the basic area. It has many things below it which will hold it in place. Nevertheless, it has emotional charge and therapy is slowed by that charge. The file clerk hands out the scalding. Now it will not *erase*, but it will reduce. Here is a job which will take more time than an erasure. And there may be several aspects to that job.

The somatic is contacted, the incident is begun as close to the beginning as the auditor can get, and is then recounted. This scalding, let us say, has apathy as its emotional tone (tone 0.5). The preclear slogs through it apathetically, well exteriorized, watching himself be scalded. Then suddenly, perhaps, an emotional discharge may come off, but not necessarily. The preclear returns to the beginning and recounts (reexperiences) the whole thing once more. Then again and again. Soon he begins to get angry at the people involved in the incident for being so careless or so heartless. He has come up to anger (tone 1.5). The auditor, although the patient would like to tell how vicious his parents are or how he thinks laws ought to be passed about scalding children, patiently puts the preclear through the incident again. Now the preclear ceases to be angry and finds that he is bored with the material. He has risen up to boredom on the tone scale (tone 2.5). He may protest to the auditor that this is a waste of time. The auditor puts him back through the incident again. New data may show up. The somatic may or may not be still present at this period but the emotional tone is still low. The auditor puts the preclear through the incident again and the preclear may, but not always, begin to be sarcastic or facetious. The incident is again recounted. Suddenly the preclear may be amused about it (but not always) and the incident, when it obviously has reached a high tone, may be left. It will probably sag in a few days, but that is a matter of no great importance for it will be erased wholly on the return from basic-basic. In any case it will never be as aberrative as it was before the reduction.

A reduction will sometimes result in the whole engram's apparently disappearing. But it is obvious when this will occur. Without much lifting in the tone scale, the incident, by repetition, simply goes out of sight. This is reducing to *recession*. In a few days that incident will be back in force again, almost as strong as ever. There is material before it and emotional charge after it which make it unwieldy.

Several things can happen, then, to an engram in the process of work. It can reduce, which is to say, discharge emotionally and somatically and be of no great aberrative power thereafter. It can reduce to recession, which is to say it merely goes out of sight after several recountings. It can erase, which is to say, vanish and cease to be thereafter, so far as the engram bank is concerned.

A little experience will tell an auditor what engrams are going to do after he has contacted them. Erasure takes place, ordinarily, only after basic-basic has been reached or, for that matter, when the basic area is being worked. The reduction occurs with an emotional discharge. The reduction to recession happens when there is too much in the engram bank suppressing the incident.

Every now and then even the best auditor will get hold of an engram and decide to grind it out now that it has been contacted. It is a sorry job. Perhaps it is better to grind it out than to merely restimulate it and let the patient be irritated by it for a couple of days. Perhaps not. But in any case, that engram which reduces only to recession was better not contacted in the first place.

New auditors are forever charging at birth as an obvious target. Everybody has a birth: in most patients it can be located rather easily. But it is a painful incident and until the basic area has been thoroughly worked and until late-life painful emotion has been discharged and until the file clerk is ready to hand up birth, the incident is better left in place. It will usually reduce to recession and afterwards keep popping up to plague the auditor. The patient gets obscure headaches, gets sniffles, feels uncomfortable afterwards unless birth is taken on the return (from the basic area). The auditor is wasting time, of course, by trying to remove these headaches and sniffles, because birth, with the whole prenatal life before it, will not properly reduce or erase but only recede. It is too often the case that birth, if prematurely contacted, will give the patient a headache and a cold. These discomforts are minor and of no great importance, but the work the auditor may have invested in working an incident which will only reduce to recession is lost work. True, the file clerk occasionally hands out birth: if he does, there is an emotional charge on it which will discharge and the incident will reduce properly. The auditor by all means should take it. True, a case sometimes stalls down and the auditor runs birth anyway just to see if he can speed things up. But merely going back to birth to put one's hands on an engram because he knows it is there will bring about discomfort and lost time. Go prenatal as far as you can and see what the file clerk will hand forth. Try repeater technique in the basic area. You may get incidents which will erase. If there is nothing there, find out about a painful emotion engram in late life, the death of a friend, the loss of an ally, a failure of a business, something. Blow a charge from it and reduce it as an engram and then go back prenatally as early as possible and see what has turned up. If the file clerk thinks you need birth he'll give it out. But do not ask for birth just to have an engram to work, because it may prove to be a thoroughly uncomfortable and fruitless endeavor. Birth will come up when it will come up and the file clerk knows his business.

Charging into any late period of "unconsciousness" such as surgical anesthetic, where physical pain is present in large quantities, can bring about this needless restimulation. You can, of course, fare better with such things in reverie than in hypnosis or narcosynthesis where such a restimulation might bring about severe results. In reverie the effect is light.

Handling the Somatic Strip

There are two little men on each side of the brain, a set for each lobe, hanging by their heels. The outer one is the "motor strip,"[5] the inner one, the "sensory strip."[6] If you wish to know more about the structure of these pairs, Dianetic research will have the answer in a few more years. Currently there is something known about them, a description. To an engineer who knows Dianetics the current description which will be found in the library is not entirely reasonable. These are, possibly, switchboards of some sort. Readings can be taken in the vicinity of them—just aft of the temples—if you have a very sensitive galvanometer,[7] a galvanometer more sensitive than any on the public market today. Those readings show emanations of a field of some sort. When we have established the precise type of energy flowing here, we can probably measure it with better precision. When we know exactly where the thinking is done in the body we will know more about these strips. All Dianetic research has established to date is that, beneath a welter[8] of labels, nothing is actually known which is worth recounting about these structures beyond the fact that they have something to do with coordination of various parts of the body. We do, however, refer to them for lack of something better, in the course of therapy. Now that we know something about

---

5. motor strip: the mind's control system through the motor controls. There are two panels on each side of the skull, one on top of the other, and they control opposite sides of the body. One of the panels on each side is where the thoughts register, and the other panel is where the muscle control is set up.

6. The *sensory strip* could be considered the "mental" side of the switchboard, the *motor strip* the physical side.

7. galvanometer: an instrument for detecting and measuring small electric currents.

8. welter: a disorderly mixture.

function, further research certainly cannot help but yield precision answers about structure.

The auditor can turn somatics on and off in a patient like an engineer handles switches. More aptly, he can turn them on and off in the body like a conductor runs a streetcar along a track. Here we have the game referred to previously when we talked about the time track.

In a patient who is working well, the "somatic strip" can be commanded to go to any part of the time track. Day by day, hour by hour, in normal life the somatic strip ranges up and down this track as engrams are restimulated. The auditor, working a patient, may find his own somatic strip obeying his own commands and some of his own somatics turning on and off, a fact which is at worst mildly uncomfortable. The whole body, the cells, whatever it is that is moving we do not really know. But we can handle it, and we can assume that it at least passes through the switchboard of the little men who hang by their heels.

"The somatic strip will now go to birth," says the auditor.

The patient in reverie begins to feel the pressure of contractions thrusting him down the birth canal.

"The somatic strip will now go to the last time you injured yourself," says the auditor.

The preclear feels a mild reproduction of the pain of, perhaps, a bumped knee. If he has sonic and visio recall, he will see where he is and suddenly realize that it was in the office: he will hear the clerks and typewriters and the car noises outside.

"The somatic strip will now go into the prenatal area," says the auditor.

And the patient finds himself in the area, probably floating along, not uncomfortable.

"The somatic strip will now go to the first moment

of pain or discomfort which can now be reached," says the auditor.

The patient drifts around a moment and suddenly feels a pain in his chest. He begins to cough and feels depression all over him. Mama is coughing (often source of chronic coughs). "Roll the cough," says the auditor. The patient finds himself at the beginning of the engram and begins to run it. "Cough, cough, cough," says the patient. He then yawns. " 'It hurts and I can't stop,' " he quotes his mother. "Go to the beginning and roll it again," says the auditor. "Cough, cough, cough," begins the patient, but he is not coughing as badly now. He yawns more deeply. " 'Ouch. It hurts, it hurts, and I can't seem to stop,' " quotes the preclear, listening directly if he has sonic, getting impressions of what's said if he does not have. He has picked up words now that were suppressed in it by "unconsciousness." "Unconsciousness" is beginning to come off with the yawns. "Roll it again," says the auditor. " 'I can't stop,' " says the preclear, quoting all that he finds this time. The somatic is gone. He yawns again. The engram is erased.

"The somatic strip will now go to the next moment of pain or discomfort," says the auditor.

The somatic does not turn on. The patient goes into a strange sleep. He mutters about a dream. Suddenly the somatic gets stronger. The patient begins to shiver. "What occurs?" says the auditor. "I hear water running," says the preclear. "Somatic strip will go to the beginning of the incident," says the auditor. "Roll it." "I keep on hearing water," says the preclear. (He must be stuck, the somatics did not move. This is a holder.) "Somatic strip will go to whatever it is that is holding," says the auditor. " 'I'll hold it in there a while and see if it does some good,' " quotes the preclear. "Pick up the beginning of the incident now and roll it," says the auditor. "I feel myself being jostled," says the preclear.

"Ouch, something bumped me." "Pick up the beginning and roll it," says the auditor. "'I'm sure I must be pregnant,'" quotes the preclear. "'I'll hold it in there a while and see if it does some good.'" "Is there anything earlier?" says the auditor. The preclear's strip goes to the earlier moment where he feels pressure as she tries to get something into the cervix. Then he rolls the engram and it erases.

This is handling of the somatic strip. It can be sent anywhere. It will pick up the somatic first, usually, and then pick up the content. Using repeater technique, the somatic is "sucked down" to the incident and the somatics turn on. Then the incident is run. If it does not lift, find an earlier incident simply by telling the somatic strip to go to the earlier incident.

If the somatic strip does not move, which is to say, if somatics (physical sensations) do not turn on and off, then the patient is stuck somewhere on the track. He can be stuck in present time, which would mean he has a bouncer thrusting him all the way up the track. Use repeater technique or merely try to send the somatic strip back. If it won't go, get various bouncer phrases like "Can't go back," "Run a mile," etc., and with them suck the somatic strip down to the incident and run it.

The somatic strip may move through an incident with full sensation and yet, returning over the same ground several times, will not bring out data. Time after time this can be done without result in some engrams: the somatics remain almost the same, undulating through the incident each time but with no other content. Then the auditor is "bucking" a denyer, a phrase such as "This is a secret," "Don't let him know," "Forget it," etc. In such a case he sends the somatic strip to the phrase which denies the data: "Go to the moment a phrase is uttered denying this data," says the auditor. After a moment, "'If he found out about this, it would kill him,'" quotes the preclear, either from sonic or from impressions. Then the auditor sends the somatic strip back to the start of the incident and it goes on through it, this time with other perceptic content. The somatics, unless the incident is very late prenatal with basic area full of material, undulate (fluctuate according to the action of the engram) and diminish to either reduction or erasure on consecutive recountings.

The auditor tells the somatic strip to go earlier, sometimes it goes later. This is a *misdirector.* "Can't tell which way I am going," "Going backwards," "Do just the opposite": these are the type of phrases of the misdirector. The auditor recognizes that he has one in the preclear—guesses it or discovers it from the preclear's wording of the complaint about the action—and by repeater or direct command of the strip, picks up the phrase and the engram, reduces or erases it and continues.

If the somatic strip does not respond according to command, then a bouncer, a holder, a misdirector or a grouper has been restimulated and should be discharged. The somatic strip will be where the command is which forbids it to function as desired.

There are good and bad conductors of this somatic strip. The good conductor works closely with the file clerk, using such broad orders as "The somatic strip will pick up the earliest moment of pain or discomfort which can be reached," or "The somatic strip will go to the highest intensity of the somatic you now have" (when a somatic is bothering the patient). The bad conductor picks out specific incidents which he thinks might be aberrative, bullies the somatic strip into them and somehow beats them down. There are moments when it is necessary to be quite persuasive with the strip and moments when it is necessary to pick out incidents of physical pain, but the auditor is the best judge of what should take place. As long as the strip will work smoothly, finding new incidents and running over them, he should not tamper with it beyond making sure that he reduces everything the strip contacts.

A very fine way to thoroughly wreck a case is to put the somatic strip into an incident, decide something else is more important and go rushing off to it, get that half-lifted and go off to something else. By the time three or four incidents have been so touched but not reduced, the strip stalls down, the track starts to bunch up and the auditor has a snarl which may take him many hours of therapy or a week or two of rebalancing (letting the case settle) to bring it back to a workable state.

The patient will sometimes want a somatic turned off. It has been bothering him. That means that the strip is somehow hung up in some incident which therapy or the patient's environment has restimulated. Ordinarily it is not worth the time and trouble to locate the incident. It will settle out of its own accord in a day or two and it may be an incident which cannot be reduced because of the earlier engrams.

The somatic strip is handled in a late incident just as it is sent to an earlier one. Despair charges are contacted in the same way.

If you want a test to see if the strip is moving, or to test recall, send it back a few hours and find out what you get. While the prenatal area is easier to reach than yesterday in many cases, some idea will be gained of how the patient is working.

Present Time

The beginning is conception. Your patients sometimes have a feeling that they are sperms or ovums at the beginning of the track: in Dianetics, this is called the *sperm dream*. It is not of any great value so far as we know at this time. But it is very interesting. It does not have to be suggested to the preclear. All one has to do is send him to the beginning of the track and hear what he has to say. Sometimes he has an early engram mixed up with conception.

At the late end of the track is, of course, now. This is present time. It happens now and then that patients are not getting back to present time because they have struck holders en route. Repeater technique with holders will generally free the strip and get it to present time.

A patient may get a trifle groggy with all the things which have been happening to him in the course of a therapy session. And he may have reduced resistance to engrams as he comes back up the track and may thus trip a holder. The auditor should be very sure the patient is up in present time. Occasionally the patient will be so thoroughly stuck and the hour so advanced that the effort to bring him all the way up is not feasible at the time. A period of sleep will generally accomplish it.

There is a test whereby the auditor can tell if the preclear is up to present time. He snaps a question at the preclear, "How old are you?" The preclear gives him a "flash answer." If it is the preclear's right age, the preclear is in present time. If it is an earlier age, there is a holder there, and the patient is not in present time. There are other methods of determining this but it is not very important, by and large, if the patient does fail to make it.

Snapping questions at people, asking how old they are, elicits some surprising answers. Being stuck on the track is so common in "normal" people that a day or two or a week or two of failure to reach present time in a preclear is far from alarming.

Anyone who has a chronic psychosomatic illness is definitely stuck somewhere on the time track. Snap questions about it get "three," or "ten years," or some such answer quite ordinarily even when asked of people who suppose they are in good health. Reverie reveals to them where they are on the track. Sometimes, in the first session, a preclear shuts his eyes in reverie to find himself in a dentist's chair at the age of three. He has been there for the last thirty years or so because the dentist and his mother both told him to "stay there" while he was shocky with pain and gas—so he did, and the chronic tooth trouble he had all his life is that somatic.

This doesn't happen very often, but you can find someone you know, it is certain, who would flash answer "ten years" and, being put in reverie, would find himself, as soon as the engram came to view, lying flat on his back in a ballpark or some such situation, with somebody telling him not to move until the ambulance came: that's his arthritis!

Try it on somebody.

The Flash Answer

A device in common use in therapy is the *flash answer*. This is done in two ways. The first mentioned here is the least used. "When I count to five," says the auditor, "a phrase will flash into your mind to describe where you are on the track. One, two, three, four, five!" "Late prenatal," says the preclear, or "yesterday," or whatever occurs to him.

The flash answer is the first thing which comes into a person's head when a question is asked him. It will come from the engram bank, usually, and will be useful. It may be "demon talk" but it is generally right. The auditor merely asks a question, such as what is holding the patient, what denies him knowledge, etc., prefacing

393

the question with the remark, "I want a flash answer to this."

"I want a flash answer to this," says the auditor. "What would happen if you became sane?" "Die," says the patient. "What would happen if you die?" says the auditor. "I'd get well," says the patient. And with this data they then make an estimate of the current computation on allies or some such thing. In this case, the ally said to the preclear when he was ill, "I'd die, just die if you didn't get well. If you're sick much longer I'll go insane." And a former engram said the preclear had to be sick. And this is, after all, just an engram. So repeater technique is used on the word *die* and an ally is uncovered that the preclear never knew existed and a charge is blown.

Much valuable data can be recovered by clever use of the flash answer. If there is no answer at all, it means that the answer is occluded and that is almost as good a reply as actual data since it means some kind of a cover-up.

Dreams

Dreams have been used considerably by various schools of mental healing. Their "symbology" is a mystic foible forwarded to explain something which the mystics did not know anything about. Dreams are crazy house mirrors by which the analyzer looks down into the engram bank.

Dreams are puns on words and situations in the engram bank.

Dreams are not much help, being puns.

Dreams are not much used in Dianetics.

You will hear dreams from patients. Patients are hard to shut off when they start telling dreams. If you want to waste your time, you will listen.

Valence Shift

A mechanism used in Dianetics is the valence shift. We know the way a patient gets into valences when he dramatizes his engrams in life. He becomes a winning valence and he says and does rather much what the person in the winning valence did in that engram.

The theory behind it is this: returned to a time the patient may consider too painful to enter, he can be shifted into a valence which felt no pain. A dull way to persuade him is to tell him he does not have to feel the pain or the emotion and let him go through it. This is very bad Dianetics because it is a positive suggestion and every safeguard must be taken to keep from giving suggestions to the patient, for he may be very suggestible even when he pretends not to be. But there is the valence shift and this permits the patient to escape the pain and still remain in the engram until he can recount it.

Example: Father beating Mother, unborn child knocked "unconscious." The data is available in the father valence with no pain, in the mother valence with her pain, in the child's valence with his pain.

The way to handle this, if the patient positively refuses to enter it although he has somatics, is to shift him in valence. The auditor says, "Go into your father's valence and be your father for the moment." After some persuasion the patient does so. "Bawl your mother out," says the auditor. "Give her a fine talking-to." The patient is now on that circuit which contains no "unconsciousness" and approximates the emotion and the words his father used to his mother. The auditor lets him do this a couple or three times until the charge is somewhat off the engram. Then he turns the patient's valence into the mother: "Be your mother for the moment now and talk back to your father," says the auditor. The patient shifts valence and is his mother and repeats his mother's phrases. "Now be yourself," says the auditor, "and re-count the entire incident with all somatics and emotion, please." The patient is able to reexperience the incident as himself.

This works very well when one is trying to get at an ally. "Shift valence," says the auditor to the returned patient, "and plead with your mother not to kill the baby." "Now be a nurse," says the auditor, with the preclear returned to some incident he seems very fearful about entering, "and plead with a little boy to get well." The patient will correct the auditor's concept of the script and usually will proceed.

The patient will often refuse to go into a valence because he hates it. This means there must be consider-able charge in the person he refuses to be.

This mechanism is rarely used but is handy when a case is stalling. The father did not obey the holders or commands, he uttered them. The nurse would not obey her own commands. And so forth. Thus many holders and denyers can be flushed to view. It is useful in the beginning of a case.[9]

Types of Chains

Engrams, particularly in the prenatal area, are in chains. That is to say, there is a series of incidents of

---

9. Valence shift is seldom used except where an engram is suspected which will not otherwise be approached by the patient. He will often approach the engram with valence shift when he will not approach it as himself. Valence shift is somewhat undesirable when employed on a suggestible subject since it violates the Dianetic rule that no positive suggestion be used beyond those absolutely necessary in returning and recounting and uncovering data. Therefore valence shift is seldom employed and rarely on a suggestible person. It should be considered a last resort and practiced only when the preclear is entirely and com-pletely unable to confront and attack an engram which the auditor is certain is present: and this is rare.

similar types. This is useful classification because it leads to some solutions. The chains one can most easily contact in a preclear are the least charged. The most aberrative chains will usually be the hardest to reach because they contain the most active data. Remember the rule that what the auditor finds hard to reach, the analyzer of the patient found hard to reach.

Here is a list of chains—not all the possible chains by any means—found in one case which had passed for "normal" for thirty-six years of his life.

Coitus chain, Father. First incident, zygote. Fifty-six succeeding incidents. Two branches, Father drunk and father sober.

Coitus chain, lover. First incident, embryo. Eighteen succeeding incidents. All painful because of enthusiasm of lover.

Constipation chain. First incident, zygote. Fifty-one succeeding incidents. Each incident building high pressure on child.

Douche chain. First incident, embryo. Twenty-one succeeding incidents. One each day to missed period, all into cervix.

Sickness chain. First incident, embryo. Five succeeding incidents. Three colds. One case grippe.[10] One vomiting spell—hangover.

Morning sickness chain. First incident, embryo. Thirty-two succeeding incidents.

Contraceptive chain. First incident, zygote. One incident. Some paste substance into cervix.

Fight chain. First incident, embryo. Thirty-eight succeeding incidents. Three falls, loud voices, no beating.

Attempted abortion, surgical. First incident, embryo. Twenty-one succeeding incidents.

---

10. grippe: influenza.

Attempted abortion, douche. First incident, fetus. Two incidents. One using paste, one using Lysol, very strong.

Attempted abortion, pressure. First incident, fetus. Three incidents. One Father sitting on Mother. Two Mother jumping off boxes.

Hiccough chain. First incident, fetus. Five incidents.

Accident chain. First incident, embryo. Eighteen incidents. Various falls and collisions.

Masturbation chain. First incident, embryo. Eighty succeeding incidents. Mother masturbating with fingers, jolting child and injuring child with orgasm.

Doctor chain. First incident, first missed period. Eighteen visits. Doctor examination painful but doctor an ally, discovering Mother attempting an abortion and scolding her thoroughly.

Premature labor pains. Three days before actual birth.

Birth. Instrument. Twenty-nine hours' labor.

In that Mother was a subvocal talker, this made a sizable quantity of material to be erased, for the remainder of the patient's life was in addition to this. This was a five-hundred-hour case, nonsonic, imaginary recalls which had to be canceled out by discovering lie factories before the above data could be obtained.

There are other chains possible but this case was picked because it contains the usual ones found. Mother's lover is not very unusual, unfortunately, for he puts secrecy into a case to such an extent that when the case seems very, very secret, then a lover or two will seem indicated. But don't suggest them to a preclear. He may use them for an avoid.

Dianetic Don'ts

Don't give any patient a positive suggestion as therapy in itself or to assist therapy.

Don't fail to give a canceler at every session's beginning and use it at every session's end.

Don't *ever* tell a patient he can "remember this in present time" because the somatic will come to present time and that is very uncomfortable.

Don't ever, ever, ever, ever tell a patient that he can remember everything that ever happened to him in present time because that groups everything in present time if the patient has slid into a deep trance. And that makes it necessary to unsnarl a whole case. Want to waste two hundred hours?

Don't ever retaliate in any way when a patient in reverie gets angry at you. *Follow the Auditor's Code.* If you get angry with him you may throw him into an apathy which will take you many hours to undo.

Don't evaluate data or tell a patient what is wrong with him.

Don't crow.[11] If the preclear is your wife or husband or child, don't rub it in that the favorite argument phrase was out of an engram. Of course it was!

Don't question the validity of data. Keep your reservations to yourself. Audit the information for your own guidance. If the patient doesn't know what you think, the engrams will never get a chance to evade.

Don't ever snap a patient to present time just because he begs for it. If he is in the middle of an engram, the only way out of it is *through* it. The power of the engram is slight when the patient is returned to it. It turns on hard when the patient comes to present time. The patient will have a nervous shock if he is snapped to present.

Don't ever get frightened, no matter what kind of squirming or squalling a patient may do. It isn't serious, any of it, although it is sometimes dramatic.

---

11. crow: to express gleeful triumph.

Don't ever promise to clear a case: promise only to release it. You may have to go away or work on something more urgent. And a broken promise to a preclear will be taken very hard.

Don't interfere with the private life of a preclear or give him guidance. Tell him to make up his own mind about what he should do.

Don't break the Auditor's Code. It is there to protect *you*, not just the preclear. Therapy can't hurt him if you do but half a job on it and do half of that wrong; breaking the code can make you very uncomfortable because it will make you a target of the preclear and cost you considerable extra work.

Don't leave engrams half-reduced when you are given them by the file clerk.

Don't get inventive about Dianetics until you have worked at least one case out. And don't get too inventive until you have worked a case which has sonic, a case which has shut-off sonic and a case which has imaginary sonic. Clear these and you will know. And you will have met enough engrams to get some ideas that can be of great benefit to Dianetics. If you don't get ideas after that and after you yourself are in therapy and cleared, there's something wrong. Dianetics is an expanding science; but don't expand it until you know which way it travels.

Don't mix gasoline and alcohol, or Dianetics and other therapy except purely medical, dispensed by a professional *medical* doctor.

Don't get a case snarled up and then take it to a psychiatrist who knows no Dianetics. Only Dianetics can unsnarl Dianetics and yesterday's methods won't help your patient one slightest bit when all he needs is another run through the one you snapped him out of too fast. Take a cinch on your nerve and send him back through the incident again. In Dianetics, today's obvious nervous breakdown is tomorrow's most cheerful being.

Don't quit, don't balk. Just keep running engrams. And one day you'll have a release. And another day you'll have a clear.

Types of Somatics

There are two kinds of somatics, those which properly belong to the patient and those which belong to his mother or some other person. The first actually happened, so did the second. But the patient should not have his mother's somatics. If he does, if he is found complaining of headaches whenever his mother has a headache, there is an engram, very early, which says he must have whatever she has: "The baby is part of me," "I want him to suffer as I suffer," etc. Or the phrase may be some entirely misunderstood thing literally taken. However, all this "comes out in the wash" and should be no great concern of the auditor's.

"Unconsciousness"

While "unconsciousness" has been covered elsewhere in various ways, in therapy it has two special manifestations: the yawn and the "boil-off."

The engram of physical pain contains deep "unconsciousness" and if it is going to lift, particularly in the basic area, it comes off in yawns. After a first or second recounting, the patient starts to yawn. These yawns are turning on his analyzer.

In a very extreme engram—a prenatal electric shock which mother received—five hours of "unconsciousness" "boil-off" have taken place during therapy. The shock lasted for less than a minute but so close did it bring the individual to death that when the incident was first contacted in therapy, he swam and floundered and had strange dreams, muttered and mumbled for five hours. That is a record. Forty-five minutes of this "boil-off" is rare. Five or ten minutes of it is not uncommon.

The auditor will take a patient into an area. No somatic turns on. But the patient begins to drowse into a strange kind of sleep. He rouses from this from time to time, mutters something, usually idiotic, rouses again with a dream and generally makes no progress to all appearances. But progress is being made. A period when he was almost dead is coming up to the surface. Soon a somatic will turn on and the patient will run an engram a few times on command, will yawn a little and then brighten up. Such a quantity of "unconsciousness" was, of course, sufficient to keep his analyzer about nine-tenths shut off when he was awake, for, if it was near basic, it was part of every other engram. Such an engram, with such deep "unconsciousness," when released, produces a marked improvement in a case, as much as a painful emotion engram at times.

It is up to the auditor to sit it through no matter how long it takes. It may make an uncleared auditor very sleepy to watch all this but it should be done. He will rarely strike one that lasts an hour but every case has such a period lasting from ten minutes to a half hour.

He should stir the patient up once in a while and try to make him go through the engram. There is a very special way to stir a patient into life: *don't touch his body* for it may be highly restimulative and make him very upset. Touch only the bottoms of his feet with your hand or your own feet and touch them just enough to jog him into attention for a moment. That keeps the "boil-off" in progress and does not permit the patient to sag into ordinary sleep.

The "boil-off" can be confused, by an inexperienced auditor, with an engram command to sleep. However, if the auditor will observe the patient closely, he will find that in the "boil-off" the patient gives every appearance of being drugged, while in a sleep command he simply goes to sleep and does it very smoothly. The "boil-off" is a trifle restless, full of mutterings and flounderings and dreams. The sleep is smooth.

An engramic command to go to sleep, acting on the returned preclear, is broken by sending the somatic strip to the moment when the sleep command is given. If the preclear contacts it and goes over it, he will quickly awaken on the track and continue with therapy.

The "boil-off" may be full of yawns, mutterings or grunts. Sleep is usually quiet and gentle.

Just why this is called a *boil-off* and just why auditors are fond of the term is obscure. It was originally and sedately named "comatic[12] reduction" but such erudition[13] has been outvoted by the fact that it has never been used.

If you are fond of listening to dreams, you will find them in plenty in the "boil-off." As images on the desert are distorted by the glass snakes of heat waves, so are the engramic commands distorted to the analyzer through the veil of "unconsciousness."

Locks

It is one of the blessings of nature that the lock is something which needs minor attention. A lock is an

---

12. comatic: of a coma (a period of deep, prolonged unconsciousness usually resulting from a severe injury or illness).

13. erudition: exhibition of knowledge not easily understood by the average person.

incident which, with or without charge, is in conscious recall and which *seems* to be the reason the aberree is aberrated. Perhaps this was another way the bank protected itself. A lock is a moment of mental discomfort containing no physical pain and no great loss. A scolding, a social disgrace: such things are locks. Any case has thousands and thousands of locks. The auditor will discover them in plenty if he cares to waste time looking for them. The treatment of these locks was the main goal of an old art known as "hypnoanalysis." Most of them can be reduced.

The key-in of an engram takes place at some future date from the time the engram was actually received. The key-in moment contains analytical reduction from weariness or slight illness. A situation similar to the engram, which contained "unconsciousness," came about and keyed in the engram. This is a *primary lock*. Breaking it, if it can be found, produces the effect of keying out the engram. But it can be considered a waste of time even if it has some therapeutic value and was used, without understanding, by some past schools.

If an auditor wants to know how the case was reacting to life, he can find some of these thousands and thousands of locks and look them over. But that is probably all the interest he has in them, for locks discharge. They discharge automatically the moment the engram holding them is erased. A whole life rebalances itself when the engrams are gone and the locks need no treatment. Neither does the preclear, now cleared, need education as to how to think: like the blowing of locks, this is an automatic process.

These locks lie down amongst the engrams sometimes. The preclear may be deep in the prenatal area and suddenly think about a time when he was twenty or, as is common in therapy, think about an engram he heard from somebody else. This is a good clue. Pay no further heed to the lock: find the engram to which it attached itself, for there is an engram immediately with it. In dreams, these locks in distorted form come swimming up out of the bank, complicating the dream.

The Junior Case

Do not take on a Junior for your first case if you can avoid it. If Father was named George and the patient is called George, beware of trouble. The engram bank takes George to mean George and that is identity thought deluxe.

Mother says, "I hate George!" "That means Junior," says the engram, though Mother meant Father. "George is thoughtless." "George must not know." "Oh, George, I wish you had some sex appeal, but you haven't." And so go the engrams. A Junior case is seldom easy.

It is customary to shudder, in Dianetics, at the thought of taking on a Junior case. An auditor can be expected to slave his hardest when he has a case with nonsonic, which is off the time track and which is named after Father or Mother. Such cases resolve, of course, but if parents knew what they did to children by giving them any name which might appear in the engram bank, such as that of parents or grandparents or friends, it is certain the custom would vanish instanter.

Restimulating the Engram

"Ask often enough and you will receive," is always true when working the engram bank. Simply by returning into an area enough times engrams will appear. If it is not there today, it will be there tomorrow. But if it is not there tomorrow, it will be there the day after and so forth. Emotional discharges are most certainly located by asking for them time after time, returning the patient over the part of the track where the charge is expected to lie. What repeater technique will fail to do can be done by returning the patient, session after session, to a portion of his life. Sooner or later it will come into view.

Occluded Life Periods and People

Whole areas of the time track will be found occluded. These contain suppressors by way of engram command, ally computations and painful emotion. Persons can vanish utterly from sight for these reasons. They come to view after a few engrams have been lifted in basic or the area has been developed as above.

Animosity Toward Parents

It always happens, when one clears a child or adult, that the preclear goes through stages of improvement which bring him up the tone scale and cause him, of course, to pass through the second zone, anger. A preclear may become furious with his parents and other offenders in the engram bank. Such a situation is to be expected. It is a natural byproduct of therapy and it cannot be avoided.

As the case progresses, the tone level, of course, rises and places the preclear in a state of boredom toward the villains who have wronged him. At last he reaches tone 4, which is the tone of the clear. At this time he is very cheerful and willing to be friends with people whether they have wronged him or not: of course he has the data about what to expect of them, but he nurses no animosity.

If a parent feels that the child, knowing all, would turn against him, then the parent is mistaken. The child has already, as an aberree, turned very thoroughly against the parent whether his analyzer knows all or not, and the most uncertain and unlovely conduct may result from further hiding of the evidence.

It is a matter of continual observation that the good release and the clear feel no animosity whatever toward their parents or others who had caused their aberrations and indeed stop negating, defending and fighting so irrationally. The clear will fight, certainly, for a good cause and he will be the most dangerous opponent possible, but he does not fight for irrational reasons like an animal, and his understanding of people is very much enlarged and his affection can at last be deep. If a parent wishes love and cooperation from a child, no matter what he has done to that child, permit therapy and achieve that love and cooperation with the child self-determined and no longer secretly in apathy or rage. After all, the clear has learned the source of his parents' aberrations as well as his own; he recognizes that they had engram banks before he did.

Propitiation

In the process of work a stage will be passed, in the upper range of apathy, of propitiation. This conciliation is an effort to feed or sacrifice to an all-destructive force. It is a state wherein the patient, in deep fear of another, offers expensive presents and soft words, turns the other cheek, offers himself as a doormat and generally makes a fool out of himself.

Many, many marriages, for instance, are marriages not of love but of that shabby substitute, propitiation.

People have a habit of marrying people who have similar reactive minds. This is unfortunate, for such marriages are destructive to both partners. She has a certain set of aberrations: they match his. She is pseudomother, he is pseudofather. She had to marry him because Father tried to murder her before she was born. He had to marry her because Mother beat him when he was a child. Incredible as it may seem, these marriages are very common: one or the other partner becomes mentally ill, or both may deteriorate. He is unhappy, his enthusiasms crushed; she is miserable. Either with another partner might be a happy person, yet, out of fear, they cannot break apart. They must propitiate each other.

The auditor who finds a marriage in this condition and attempts to treat one of the partners had better treat both simultaneously. Or such partners had better treat each other and soon. Tolerance and understanding are almost always fostered by mutual help.

Propitiation is mentioned here because it has a diagnostic value. People who start bringing the auditor expensive gifts are propitiating him, and it probably means that they have a computation which tells them, engramically, that they will die or go crazy if they become sane. The auditor may enjoy the gifts, but he had better start looking for a sympathy engram not yet suspected or tapped.

Love

Probably no single subject in the concerns of man has received as much attention as love.

It is not untrue that where one finds the greatest controversy, there he will also find the least comprehension. And where the facts are least precise there one can also find the greatest arguments. And so it is with love.

Without doubt, love has ruined more lives than war and made more happiness than all the dreams of paradise.

Entangled with a thousand songs a year and submerged beneath a solid tonnage of poor literature, love should have a proper chance to be defined.

It has been discovered that there are three kinds of love between woman and man: the first is covered under the law of affinity and is the affection with which mankind holds mankind; the second is sexual selection and is a true magnetism between partners; the third is compulsive "love" dictated by nothing more reasonable than aberration.

Perhaps in the hero and heroine legends there have been cases of the second kind, and surely as one looks about him in this society he can discover numbers of happy partnerships based on a natural and strongly affectionate admiration. The third kind we find in plenty: tabloid[14] literature is devoted to it and its travails; it crams the courts with urgent pleas for divorce, with criminal acts and civil suits; it sends children weeping into the corner away from quarrels; and it launches from its broken homes broken young women and men.

Dianetics classifies this third kind of love as "reactive mind partnership." Here is a meeting of minds—but the minds are on the lowest computational level possessed by man. Driven together by compulsion, men and women mate who will find in that mating nothing but sorrow and reduction of their hopes.

He is pseudobrother who beat her regularly or he is pseudofather whom she had to mind. Maybe he is even pseudomother who screamed ceaselessly at her but whom she had to placate, and he might be the doctor

---

14. tabloid: a newspaper usually half the ordinary size with many pictures and short, often sensational news stories.

who hurt her so savagely. She may be his pseudomother, his pseudograndmother whom he had to love despite the way she undermined his decision; she may be a pseudonurse in some operation long gone or the pseudo-teacher who kept him after school to whet her sadism upon him.

Before the marriage takes place they only know there is a compulsion that they must be together, a feeling that each must be extremely nice to the other. And then the marriage takes place and more and more restimulation of ancient pain is felt until at last each is ill and life, complicated now perhaps by unhappy children, is an unhappy ruin.

The mechanism of propitiation carries with it covert hostility. Gifts given without cause and beyond the ability to expend, self-sacrifices which seem so noble at the time compose propitiation. Propitiation is an apathy effort to hold away a dangerous "source" of pain. Mistaken identity is one of the minor errors of the reactive mind. To buy off, to nullify the possible anger of a person perhaps long since dead but living now again in the partner, is the hope of propitiation. But a man is dead who will not sometimes fight. The hostility may be masked, it may be entirely "unknown" to the individual who indulges it. Certainly it is always justified in the mind of the person who exerts it and is supposed to be a natural consequence of some entirely obvious offense.

The wife who makes inadvertent blunders before the guests and by them accidentally gives away the truth of her husband's favorite myth, the wife who forgets the little favors he has asked, the wife who suddenly stabs him with a "logical" pin in the region of his hopes: these are wives who live with partners whom they must, out of some wrong done years before the courtship and by some other man, propitiate, and these are wives who, propitiating, numb the hopes and misunderstand the sorrows of their mates.

The husband who sleeps with another woman and "accidentally" leaves the lipstick on his tie, the husband who finds her excellent cooking bad and idleness in her days, the husband who forgets her letters he must mail, the husband who finds her opinions silly: these are husbands who live with partners whom they must propitiate.

A soaring, roller-coaster curve of peace and war in the home, failures to understand, mutual curtailment of liberty and self-determinism, unhappy lives, unhappy children and divorce are caused by reactive mind marriages. Compelled by an unknown threat to marry, repelled by fear of pain from trust, this "meeting of minds" is the primary cause of all marital disaster.

The law lacked definition and so invoked great difficulty in the path of those involved in such marriages. The track of it is the dwindling spiral of misery which accompanies all chronic restimulation and leads only down to failure and to death. Someday there will, perhaps, exist a much more sentient law that only the unaberrated can marry and bear children. The present law only provides that marriages must be at best most difficult to part. Such a law is like a prison sentence for the husband, the wife and the children—all and every one.

A marriage can be saved by clearing its partners of their aberrations. An optimum solution would include this in any case since it is most difficult for a wife or a husband to rise, even when divorced, to any future plane of happiness: and where there are children, if clearing is not effected, a great injustice has been done.

It is usually discovered that when both partners in a reactive mind marriage are cleared of aberration, life becomes considerably more than tolerable; for human beings often have a natural liking even when no sexual selection has been present. The restoration of a marriage

411

by clearing the partners may not bring about one of the great loves that poets strummed about, but it will at least bring a high level of respect and cooperation toward the common goal of making life worthwhile. And in many marriages so cleared it was discovered that the partners, beneath the dirty cloth of aberration, loved each other well.

A major gain to such a clearing is for the children's sake. Nearly all marital discontent has as its major factor aberration on the second dynamic, sex. And any such aberration includes a nervous disposition toward children.

Where there are children, divorce does not answer, clearing does. And with clearing comes a fresh new page of life on which happiness can be written.

In the case of the reactive mind marriage, turnabout clearing is often complicated by the concealed hostilities which lie below the propitiative mechanism. It is wise for the partners to look outside the home, each interesting a friend in a therapy turnabout. If such mutual clearing is begun, with the partners working on each other, much restraint of anger and exertion of patience must be practiced, and the Auditor's Code must be most severely followed. It requires a saintly detachment to bear the tone 1 of the partner who, returned to a quarrel, seasons the recountings with further recrimination. If it must be done, it can be done but, when many quarrels and travails have beset a couple, it is easier if they each look without the home for a therapy partner.

Additionally, there is a kind of "rapport" established between any auditor and preclear and, after the therapy session is done, a strengthening of the natural affinity is such that a small deed or word may be taken as a savage attack with the result of a quarrel and the inhibition of therapy.

Men can be considered to be best audited by men

and women by women. This condition is changed when one deals with a woman who has such severe aberrations about women that she is in fear around them or when one is auditing a man who has deep fear of men.

The dynamics of men and women are somehow different and a wife, particularly if there have ever been quarrels of any magnitude, sometimes finds it difficult at times to be sufficiently insistent to audit her husband. The husband may audit, in the usual case, without great difficulty but when in therapy himself, his feeling that he must rise superior to the situation forces him to attempt autocontrol, a thing which is impossible.

The Erasure

Sooner or later—if you keep trying—you will get basic-basic, the earliest moment of "unconsciousness" and physical pain. You will know when you have it, perhaps, only because things start to erase rather than reduce. If the patient still has a sonic shut-off, you can still erase: sooner or later that sonic will turn on, perhaps not even until the case is almost finished. You will reach basic-basic sooner or later.

The erasure, then, is more or less the same procedure as the entrance. You erase all the early engrams, always the earliest you can find, and you keep discharging painful emotion engrams either in the basic area or in the later periods after birth and later in life. You erase as much as you can find in the early part of the case, then you release all the emotion you can find later in the case (erase everything in each engram you touch) and then you come back and find early material.

The reactive engram bank is a hurrah's nest.[15] The file clerk must have a great deal of trouble with it. For

---

15. hurrah's nest: state of utmost confusion; a mess.

things are keyed in early and late, sometimes all he can get is material under certain topics; sometimes all he can get is material under certain somatics (all teeth, for instance); sometimes he can go in an orderly parade forward in time and give consecutive incidents: this last is the most important proceeding.

Not until you have worked out every moment of physical pain and discharged all the moments of painful emotion will the case be cleared. There will be times when you are sure that you are almost to the goal only to discover, going into the prenatal area again, a new series of material uncovered by the later life painful emotion you have released.

One day you will find a case which will not have any occlusions anywhere on the track, which will no longer be interested in engrams (apathy cases aren't interested at the start; clears, at the top level, are not interested either, making a cycle, though the clear is a long way from apathetic), which will have all recalls, which will compute accurately and make no errors (within the limitations of the data available) and which, in short, has an exhausted engram bank. But do not be too optimistic, ever. Keep looking until you are sure. Observe the case to make certain no aberrations are displayed about anything, that dynamics are high in it and that life is good. If this person now feels he can solve all the problems of life, lick the world with one hand tied behind him and feel a friend to all men, you have a clear.

The only way you can go wrong is to compute with the idea that human beings are full of error and evil and sin and that if you have made a person less unhappy and above normal he is to be judged a clear. This is a *release*.

In gold panning, it is true that every tenderfoot mistakes iron pyrites—fool's gold—for gold. The tenderfoot will crow with delight over a bright bit of something in his pan which, actually, is worth a few dollars a ton. And then he sees real gold! The moment he sees real gold in that pan, he knows what gold really looks like. It cannot be mistaken.

Aside from the fact that psychometry[16] would show a clear phenomenally intelligent, would show his aptitude and versatility wide, there is another quality, the human quality of a freed man. You take a *release* through psychometry and show him to be above normal, too. But a clear is a clear and when you see it you will know it with no further mistake.

That a clear is no longer interested in his extinct engrams does not mean he is not interested in the troubles of others. That a person is not interested in his own engrams does not necessarily argue a clear but may well be another mechanism, the apathy of neglect. To have engrams and neglect them is a common aberration with the reactive mind on a tone scale level of apathy. To have no engrams and neglect them is another thing. Every apathy case, neglecting his engrams as an answer to his woe, insisting he is happy, insisting, as he racks himself to pieces, that there is nothing wrong with *him*, will, in work, particularly after basic-basic is lifted, become interested in his engrams and more interested in life. It is easy to tell the apathy case from the clear for the two are at opposite ends of the spectrum of life: the clear has soared up toward victory and triumph; the apathy case knows victory and triumph are not for him and explains they are not worth it.

What the life span of a clear is cannot be answered now; ask in a hundred years.

How can you tell a clear? How close does the man measure to optimum for man? Can he adjust to his environment smoothly? And far more important, can

---

16. psychometry: same as psychometrics: measurement of psychological variables, as intelligence, aptitude and emotional disturbance.

he adjust that environment to him?

Sixty days and again six months after a clear has apparently been effected, the auditor should again make a search for any neglected material. He should question the possible clear carefully as to the events of the past interval. In such a way he can learn of any worries, concerns or illnesses which may have taken place and attempt to trace these to engrams. If he cannot then find engrams, the clear is definitely and without question, cleared. And he will stay that way.

If a case merely stalls, however, and while aberration seems to be present, engrams cannot be found, the cause probably lies with thoroughly masked despair charges—painful emotional engrams. These are not necessarily postnatal, they can be within the prenatal period and involve circumstances which are very secret—or so the engrams announce. Also, some cases have stalled and proven "impenetrable" because of a current or immediately past circumstance the patient has not revealed.

There are two reasons which can delay a case:

a. the person may be so aberratedly ashamed of his past or so certain of retribution if he reveals it that he does nothing but avoid; and

b. the person may be in fear because of some existing circumstance or threat.

The auditor is not interested in what the patient does. Or in what the patient has done. Dianetics treats[17] of what has been done *to* the person exclusively in therapy. What has been done *by* a patient is of no concern. The auditor who would make it any concern is practicing something other than Dianetics. However, a patient, because of his engrams, may become obsessed with the idea that he must hide something in his life

---

17. treat: to deal with a subject in writing or speech; speak or write (*of*).

from the auditor. The two general classes above cover the general conditions.

These active reasons, as under (a), may be such a thing as a prison sentence, a murder hitherto unknown (although many people think they have done murder who have not even threatened it to anyone), abnormal sexual practices or some such circumstance. The auditor should promise not to reveal any confidential matter, purely as a matter of routine and explain the principle of "done *to,* not done *by.*" And no auditor would taunt or revile a patient for having been victimized by his engrams. As under (b) there may exist some person, even the wife or husband, who has cowed[18] the patient into secrecy. One case is at hand where no advance was made although there were many incidents contacted: the incidents would not reduce or erase no matter where they were. It was discovered that this case, a woman, had been beaten savagely and often by her husband and that she had been threatened with death if she told the auditor a word of these acts; and yet these acts contained the whole despair charges of the case and had to be released. Seeing this, finally suspecting, the auditor was able to gain her confidence and locate the despair charges. Even if he had not gained her confidence, by constant restimulation of late-life areas he would have provoked her tears. In another case, that of a small child, "dub-in" recall was so obvious and lie factories were so busy that the auditor at last realized that he was attempting to penetrate not just the secrecy on an engram but the secrecy imposed upon a child by someone at hand. The mother, in this case, out of the idea that she would be apprehended, had furiously threatened the child to say nothing about his treatment at home. There was more

---

18. cow: to subdue by frightening with threats or force.

than this behind the case: there were eighty-one attempted abortions, an incredible number.

Anything is the business of an auditor if it has become an engram. If society has jailed a man, if all is not well in the home, these are things done *to* a person. What the person did to "deserve" this treatment is of no concern.

The Foreign-Language Case

Now and again an auditor will encounter a strange sort of holdup in a case. He will be unable to get anything to clear or make sense in the prenatal area, and sometimes in childhood as well as the prenatal area. He may be encountering a "foreign-language case." Occasionally, the child did not know he was born to other parents (who may have spoken a foreign tongue) than those he has known as his parents. This is a special sort of mix-up of its own which is rather easily resolved simply by running engrams. It is always possible for the patient to forget that his parents spoke some other tongue in the home. Another tongue than the one the patient is using or other than that of the country in which the patient resides is, in one way, an asset: it gives a prenatal area which is very difficult to restimulate although it may still be acting upon the patient's mind. But it is no asset to the auditor, who must now deal with a patient who does not know the language, who may not have sonic recall and yet has an engram bank full of data which once had meaning and really is his basic language.

The best remedy for such a case is to get an auditor who knows both the language used in the prenatal area and the present tongue. Another remedy is to take a dictionary to the case and figure out the bouncers, *et al.*, from the dictionary. Another way is to return the patient often enough into the infant period that he begins to pick up the language again (making the file drawer of it come forth) and then ask the patient for phrases which, in the foreign tongue, would mean this or that. Gradually he may recover the language and so exhaust the bank. This is an extremely difficult case only when there was no childhood use of the other tongue. Given childhood use of that tongue, the auditor simply keeps returning the patient to childhood when he knew the tongue and then returning him into the prenatal area; the patient can translate what is happening. The clichés of other tongues than that the auditor speaks are often quite productive of other literal meanings than comparable clichés in the auditor's tongue. This difference of cliché is a very responsible agent in the social aberrations of one nation as they differ from those of another. "I have hot," says the Spaniard. "I am hot," says the Englishman. Engramically, they mean different things, even if they mean the same to the analyzer.

Mechanisms and Aspects of Therapy—Part Two

Extrasensory Perception

Every time the auditor has a case with dub-in recall or which is highly charged with emotion, the case may return into the prenatal area and start describing scenery. This is the awe and wonder of some beholders. There is the patient in the womb and yet he can "see" outside. The patient tells about Father and Mother and where they are sitting and what the bedroom looks like, and yet there he is in the womb. Some pretty theories can be advanced for this: one of them is that the tortured fetus develops extrasensory perception in order to see what is coming next. ESP is an excellent theory and some observation may confirm it, *but not in the fetus.*

One must recall that the fetus, even if it has highly developed and clever cells, is yet not a truly rational organism. The presence of the engram does not necessarily mean that the fetus could think. The engram became most severely aberrative when the child finally learned speech. The engram is not a memory but a recording of pain and percepts.

Returning a grown man or a child into the prenatal area returns there an experienced mind which, connecting with these engrams, forms conclusions. To listen to some preclears one would think they read Keats[1] and drank lemonade every afternoon at four throughout the prenatal period.

---

1. Keats, John: (1795–1821) English poet.

To return *reason* and analytical power back into a period when neither reason nor analytical power existed, of course, impinges upon the returned individual many ideas. All he is supposed to run are the engrams and their contents. He may additionally, by dream mechanisms and current computation, try to fashion in a whole technicolor picture of the scenery.

This prenatal ESP does not in fact exist. It has been proven, after considerable test, that whenever the returned preclear thinks he sees something, the scenery itself is mentioned in the engrams and gives him an imaginary picture of it. There is no prenatal ESP, in other words. There are only descriptions and actions which suggest scenery and these suggestions, operating now upon the imagination, bring about the supposed visio.

This is most chronic with patients who have high-powered lie factories. When the auditor sees this, he begins to form a notion of the case he is engaged upon; he knows "dub-in sonic" may be used and he should find and discharge all painful emotion he can reach, for it is this painful emotion which so disposes a case to avoid. He can find, then, the lie factory itself, not the lie factory of the lie factory which produces lie factories, but the actual engram which causes all this delusion.

However, never bring a preclear up short on this material. Don't tell him it is imaginary, you'll drive the lie factory into higher effort. For there are sympathy computations here, despairful losses, great prenatal pain and childhood neglect. And it would take little to shatter what self-confidence this patient has managed to assemble. Therefore walk softly, look for despair charges, allies, sympathy engrams and get the lie factory. Then the case will settle down and progress to clear.

Electric Shock

It has been found important, in entering a case, to locate and relieve all engrams caused by electric shock of whatever kind. These seem to produce a grouping of engrams, whether they are received prenatally (as some have been), accidentally or at the hands of psychiatrists. Any electric shock seems to have more than usual force in the engram bank and apparently deranges the memory files of both past and future events surrounding the shock area. Further, electric shock injury contains a great depth of "unconsciousness" which thereafter holds the analytical mind in a reduced state.

Tacit Consent [2]

In the case of two preclears working on each other, each one assuming in his turn the auditor's role, a condition can arise where each prevents the other from contacting certain engrams.

For example, preclear A has an ally computation concerning a dog. He unknowingly seeks to protect this "prosurvival" engram within himself although, of course, failure to release it will hinder therapy. As he audits preclear B he has a tendency to project his own problems into preclear B, which is to say he has some slight confusion of identity. If preclear B is known to have some "prosurvival" engram about a dog, then preclear A, auditing, will actually avoid making preclear B contact B's own engram. This is a mistaken idea that by letting B keep his dog engram, A can retain his dog engram. This is "tacit consent." It might be summed as a bargain: "If you don't make me get well, I won't make

---

2. tacit consent: mutual avoidance of certain subjects.

you get well." This should be guarded against: once known that such a condition exists and that such reluctance to clear the other is manifested, "tacit consent" ceases.

It may also happen that a husband and wife may have a mutual period of quarrels or unhappiness. Engaged upon clearing each other, working alternately as auditor, they avoid, unknowingly but by reactive computation, the mutual period, thus leaving in place painfully emotional engrams.

Tacit consent is not easily recognized by the individuals so involved, and preclears, alternating as auditors, should be very wary of it for it cannot do other than slow a case.

Emotion and Pain Shut-offs [3]

A case which manifests no emotion or cannot feel pain when emotion and pain should be present in some incident is suffering from a "feeling" shut-off: this most likely will be found in the prenatal area. The word *feeling* means both pain and emotion: thus the phrase, "I can't feel anything," may be an anesthetic for both.

If an exteriorized view of the incident (where the patient sees himself and is not in himself) or what pretends to be prenatal "ESP" is present, the emotional shut-off probably stems from painful emotion engrams in late life or at least postbirth. If there is no exteriorized view and the patient is within himself, and yet no sharpness of pain or emotion manifests itself while he is running through an engram, an early emotional shut-off

---

3. The somatic strip works in all shut-offs whether the patient feels it or not. The somatic strip also obeys but no somatic turns on when the incident is occluded by "unconsciousness," the somatic appearing after the "boil-off."

or an early pain shut-off should be suspected and should be located by repeater technique. Run the words "no emotion" until a paraphrase is obtained: run the words "I can't feel," or some other phrase meaning the same thing and the patient, if the engrams are available and are not suppressed by others, will eventually respond.

It may happen that a case may "work" very well, which is to say, that engrams present themselves and can be run and reduced, without emotion manifesting itself as part of the content and with somatics which are dull and not so much pain as simply pressure. If the pain and emotion shut-offs do not yield at first to repeater technique, many engrams may have to be run in the basic area without pain or emotion but only with pressure and word content. In such a case, pain and emotion can eventually be contacted, after which therapy is more beneficial.

Exteriorized Views

Whenever you find a patient, returned, outside himself and seeing himself, that patient is off the track. He should not be told so, but the despair charges, which is to say, the painful emotion engrams, should be found as soon as possible and discharged. This is something of the same mechanism as the ESP described above.

Telepathy

Every few cases some preclear may try to palm off telepathy as an aberrative factor. This is more rainbow chasing. There may be telepathy but, so far as research has shown, the fetus doesn't receive any and even if he receives it, it is not aberrative in any way.

Exhaustive tests were made on telepathy and ESP and in every case an explanation was found which did not need to go into mind reading or radar sight.

When a patient tries to tell the auditor that he is reciting Mother's thoughts received prenatally, be certain that somewhere around there is an engram in which she says these exact words aloud. Mothers, especially when aberrated severely and especially when aberrated severely enough to attempt abortion, have many engrams they dramatize. The power of the dramatization commonly manifests itself as monologues. Some mothers have a very great deal to say to themselves when alone. All of this speech is, of course, transmitted to the child when he is injured, and he may be injured without Mother being injured as in an attempted abortion. For considerable time after such an injury the child is usually "unconscious" and in pain; he therefore records in engrams these monologues (and often the voice is quite loud). He doesn't hear it: it is simply cellularly recorded. All such monologuing is aberrative, of course, and produces some remarkable patterns of insanity and neurosis.

But of telepathy, there is none that is aberrative so far as we know at this time. So the auditor should not accept telepathy any more than he would accept ESP.

Prenatal Living Conditions

It is very noisy in the womb. A person may think he has sonic and yet hear no "womb" sounds, which means that he does not have sonic but only "dub-in." Intestinal squeaks and groans, flowing water, belches, flatulence and other body activities of the mother produce a continual sound.

It is also very tight in later prenatal life.

In a high blood pressure case, it is extremely horrible in the womb.

When Mother takes quinine,[4] a high ringing noise may come into being in the fetal ears as well as her own—a ringing which will carry through a person's whole life.

Mother gets morning sickness, has hiccoughs and gets colds, coughs and sneezes.

This is prenatal life.

The only reason anybody "wanted" to "return to the womb" was because somebody hit Mother and yelled "Come back here!" so the person does.

The Engram Filing System

Engrams are not filed in the orderly fashion managed by a cleared standard bank. Engrams are filed in a way which would defy Alexander. Hence, it is difficult to know when the proper consecutive item will appear.

Time, topic, value, somatic and emotion are the methods of filing.

The return from basic-basic may be an apparent orderly progress into late life. Suddenly a despair charge is triggered and discharged. The auditor looks back at the prenatal area and finds a whole new series of incidents in view. Progress is then begun back to present time, step by step, another discharge is triggered and another series of prenatals comes into sight. These are erased and progress is made back toward present time when still another despair charge is released and still more prenatals come to view. These are erased and so forth and so on.

---

4. quinine: a bitter medicinal drug used to treat malaria and in tonics.

The engram filing system gives out data by somatic, time, topic, value or emotion. Usually the file clerk hands out material on the basis of time and topic. Emotion in the bank keeps the file clerk from getting at a certain series of incidents; when the emotion is discharged, the incidents become available and incidents are brought out until another emotional charge stops the file clerk. The wit of the auditor is most used, not in getting prenatals, but in finding these later life emotional charges and discharging them.

All in all the engram filing system is very poor, unlike the standard bank. But it is also very vulnerable now that we understand it.

The engram filing system data can be erased. Standard bank data cannot be erased. Pain is perishable—pleasure endures.

Alleviation

The psychoanalyst or general counselor in human relations is occasionally faced with a type of problem which Dianetics, applied in small quantity, can resolve easily.

It is possible, when a person has been too disturbed by an event of the day to address himself to the problem at hand, to alleviate his disturbance with a few minutes of work.

A sudden change in the aspect of a patient, a sudden deterioration of his serenity, generally stems from some incident which has caused him mental anguish. Although this change of mind has its source in the restimulation of an engram, the moment of restimulation, which is a lock, may be addressed and alleviated with success.

Using reverie or merely asking the patient to close his eyes, the analyst can request him to return and be in the instant wherein he was disturbed. That instant may be in the same day or the same week as the office call. A moment of analytical shutdown will be discovered wherein some restimulative person or circumstance upset the equilibrium of the patient. This moment is a lock. It can be recounted, ordinarily, as an engram and the latest source of tension will relieve so that work can be continued. The engram itself, upon which the lock depended, may not be accessible without a full Dianetic address to the problem.

The auditor, finding a patient much disturbed, can often save time by relieving the lock which caused the immediate disturbance of the preclear.

Locating locks on a wholesale basis is unremunerative from a Dianetic viewpoint since there are thousands and thousands of them in every case. Locating the last lock, which is hindering work, may be of benefit.

The Tone Scale and Reduction of Engrams

Because it is very important, the mechanism of the reduction of a late painful emotion engram must be specifically detailed.

The uses of reduction on late engrams are wide and various. When the auditor gets into trouble with his preclear by some violation of the Auditor's Code, he can treat the violation as a painful emotion engram and reduce it, at which moment the effect of his blunder will be gone in the preclear. The auditor merely returns the preclear back to the blunder and runs the error itself as an engram. When the husband has quarreled with his wife or she has found out some unpleasant thing about his activities, he can treat the quarrel or the discovery as a painful emotion engram and release it with the result of no further worry about it by his wife. When the little boy's dog has just been run over, the incident can be treated as a painful emotion engram and released. When the preclear's wife has just left him, treat the leaving as a painful emotion engram and release it. Whatever the shock or upset, it can be reduced in an individual by regular reduction technique and the individual will cease to be troubled by it in the painful emotion sense.

It does not matter whether the engram occurred two hours or ten years ago, painful emotion can be reduced from it. It is run exactly like any other engram, beginning at the beginning of the first shock with the patient returning to it and continuing far enough along it to adequately embrace its first impact.

The aspect of this reduction is a pattern which does not much vary. If the news struck the individual into apathy, then, as he recounts, he will, unless there is a severe emotional shut-off elsewhere, progress through the incident a time or two, perhaps, before he contacts it properly. Then there will come the tears and despair of apathy. Another two or three runs should bring up anger. Then further recounting (always from beginning to end as reexperience) brings the tone up into boredom. Further recounting should bring it to tone 3 or 4, release or, most favorably, laughter.

This progress of the tones is the clue which led to the establishment of the tone scale from 0 to 4. A tone 4 is laughter.

There is sometimes a stage in the tone 2 area where the patient begins to be offhand and flippant. This is not tone 4, it denotes more data present. He may resist recounting at this point, saying the incident is released. The auditor must insist on further recounting whenever he finds the preclear unwilling to recount again, for here is data being suppressed and more charge is present. The flippancy is generally found to be an escape mechanism and is sometimes uttered in the very words which are yet concealed. More recounting (without the auditor insisting any certain words be found) is then done until the patient reaches tone 4.

Here we have, in vignette,[5] the behavior of the whole engram bank in the process of therapy. The entire bank rises from its initial tone level eventually up to tone 4, higher and higher as more and more engrams are erased or reduced. The bank's rise is not, however, a smooth upward curve for new engrams will be contacted with apathy in them and some have manics in them. The painful emotion engram, however, does a rather smooth rise. If it is going to release at all it will rise up the scale. If it does not rise up the scale—apathy to anger, anger to boredom, boredom to cheerfulness or at least no concern—then it is suppressed by an incident with similar content.

An engram may begin at tone 1—anger—and rise from there. If it is found to be in tone 2 at the start—boredom—it is hardly an engram.

It may, however, be in a false tone 2 and suppressed by other data so that the patient merely appears bored and careless about it. A few recountings may bring about release of it, at which moment it will sag instantly to apathy—tone 0—and then come on up the scale of the tones. Or another engram may have to be contacted.

The whole physical being follows this tone scale throughout a course of therapy. The mental being follows this tone scale. And painful emotion engrams follow it.

On an erasure down in the basic area or when returning from basic-basic, two or three runs will erase an engram of whatever kind unless it is the basic on a new chain of similar incidents. But engrams which show no emotion anywhere on the track are suppressed by emotional or feeling shut-offs, late painful emotion or

5. vignette: a short description or character sketch.

early engrams, which simply shut off the pain or emotion in so many words.

A case should be kept "live." There must be variability of emotion. A monotone recounting, which is to say, one which does not vary the engramic tone but merely reduces, is necessary in the basic area at times, but any time a patient becomes orderly and "well drilled" and expresses no concern over his engrams as he recounts them, there is late painful emotion to be tapped or early emotional shut-off. Conversely, if the patient is too continuously emotional about all and anything, if he weeps a while and then laughs hysterically, therapy is being done but one should be alert for something engramic in the prenatal area which says he has to be "too emotional"—which is to say, he has engrams which make him emotional by their command content.

The tone scale is very useful and is a good guide. It will be most prominent in reducing postspeech engrams, but will also appear earlier.

Any painful emotion engram can be run. If it is properly reducing and not suppressed elsewhere, it follows the tone scale upwards to tone 4.

If the Patient Does Not Work Well on Repeater Technique

If, when the patient repeats a line the auditor has given him, the patient does not move to an incident, three things can be wrong: first, the patient cannot move on the track; second, the phrase may be sensibly withheld by the file clerk until such time as it can be cleared; or third, the phrase does not exist as engramic material.

The patient may also have strong "control yourself" engrams which manifest themselves by his snatching control from the auditor, being very bossy or simply refusing cooperation. Repeater technique, when directed at "control yourself" and "I've got to operate" and allied phrases, can then work.

The usual reason repeater technique does not work is that the patient is in a holder. If he is returned but does not shift on the track when repeater technique is given him, use repeater technique on the holders.

Remember that a "feeling" shut-off can deny all somatics so that the patient does not feel them. If the patient seems insensible to trouble on the track, be sure that he has a feeling shut-off.

A large emotional charge may also inhibit repeater technique. The somatic strip does not go well into emotional charges—painful emotion engrams—and repeater technique is therefore indicated.

If repeater technique does not work, although it is seldom necessary, one may request the patient to imagine "the worst thing that could happen to a baby" and so forth, and from his conversation may be garnered[6] new phrases for repeater work which will take the patient into an engram.

Single Word Technique

Words as well as engrams exist in chains. There is always a first time for the recording of each word in a person's life. The whole common language may lie within the engram bank. The possible combinations of that common language may well approach infinity. The ways various denyers, bouncers, *et al.*, can be phrased are always beyond count.

Two "happy" facts exist, however, to reduce the auditor's labors. First, the dramatis personae[7] of his

---

6. garner: to acquire or earn.
7. dramatis personae: the characters in a play or story.

engrams are at this date aberrated. Each aberree has standard dramatizations which he repeats over and over in restimulative situations. The reaction, for instance, of the father to the mother is repetitious: if he utters a set of phrases in one engramic situation, he will utter it in subsequent similar situations. If the mother, for example, has an accusative attitude toward the father, then that attitude will be expressed in certain terms and these terms will appear in engram after engram. The second fact is that where the father or mother is abusive to the other, the other will eventually begin to suffer contagion of aberration and will repeat the other's phrases. In a firstborn child, where parental brutality is present, one can observe the parents through the engrams of the patient and see one or the other gradually take up the other's phrases either to worry about themselves or to redeliver them. All this tends to make the engrams appear in chains of incidents, each incident much like the next. When one has the basic on each type of chain, the subsequent incidents on that chain are sufficiently similar to permit many incidents to be reduced or erased immediately after the first is found. The *first* incident on the chain, the basic for that chain, holds the others more or less in place and out of sight; therefore, the basic of the chain is the goal.

Each word in the bank can be discovered to have been delivered to the bank for the first time. Words also reduce in chains with the virtue that each subsequent appearance of the word in the bank locates automatically a new engram, which, of course, is reduced or erased as soon as it is contacted or as soon as its basic can be located.

Single word technique is very valuable and useful. It is a special kind of repeater technique. On most patients, the repetition by themselves of one word will cause the associated words to suggest themselves. Thus, one asks the patient to repeat and return on the word *forget*. He starts repeating the word *forget* and shortly has an associated set of words, making a phrase, such as "You can never forget me." Here we have a phrase in an engram and the remainder of the engram can then be run.

When a late engram has had to be contacted to progress a case and yet will not relieve, it is possible to take each word or phrase of that late engram and run it back with repeater technique. Thus the earlier engrams which hold this late engram in place can be located and reduced, and eventually one will have reduced the late engram itself. This, by the way, is a common and useful practice.

There is a law about this: *When any phrase or word in an engram will not reduce, the same phrase or word occurs in an earlier engram.* One may have to discharge late emotion to get the earlier phrase, but ordinarily single word repeater or phrase repeater will attain it.

There are only a few dozens of words necessary to get almost any engram. These would be the key single word repeaters. They are such words as these: *forget, remember, memory, blind, deaf, dumb, see, feel, hear, emotion, pain, fear, terror, afraid, bear, stand, lie, get, come, time, difference, imagination, right, dark, black, deep, up, down, words, corpse, dead, rotten, death, book, read, soul, hell, god, scared, miserable, horrible, past, look, everything, everybody, always, never, everywhere, all, believe, listen, matter, seek, original, present, back, early, beginning, secret, tell, die, found, sympathy, mad, crazy, insane, rid, fight, fist, chest, teeth, jaw, stomach, ache, misery, head, sex, Anglo-Saxon four-letter words of sex and profanity, skin, baby, it, curtain, shell, barrier, wall, think, thought, slippery, confused, mixed, smart, poor, little, sick, life, Father, Mother, familiar names of parents and any others of household during prenatal and childhood period, money, food, tears, no, world, excuse, stop, laugh, hate, jealous, shame, ashamed, coward,* etc.

Bouncers, denyers, holders, groupers, misdirectors, *et al.*, each have their common single words and these are few. The bouncer would contain: *out, up, return, go, late, later,* etc.

The holder would contain: *catch, caught, trap, trapped, stop, lie, sit, stay, can't, stuck, fixed, hold, let, lock, locked, come,* etc.

The grouper would contain: *time, together, once, difference,* etc.

The single word technique shines nowhere brighter than in the Junior case—where the patient carries the name of one or another parent or grandparent. By clearing out the patient's name from the prenatal engrams (where it is applied to another person but misinterpreted by the patient as himself), the patient can regain his own definition and valence. Always use the patient's first name and last name (separately) as repeater, Junior or not.

If the engram bank is blank on a phrase, it probably is not blank on a common word. Any *small* dictionary will provide an ample fund for single word technique. Use also any list of familiar first names, male and female, and you may discover allies or lovers not otherwise contactable.

The painful emotion engram sometimes yields slowly by simply directing the somatic strip to it. Sometimes the patient finds it difficult to approach an overcharged area. Single word technique using the name of the ally, if known, or words of sympathy, endearment, death, rejection or farewell, and the love name of the patient as a child in particular, will often yield swift results.

By the way, in using repeater technique, word or phrase, the auditor *must* not stir the case up too much. Get what shows and reduce that. Reduce the somatic the person manifests when he goes into reverie and always try to find it for a while, even if you don't succeed. If you stir up something en route down a chain which won't reduce, mark it to be reduced when you have the basic.

Using single word technique one often obtains phrases which would otherwise remain hidden but which come into view when the key word is tapped. Using *hear* as a single word, for instance, the following phrases came to light which had thoroughly impeded the progress of the case. No effort was being made to contact such an engram in the prenatal area. Indeed, the "fight" chain had never been suspected since the patient had never dramatized it, and, because such a violent prenatal fight chain existed, the fact that his parents fought violently in the home was utterly struck from the standard banks so that he would have denied such a thing with shocked surprise had it been suggested. The somatic was unusually severe, caused by the father kneeling on the mother and choking her.

Patient repeated "hear" several times, the auditor asking him to return to an incident containing that word. The patient continued to repeat and then suddenly sank into a stupor when he reached the prenatal area. He remained in this "boil-off" for about thirty minutes and then, the auditor rousing him occasionally to make him repeat the word "hear," manifested a strong somatic. "Hear" became "Stay here!" The somatic became stronger and "Stay here" was repeated until the patient could move freely on the track through the engram. He contacted his father's voice and was most reluctant to carry on with the engram, due to its intense emotional violence. Coaxed and edged into it by the auditor, the engram was recounted.

Father: "Stay here! Stay down, damn you, you bitch! I'm going to kill you this time. I said I would and I

will. Take that!" (Intensified somatic as his knee ground into the mother's abdomen.) "You better start screaming. Go on, scream for mercy! Why don't you break down? Don't worry, you will! You'll be blubbering around here, screaming for mercy! The louder you scream the worse you'll get. That's what I want to hear! I'm a punk kid, am I? You're the punk kid! I could finish you now but I am not going to!" (Auditor suddenly has trouble, patient taking last phrase literally and stopping his recounting; auditor starts him again.) "This is just a sample. There's a lot more than that where it came from! I hope it hurts! I hope it makes you cry! You say a word to anybody and I'll kill you in earnest." (Patient now running ahead with such an emotional surge that commands are less active on him. This command to remain quiet disregarded.) "I'm going to bust your face in. You don't know what it is to be hurt!" (Somatic lessened by removal of the knee.) "I know what I'm going to do to you now! I'm going to punish you! I'm going to punish you and God is going to punish you! I'm going to rape you! I'm going to stick it into you and tear you! When I tell you to do something you've got to do it! Get up on the bed! Lie down! Lie still!" (Crack of bones as she is struck in the face with a fist. Blood pressure coming up and hurting baby.) "Lie still! You'll always be here! I'm going to finish this! You're unclean! You are dirty and diseased! God's punished you and now I'm going to punish you!" (Coitus somatic begins, very violent, further injuring child.) "You've got something terrible in your past. You think you've got to be mean to me! You try to make me feel like nothing! You're the one that's nothing! Take it, take it!" (String of sexual banalities screamed for about five minutes.)

The patient recounted this three times and it erased. It was basic-basic! Three days after conception, as nearly as could be judged by the subsequent days to the missed period. It threw into view almost all the other important data in the case, which then resolved and was cleared.[8]

The single word might have landed the patient on some other of the *hear*s in the case. In this event it would be necessary to pick it up at its earliest moment or the remainder of the engram might not erase or reduce.

The word *hear* might also have landed the patient later on the track, in which case the engrams would have had to have been traced back earlier until one was found which would erase, reducing each one as it was encountered until the earliest was reached, when all would erase.

In using single word repeater, as in phrase repeater, the auditor should not permit a rapid, unmeaning repetition but a slow repeat, the auditor requesting the somatic strip to return the while and asking the patient to contact anything else which might associate with the word.

Caution: If the patient is not moving on the track, do not give him repeater words or phrases at random as these will pile up engrams where the patient is stuck. Use only efforts to get the patient moving on the track by discovering and reducing the phrase that is holding him.

---

8. Apropos of this text, it crossed the "fight chain" with the "coitus chain," occluding both. Wherever this engram originated or where the engrams which are compounded into it came from, is of course a matter of antiquity. This was home conduct for Papa, a character confirmed by the fact that both his wife and child were almost psychotic. Papa was not "psychotic." He was a "bold, forceful" and "forthright" man, president of a bank and renowned for his hardheadedness. The son was a drunkard, a soapbox atheist, and negated against everything his father represented including money. The son, while still in therapy, incautiously told his father of this engram and the father raved wildly against Dianetics for two days and then came down with "rheumatic fever," in which state he sent for the auditor in the case to clear him, which was done. Both cases were sonic shut-offs, pain and emotion shut-offs.

Caution: Basic-basic does not always have words in it, often being only painful and accompanied with womb sounds. It will, nevertheless, hold everything in place by its perceptics.

Special Classes of Commands

There are several distinct classes of commands. They are outlined here for ready reference with some samples of each.

Aberrative commands can contain anything. The auditor does not much concern himself with them. Refer back to our young man and the coat in Book Two and there we find, in the guise of hypnotic commands, some idea of what aberrative commands are. "I am a jub-jub bird," "I can't whistle Dixie," "The world is all against me," "I hate policemen," "I am the ugliest person in the world," "You haven't any feet," "The Lord is going to punish me," "I always have to play with my thing," may be very interesting to the patient and even amusing to the auditor and may have caused a considerable amount of trouble in the patient's life. Where Dianetic therapy is concerned, these all come up in due course. Looking for a specific aberration or a specific somatic is sometimes of interest and sometimes of some use, but it is not usually important. These aberrative commands may contain enough data to make the patient a raving zealot, a paranoid or a catfish, but they are nothing to the auditor. They come up in due course. Working on them or about them is secondary and less.

The primary business of the auditor in any case is to keep the patient moving on the track, keep his somatic strip free to come and go and *reduce engrams*. The moment the patient acts as though or responds as though he was not moving, or the moment the file clerk will not give forth data, then something is wrong and that something has to do with a few classes of phrase. There are thousands of such phrases contained in engrams, variously worded, but only five classes:

Denyers

"Leave me alone," which means, literally, that he must leave the incident alone.

"I can't tell" means he can't tell you this engram.

"It's hard to tell" means it is *hard* to tell.

"I don't want to know" means he has no desire to know this engram.

"Forget it" is the classic of the subclass of denyer, the forgetter mechanism. When the engram simply won't come to view but there is a somatic or a muscle twitch, send the somatic strip to the denyer. It is often "Forget it" or "Can't remember" as a part of the engram. "I don't know what's going on" may be Mama telling Papa something, but the preclear's analyzer, impinged, then doesn't know what's going on.

"It's beyond me" means he is right there but he thinks he isn't.

"Hold on to this, it's your life!" makes the engram "vital" to existence.

"It can't be reached," "I can't get in there," "Nobody must know," "It's a secret," "If anybody found out, I'd die," "Don't talk," and thousands more.

Holders

The *holder* is the most frequent and the most used since whenever the preclear can't shift on the track or come to present, he is in a holder. A holder combined with a denyer will still hold: if it can't be found, look for the denyer first, then the holder.

"I'm stuck" is the classic phrase.

"That fixed it" is another.

"I'm caught" doesn't mean to the preclear what Mama meant when she said it. It may mean to her that she is pregnant but it tells the preclear he is caught on the track.

"Don't move," "Sit there until I tell you to move," "Stop and think" (on this last phrase, when it is uttered on a first recounting, the auditor may have to start him going again for he does just that: he stops and thinks, and he would stop there and think for some time. The auditor will see this strange obedience to this literal nonsense as he works a case).

And thousands more. Any way words literally understood can stop a person or keep him from moving.

Bouncers

The *bouncer* could best be demonstrated by a curve. The preclear goes back into prenatal and then finds himself at ten years of age or even present time. That's a bouncer at work. He goes early on the time track: it says come back up.

When the preclear can't seem to get earlier, there is a bouncer ejecting him from an engram. Get a comment from him on what's happening. Take the comment or some phrase which would be a bouncer and use repeater technique until he settles back down on the engram. If he contacts it easily, it won't bounce him again.

"Get out" is the classic bouncer. The patient usually goes toward present time.

"Can't go back at this point" may mean Mama has decided she will have to have the baby after all or finish the abortion, but to the preclear it means he must move on up the time track or that he can't get any earlier period.

"Get up there."

"Run a mile." ("Beat it," would not be a bouncer; it would mean the preclear should beat the engram.)

"I must go far, far away," so he does.

"I'm growing up," "Blow you higher than a kite," "Batter up."

And thousands more.

Grouper

The *grouper* is the nastiest of all types of command. It can be so variously worded and its effect is so serious on the time track that the whole track can roll up into a ball and all incidents then appear to be in the same place. This is apparent as soon as the preclear hits one. The grouper will not be discovered easily, but it will settle out as the case progresses and the case can be worked with a grouper in restimulation.

"I have no time" and "Nothing makes any difference" are the classic groupers.

"Everything comes in on me at once" means just that.

"They're all in there together," "Screwed up," "Balled up," "It's *all* right here."

"You can remember all this in present time" (a serious auditor error if he uses this to a suggestible patient, for it will gloriously foul a case).

"You associate everything."

"I am tangled up," "Jam everything in there at once," "There's no time," and thousands more.

Misdirector

This is an insidious character, the *misdirector*. When it appears in an engram, the patient goes in wrong directions, to wrong places, etc.

"You're doing it all backwards."

"All up now" is a grouper and a misdirector.

"Always throwing it up to me" puts the preclear up the track some distance and from there he tries to pick up engrams.

"You can't go down" is partly bouncer, partly misdirector.

"We can't get to the bottom of this" keeps him off from basic-basic.

"You can start over again" keeps him from finishing the recounting, whereupon he goes back to the beginning of the engram instead of running it.

"Can't go through that again" keeps him from recounting.

"I can't tell you how it began" keeps him starting his engrams in the middle and they will not then reduce. There are many such phrases.

"Let's settle down" and all "settlings" make him drift backwards down the track.

"I am coming down with a cold" puts the aberree in a common cold engram. This can be counted upon to make every cold much worse.

"Come back here" is really a *call back* but it directs him away from where he should be. A patient who reaches present time with difficulty and then begins to go back has a "Come back here" or a "Settle down."

"Down and out" misdirects him, not only away from present time but to the bottom of the track and off it. This is a misdirector and a derailer all at once.

"Can't get past me" is a misdirector on the order of a reverser. "You don't know down from up" is the classic phrase.

"I'm all turned around."

A special case is the *derailer* which "throws him off the track" and makes him lose touch with his time track. This is a very serious phrase since it can make a schizophrenic and something of this sort is always to be found

443

in schizophrenia. Some of its phrases throw him into other valences which have no proper track, some merely remove time, some throw him bodily out of time.

"I don't have any time" is a derailer as well as a grouper.

"I'm beside myself" means that he is now two people, one beside the other.

"I'll have to pretend I am somebody else" is a key phrase to identity confusion.

"You're behind the times" and many more.

There is another special case of the misdirector. The auditor says to go to "present time" and the file clerk throws out a phrase with *present* in it. It does not matter if the present in the phrase was a Christmas present, if it is in the prenatal area, the preclear goes there, ignoring what the auditor meant.

"That's all at present," is a vicious phrase, putting everything in present time.

"It's a lovely present."

And others.

Now is sometimes confused with present time but not often. The auditor should not say "Come to now," because if he did he would find more *now*s than he could comfortably handle. *Present* is a rarer engramic word and is therefore used. *Now* appears too frequently.

Several severely aberrated persons who had little memory of the past have been found to be entirely off their time tracks, regressed into the prenatal area and stuck, when the case was entered. As far as their wits were concerned, they had only a few months of past from where they were back to conception. And yet these people had managed somehow to function as normals.

Emotional charges usually hold the person off his track and, indeed, are the only things which give these engram commands any power according to current findings.

Differences

There are two axioms about mind function with which the auditor should be familiar.

I. The mind perceives, poses and resolves problems relating to survival.
II. The analytical mind computes in differences.
   The reactive mind computes in identities.

The first axiom is of interest to the auditor in his work because with it he can clearly establish whether or not he is confronting a rational reaction. The seven-year-old girl who shudders because a man kisses her is not computing; she is reacting to an engram since at seven she should see nothing wrong in a kiss, not even a passionate one. There must have been an earlier experience, possibly prenatal, which made men or kissing very bad. All departures from optimum rationality are useful in locating engrams, all unreasonable fears and so forth are grist to the auditor's mill. The auditor, with the above law, should study as well the equation of the optimum solution. Any departure from optimum is suspect. While he cares little about aberrations, at times a case will stall or seem to have no engrams. He then can observe the conduct of his patient and his patient's reactions to life in order to gain data.

The second law is Dianetics' contribution to *logic*. In the philosophic text this is more fully entered. Aristotle's pendulum and his two-valued logic were abandoned, not because of any dislike of Aristotle but because broader yardsticks were needed. One of these yardsticks was the spectrum principle whereby gradations from zero to infinity and infinity to infinity were used and absolutes were considered utterly unobtainable for scientific purposes.

In the second axiom the mind can be conceived to recognize differences very broadly and accurately, in its nearest approach to complete rationality and then, as it falls away from rationality, to perceive less and less difference until at last it achieves a near approach to utter inability to compute any difference in time, space or thought and so can be considered completely insane. When this follows one thought only, such as a sweeping statement that "All cats are the same," it is either careless or insane, since all cats are not the same, even two cats who look, act and sound alike. One could say, "Cats are pretty much the same," and still be dealing with rather irrational thought. Or one could recognize that there was a species *Felix domesticus* but that within it cats were decidedly different, not only from breed to breed but cat to cat. That would be rationality, not because one used Latin but because he could tell the difference amongst cats. The fear of cats has as its source an engram which usually does not include more than one cat and that is a very specific cat of a specific breed with a certain (or perhaps uncertain) personality. The preclear who is afraid of all cats is actually afraid of one cat and a cat which is most likely dead these many years at that. Thus, as we swing from complete rationality down to irrationality, there is a narrowing of differences until they nearly vanish and become similarities and identities.

Aristotle's syllogism[9] in which two things equal to the same thing are equal to each other simply does not begin to work in logic. Logic is not arithmetic, which is an artificial thing man invented and which works. To handle a problem in logic the mind flutters through an

---

9. syllogism: a form of reasoning in which a conclusion is reached from two statements, as in *"All men must die; I am a man; therefore, I must die."*

enormous mass of data and computes with dozens and even hundreds of variables. It does not and never did think on the basis that two things equal to the same thing are equal to each other, except when employing mathematics it had conceived the better to resolve abstract problems. It is an abstract truth that two and two equal four. Two what and two what equal four? There is no scale made, no yardstick or caliper[10] or microscope manufactured which would justify the actuality, for instance, that two apples plus two apples *equal* four apples. Two apples and two apples are four apples now if they are the same apples. They would not equal four other apples by any growth or manufacturing process ever imagined. Man is content to take approximations and call them, loosely, exactitudes. There is no absolute anything save in abstract terms set up by the mind to work out exterior problems and achieve approximations. This may seem to be a stretched conception, but it is not. The mathematician is very well aware that he is working with digit and analogue approximations set up into systems which were not necessarily here before man came and will not necessarily be here after he is gone. Logic, even the simple logic of wondering about the wisdom of going shopping at ten, is handling numerous variables, indefinites and approximations. Mathematics can be invented by the carload lot. There is no actual absolute, there is only a near approach. Our grammarians alone, much behind the times, insist, probably in memory of the metaphysician, on absolute reality and truth.

This is here set down partly because it may be of interest to some but mainly because the auditor must

---

10. caliper: a compass for measuring the diameter of tubes or of round objects.

realize that he has an accurate measuring stick for sanity. *Sanity is the ability to tell differences.* The better one can tell differences, no matter how minute, and know the width of those differences, the more rational he is. *The less one can tell differences and the closer one comes to thinking in identities (A=A) the less sane he is.*

A man says, "I don't like dogs!" Spot it, auditor; he has an engram about one or two dogs. A girl says, "All men are alike!" Spot it, auditor; here's a *real* aberree. "Mountains are so terrible!" "Jewelers never go anyplace!" "I hate women!" Spot them. Those are engrams right out in broad daylight.

Those engrams which inhibit the analytical mind in differentiating are those engrams which most seriously inhibit thinking.

"You can't tell the difference," is a common engram. "There is no difference," "Nothing will ever make any difference to me again," "People are all bad," "Everybody hates me." This is insanity bait, as the auditors say, and puts a man "spinbin bound."

There is another class of identity thought and that is the group which destroys time differentiation. "You don't know when it happened!" is a classic phrase. "I don't know how late it is," and others have a peculiar effect on the mind, for the mind is running on a precision chronometer of its own and the engrams can thoroughly misread the dial. On a conscious level, one goes along fairly well on analytical time. The engrams slide around back and forth according to when they are keyed in or restimulated. An engram may underlie today's action which belonged forty years ago on the time track and should be back there. It is not remarks about time difference so much that aberrate, it is the untimed character of engrams. Time is the great charlatan; it heals nothing; it only changes the environmental aspects and a man's associates. The engram of ten years ago, with all its painful emotion, may be encysted and "forgotten," but it is right there, ready to force action if restimulated today.

The reactive mind runs on a dime store wristwatch, the analytical mind runs on a battery of counter-checking chronometers of which a liner could be proud. The cells think that wristwatch is a pretty fair gimmick—and it was, it was, back there in the days when man's ancestor was washed in by the waves and managed to cling to the sand.

Thus, a primary test for aberration is similarity and identity, the primary test for rationality is differentiation and the minuteness or largeness with which it can be done.

"Men are all alike," she says. And they are too! To her. Poor thing. Like the fellow who raped her when she was a kid, like her detested father who said it.

Relative Importances and "Believe" and "Can't Believe"

The auditor will find himself confronted with two archenemies in "You must believe it," and "I can't believe."

The mind has its own equilibrium and ability and it is aided no more by engrams than an adding machine is aided by a held-down seven.[11] One of the most important functions of the mind is the computing of the relative importances of data.

In discovering and conducting research on Dianetics, for instance, there were billions of data about

---

11. Or a five as in a recent case at Harvard where a spot of solder held down *five* in an electronic computer, much to the dismay of the gentlemen who depended upon it for answers.

the mind accumulated throughout the last few thousand years. Now, with a six-foot rear-vision mirror we can look back and see that here and there people had expressed opinions or turned up unevaluated facts which are now data in some of the axioms of Dianetics or parts of its discoveries. These facts existed in the past, some exist now in Dianetics, but with a tremendous difference: they are evaluated. *Evaluation* of the data for its importance was vital before the information was of value. Dr. Sententious[12] might have written in 1200 A.D. that he believed actual demons did not exist in the mind; Goodwife Sofie, in 1782, was heard to say that she was certain that prenatal influence had warped many a life; Dr. Zamba might have written in 1846 that a hypnotized patient could be told he was crazy and that he would thereafter act crazy. Dr. Sententious might have said *also* that angels, not demons, caused mental illness because the patient had been evil; Goodwife Sofie also might have said that punk[13] water poultices[14] cured "ravings"; Dr. Zamba might also have declared that hypnotized patients needed only a few more positive suggestions to make them well and strong. In short, for every datum which approached truth there were billions which were untrue. The missing part of each datum was a scientific evaluation of its importance to the solution. The selection of a few special drops of water from an ocean of unspecial drops is impossible. The problem of discovering true data could be resolved only by jettisoning all former evaluations of humanity and the human mind

---

12. Dr. Sententious: made-up name for an "authority." Sententious: putting on an air of wisdom, dull and moralizing.

13. punk: poor in quality or condition.

14. poultice: a hot, soft, moist mass, as of flour, herbs, mustard, etc. Sometimes spread on cloth, applied to a sore or inflamed part of the body.

and all "facts" and opinions of whatever kind and starting fresh, evolving the entire science from a new highest common denominator (and it is true that Dianetics borrowed nothing but was first discovered and organized; only after the organization was completed and a technique evolved was it compared to existing information).

The point here is that monotone importance in a class of facts leads to nothing but the most cluttered confusion. Here is evaluation: opinions are nothing, authority is useless, data is secondary; establishment of relative importance is the key. Given the world and the stars as a laboratory and a mind to compute the relative importance of what it perceives, and no problems can remain unsolved. Given masses of data with monotone evaluation and one has something which may be pretty but isn't useful.

The stunned look of fresh-caught ensigns of the Navy when they first see in the metal the things about which they have so laboriously read is a testimony to more than the faulty educational system currently employed: the system seeks to train something which is perfect—the memory; it aligns little or nothing with purpose or use, and ignores the necessity of personal evaluation of all data, both as to need for it and its use. The stunned look comes from the overwhelming recognition that whereas they have thousands of data about what they see, they do not know whether it is more important to read the chronometer when they take a sextant sight or use only blue ink in writing a log book. These gentlemen have been wronged educationally, not because they have not been given thousands of data relative to ships, but because they have not been told the relative importance of each datum and have not experienced that importance. They know more facts than the less educated but they know less about factual relation.

More pertinent to the auditor, there are two species

of engramic commands which give monotone evaluation to data. The persons who have either of these as a major content in the engram bank will be similarly aberrated even if each manifests the aberration with opposite polarity.

Every now and then some unfortunate auditor finds a "Can't believe it" on his hands. This case is extremely trying. Under this heading come the "I doubt it," the "I can't be sure," and the "I don't know" cases.

Such a case is easy to spot for when he first comes into therapy he begins by doubting Dianetics, the auditor, himself, the furniture and his mother's virginity. The chronic doubter is not an easy case because he cannot believe his own data. The analyzer has a built-in judge which takes in data, weighs it and judges it right, wrong or maybe. The engramic doubter has a "held-down seven" to the effect that he has to doubt everything, something much different from judging. He is challenged to doubt. He must doubt. If to doubt is divine, then the god is certainly Moloch.[15] He doubts without inspecting; he inspects the most precise evidence, and he still doubts.

The auditor will return this patient to a somatic which tears half his head off, which is confirmed by scars, which is confirmed by aberration, and which is doubted as an incident.

The way to handle this case is to take his pat phrases and feed them to him in reverie or out of reverie with repeater technique. Make him go over and over them, sending his somatic strip back to them. Shortly a release of the phrase will take place. Feed all doubter phrases which the patient has used in this manner. Then continue the case. The object is not to make him a believer

---

15. Moloch: the god of the ancient Phoenicians to whom children were sacrificed in the Old Testament.

but to place him in a situation where he can evaluate his own data. Don't argue with him about Dianetics— arguing against engrams is senseless since the engrams themselves are senseless.

In ten or twenty hours of therapy such a patient will begin to face reality enough so that he no longer doubts the sun shines, doubts the auditor or doubts that he had a past of some sort. He is only difficult because he requires these extra hours of work. He is usually, by the way, very aberrated.

The "Can't believe it" finds difficulty in evaluation because he has difficulty giving credence to any fact more than any other fact: this produces an inability to compute relative importances amongst data, with the result that he may be as concerned with the shade of his superior's tie as with the marriage he himself is about to undertake. Similarly, the "You must believe it" case finds difficulty in differentiating amongst importances of various data and may hold equally firmly the idea that paper is made from trees and that he is about to be fired. Both cases "worry," which is to say they are unable to compute well.

Rational computation depends upon the *personal* computation of the relative importances of various data. Reactive "computation" deals exclusively with the equation that widely different objects or events are similar or equal. The former is sanity, the latter is insanity.

The "Must believe it" case will present a confused reactive bank, for the bank embraces the most unlikely differences as close similarities. The "Must believe it" engram command can dictate that one person, a class of persons or everyone must be believed, no matter what is written or said. The auditor, returning the patient, will find major aberrations held in place by a lock containing only conversation.

When Father is the actual source and is an ally of the patient, the auditor will discover that almost everything Father said was accepted *literally* and unquestioningly by his child. The father may not have been aware of having established this "Must believe it" condition and he may even be a jocular man, given to jokes. Every joke will be found to be literally accepted unless the father carefully labeled it a joke, which meant it must not be literally accepted. One case folder is to hand here where Father was the source of "Must believe": one day the father took his daughter, three years of age, down to the seacoast and, through the fog, pointed to a lighthouse. The lighthouse gave an eerie aspect in the foggy night. "That's Mr. Billingsly's place," said the father, meaning that Billingsly, the lighthouse keeper, lived there. The child nodded faithfully, if a little frightened, for "Mr. Billingsly" threw around a mane of hair—shadows—glared to seaward with one eye sweeping the water and stood a hundred feet tall and "Mr. Billingsly" let out moans which sounded quite ferocious. His "place" was a ledge of rock. As a preclear, twenty years later, the daughter was discovered to be frightened of any low moaning sound. The auditor patiently traced down the source and found, much to the delight of himself and the daughter, "Mr. Billingsly." Vast quantities of aberration, peculiar conceptions and strange notions were found to derive from casual statements the father had made. Being skilled in his task, the auditor did not bother to try to locate and erase everything the father had said—a task which would have taken years and years: he located, instead, the prenatal "You must believe me" and its engramic locks, and all the nonengramic locks, of course, disappeared and were automatically reevaluated as experienced data rather than "held-down sevens." Of course, there is always much more wrong with a case than a mere "You must believe me," but the change of viewpoint which the patient experienced immediately afterwards was startling: she was now at liberty to evaluate her father's data, which she had not been before.

Because they teach in terms of altitude[16] and authority, educational institutions themselves form a social "You must believe it" aberration. It is impossible to reduce an entire university education even if it sometimes appears desirable, but by addressing the moments when the patient was hammered into *believing* or accepting school, from kindergarten forward, many a fact-clogged mind can again be made facile which was not so before, for the facts will be reevaluated automatically by the mind for importances, not accepted on monotone evaluation as is the case in "formal education."

The "Can't believe it" is a subject so weary and dreary to the auditor that he may find himself, after a few finished cases, running adroitly away from one. The "I don't know" and the "I can't be sure" cases are not as bad as the "I can't believe it." The prize case in difficulty in Dianetics is a patient who is a Junior named after either Father or Mother, who has not only shut-down pain, emotion, visio and sonic recall but also "dub-in" for them on a false basis, with a lie factory working full blast, who is uncooperative and who is a "Can't believe it."

Monotone evaluation hinders the "Can't believe it" case's acceptance of all facts. Any case may have a few "Can't believe its," but some cases are so thoroughly aberrated by the phrase that they disbelieve not only

---

16. altitude: by *altitude* is meant a difference in level of prestige—one on a higher altitude carries conviction to one on a lower altitude merely because of altitude. The auditor may find himself unable to gain sufficient *altitude* with some patients to work them smoothly and he may have so much altitude with others that they believe everything he says. When he has too little altitude, he is not believed; when he has too much, he is believed too well.

reality but also their own existence.

The mind has a "built-in doubter" which, unhindered by engrams, rapidly sorts out importances and, by their weights, resolves problems and arrives at conclusions. The rational mind applies itself to data presented, compares it to experience, evaluates its veracity and then assigns it relative importance in the scheme of things. This is done, by a *clear,* with a rapidity which sometimes requires the splitting of seconds. By a *normal,* the time required is extremely variable and the conclusions are more-apt to be referred to another's opinion or compared to authority rather than to personal experience. That is the fundamental effect of contemporary education which, through no particular fault of its own and despite every effort it has made to free itself, yet, through lack of tools, is forced to follow scholastic methods. These, by contagion of aberration, persist against all efforts of advanced educators. The *normal* is taught on one hand to *believe* or else he'll fail and on the other to *disbelieve* as a scientific necessity: belief and disbelief cannot be taught, they must be personally computed. If a mind could be likened to a general served by his own staff, it could be seen to have a G-2[17] which, as a combat intelligence center, collected facts, weighted them for importance and formed an estimate of a situation or the value of a conclusion. As the intelligence officer would fail if he had a signed order to disbelieve everything, so does the mind fail which has a reactive command to disbelieve. Certainly a military organization would lose to every puny enemy if it had, conversely, a command to believe everything, and a man will fail if he has a reactive mind order to believe all information in the world around him.

The *believe* and *disbelieve* engrams present different

---

17. G-2: military intelligence section of the Army or Marine Corps.

manifestations, and while one cannot be said to be either more or less aberrative than the other, it is certain that the disbelieve engram, by and large, seems to make the less sociable man.

Disbelief occurs in various degrees, of course. There is, for instance, a social disbelief engram which promotes a class of literature which is as insincere as it is unwitty. Insincerity, shame of emotional demonstration, fear of praising may stem from other things than merely a disbelief engram, but a disbelief engram is most certainly present in the majority of such cases.

The auditor will find, when he is trying to enter a very strong "Can't believe it" case, that experience is disbelieved, the auditor is disbelieved, hope of results is disbelieved and that the most ridiculous and unreasonable insults and arguments may be presented. The patient may squirm in a veritable snake pit of somatics and still disbelieve that he is reexperiencing anything.

It is a sadly chronic fact that an aberree has a certain set of clichés from out of his engram bank. He will repeat these clichés for all occasions and circumstances. Mother, having an engram bank of her own and Father having his, will be found to be uttering pretty much the same sort of statement time after time. These are dramatizations. One of the parents may have had an "I don't know" ready to precede everything he or she said, which makes a whole "stack" of "I don't knows" in the engram bank which much undermines understanding. In the same way, "You must believe!" or "You can't believe!" may become "stacked" in the engram bank. Once one has heard a few engrams from a patient, he knows he will have many, many more similar engrams from that source. Once an auditor has listened to the personnel in the patient's engram bank for a very short time, he knows pretty much what he will have in many, many more engrams. Hence, any phrase is liable to be much repeated in the engram bank, with varying somatics and accompanying perceptics. If Mother is troubled with high blood pressure, and it is raised by Father—to the intense discomfort of the child and a degree which often produces a later migraine headache —she is apt to utter, "I can't believe you would treat me this way." Privately, she must have been hard to convince (one doesn't convince much against engramic "reasoning"), for he treated her this way about every three days; and every three days she was saying, "I can't believe you" or "I can't believe you would do this to me" or "I can't believe anything you say" or some such thing.

The "Can't believe" is apt to be rather hostile since "Can't believe" is often hostile conversation. "You've got to believe me" is more apt to be a pleading or whining sort of an engram. "Believe what I tell you, goddamn it," is, however, fully as hostile as an auditor might expect.

An auditor who finds a case intensely and unreasonably skeptical should expect a "Can't believe" stack in the engram bank. If he finds a patient incapable of holding an opinion of his own but weather-vaning to each new person or quoting an authority (all authorities get easily identified with Father in the reactive bank), he should suspect a "Must believe" in some form, as well as other things. There are many manifestations of either case. The chronic aspect in therapy is that the "Can't believe" suspects his own data so strongly that he alters it continually and the engrams which, after all, have just one exact package of content, will not properly reduce; the "Must believe" takes up every engram he hears about as his own and that does *him* little good.

Do not suppose that any case has a standard aspect, however. The language contains many words and combinations of words, and aberrees are not unusual who have the entire basic language and all its idioms securely connected up to some somatic or other. Cases ordinarily contain "Can't believe" and "Must believe" phrases in the same bank. Only when these phrases become top-heavy does the person respond in a set pattern. When the set pattern is of either species of phrase, then the auditor confronts a patient who must have had, at best, a most unhappy life. But either case clears. They all clear, even Juniors.

Physical Pain and Painful Emotion Commands

Besides visio and sonic, another vital recall to therapy is the somatic, which is to say, the physical pain of the incident. Running a physically painful incident without a somatic is worthless.

If physical pain is present, it may come only after considerable "unconsciousness" has been "boiled off." If the incident contains pain but the somatic is not turned on, the patient will wriggle his toes and breathe heavily and nervously or he may have jumping muscles. The foot wriggling is an excellent clue to the presence of any somatic, turned on or not turned on. Breathing heavily and jumping muscles and various twitches without pain denote two things: either a denyer is in the incident and the content isn't being contacted; or, if the preclear is recounting, the somatic may be shut off in the incident or elsewhere, either earlier by command or late by painful emotion. The patient who wriggles a great deal or who does not wriggle at all is suffering from a pain or emotion shut-off or late painful emotion engrams or both.

There is a whole species of commands which shut off pain and emotion simultaneously: this is because the word *feel* is homonymic. "I can't feel anything" is the standard, but the command varies widely and is worded in a great many ways. The auditor can pick up his own book of these from patients who, describing how they feel—or rather, how they don't feel—give them away. "It doesn't hurt" is a class of phrases specifically shutting off pain, a class which includes, of course, such things as "There isn't any pain," etc. Emotion is shut off by a class of phrases which contain the word *emotion* or which specifically (literally translated) shut off emotion.

The auditor should keep a book of all denyers, misdirectors, holders, bouncers and groupers which he discovers, each listed under its own heading. In this way he adds to material he can use for repeater technique when he sees something is wrong with the way the patient is moving on the track. But there are four other classes of phrases which he should also study and list: *shut-offs, exaggerators, derailers* and *lie factories*. He can also add to his classes.

He will discover enormous numbers of commands in engrams which can accomplish these various aspects. And he should be particularly interested in the pain and emotion *shut-offs* and the *exaggerators,* which is to say, those engramic commands which give the aspect of too much pain and too much emotion. There is no reason to give large numbers of them here. They are quite various, language being language.

Many combinations are possible. A patient can be found to weep over the most trivial postspeech things and yet have few or no somatics. Several things can cause this. Either he had a mother or a father who wept for nine months before he was born or he has an exaggerator at work which commands that he be emotional about everything: "too much emotion." In combination with this, he can have something which says he can feel no pain or can't hurt or even can't feel.

A patient who aches and suffers and yet cannot

weep would have a reverse set of commands: he has a "no emotion" command early on the track or a long chain of them, and yet has commands which dictate pain to excess: "I can't stand the pain," "The pain is too great," "I always feel I'm in agony," etc. "I feel bad," on the other hand, is a shut-off because it says there is something wrong with the mechanism with which he feels and implies disability to feel.

Both pain and emotion can be commanded into exaggeration. But it is a peculiar thing that the body does not manufacture pain to be felt. All pain felt is genuine, even if exaggerated. Imaginary pain is nonexistent. A person "imagines" only pain he has actually felt. He cannot imagine pain he has not felt. He may "imagine" pain at some time later than the actual incident, but if he feels pain, no matter how psychotic he is, that pain will be found to exist somewhere on his time track. Scientific tests have been carefully conducted in Dianetics to establish this fact and it is a valuable one. You can test it yourself by asking patients to feel various pains, "imagining them" in present time. They will feel pains for you so long as you ask them to feel pains they have had. Somewhere you will find the patient unable to actually feel the pain he is trying to "imagine." Whether he is aware of it or not, he has had pain wherever he "imagines" it and is simply doing a somatic strip return for you on a minor scale.

This aspect of pain is quite interesting in that many patients have, at one time or another in their lives, pretended to the family or the world that they had a pain. The patient thought, when he asserted this "make-believe" pain, that he was lying. In therapy, the auditor can use these "imaginings," for they lead straight to sympathy engrams and actual injury. Further, these "imaginary" pains are generally displayed to the person or pseudoperson who was the sympathy ally present in the engramic moment. Thus, if a small boy always pretended to his grandmother, and thought he was pretending, that he had a bad hip, it will be discovered eventually that some time in his early life he hurt that same hip and received sympathy during the engramic moment, which is now eclipsed from the analyzer. Patients often feel quite guilty over these pretenses. Sometimes soldiers in the recent war have come home pretending they had been wounded and, when in therapy, are afraid the auditor will find out or give them away to their people. This soldier might not have been wounded in the war, but an engram will be found which contains sympathy for the injury of which he complains. He is asking for sympathy with a colorful story and believes he is telling a lie. Without informing him of this Dianetic discovery, the auditor can often flush into view a sympathy engram which might otherwise have to be arduously hunted down.

"Cry baby" is a phrase against which the preclear will negate in an engram, thus inhibiting tears. It is quite ordinary to find the preclear confusing himself with older brothers and sisters who are in his prenatal life: their jeers, Mother's orders and so forth, then, all register. If the preclear knows of any older children, the auditor should look for them in the engrams of prenatal life, for children are quite active and often bounce up and down on Mother's lap or collide with her. Any childish phrases of derision are then not always postbirth.

It has been said during Dianetic research that if one could release all the painful emotion of a lifetime, he would have 90 percent of the clearing done. However, the painful emotion is only a surface manifestation of the physical pain engrams and would not be painful if the physical pain did not coexist or exist priorly.

When emotion and pain shut-offs exist in a case, the

patient is normally tense of muscle and nervous, given to twitching or merely tension. When pain and emotion are exaggerated by commands, one has a highly dramatizing case on his hands.

The Ally Versus the Antagonist

It is necessary for the auditor to know the reactive mind's evaluation of importances. Moronic or not, the reactive mind distinguishes violently between friend and foe, about the only piece of differentiation it does.

There is a prime test for an ally. And recall that the ally is a part of sympathy engrams, the things which are most likely to produce psychosomatic illnesses, immaturities and confusion on a grand scale. As long as it can rebel and negate, the reactive mind takes care of the enemies so far as it is able. It can, of course, be twisted by circumstance into the valence of the enemy and so cry havoc[18] and abreact[19] in general if this was a winning valence. But it will not ordinarily use the data of the enemy contained in a contrasurvival engram save to negate against it. When the general tone nears zone 1, of course, the reactive mind starts picking up and obeying antagonistic commands. Thus, if Father is the villain of the piece, an antagonist, Father's commands are not the reactively obeyed commands but the commands the aberree will usually negate against or avoid.

This is not the case, however, with the ally. The ally, the person from whom sympathy came when the patient was ill or injured, is heeded and obeyed since his "purpose" is apparently aligned with the purpose of the

---

18. cry havoc: to warn of great, impending danger.

19. abreact: to release (repressed emotions) by acting out the situation causing the conflict.

individual, to survive. If one thing about a person is right, then—according to our moronic little friend, the reactive mind—everything about that person is right, everything that person says and does is right and particularly is right whatever that person said in the engram.

The chronic psychosomatic illness is ordinarily from a sympathy engram. This is quite important, for the sympathy engram will be the last or hardest to reach, being aligned with survival purpose.

A "Must believe" from an ally means that the person *must* believe. A "Must believe" from an antagonist ordinarily brings about a circumstance that the person must *not* believe.

Here, in the ally and the antagonist, we have the age-old tale of the hero and the villain, the heroine and the villainess, Mazda and Ahriman,[20] the cowboy in the white hat and the cowboy in the black. The Hindu trinity[21] is found, as source, in Father, Mother and unborn baby. But the war of "good and evil" is found as reactive data in the engram bank in the form of the ally and the antagonist.

The very best logic of which the reactive mind is capable is two-valued, white and black, and two-valued logic finds its response only in the reactive bank. And the reactive mind works out all problems in absolutes, bringing about logical monstrosities, for there is the absolute of good, the absolute of evil and the absolute

---

20. Mazda and Ahriman: the deities in Zoroastrianism, the religious system of the Persians before their conversion to Islam. Mazda is the spirit of universal good and Ahriman is his archrival as the spirit of evil.

21. Hindu trinity: Hindu representation of the three manifestations of the Supreme Being—Brahma, Vishnu and Siva—each with a specific cosmic function: Brahma was associated with creation; Vishnu was associated with preservation and renewal; and Siva with destruction and disintegration.

of identity thought. Any rational computation demonstrates an absolute to be impossible from a standpoint of truth or workability: but the reactive mind never quibbles, it just reacts. It knows a champion when it sees one (it thinks) and it knows a villain (it supposes). The ally, the champion, is everybody who has any characteristic of the ally; and the antagonist, the villain, is everyone who has any characteristics of the antagonist. Further, anything associated with the ally is a champion and everything associated with the antagonist is villainous. If the ally is an aunt, then aunts are good. If the antagonist is a sign painter, then sign painters are all evil. Further, the doilies Auntie crocheted mean that doilies are good and that all lacework is good and that anything on which lacework sits is good and that anything which looks like lacework is good and so on in the *ad absurdum*[22] which only the reactive mind can manage without a qualm. And the signs the painter painted are evil and where they sit is evil and paint is evil and smell of paint is evil and brushes are evil so hairbrushes are evil so the dresser on which hairbrushes sit is evil and so on.

There is an axiom here which it is well not to slight in working a patient:

Any chronic psychosomatic illness has at its source a sympathy engram.

And another:

A reactive mind will not permit an individual to be aberrated or chronically psychosomatically ill unless the illness has survival value.

This does not mean that the individual has a power of choice analytically. It does mean that the reactive mind, working quietly and hitherto hidden so well, chooses, on identity computation, physical and mental

---

22. *ad absurdum:* to the point of ridiculousness.

conditions to match any circumstances even remotely similar to any concept in the engram bank.

There is such a thing as necessity level. This rises and keys out engrams and can key out the control of the reactive mind itself. Necessity level often rises. The individual can force it to rise analytically whether or not actual cause exists. A person may have no engram about going to the electric chair for murder and yet have an engram about murdering people. Necessity level rises and analytically overwhelms all impulse to kill, for the analyzer knows all about electric chairs. When the necessity level cannot rise, then one is dealing with a low dynamic individual. An artist, terribly aberrated about his work through the kind efforts of obligingly caustic critics, can yet boost himself by his necessity bootstraps to do another piece of work and damn the aunt who said he gave her too many chins in her portrait and ripped the work to shreds, or damn the critics who said he was too new and his work too swift. Necessity level can soar above the reactive mind by, as the marine sergeant said, "Sheer guts."

Given too many current restimulators, used too hard by life, an individual, caught in the dwindling spiral of reactivated engrams, may come at last to a point where he cannot longer remain well. If this is his first serious sag and if the sag is deep, a psychosomatic illness will appear and become more or less chronic and, this is important, it will stem directly from a sympathy engram.

All psychosomatic ills carry with them, if less obvious, aberrative commands, which means that a person suffering from psychosomatic illness, whether he relishes the idea or not, is also suffering from the aberration which is part of the same engram.

If the auditor wants to find the *real* holders, the *real* reasons his case appears to resist getting well, the *real* aberrative factors and illnesses, he will look to the ally or allies, for any case may have many. He will exhaust from them the painful emotion of loss or denial and backtrack immediately to find the underlying engrams.

Remember, too, that the reactive mind is not bright enough to realize that two sides of the same person are the same person. Hence we can have Mother-the-white-angel and Mother-the-howling-harridan.[23] As the white angel she is implicitly followed, as the harridan she is negated against. Father may be Father-the-beneficent and Father-the-baby-killer. And so with all allies. But only the pure, the absolute, the never-changing ally who, resolute and firm, stayed the cold, sharp hand of death and placed tenderly in the expiring hand of the wistful child the strong and flaring torch of life (or at least said, "Poor baby, you feel so bad; please don't cry,") is the model, the paragon, the gold-footed idol with free access to the gods. (This was Grandpop: he drank too much and he cheated at cards, but the reactive mind doesn't see it that way because Grandpop hauled baby through pneumonia and was darned sure baby got well—good acts if he hadn't been so melodramatic about it and if he hadn't talked so much while the poor kid was "unconscious.")

Question the patient adroitly about Father and Mother: if he isn't much disturbed by their deaths (if they are dead) or if he is simply careless of them or if he bares his teeth, they are antagonists; the allies are elsewhere. If the mother and father are indifferently or angrily or propitiatively regarded, be very sure, then, that the patient had a rough time of it between conception and birth and later and be sure, if this is the case, that there will be allies in plenty, for the child will have sought them out in every scrape or injury. But you will

---

23. harridan: a disreputable, shrewish old woman.

not find the allies, usually, by mere questions. The reactive mind considers them to be pure gold even if the engrams in which they appear have somatics enough to wreck a person for life. It hides allies. The auditor has to look for them through discharging painful emotion. The death, departure or denial by an ally is a certain painful emotion engram. One way or another, working at it from later painful emotion or earlier physically painful engrams, the ally will eventually uncover and can be entered as memory in the standard banks and erased as illness out of the engram bank.

The solution of chronic psychosomatic ills lies largely in the field of sympathy engrams. These will not erase early, however, for they are the inner bastion behind which the reactive mind crouches and observes the storming of the outer defenses by antagonists. The painful emotion of ally losses masks, at times, not only allies but antagonists as well. The sympathy engram is not the only source of psychosomatic illness by far, but it is the source of the *chronic* psychosomatic ill.

By the way, nothing in this dissertation about allies should be construed to mean that one should not show love to a child. Observers in the past have jumped at questionable conclusions when they felt that demonstrated affection aberrates a child. Lack of affection may kill him, but the reverse is not true. The only way an ally can aberrate a child *is by talking to and sympathizing with a child who is very ill or "unconscious" from injury.* If he does this, he alloys[24] the child's personality with his own, creates an eventual possibility of psychosomatic illness and aberration and may generally disable the child for life (except for Dianetics, of course). Love a child best and do for him best when he is well. Do

---

24. alloy: to weaken or spoil by adding something that reduces value or pleasure.

anything you please with him when he is well, say what you please. When he is sick or hurt, it is best to, as the bosun said, "Patch him up and keep goddamned quiet!"

Tokens

The tale of the magic amulet,[25] the lucky talisman,[26] the belief in the charm and the long catalogue of fetishes,[27] the objects and mannerisms which one keeps as sakes are the "dearly beloveds" of the reactive mind.

There is nothing wrong with a man keeping llamas in the parlor or wearing purple and green suspenders or rubbing fireplugs for luck, nor is there anything wrong with sighing over a stolen lady's slipper or smoking Pittsburgh stogies. Any *Rights of Man* should provide for such eccentricities. But the auditor can use this data to detect vital information.

In Dianetics, the term *token* is defined to embrace the objects and habits which an individual or society keeps by not knowing they are extensions of an ally.

By identity thought there are *associative restimulators* for every restimulator in the environment—those things connected with the restimulator. Being blank on the subject, the analytical mind, apprised by physical reaction that a restimulator of something is nearby, then picks up the associative restimulator but does not select the actual restimulator. (In Book Two, the young man's signal to remove his coat was a touch of the tie: he did not cite the tie in his complaint; the nearest he came to it

---

25. amulet: something worn on the body because of its supposed magic power to protect against injury or evil; a charm.

26. talisman: an object supposed to bring good luck.

27. fetish: anything to which foolishly excessive respect or devotion is given.

was the person and clothing of the hypnotic operator. These were *associative restimulators.*)

A restimulator for a contrasurvival engram might be an electric light; the aberree looks to the shade, the pull chain, the room or the person under the light to be a source of annoyance, and not only does he not know that a restimulator is present but supposes that the associated objects have some evil in themselves.

The associative restimulator for a contrasurvival engram needs no name other than that, *associative restimulator.* The pain is the thing, the things associated in any way with the thing are the thing, are other things, etc., is the reactive equation which fills the world of the aberree full of fear and fills him full of anxiety. Leave a child in a place or a room where he has been unhappy and he may become ill, for he is confronted with some restimulator and he can at best explain, like the adult, his fear in terms of things not rationally connected to the restimulator. This is the mechanism of engramic restimulation.

It is most terribly uncomfortable to any aberree who, try as he might, cannot say why he does not like some person or object or locale, and who cannot connect any of the three with the actual item which is the restimulator and does not know he has an engram about it. This method of detecting engrams leads nowhere quickly since one cannot select objects, persons or locales and know they are restimulators. They may be only associative restimulators to the actual restimulator item in the environment. (Words contained in engrams, by the way, and any other precise restimulator can "push button" the aberree into action or apathy if they are used upon him. In words it has to be the exact word; for instance, paint*ed* will not do when paint*er* is in the engram. What is paint*ed,* however, may be an associative restimulator and the aberree may declare he does not like it; that he does not like it does not mean that it will "push his buttons" and make him cough or sigh or get angry or get sick or whatever the engram containing the word dictates he should do.)

The *token* is a very special kind of restimulator. While the auditor may not find much use for the associative restimulator as applied to contrasurvival engrams, he can employ the token as a means of detection to locate allies.

The *token* is any object, practice or mannerism which one or more allies used. By identity thought the ally is survival; anything the ally used or did is, therefore, survival. The valence of the ally is that one most frequently employed by the aberree. While the clear can shift himself into valences he imagines or beholds at will and convenience, and out of them at will and can stabilize his own at will, the aberree skids around into valences without his knowledge or consent and is most likely to be in any valence but his own. The person who seems to be a different person every time he is met or a different person to each person he meets, with special valences manifesting here and others manifesting there, is shifting into various winning valences; interfered with in his shifts, he goes into secondary valences; if forced into his own valence he becomes ill. It is understood, of course, that all valences manifest something of himself.

Shifting into ally valences is the fundamental practice of the aberree. He will feel most at ease when his own valence is alloyed to some degree with an ally valence. So long as the ally or the pseudoally is not available, the aberree reminds himself of the ally valence with tokens. These tokens are the things the ally possessed, practiced or did.

An aberree will often inextricably associate himself with a pseudoally, as in marriage, and then make the astonished discovery that he is not partnered with the

471

optimum ally conduct. (Mother was an ally, Mother baked bread; wife is pseudomother though she nor he knows it, wife does not bake bread. Mother frowned on lipstick; wife wears lipstick. Mother gave him his way; wife has a bossy attitude. Wife is pseudomother because she has similar voice tones only.) The aberree then reactively and unknowingly attempts to coax wife or partner into the ally valence by assuming that the moment of the sympathy engram is present time—a mechanical shift caused only by the restimulation of the sympathy engram because of voice tones or some such thing—and proceeds to manifest the ghost of the engram illness or injury or operation as a psychosomatic sickness. The computation of the reactive mind is simple—just like Simple Simon—one forces the ally into being by manifesting the somatic with which the ally sympathized. This can also be an effort to turn a partner, in which the reactive mind thinks it has discovered an ambivalent friend-enemy, into the sympathy valence. Wife is cruel. Mother was cruel until the injury, then she was nice. Manifest the injury as a chronic psychosomatic illness and wife will be nice. Actually wife isn't nicer, so the computation gets stronger, the illness gets stronger, and down into the dizzy dwindling spiral we go. The psychosomatic illness is also a denial of dangerousness, a plea of helplessness—a shade of opossum playing, fear paralysis: "I'm no menace to you. I'm sick!"

The aberree goes into his own valence of the time of the sympathy engram in his bid for sympathy and his denial of his own dangerousness. The valence of himself, of course, is complicated by the age-tab and somatic of the engram in which he was immature and not well.

The psychosomatic illness is, as well, a token, which is to say it is a reminder of a time when he once had love and care and was told so. He needs it about as much as he needs to be atom bombed, of course, but this is good, solid, reactive mind "survival" and the reactive mind is going to make it so he can survive if it kills him.

This is all mechanical and is actually merely re-stimulation of an engram, but it is better understood as a low order of computation.

In the absence of an ally, and even in the presence of the ally, he uses reactive mimicry. Conscious mimicry is a wonderful way to learn. Reactive mimicry is most alloying to the personality. Reactively, he once had an ally and imitates the ally. Consciously he may not even recall the ally or the habits of the ally.

The ally, remember, is somebody who has entered the interior world of the mind when the analyzer was shut down by illness or injury or an operation and gave forth sympathy or protection. The ally is part of the sympathy engram. If a child had grandparents he liked and was lucky enough not to be ill around them or be talked to by them in sympathetic terms when he was ill or injured, the grandparents would still be much loved. In Dianetics an ally is only someone who has offered sympathy or protection in an engram. We don't have to have engrams to be loved or to love: quite the contrary, one is better loved and loves more without engrams.

The token applies, Dianetically, only to the ally and is an object, practice or mannerism similar to an object, practice or mannerism of the ally.

The ally smoked Pittsburgh stogies, so the aberree may smoke Pittsburgh stogies no matter what they do to his throat or his wife. The ally wore bowlers, the lady aberree dotes on riding habits but has never ridden a horse. The ally knitted, the aberree specializes in wearing knit things or a lady at least makes a pretense of knitting and sometimes wonders why she ever took it up, she is so bad at it. The ally used profanity, the aberree uses the same profanity. The ally wipes his nose on his sleeve and picks his nose, the aberree wipes his nose on a dinner jacket and fiddles with his nostrils.

The token may be a reminder of pure ally or it may be a reminder of the friend side of an ambivalent friend-enemy. And it may be a winning valence that was also ambivalent toward the aberree. The token is never an associative restimulator in the meaning that it reminds of some antagonist, for associative restimulators are abhorred.

The most chronic token, the most constant habit, practice or mannerism of the preclear is a direct arrow to the pure ally. And the pure ally is the one the reactive mind will guard to its highest level of the beset donjon[28] keep.[29] And that is the target of the auditor. He may have to relieve the majority of the engram bank before he can erase the engram which is most likely to aberrate the individual, to saddle him with strange practices and to make him chronically ill.

Observe your preclear and see what he does and says that is strange to his personality, things he does but does not much seem to enjoy. See what he uses and what his mannerisms are. Amongst this collection you may, by asking discreet questions, jog an ally into his memory which he had forgotten and so jogging, reach swiftly toward the sympathy engram in which that ally is contained or reach toward, for an emotional discharge, the painful emotion engram of the loss of that ally, his illness or incidents concerning him.

Another but special token is that which stems from a "die if you don't" command. Fathers, for instance,

---

28. donjon: the fortified main tower of a castle.

29. keep: the strongest, innermost part or central tower of a medieval castle.

suspicious of paternity,[30] sometimes claim while trouncing[31] or upsetting mothers that they will kill the child if it isn't just like Father. This is a very unhappy type of token, to say nothing of being, usually, a bad engram; it can go to the extent of remodeling structure, of making noses long or hair absent; it may compel an aberree into a profession he does not admire and all out of the engramic command that he must be like the parent. As this type of command is usually given before birth it is often addressed, unknowingly, to a girl, fathers not being gifted ordinarily with clairvoyance; in such a case it will bring about a most remarkable structural change in a woman and form some unusual mannerisms, "ambitions" (like a dog that gets whipped if he doesn't fetch the duck) and some habits which, to say the least, are astonishing. Father, postbirth, to accomplish the reactivation of such an engram, must be quite ambivalent so that the friend-enemy computation comes into being. Not to be like Father is to die: to force Father into his sympathy-engram self the reactive mind must manifest the token of illness. Token and likeness is the answer to such a computation. And recall, all such computations are not simple but are made further complex by the addition of dozens of other engramic computations.

The friend-enemy is rather easy to find as an enemy, not too hard to find as a friend. Standard technique with its repeater and return, *et al.*, would in themselves at last locate any engram and erase the bank so that it properly refiles. The use of the token facilitates the auditing.

In the case of the pure ally, the champion of the right, standard technique also at last arrives. But here, how smooth the use of the token sometimes makes the road! For the token may be as alarmingly strange as an

---

30. paternity: the state of being a father; fatherhood.

31. trounce: to beat.

elephant in a bird cage. It takes a *real* ally to keep some of these odd habits around.

Measure the preclear against his environment and education and his society and profession. See what doesn't seem to belong amid the things he uses, the objects he adores and the mannerisms his friends find so strange. Then find out if he or the spouse knew of anyone who did those things or liked those things.

Do not suppose from all this that our *clear* has jettisoned all strange mannerisms. Self-determinism is individuality in the extreme; personality is inherent and, revealed by clearing, looms up high above the aberree. The engrams compress a man and make him small and afraid. Released, his power comes into play. The sympathy engram is to a man like a crutch when he has two sturdy legs. But oh, the preclear sobs where he loses old Uncle Goston, whose habit of spitting on the floor, as transplanted, so astonished our preclear's friends and business associates. But the grief is brief, usually the half hour it takes to run the sympathy engram out. Suddenly the preclear recalls Uncle Goston, recalls a thousand things Uncle Goston and he used to do, for the engram had Uncle Goston occluded and amongst those missing from the sight of "I." Although it might have said in the engram, "All right, there, there, there, Billy. I'll take care of you. Don't thrash around so. You'll be all right. There, there, there. Poor little fellow. What a terrible rash you've got. How feverish. There, there, there, Billy. You'll be all right as long as I am here. I'll take care of my Billy. Go to sleep now. Go to sleep and forget it." And Billy was all the time "unconscious" and never "knew" about it.

Afterwards he got a partner who looked like Uncle Goston (but happened to be a fool), and when bankrupt somehow developed a rash and a chronic cough and got very "feverish" about his business affairs. He took to spitting on the floor no matter where he was; and his health got worse and he got worse: but if you had asked him about any uncles before he went into therapy, he would have been very vague. "Give me a flash reply," says the auditor. "Who used to spit on the floor?" "Uncle Goston," answers the preclear. "Gosh, that's funny (hawk, spit), I hadn't thought of him for years. He was never around much, though." (Not more than ten years constantly, the auditor may discover.) "Don't suppose he's important. Let's take up Mrs. Swishback, that teacher I had——" "Let's return now to the time Uncle Goston helped you," says the auditor. "The somatic strip will now go back to the time your Uncle Goston helped you." "I feel like my skin's on fire!" complains the preclear. "This must be—hey, it's my allergy! But I don't see anybody. I don't—— Wait, I get an impression of somebody. Somebody—— Why, it's Uncle Goston!" And he runs it and the rash goes away. But maybe the auditor had to get a hundred engrams before he got this one. And then the preclear suddenly remembers about him and Uncle Goston and the time—but get on with therapy.

Complete remembering seems to be a synonym for complete sanity. But don't suppose that just because a clear gets rid of his Uncle Gostons and his habit of spitting on the floor that he will not now indulge in any eccentricity. The difference is, he is not compelled into eccentricity without his consent. Good Lord, what a cleared mind can think up to keep itself from being bored!

What to Do If a Case Stops Progressing

Even in the easiest cases there will come times when progress seems to stop. Here is a list of possibilities of why:

1. The preclear is not moving on the track despite appearances, but is being subject to one of the five types of commands which can inhibit his free motion or information. The commonest of these is a holder and the preclear may be found to be in an engram and in a strange valence.

2. There is an emotional or pain shut-off. These can always be detected even at the beginning of a case. The patient's muscles will tremble or twitch when he is in an engram but he will not feel the somatic: this is inevitably a pain shut-off. Out of therapy the patient may be very tense, his neck muscles in particular may be tight: this is often an emotional shut-off. Either of these conditions can be observed in many aberrees before beginning therapy. If they appear while therapy is in progress, look for pain or emotional shut-offs.

3. There is an exaggerator of emotion and a pain shut-off so that the patient weeps over anything but wriggles and twists when asked to approach pain. He is feeling emotion without feeling the pain.

4. There is an emotional charge in some area which has not been discharged but which is ready to discharge. Or, conversely, if you have been trying to get an emotional discharge in a late painful emotion engram and have had no success, there is a feeling shut-off in the prenatal area.

5. The Auditor's Code has been broken. Change auditors or reduce the moments when the code was broken.

6. There is an emotional upset in the patient's life current with therapy. Question him closely and remove the charge, if possible, of the emotional upset as an engram.

7. The auditor has missed an important point in this book. Study it.

If a Case "Refuses" to Get Well

It has long been a popular idea, if an erroneous fact, that people desire to retain their neuroses. In any case which "resists" therapy, you may be certain that the engrams are resisting, not the patient; do not, therefore, attack the patient but the engrams.

There are many computations which give the appearance of resistance. The commonest of these is the ally computation, which derives from engrams containing allies who seem to plead that the patient is not to rid himself of anything. An ordinary situation is one in which some relative or friend of the mother's is advising the mother against aborting the child. The ally is pleading, "Do not get rid of it!" The preclear knows this person to be a friend of his of the highest order. The preclear may interpret this to mean that he is not to get rid of his engrams.

Another computation is the stupidity computation, wherein the preclear begins to believe he will be stupid or lacking a mind if he gives up engrams. This stems, for example, from the mother saying she will lose her mind if she loses the child: she calls the child "it." A whole chain of these may appear in a case, giving the preclear the idea that if he parts with any engrams, he will lose his mind. This is the primary reason why past schools believed that the mind was composed of neuroses instead of an inherent personality. The engrams, even though unknown, appeared very valuable, which they are not—none of them.

Yet another computation is one of secrecy. It seems to the preclear that his life depends upon holding some secret. This is common in a case where the mother has had a lover. Mother and the lover both enjoin[32] secrecy. The preclear, obeying engramic commands, believes that

---

32. enjoin: to order, to command.

he has much to lose if he tells this secret even though those who enjoined it were not even aware that he was present, or if they knew, that he was "listening." One secrecy computation stems from the mother's fearing to tell the father that she is pregnant: if the mother is an ally of the child, then the child will be extremely tenacious of this type of engram.

All cases have one or more computations which inhibit a delivery of engrams. Some have all the above and more. This is no great worry to the auditor for, by repeater technique, he can open the engram bank.

Drugs

The so-called hypnotics have no great use in Dianetics except, on occasion, when a patient is psychotic and narcosynthesis is employed. By hypnotic is meant such preparations as phenobarbital,[33] hyoscine,[34] opium[35] and so on. These sleep-producing drugs are undesirable save only as a sedative and would be administered as sedatives by a medical doctor. Any patient who *needs* a sedative already has a medical doctor whose business it is. The auditor should not, then, concern himself with hypnotics or anything producing sleep. Some preclears will beg to be given sleeping drugs to "facilitate therapy" but any such drug is an anesthetic and shuts down somatics, inhibiting therapy. Further, none but the insane should be worked in amnesia trance, particularly a drug trance, for the work is longer than necessary and the results slow, as elsewhere explained. Dianetics wakes

---

33. phenobarbital: a medicinal drug used to calm the nerves and induce sleep.

34. hyoscine: same as scopolamine, an alkaloid used in medicine as a sedative, hypnotic and sometimes with other drugs to relieve pain.

35. opium: a drug made from the juice of certain poppies, smoked or chewed as a stimulant or narcotic, and used in medicine as a sedative.

people up; it does not try to drug them or hypnotize them. Hence, the hypnotic drug is worthless to the auditor.

Patients who wish to be knocked over the head with lead pipes or otherwise put into a deep trance should not be allowed to have their way even when they humorously present their own lead pipes.

The trick is to put "I" in contact with the file clerk. All hypnotics work to shut down "I." While the file clerk can be reached and sonic and visio are available and even while, with much labor, a clearing can be so effected, even the most "hopeless" case is better worked in contact; the work is faster, more satisfactory and less troublesome.

When one discovers the science of mind, he inevitably discovers numerous other things not properly in his province. Amongst these is the confusion which has unwittingly existed about hypnotics. Those things labeled "hypnotics" as named above are not hypnotics at all but anesthetics. And those things labeled anesthetics are not anesthetics but hypnotics. This will become brilliantly clear to the auditor when he finds himself tangling with his first "anesthetic" nitrous oxide engram in some preclear. Perhaps there will have been another engram wherein morphine[36] was administered for days and even weeks, leaving the patient in a stupor which, by the definition "hypnotic," should have been a trance: the aberrative material will be there but it will be found to be slight compared to a chloroform or nitrous oxide engram.

Ether, chloroform and nitrous oxide, the "anesthetics," place the patient in a deep hypnotic trance: the reactive bank is wide open and all reception is sharp, clear and aberrative in the extreme. Of the three, nitrous

---

36. morphine: a drug made from opium, used for relieving pain.

oxide is easily the worst, being no anesthetic which would dull pain at all but a first-class hypnotic. In nitrous oxide the pain is filed and the content is filed with high and brilliant fidelity.[37] Some years ago some investigator wondered if nitrous oxide did not make the brain decay. Fortunately brains do not decay that easily; but nitrous oxide does bring into being particularly severe engrams. The serious, late-life engrams which the auditor will encounter may include, at the list's top, a nitrous oxide dental or surgical or obstetrical[38] engram. Nitrous oxide engrams are particularly bad when they involve exodontistry; they often form the most severe late-life engram. Aside from the fact that all exodontists have in the past talked too much and have offices which are far too noisy with street sounds, running water and flapping drill belts, nitrous oxide is not at all anesthetic and sharpens rather than dulls pain.

In reverse, nitrous oxide makes an excellent hypnotic for institutional therapy. It is far from the best obtainable from the chemists, that is certain, for some brilliant chemist will certainly be able to bring out a good gas hypnotic now that Dianetics is known and the need of it in institutions is realized.

There are some drugs which assist reverie, however. The commonest and most easily obtainable is plain, strong coffee. A cup or two of this occasionally alerts the analyzer enough so that it can reach through deeper layers of "unconsciousness." Benzedrine[39] and other commercial stimulants have been used with some success, particularly on psychotic patients. These bring the mind enough awake to permit it to overcome engramic

---

37. fidelity: accuracy.

38. obstetrical: of or regarding obstetrics, the branch of medicine and surgery that deals with childbirth.

39. Benzedrine: (trademark) an amphetamine, a drug used as a stimulant.

commands. Such commercial stimulants have the disadvantage of exhausting a Q^{40} quantity in the mind.

This Q quantity has not been much studied. It is as though the brain burns a certain amount of Q when it is exhausting engrams. For instance, therapy every day may bring results more rapidly but it will also bring some stale sessions. Therapy every two or three days produces the best results as observed. (Therapy once a week permits the engrams to sag and slows a case, one week being too long.) Benzedrine burns up Q. After a few sessions with Benzedrine the current stock of Q is exhausted and the work has been observed to deteriorate either until a higher dosage was administered—and there is a close limit to that—or until more Q was manufactured.

Here, with all this, must be included an important and vital fact. It should be on a page by itself and underscored. All patients in therapy should be given a dosage of vitamin B_1 orally or by injection at the minimum of 10 mg per day. Reducing engrams exhausts Q which seems to depend in some measure on B_1. You can be absolutely certain of nightmares in a patient who is not taking his B_1. Taking liberal doses of that, he will have no nightmares. D.T.'s[41] are probably caused by a similar exhaustion of Q quantity. D.T.'s are best treated by B_1 and Dianetics. Something like D.T.'s on a very minor scale has been observed to develop in occasional patients who were negligent about their B_1. With it, in therapy, they thrive.

Alcohol is rarely an assist to the auditor. In fact, alcohol is rarely an assist to anyone. A depressant, classifiable at best as a poison, alcohol has the single

---

40. Q: symbol used to represent an undefined, but observable as existing, form of energy or force.

41. D.T.'s: delirium tremens: a form of delirium (a disordered state of mind) with tremors and terrifying delusions.

virtue of being highly taxable. *All* alcoholics are alcoholic because of their engrams. All alcoholics, unless
they have injured their brains—which case is cited only
because it is possible, not because research in Dianetics
demonstrated any real evidence of it—can be released.
Alcoholism is engramic. It has become, in some very
understandable way, a class of contagious aberration
whereby the reactive mind confuses alcohol and "being
a good sport" or "having fun" or "forget your troubles."
Some of these things can also be obtained by strychnine[42] and cyanide.[43] Alcohol has its uses: one can put
specimens of frogs and such in it; one can clean the
germs off needles with it; it burns well in rockets. But
one would not consider preserving his stomach in a glass
jar and, unless insane, does not think of himself as a
needle. While some drunks think they act like rockets,
few have been observed to reach an altitude of more than
the floor. It is not only a poor stimulant-depressant,
it is also a hypnotic in the finest sense: what is done
to a drunk becomes an engram.[44] The chronic alcoholic
is physically and mentally ill. Dianetics can clear him
or even merely release him without too much trouble
for alcohol is apparently not physiological in its addictive
effect. With the whole range of chemistry to choose
stimulants and depressants from, why the government
chooses a superiorly aberrative and inferiorly stimulative
compound to legalize is a problem for the better mathe-
maticians, possibly those who deal exclusively in tax
income problems. Opium is less harmful, marijuana
is not only less physically harmful but also better in

42. strychnine: a bitter, highly poisonous substance, used in very small
doses as a stimulant.

43. cyanide: a very poisonous chemical substance.

44. I am not being paid by the W.C.T.U. [Women's Christian Temperance Union, an organization that campaigns against alcohol use] to
write this; it is only that I have had to clear too many alcoholics.

the action of keeping a neurotic producing, phenobarbital does not dull the senses nearly as much and
produces less aftereffect, ammonium chloride and a
host of other stimulants are more productive of results
and hardly less severe on the anatomy: but no, the
engrams, contaging unpleasantly along from the first
crude brew which made one of our ancestors drunk,
decree that alcohol is the only thing which is to be drunk
if a person wants to "forget it all" and "have a good
time." There is really nothing wrong with alcohol save
that it depends mainly on engrams and other advertising
for its effect and is otherwise remarkably inferior in
performance: that it makes such aberrative engrams is
probably its main claim to fame and infame. Making
one drug immoral and another one taxable is a sample
of the alcohol engram in society. However, although it is
immensely legal, it is doubtful if the auditor will find
any use for it in therapy.

And speaking of drugs, that three-thousand-cycle
note[45] in your ears came either from a nitrous oxide
engram or Mother taking lots of quinine before you
were born in the hope that she would not be a mother,
saying the while, "It makes my ears ring so: it just keeps
on and on and on and will not stop!"

Autocontrol

Since the beginning of Dianetics research in 1930,
patients have, in the majority, had some belief that they
could run their cases in autocontrol.

Not understanding that an auditor is only interested
in what has been done *to,* not done *by* a patient, some
shyness or imagined guilt often prompts this vain hope

---

45. three-thousand-cycle note: a ringing sound with three thousand
vibrations, or cycles, per second.

that one can accomplish therapy alone.

It cannot be done. That is a flat statement and it is a scientific fact. The auditor is necessary for a large number of reasons. He is not there to control or order the preclear about, but he is there to listen, to provide insistence, to compute the trouble the preclear is having and remedy it. The work is done on these equations:

- The dynamics of the preclear are less than the force in his reactive bank.
- The dynamics of the preclear plus the dynamics of the auditor are greater than the force in the preclear's reactive bank.
- The analytical mind of the preclear is shut down whenever he reaches an engram and he is then unable to pursue it and recount it enough times to discharge it without auditor assistance.
- The analytical mind of the preclear plus the analytical mind of the auditor can discover engrams and recount them.

(There is another equation, not elsewhere mentioned, but germane to the Auditor's Code, which demonstrates mathematically the necessity of that code:

- The force of the preclear's engram bank plus the force of the auditor's analytical mind is greater than the analytical mind and the dynamics of the preclear.

This explains the necessity of never attacking the preclear personally. It also explains the behavior of the aberree under attack in usual life and why he grows angry and apathetic, for this equation overwhelms his analyzer.)

These equations demonstrate actual natural laws.

Autocontrol finds the preclear attempting to attack something which has never been overcome by his analyzer although his analyzer has never been trying, interiorly, to do anything else but attack that bank so long as the analyzer would operate. The fact that the preclear's analyzer shuts down whenever he comes into an area of "unconsciousness" was why the engrams could take him over and use him as a puppet when they were restimulated—they simply shut down the analyzer.

Many efforts by many patients have been made to put Dianetics on an autocontrol level. They have all failed and thus far it is believed to be utterly and completely impossible. The preclear in autocontrol reverie may be able to reach some locks; he can certainly reach pleasant experiences and achieve data recall by return; but he cannot attack his own engrams without a standard auditor-preclear arrangement.

Aside from Dianetic reverie, some preclears have been foolish enough to attempt autohypnosis and thus reach their engrams. Hypnotism in any form is unwarranted in Dianetics. Autohypnosis used in Dianetics is probably as close to fruitless masochism as one can get. If a patient places himself in autohypnosis and regresses himself in an effort to reach illness or birth or prenatals, the only thing he will get is ill. Of course, people will try. None are ever convinced until they have tried, once they begin to agitate about autocontrol. But be sure to have a friend and this book handy so that he can audit away the headaches and such that suddenly turn on.

Dianetic reverie, which means with an auditor present, is not dangerous or severe. Autocontrol is often very uncomfortable and often fruitless. It should not be attempted.

The clear alone can autocontrol his whole time track back to conception and does when he wants specific data from anywhere in his life. But he is clear.

Organic Mental Alterations

There are several things which can happen to the nervous system, including the brain, which can cause structural change. These are called, in Dianetics, organic mental alterations. They are not called "organic neuroses" or "organic psychoses" because the alteration of structure does not necessarily produce aberrations. There has been a confusion in the past between behavior caused by organic differences and behavior caused by engrams. This confusion came about because the engram bank and the reactive mind were not known.

Any human being with an organic mental alteration also has engrams. The behavior dictated by the engrams and the action caused by alteration are different things. Engrams carry dramatizations, delusions, tantrums and various inefficiencies with them. Alterations establish inabilities to think or perceive or record or recall. For instance, the radio set may have new filters and circuits added to it which change and vary its performance and reduce it from optimum; these would be engrams. The radio set might have original tubes or circuits deleted from it or it might have some of the wires crossed; this would be organic mental alteration.

The sources of organic mental alteration are as follows:

1. Variation of the blueprint of structure by reason of a changed gene pattern. Some parts of the body would grow too much or too little to establish any alteration of structure. This is usually so gross a change that it is obvious. The feebleminded and so on may suffer either from engrams or an altered blueprint, but usually both.

2. Alteration of the nervous system by disease or growths, which divides into two classes:
   a. Disease destruction as in paresis.
   b. Additional construction as in the case of tumors.

3. Alteration of the nervous system by drugs or poisons.

4. Alteration by physical disorder as in the case of a "paralytic stroke" wherein certain tissues are inhibited or destroyed.

5. Physical change in structure due to injury as in the case of a head wound.

6. Alteration of structure by surgery as a necessity to remedy injury or disease.

7. Iatrogenic alterations (caused by doctors) undertaken under a misapprehension of brain function. These can be divided into two classes:

   a. Surgical, to include such things as the transorbital leukotomy, prefrontal lobotomy, topectomy and so forth.

   b. Shock "therapies" of all kinds including electric shock, insulin shock, etc., etc., etc., etc., etc., etc., etc., etc., etc., etc., etc., etc.

The first six sources of organic mental alteration are much less common than has been supposed. The body is an extremely hardy mechanism and its repair facilities are enormous. If an individual can be made to speak or follow orders at all, it is conceivable that the techniques of Dianetics can be applied to reduce the engrams in the engram bank, bringing about considerable improvement in the condition and mental ability of the individual. When these various sources are so severe that they inhibit any use of therapy, and when it is certain that no recourse to therapy is possible and that it is utterly impossible to reach the engram bank by standard technique, hypnotism or drugs, such cases can be considered beyond help of Dianetics.

Category 7 presents another problem. Here we have selective experimentation at work and it would be flatly impossible to conceive, without months of study of their experimental subjects, how many brands and varieties of operation have been performed and how many odd and bizarre shocks have been used.

All iatrogenic alterations of the nervous system can be considered under the heading of "reduced ability," in other words, inability. In each case something has been done to reduce the ability of the individual to perceive, record, recall or think. Any of these complicate a case for Dianetics, but they do not inevitably bar Dianetics from working.

In shock cases, such as electric shock, tissue may have been destroyed and the memory banks may in some way have been scrambled, the time track may be altered and other conditions may exist.

In all such iatrogenic alterations, the results of Dianetics must be considered equivocal. **But in all such cases, particularly those of electric shock, Dianetics should be used in every possible way in an effort to improve the patient.**

All shocks and operations should be picked up for what they are—engrams.

No person who can perform routine tasks or whose attention can be attracted and fixed should feel despair or be considered hopeless.

Any person who has been subjected to such treatment may not be able to reach optimum mental efficiency but he may be able to reach a level of rationality even yet in excess of the current normal. The thing to do is try. In spite of what has happened or what has been done, in the large majority of cases there may be a chance of excellent recovery.[46]

---

46. Attempted abortion sometimes may do strange things to a brain. This can be considered under the heading of injury. Most sonic recalls can be recovered. If various recalls cannot be recovered engrams can still be removed. Intelligence in such cases will rise and is often already extremely high.

Organic Derangement

A standard class of prenatal engrams has as its content the worry of the parents that the child will be feebleminded if not now aborted in earnest. This adds an emotional overload to such engrams and it adds, as importantly, an aberrative condition in the now grown patient that he is "not right," "all wrong," "feebleminded" and so forth. The difficulty of aborting the child is nearly always underestimated: the means used are often novel or bizarre: the worry because the child has not come out of the womb after the abortion attempt is acute, and the concern that he is now damaged beyond repair all combine to make severely aberrative engrams and, because of their content, engrams which are difficult to reach.

The aberrative quality of the "feebleminded" species of remark is, of course, high. The worry that the child may be born blind or deaf or otherwise incapacitated is common. The former class of engramic remarks can bring about actual feeblemindedness; the latter concern over blindness and so on bring about, at best, impaired visio and sonic recall.

The shut-off of the recalls is occasioned as well by an engramic belief in the society at large that the unborn child is blind, unfeeling and not alive. This belief is introduced into AA (attempted abortion) engrams by people's self-justification remarks while attempting an abortion: "Well, he can't see, feel or hear anyway." Or, "It doesn't know what's going on. It's blind, deaf and dumb. It's a sort of growth. It isn't human."

The greater part of all sonic and visio recall shut-off has as its source the remarks made at such times or by painful emotion and other engramic data. Hundreds of hours of therapy may pass before these recalls turn on.

The bulk of all shut-offs will turn on in the course of

therapy. There are thousands of engramic remarks and emotional situations which will deny the preclear his recall and that recall can be expected ordinarily to restore.

A very low dynamic patient (for people have various native strengths of the dynamic) may have recalls shut off rather easily. A high dynamic patient would require much more aberration before the recalls are closed down. These recalls can be turned on simply by running out the physically painful and painful emotion engrams.

It must not pass unremarked, however, that the abortion attempts actually can, if rarely, derange the brain and nervous mechanisms beyond the fetal ability to repair. The result of this is actual, physiological disability.

Children and adults now classified as feebleminded may then be separated into two groups: the actual, physiological class and the aberrated class. Further, recall shut-offs must be classified into two classes as well, regardless of the dynamic and intelligence of the individual: those occasioned by brain damage received during an attempted abortion and those which are solely aberrational and derived from engramic commands and emotion.

The ability of the fetus to repair damage is phenomenal. Brain damage can ordinarily be repaired perfectly regardless of how many foreign substances were introduced into it. Just because the brain was touched in an attempted abortion is no reason to suppose that the recall shut-off has this as a source, for this is the rarer of the two causes.

It is understood that this is being read by many with recall shut-offs and it is understood that it may well produce a considerable upset. But remember this, *sonic and visio recall are not vital to a nearly full release*. This comment about organic damage does not mean that a release cannot be effected which will leave the person more competent and happier, for this can always be done regardless of the recalls. And remember this, recalls almost always turn on even if it takes five hundred hours or more. This condition is only remarked because it will be found in some few cases.

The "tests" and "experiments" with human brain vivisection in institutions are not, unfortunately, valid. For all the pain and trouble and destruction caused by these "experiments," they were done without a proper knowledge of aberration and mental derangement. None of such data is of any value beyond showing that the brain can be cut in various ways without entirely killing the man. For the patients used responded both to engramic disorder and the physical disorder caused by the psychiatrist, and there is no way to differentiate between these after the operation except by Dianetics. Conclusions drawn from this data are then invalid conclusions, for the response of the patient after the operation might have stemmed from a number of sources: engramic, the engram of the operation itself, attempted abortion damage early in life, brain disability on account of the operation and so forth. Hence, draw no conclusions that impairment of conceptual thinking, for instance, results only when a part of the brain is removed, that recall is shut off only when the brain is vivisected and so on. From a scientific standpoint no such "findings" were conclusive of anything except that the brain can be damaged late in life without entirely killing a man and that surgery of any kind often brings about a mental change in the patient. True, it may have been discovered that this or that portion of the switchboard called the brain, when removed, removed also some ability to perform.

Dianetic First Aid

It will be of interest to those associated with emergency hospital work particularly that the healing and recovery of any patient can be enormously benefited and the term of illness shortened by removing the engram occasioned at the moment of injury.

The accident case sometimes dies, in a few days, from shock, or does not recover and will not heal swiftly. In any injury—a burn, cut, a bruise of whatever kind—a trauma lingers in the injured area. The moment of the injury created an engram. This engram inhibits the release of the trauma. The fact that the injured part still hurts is an organic restimulator which depresses the ability of the patient to recover.

Using reverie or merely working the patient with his eyes closed, and working the patient as soon after the injury as possible, the doctor, nurse or relative can return the injured person to the moment when the injury was received and usually recover and exhaust the incident as a usual engram. Once the engram of the injury is reduced, the general mental tone of the patient improves. Further, the injured area is no longer inhibited from healing.

Some experimental work on this demonstrated that some burns would heal and disappear in a few hours when the engram which accompanied their reception was removed. On more serious injuries tests showed definite and unmistakable acceleration of the rate of healing.

In operations, when anesthetics have been used, Dianetics is useful in two ways: (1) as a preventive measure and (2) as a recovery measure. In the first, no conversation of any kind should be held around or with the "unconscious" or semiconscious patient. In the second, the trauma of the operation itself should be recovered and relieved immediately afterwards.

A Problem in Mutual Therapy

R and his wife C cleared each other in eight months with Dianetics, working four hours a night, four nights a week, each of them auditing the other for two hours of the four. This mutual arrangement had been complicated by the fact that whereas R was very eager to be cleared, his wife was quite apathetic about the work: he had managed only after much persuasion to get the cases started.

He was a high dynamic case with much emotion encysted; she was an apathy case who entirely neglected her troubles (black panther mechanism). He was troubled with a chronic ulcer and anxieties about his job; she was troubled with a general allergic condition and a chronic carelessness in domestic affairs. They were not to any great degree mutually restimulative, but they had problems about tacit consent, avoiding the subjects which had most upset them while together, such as a miscarriage she had had and the loss of their home by fire many years before, as well as other shocks. Further they were faced by R's intensity on the one hand and his introversion, which caused him to slight her therapy, and C's apathy on the other hand, which at once aided R's effort to take more time as the preclear than she and which made her less interested in being a good auditor.

Further complication took place because C did not understand the Auditor's Code or its use and on several occasions had become angry and impatient with R when he was in session and returned, an attitude which tended to force R into an anger valence.

Along this uncertain course therapy had been continuing. R was then informed of tacit consent and told he had better release some of their mutual painful emotion. He thereafter addressed the engram of the burning home and suddenly found himself able to audit some early sympathy engrams of his wife's which had not heretofore been available. It was discovered that her allergies stemmed from a father sympathy computation and that R was the pseudofather. This resulted in a marked improvement in C's case. She began to suffer less from her allergies, and a chronic heart pain she had had so long that she no longer heeded it vanished as well. She became interested in being a good auditor and studied the subject. She became slightly annoyed with R when he demanded more than his share of therapy time. (This increase of interest is always true of any apathy case which began with neglect of engrams.)

R, however, was much inhibited by her periods of anger and found that he now operated almost exclusively under autocontrol, a condition wherein *he* decided what should be run and what should not be run in himself. This autocontrol is, of course, useless, since if he knew about his aberrations and the data in his engrams, they would not be engrams. He, therefore, started on a period of refusing to display any emotion since she had mocked him about it, would not follow her directions and was, in short, obeying the engrams which she had given him when angry with him during past sessions. C was advised to pick up the moments of anger she had displayed as an auditor during therapy and when these were reduced, it was found that R worked well again and cooperated.

His ulcer stemmed from an attempted abortion. His father, an extremely aberrated individual, had sought to abort the baby when it was seven months in the womb. The mother remonstrated[47] that the baby might be born alive. The father said that if it were alive when born he would kill it as soon as it came out. He had said, further, that the mother had to hold still while he operated.

---

47. remonstrate: to make a protest.

On another occasion the father had said that he would lock the mother in a closet until she decided to abort the child. (This case was much complicated because the mother had been afraid to tell the father and had pretended not to be pregnant for three months, giving the husband the belief that the child, seven months along, was actually only four months along. Therefore, there was much secrecy in the case, much confusion and conflicting data.) This meant that R had a severe *holder* in the prenatal area: he was held by the engram which included a penetration of his stomach. This was the *key* engram, which is to say other engrams, by the mechanism of similar somatic and content, had gathered around it to suppress it. This was the tangle of incident which C was confronting unknowingly: it had become more tangled by her anger. R would now cooperate but his time track had wound into a ball around the holder engram, the key. Two exodontistries for the removal of wisdom teeth with nitrous oxide anesthesia were also suppressing the prenatals.

C worked for some time trying to get at the late extraction engrams, which contained an enormous amount of conversation between the dentist and his assistants and R's mother, who, unfortunately for his sanity, had accompanied him to the dentist's office.

R was made intensely uncomfortable by the continual restimulation of engrams which yet could not be reached. He was no more uncomfortable than he had often been in the past and his discomfort would have been absent had C understood and followed the Auditor's Code. The case made no progress for several weeks.

C's therapy was progressing. It was intensely restimulative to R to work upon her and increased his discomfort, but the more he worked on her the better auditing she did and the more intelligent she was (her IQ went up about fifty points after five weeks of therapy).

C desired to know how she could break the impasses in his case and was informed that she was now practicing tacit consent, for she had many times been needlessly thoughtless of R long before therapy was undertaken and she now realized what she had done to him and yet could not bring herself to face the fact that she was a responsible party to so much of his unhappiness. She had quite ordinarily used angry language to him which she well knew would "push button" him into doing something or into retreating from a quarrel, which language had been restimulative to him long before therapy.

C thereupon entered into painful emotion engrams late in R's life and, by working early physically painful engrams which said R could "feel nothing" alternately with late engrams when he was feeling intensely on an emotional plane but could not exhibit it, began to release the emotion in the case. R then showed steady improvement. Late painful emotion was released and early prenatals would show to be reduced, at which more late emotion would be visible for reduction.

It was suddenly disclosed in the case that the reason R was so easily upset by C lay in the person of a nurse who had attended R during his tonsillectomy when he was five years of age. C had some similarity of mannerism to this nurse. This was a sympathy engram, and when it was released the time track began to straighten out and the abortion engrams could be more easily contacted.

It so happened that R had been well off his time track most of his life, his memory occluded, his recall in poor condition. This was found to lie in the hidden key engram, the abortion attempt wherein his father had vowed to kill him if he came out and had added that the child could not see, feel or hear anything anyway, engramic material which was demonstrated by R's inability to move on his time track.

The moment the key was found—two hundred and eighty hours of therapy had elapsed—R came back on the time track, could move on it, and the erasure of his engrams proceeded in an orderly fashion.

C had been cleared about two months before R reached the final engram. C's allergies, however, disappeared long before her case was cleared completely, and R's ulcer and some other psychosomatic difficulties also vanished well before his case was finally cleared.

A Problem in a Restimulated Case

G was cleared in ten months of sporadic sessions. His case had the initial diagnosis of nonsonic, nonvisio, pain and emotional shut-off, permanent light trance, permanent "regression" at the age of three years. This is to say that the instant he went into reverie he was startled and frightened to find himself in a dental chair, three years old, and having a tooth pulled, an engram in which he had been situated, unknowingly, about half of his ensuing life. It had been the partial cause of his chronic tooth decay and his inability to sleep as negation against the anesthetic. The situation was obvious since he immediately began to wrestle about and lisp, which condition was instantly remedied by running the engram so that he could come to present time, which he did.

He had had considerable difficulty in life, was a high dynamic but manifested apathy. It was discovered after seventy-five hours, at which time release took place, that his wife was sometimes his pseudograndmother and also, by ambivalence, was his pseudomother. As his sympathy computation demanded that he be ill so that his grandmother would stay with him and as his contrasurvival engrams demanded that his mother was only nice to him when he was ill, the reactive computation added up to the fact that he must be ill continually, which demand had been obeyed by his body for twenty-three years. All this was recovered and remedied, of course, only by reducing engrams.

The erasure began to take place at the end of about two hundred hours of therapy and was proceeding when the case suddenly stopped all progress. For fifty or more hours of therapy, few engrams could be located; those which were located could not be reduced, no painful emotion could be reached and whatever engrams were reached and reduced were located and treated only because the auditor in this case used highly skilled forcing techniques which are almost never necessary and should not be employed save in psychotic cases. Such endeavor had not been necessary at the beginning of the case. Something was obviously wrong.

On close questioning it was discovered that G's wife was violently opposed to Dianetics, that she never lost any chance of leveling the most scathing attacks against it to G and particularly when he was in the company of friends. She derided him as being psychotic. She sought a lawyer to give her a divorce (announcing it after he had entered therapy but actually having had continual consultation on it with a lawyer for two years past) and generally agitated and disturbed G to such an extent that he was continually receiving painful emotional engrams even though he did not display any emotion against her.

They had a child, nine years of age, a boy. G was very fond of the boy. The child had had an unusual number of childhood illnesses and suffered from eye trouble and chronic sinusitis; he was backward in school. The wife was somewhat sharp with the child. Anything he did made her nervous.

The auditor in the case, on learning the facts about

her attitude toward her husband in general and Dianetics in particular, held a conference with her about her husband. She was found to be unopposed to therapy for herself. Shortly after the conference, G and this woman had a brief quarrel in which G made the remark that she must be aberrated. She took intense affront at this and said that he must be the one who was crazy since he was interested in Dianetics. He countered with the fact that of the two he must be the least aberrated since he was taking steps to do something about it. Further, he pointed out that she must be aberrated or she would not be as quarrelsome with the child as she was, a fact which definitely indicated that she must have a block on her second dynamic, sex.

The following day he came home from work and found she had withdrawn the money from the bank and gone to another town, taking the boy with her. He followed and found her staying with some of her relatives. She had told them that he beat her and had gone so crazy that he had to have therapy. The truth of the matter was that he had never touched her brutally in his life. In this meeting, before witnesses, she began to rave and revile any "system of psychiatry" which believed in prespeech memory. He pointed out to her that many schools of the past had believed in prespeech memory, that the whole background of psychiatry had long talked about "memories of the womb" without knowing what they were, and so forth.

Her relatives, seeing him so calm about it, forced her to return home with him. En route she made a dramatic gesture, although in no way threatened, of committing suicide by leaping out of the car.

The auditor in the case had a private conversation with her on her return. He had somewhat belatedly deduced the fact that there was something in her life which she was afraid her husband would find out and that, confronted with a science which could recover all memory, she had become wildly emotional about it. She at length admitted, under close questioning, that this was the case, that her husband must never know. She was so disturbed that the auditor, with her consent, gave her a few hours of therapy. It was instantly discovered that her father had many times threatened to kill her mother and that her father had not wanted her. Further, it was found that her father's name was Q and that her engram bank was strewn with remarks such as "Q, please don't leave me. I will die without you." Additionally, when she was no longer in session, she suddenly volunteered what was to her a hysterically humorous fact that all her life she had been having affairs with men named Q no matter what their shape or size or age. This was far from a release but in view of the fact that his other patient, G, was jeopardized by all this unnecessary hubbub and that therapy was being stalled, the auditor further questioned her. She divulged that she had tried many times to abort their son because she was terribly frightened that he would be a blond whereas she and her husband had dark hair. Further, the engrams of that child, she knew, contained data which she considered incriminating beyond mere abortion; while pregnant she had had intercourse with three men other than her husband.

The auditor pointed out to her that this guilt feeling, no matter how real, was still engramic in her and that it was doubtful if her husband would kill her on receipt of these tidings. He told her that she was condemning a child to a second-rate existence and that she was reducing her husband to apathy by her fears and causing the auditor far more work than was necessary. In her husband's and the auditor's presence she confessed her infidelity and learned with some amazement that her husband had known about it for years. He had not known about her attempts on their child.

She was requested to study a therapy manual and clear the child which, with her husband's help, she did. The auditor continued G on to clear, who then cleared his wife.

Advice to the Auditor

The hidden source of human aberration was hidden for a number of very specific reasons. The auditor will encounter all of these and, although with these techniques the ability of the reactive engram bank to deny him is precisely nil, he should know the nature of the beast he has under attack.

The mechanisms of protection which the engram bank had—although they are not very good now that we know how to penetrate this armor of insanity's cause—are as follows:

1. Physical pain.
2. Emotion in terms of captured units.
3. "Unconsciousness."
4. The delayed character of the key-in.
5. Delay between restimulation and illness.
6. Utter irrationality.

Of the physical pain we know much—that the mind, in memory, sought to avoid it just as the mind in life seeks to avoid it as an outside source: hence, memory blockage.

Emotion of loss piles up to make a buffer between the individual and the reality of death.

"Unconsciousness" is not only a mechanism of hiding data, it is also a block to memory which cannot jump the gaps of past moments when the fuses were blown.

An engram might slumber for the better part of a lifetime and then, given the correct set of restimulators in the right moment of physical weariness or illness, manifest itself, making an *apparent* cause of insanity or lesser aberration many years after the actual incident had taken place.

Another aspect of the bank protective mechanism was the restimulator lag, which is to say that when a keyed-in engram was restimulated it often required two or three days for action to take place. (Example: Say a migraine headache has as its restimulator a rhythmic bumping sound; that sound is heard by the individual who has the engram; three days later he suddenly has a migraine.) Given this lag, how could one locate the cause of a specific restimulation of a sporadic illness?

The utter irrationality of an engram, the ultimate in irrationality, that everything equals everything else in the engram and that these are equal to things in the exterior environment which are only vaguely similar is a feat of idiocy which any sentient man might be expected to overlook as a "thought process."

Man has been looking for this source for some thousands of years; but he was looking for something which was complicated on the grounds that anything which could be so harrowing, so destructive, so vicious and so capable of producing complex manifestations must therefore have a complex source; on examination it is remarkably simple.

The auditor will have very little to do with trying to draw a line between sanity and insanity, they are such relative terms. He will be asked to compare Dianetics with old standards such as the complex classifications of Kraepelin:[48] it can be done but it has the usefulness of Aristotelian natural history, of interest only to the historian.

---

48. Kraepelin, Emil: (1856–1926) German psychiatrist. Divided mental disturbances into various classifications.

If an individual is incapable of adjusting himself to his environment so as to get along with or obey or command his fellows, or, more importantly, if he is incapable of adjusting his environment, then he can be considered to be "insane." But it is a relative term. Sanity, on the other hand, closely approaches, with Dianetics, a potential absolute meaning, for we know the optimum mind. Modifications of education and viewpoint may make the rational action of one person appear irrational to another but this is not a problem of sanity—it is a problem of viewpoint and education, with which the auditor will have but small concern.

Thus the patients the auditor will encounter will fall into the three general Dianetic classes of nonsonic recall, imaginary recall and sonic recall. The question of sanity does not arise: the question of how difficult or how long the case may be is fairly well determined by the degree of these three conditions.

However, the auditor will find that he may have in his hands a truly "insane" case, one which is "psychotic." The treatment of such a case depends on which of the three above classes the psychotic patient may be entered. The problem is to deintensify the engrams of the patient as swiftly as possible.

The conditions and mechanisms which hide the engram bank do not vary: they are uniformly present in every patient, in every human being. The techniques of Dianetics may be improved upon—and what scientific technique, particularly in its first few years of existence, cannot—but they also do not perform selectively but are applicable to all individuals.

Hence, if we have an "insane" patient, the fundamental problem does not change and Dianetic technique works as in any other case. The task is to reduce the intensity of charge in the case so that it can be resolved by standard technique.

Insane patients are often found stuck on the time track, in which case a holder is fed to them, one kind after another, until they are moving again. If the patient is regressed, he has become so thoroughly stuck that he has lost touch with the present time. Any patient can begin to *relive* instead of merely return and the auditor, as the remedy for this, merely snaps at them that they can remember this, which places them in a *returned* status again. Insane patients are often found listening to one engram over and over, in which case it is again only necessary to fix attention and feed them holders until they are once more moving on the track. Insane patients are sometimes discovered completely off the time track, listening to demons or seeing illusion. The problems are always the same: use repeater technique when, by one means or another, their attention has been fixed, and then either get them moving on the track or get them back on the time track. The schizophrenic is usually a long way off his time track.

The best way to deintensify a case so that it can be entered in routine therapy is to discover and discharge painful emotion engrams. If ordinary means fail, get the help of a medical doctor, place the patient under nitrous oxide or sodium pentothal and reach a deep level of trance where the patient will be found, ordinarily, to be capable of moving on his track even though he was off his track when awake. Find a late despair engram and discharge it as described in the chapter on emotion. The technique for deep trance is no different except that very cautious safeguards must be taken to say nothing which will aberrate the patient further but to limit all conversation to therapy patter, being very careful to include the canceler.

The insane patient is obeying some engramic command, perhaps many, no matter what he is doing. That command may dictate, by the patient's misinterpretation, some strange action; it may dictate demons; it may dictate anything. But diagnosis merely consists of observing the patient in order to discover, by his actions, what the engramic command might be.

This volume does not cover Institutional Dianetics beyond these few remarks, but an auditor who knows the fundamentals in this volume and with any understanding can bring about a "sanity" in patients in a short time which the boards of these institutions normally consider a miraculous recovery. The patient, however, is very far from a *release,* and many more hours should be spent in discharging further painful emotion and reducing engrams before an auditor should consider it safe to permit him to leave therapy.

The auditor should be extremely cautious, at least for the next twenty years, about any case which has been institutionalized, for he may be getting a case with iatrogenic psychosis—caused by doctors—in addition to the patient's other engrams. Dianetics may help a mind a little in which the brain has been "ice picked" or "apple cored," but it cannot cure such insanity until some clever biologist finds a way to grow a new brain. Electric shock cases are equivocal: they may or may not respond to treatment, for brain tissue may have been burned away to a point where the brain cannot function normally. In entering any such case, the auditor will be perplexed by the scrambled condition of the standard bank, to say nothing of the circuits by which he should be able to reach the engram bank. Syphilis and other brain erosions should be similarly classified and should be approached or undertaken only with the full knowledge that Dianetics may not be able to help the dismembered machine at all. There have been many thousands of these brain "operations" and hundreds of thousands of electric shock treatments: thus the auditor should be alert not to engage upon what may be a hopeless cause when there exist so many cases which can better be helped. Any case which has been institutionalized should be suspected. And if anything unusual in the way of memory scramble or lack of coordination is observed, searching inquiry may reveal hidden institutionalization. Further, an auditor called upon to assist a case which is about to be institutionalized should always be wary. The case which is being sent to an institution may be a case which has been in one before, regardless of the protestations of relatives or friends that such is not the circumstance.

Similarly, combat exhaustion cases should be warily undertaken, for the case was probably processed before quitting the service, at which time electric shock or brain operation or narcosynthesis may have been applied without the knowledge or consent of the patient.

These warnings are given not because the auditor will be in any particular physical danger—patients seldom do anything but cooperate, sane or insane, when Dianetics is applied, even if they snarl about it—but because much work may be expended only to discover that the entire mental machinery has been wrecked beyond repair.

If the auditor undertakes an electric shock case, he should address his primary attention to the release of that shock as an engram, for there is all manner of careless chatter contained in these institutional engrams, which may further inhibit treatment. This is aside from the fact that any electric shock, anywhere in the body, has a tendency to derange the engram bank and bind it so that its incidents are more than usually snarled.

For no other reason than the advance of Dianetics, and the conservation of an auditor's time, it should also be remarked that the third degree methods of some police departments and general police abuse of criminals or ordinary citizens may have to be released in a case before it can be further treated. Prison terms may contain large despair charges sufficient to derange the mind and yet may be hidden by the patient under the mistaken idea that the auditor is interested or will be disappointed in his "character."

Various other things enter into the engram bank which would not be suspected as obstacles to therapy unless mentioned. Hypnotism can be extremely aberrative and may hold up a case. An auditor should have some working knowledge of it so that he can release the engrams it makes, not so he can work Dianetics. Hypnotism is the art of implanting positive suggestions in the engram bank. Here they may append themselves to engrams and become locks on those engrams. As most engram banks contain a sample of most common words, hypnotism is almost certain to be aberrative. The reduction of analytical power by artificial means places the subject in an optimum condition for the receipt of an engram. The hypnotist uses the forgetter mechanism with most of his suggestions and most people have similar engramic remarks which make it impossible for the hypnotist's suggestion to release. Hypnotism can be considered as a "high-powered" lock and may be a serious obstacle in the patient's engram bank. With clearing, the suggestions, having no anchors of pain below them in engrams, vanish as locks. But hypnotic suggestions may have to be found and cleared before a case can proceed. Hypnotism is very commonly used in this society and it is very often the case that, with the forgetter mechanism, the patient is unable to recall whether he had ever been hypnotized or not. Return technique will discover it; repeater technique, making the patient return with repetition of hypnotic patter (by the patient) such as "Go to sleep, go to sleep, go to sleep," can be depended upon to locate it.

Not all hypnotism is in the parlor. Perverts quite

commonly use it despite the fact that the "moral" nature is supposed to rise in a hypnotized subject. Incidents even with people of repute have been found in patients when examining their childhood. These incidents were often entirely occluded to the patient, so thoroughly cowing were the commands contained in the hypnotic suggestion.

Dianetics and hypnotism can be combined, but so can Dianetics and astronomy. The auditor will find himself working with hypnotic patients and will have to be very careful with patter in order to install minimal words of his own in the engram bank so as not to turn Dianetics into hypnotism.

Any benefit derived from hypnotism is in the field of research or the installation of a temporary manic engram. The latter has far more harm than value. Hypnotic anesthetic is vastly overrated. And hypnotism as a parlor game is a thing which no society should tolerate, for it may be sufficiently destructive to cause the engrams to restimulate to a point of insanity. And the hypnotist never knows the content of the engram bank. Any good hypnotist, if he can conquer his desire to talk, should make a good auditor: but if he tries to combine Dianetics and hypnotism he will find himself with a very thoroughly sick patient on his hands. *Never install a positive suggestion of any kind in a patient no matter how much he may beg for one. It has proven nearly fatal.*

An entire case can be worked in deep amnesia trance. It is often possible to waken a sleeping person into a deep trance simply by speaking to him quietly several nights in succession at the same hour and finally getting him to respond to the invitation to talk. Dianetic therapy can then be entered upon and pursued and will succeed particularly if the auditor is not careless enough to artificially restimulate a late physical pain engram, treating in the postbirth life mainly engrams of painful emotion. If the person on whom the therapy is being done is aware of the action, he can be put into reverie so that earlier data can be reached, "I" being more powerful than the weak if wise attention units which constitute basic personality. He is alternately worked in amnesia trance and then in reverie. The case will resolve eventually even if reverie is not used. But there are grave responsibilities with amnesia trance: a canceler must always be installed and used in every session. Minimal conversation must be employed. All auditor desires should be stated as questions if possible, as these are not aberrative to the degree that commands are. This method has been successful and can be used, but reverie, even if it appears slower, even if sonic is not present, is far more satisfactory for the excellent and incontrovertible reason that the patient recovers more swiftly and recovers on a steady upgrade, whereas amnesia trance may incapacitate him for days together, when incidents are apparently lifted in deep trance but nevertheless "hung up" in the awake state. Amnesia trance is definitely not advised: it has been subjected to much research and has been found to be both uncomfortable for the patient and harassing to the auditor. However, if other methods cannot be used for one reason or another (and none of those reasons include the desire of the preclear who, if the auditor would let him, might crave drugs, hypnotism and positive suggestion in an effort to escape his engrams and who, if allowed, would have himself a wonderfully messy case for the auditor to unsnarl), amnesia trance can be employed, but always with the greatest caution and always with the full knowledge that the patient's recovery is retarded by as much as a factor of three, for working on a level with the engram bank leaves the analyzer circuits unused in the discharge. Reverie is best.

External Problems With Patients

It may happen that a patient who has made progress suddenly ceases to make further progress. The answer may lie elsewhere than therapy. The environment of the preclear may be so intensely restimulative that he is distracted, always in restimulation and thus works slowly. It may be discovered, in such a case, that the preclear (as in one case) has made a bargain with a wife or husband who desires divorce that he or she wait until the preclear is cleared. Other situations of a life nature can place an environmental value on not being cleared. The auditor has no business with the private lives of his preclears, but in a case where therapy itself is made difficult by existing situations, the auditor, with his time at stake, has every right to discover the reason. All these reasons will compute into some environmental advantage in not being clear. Removing the preclear temporarily from his home, for instance, may change his environment and advance therapy. The auditor has a right to ask that, clear or not, the patient resolve the problem on his own initiative. It is common with preclears that they do not realize that they are *releases,* for so glittering is the goal of *clear* that they cease to compare themselves to the normal which they have already overpassed.

A patient can commonly be expected to introvert to a very marked degree in the course of Dianetic therapy. As the case progresses this introversion reaches an acute stage about three-quarters or thereabouts through and thereafter recedes. Ambiversion[49] is a marked characteristic of the *clear.* When introversion has been marked, a fairly good gauge of the advance of the case is in the

49. ambiversion: a condition or character trait that includes elements of both introversion and extroversion.

preclear's interest in exterior things.

Nearly all preclears talk a great deal about their engrams up to the point when they are very solid releases. If they don't or won't talk about their engrams in common conversation, the auditor can suspect something highly protected in the engram bank concerning the necessity to hide something: the auditor can act accordingly. Although the auditor may weary of such conversation, it nevertheless reveals much new material to him if he observes the phrases which the preclear uses about engrams.

It is very, very true that aberration is caused by what has been done *to* not what has been done *by* the patient. The actions of the patient in dramatizing, in committing crimes and so forth are not aberrative to the patient. Therefore the preclear's activities need be no concern whatever of the auditor's. Whole cases have been completed without the auditor's knowing what the preclear did for a living. While responsibility for his actions is necessarily demanded of him by an aberrated society, antisocial activity is the result of engrams which dictate it. The patient is not responsible for what he himself has done. Cleared, the matter is different. A clear can be considered entirely responsible for his own actions, for he can compute rationally on the basis of his experience. But the aberree has little or no real control over his actions. Therefore, the auditor should make it plain that he does not care what the aberree who becomes a preclear has done in life. The problem on hand between the auditor and the preclear is an engram bank which contains, exclusively, what other people have done in life and what has been done to the preclear in moments when he could not protect himself. This approach is not only truth, it has a therapeutic value, for in so explaining himself an auditor can often obtain cooperation which would otherwise be denied.

The auditor should never violate the Auditor's Code with a patient. Extended terms of therapy inevitably result from such violations.

Restimulation

The mind is a self-protecting mechanism—but so is Dianetics. A science of thought which works would so closely approximate the working principles of the mind that it would follow in parallels the injunctions[50] and provisos[51] of the mind itself. Such is the case with Dianetics: the mind is diagnosed by its reaction to therapy, therapy is improved by the reactions of the mind to it. This is a working principle of great value since it explains much observed phenomena and predicts most of the remainder. Part of this parallelism is the self-protection feature.

It is almost impossible to injure a mind: it is an extremely tough organism. Of course, when one begins to hew[52] and saw upon it with metal or poison it with drugs or bacteria or throw its natural armor aside as with hypnotism, unfortunate things can occur.

Charlatanism is almost impossible where Dianetics in any of its principles is being practiced. One either practices all Dianetics and gets results or practices himself into a decline: that is a mechanical, scientific fact. Dianetics, as a self-protecting science, demands practice by clears or at least good releases. A clear very closely follows in all his conduct the better aspects of the

---

50. injunction: an order or command that something must or must not be done.

51. proviso: something that is insisted upon as a condition of an agreement.

52. hew: to chop or cut with an ax or sword, etc.

Auditor's Code: his ethical level is very high. Hence, anyone starting a practice of Dianetics is going to find himself, no matter what his original intention, thrust toward the goal of being a clear.

There is an excellent reason for this. There is a principle known as restimulation of the auditor. We have an understanding now of what makes an engram come into restimulation. When it comes into restimulation, it forces the pain or the action of the engram into being in the organism. The observation of some percept in the environment which approximates a recording (sound or sight or organic sensation) in the engram brings the engram into greater or lesser play. Similarly, when an auditor is not cleared himself or when he is not in therapy himself working toward the goal of a clear, he becomes restimulated. He is, after all, listening constantly to engramic material in a patient. This engramic material is the very stuff of which insanity is made. Anyone has engrams: sooner or later a patient is going to start going over an engram of his own which will approximate the auditor's own engrams. This leads to great discomfort for the auditor unless the auditor is in therapy and can have the discomfort so brought forth released. So long as one is merely working late locks this is not so much the case and has made it possible for practitioners and mental healers of the past to escape much of the penalty of their own aberrations, but when one deals with the root material of these aberrations, a constant hammering by restimulators can bring about a serious condition. This is the mechanism which causes people in asylums to fall prey themselves to psychoses, although one must have had them in the first place for them to have been restimulated.

The auditor may run one or two cases without any serious repercussion: indeed, no matter what the repercussion, it can be eliminated by Dianetics. To save his own comfort, however, he should himself be cleared or released as soon as possible. He can work as a release without too much trouble, and this makes it possible for him to make a mutual compact where he is worked on while he is working the other. A condition can then come about where two preclears are each auditors. This alternation between the couch and the auditor's chair will usually work very well.

Two persons, however, after they have begun work, may discover that they are mutually restimulative—which is to say each is a pseudoperson in the other's engrams or one is restimulated (voice tone, incidents) by the other. This should be no bar to therapy. It has been overcome and therapy has gone forward despite the most severe restimulative circumstances. A common avoidance technique on the part of a subject is to claim the auditor restimulates him: it is not sufficiently important to stop therapy. It may be, however, that two people can enter a third into the chain and, by one clearing the next, considerably ease the tension. The triangular work plan, where no person is working on the person who is working him, is quite successful.

A husband and wife who have quarreled long and often may find it too restimulative to clear each other. It is possible to do if other arrangements cannot be made and it is often done: but if therapy does not go well, he should find a therapy partner and so should she. Mothers who have attempted abortion on their children or otherwise maltreated them can accomplish therapy on those children, but in any case of restimulative circumstance such as this, the greatest precaution must be taken by the auditor to adhere severely to the Auditor's Code—to do otherwise might bring much more stress into therapy than is necessary. In such a case, the mother had better herself have at least a release accomplished upon her before she attempts to clear her children—and she should not touch those children until they are at least eight.

The subject of auditor-restimulation, where the auditor restimulates the preclear or the preclear restimulates the auditor, does not include the routine aspect of therapy that the preclear is always being artificially restimulated via standard therapy. An engram can be restimulated by being touched several times and so it will lift. The auditor-restimulation problem is a specific one where the auditor is a pseudoenemy, a similarity to a person who has harmed the patient. Wild antagonism on the part of a patient to an auditor is usually traced to this. Some patients have such a hatred of men that only women can work them, some have such a hatred of women that only men can work them. But even when there is a wild antipathy, if there exists no other auditor or person who can be trained quickly as one, therapy can proceed anyway and it will accomplish results.

Rebalancing a Case

Any case dropped out of therapy will rebalance itself in a few weeks, which is to say, it will settle to a new high for the individual. Unless drug hypnotism or some other Dianetically illegal method is used, all cases will so rebalance, much benefited. Restimulations can be expected to die down if they are due to therapy. The patient will gradually find his own level in the released state. Cases do not have to be carried forward to *clear* if auditor time is short, but it is of course better if they are and, indeed, the majority of patients will insist that they be.

Working Time in Therapy

The usual period of a Dianetic treatment is two hours. In these two hours, with the usual patient, everything is going to be accomplished which can be accomplished on that day. Working every day is not necessary, but working every two days or every three days is desirable. Working with periods a week apart is not optimum, for the case tends to rebalance. Further, there is a "sag" in a case, usually every fourth day when it is not worked in periods as short as three days. The fourth day "sag" is a natural mechanical thing: an engram, keyed in, when it is restimulated in life, takes about four days to cut in sharply. In therapy, three days is sometimes required to "develop" an engram. This does not mean that three days have to elapse before it is available and it does not mean that work has to stop for three days, but it does mean that engrams, not being memories and articulate as such, take three days, sometimes, to come to the surface.

To be more clear, an engram can be asked for on day one and will be found on day three. Meanwhile the auditor is getting other engrams. This process is so automatic that it requires no attention and will not come to notice except in cases that are being worked once a week. The engram is asked for on day one, is ready to reduce on day three, sags on day four and is rebalanced by day seven.

The three-day aspect is interesting in another sense. This time of three days is just an observation of the average behavior of preclears. Precision investigation may fix it at 2.5 days or 3.6 days (it varies in individuals), but three days is close enough for our purposes. When one is doing just a release on a case, he will sometimes find that it is necessary to take a late engram and run it: the physical pain engram of later life (post-birth) will appear to rise, will remain constant for three days and then will "sag." When it sags, the auditor will have to go back to it and run it again. Taking out these "sags" will eventually make the later life engram stay in a recessed state.

Euphoria often sets in on a case when the auditor touches an engram which contains a manic. The patient will then go around saying how wonderful Dianetics is because he is now in magnificent condition and is so happy. Watch out. In three or four days this manic will have sagged back to a depressive state. Be wary if somebody experiences one of these skyrocket "recoveries" for it is about as permanent as the fire of a burning match. It goes out and leaves very cold ashes. The auditor, seeing this euphoria, had better enter the case again and reduce the engram it contains more thoroughly or get a more basic engram.

The length of time it takes to clear a person is quite variable. By blowing despair charges and working a few early engrams, an auditor can get a better state of being in the patient than in any past therapy in twenty or thirty hours: this is a release. It compares to two or three years of past therapeutic work. The length of time it takes to get a clear cannot be compared to any past standard because a clear is something no past standard ever dreamed about.

In a sonic case, where recall is in good condition, a clear can be obtained in a hundred hours. In a case which has thoroughly shut-down recalls, anything can happen up to, in extremity, a thousand hours. Similarly, the imaginative case which has things which never happened may be long.

Look at it this way: we can get the results of two or three years of psychoanalysis in a score or two of hours of Dianetics, and what we accomplish with Dianetics does not have to be done again, which is not true with psychoanalysis. This is the *release*. He can go about his business in a far more competent fashion, his emotional charges being largely freed. In the clear we are attempting and can achieve a supernormal state of mind. Thousands and thousands and thousands of hours were spent in the education of a man: the expenditure of two or even ten thousand hours of work to make him rank above what would formerly have been possible for him is work well spent. But we do not have to spend anything like this amount of time. People have been cleared in anything from thirty hours, when they had sonic and little volume, to five hundred hours when they had shut-down recall plus imaginary recall. What an auditor can do with his first few cases by way of time is a question mark. He will get to the clear eventually and certainly in less than twelve hundred hours in a severe case. All the time he is working toward a clear he is achieving a higher and higher release which, after at least fifty hours, rises well above the current norm and keeps right on soaring. Improvement is such that from week to week the change is physiologically noticeable and psychologically startling. If one thinks the reach for clear is a short jump and a small gain, then he has no conception of just how high that goal is.

Most auditors will try for release at first and are wise if they do. When their own case is finally cleared, only then will they suddenly realize that the state was worth far more time than was expended to attain.

It is impossible to forecast, with a new auditor, just how much time he will consume in making errors, learning his tools, attaining skill. It is therefore impossible to estimate for him how long it will take him to gain a clear in a patient. A well-trained auditor never takes more than eight hundred hours with the worst of cases: five hundred is high.

Data From Relatives

The auditor will always be plagued by the anxiety of the patient to get data from relatives or friends. The request for this data itself is restimulative both to the preclear and the relative. Mothers have been made very ill by being given the restimulators of their own past illnesses by the child who has "suddenly found out."

It is a uniform experience that the data obtained from relatives, parents and friends by the preclear is absolutely and utterly worthless. Here we are depending upon an aberree's memory when we have at hand, with Dianetics, a reliable source of accurate material. Auditors have had cases progress very smoothly and then suddenly stop progress: on inquiry it is discovered that the preclear has been running around to his parents and relatives for material and they, wanting nothing more than that he forget all about what they have done to him, throw him red herrings which have to be carefully eliminated. These are the villains of the piece, the people who have done the things to the preclear which made him an aberree. If one expects accurate data from them, one might as well expect the moon to be green cheese.

If the auditor wants data from these people and requests it, bypassing the preclear, he may get somewhere. But any data so received has a value which, in intelligence, is used to label "Incompetent Source—Improbable Material."

Warn a preclear not to bother his relatives and parents and explain to him that he can make them ill by asking for data, on the restimulator principle. If we want confirmation of the data received, the only way to get it is put the parent or relative in therapy. At such time, we shall get the basic dramatization sources: in the prenatal life and childhood of the parent. This is a problem of research, not of therapy.

521

If the auditor has Mama available, he can run off the child's birth and then Mama giving birth, keeping the two apart, and get his check on the accuracy of therapy. And there are other data that can be so compared, using proper safeguards.

The subjective reality, not the objective reality, is the important question to the auditor. First, last and always, *does the patient get well?*

Stopping Therapy

The woman scorned has a violent rival in the preclear on whom therapy has been stopped by the auditor's decision.

Keeping the preclear in therapy, no matter how seldom are the sessions, satisfies in some measure the effort his basic personality makes to fight clear of the aberrations.

The basic personality, the file clerk, the core of "I" which wants to be in command of the organism, the most fundamental desires of the personality, may be considered synonymous for our purposes. There is an enormous surge of this basic self—which is really the individual himself—to conquer the engrams. The engrams, borrowing life from their host, appear as things which do not want to be conquered. As mechanistic as all this actually is, the auditor will often find himself wondering at the resistance the engrams can make and marveling at the efforts of the basic personality to conquer the engrams. He works *with* the basic personality, the individual himself, and ignores the engramic efforts to interfere. But there is a situation in which the basic personality seems to give free play to the engrams in an effort to accomplish therapy.

In work, a "patient" might have been skeptical,

sarcastic or even vicious to the auditor. Or the patient may have been thought to be completely neglectful of his engram bank. Or the patient may even rage that he hates therapy. For some of these reasons the auditor may injudiciously decide to cease working the patient. The patient is so informed. For a short while, perhaps, the patient may manifest no reaction, but in a few minutes, a few hours or a few days, basic personality, denied a route out, may begin to use every weapon to hand to compel the auditor to resume therapy.

Disturbed by cessation of therapy, even though he may have insisted upon its being stopped, the ex-patient may begin either to rapidly decline or to attack, to his face or behind his back, the auditor and even therapy itself. The woman scorned has rarely made such thorough upsets as ex-patients who have been refused continuance of therapy. Auditors have been personally reviled, have had other preclears searched out and undermined by violent attacks upon therapy itself, have been targeted by all manner of accusations and whispering campaigns and have been made most uncomfortable by preclears who have had further therapy denied to them before a release had taken place. Even solid, legitimate releases, whose psychosomatic ills have disappeared and who should be quite cheerful, have been observed to create turbulence when the auditor would not take them through to clear. Any number of mechanisms may be used by the ex-patient, as many mechanisms as men use to force other men into action. One of the mechanisms is a resumption of apathy and a "swift decline." Another is wild campaigning against therapy. Another is personal attack of the auditor. Each has, as its provable intention, the resumption of therapy.

The mind knows how the mind works. And the mind which has tasted a way out of pain and unhappiness may be expected, if that way is blocked, to use all methods to cause therapy to be resumed.

No matter how thoroughly disagreeable the ex-patient has been, the moment the auditor starts therapy upon him again, the attitude alters. No further destructive efforts are made against the auditor or therapy but all is almost as well as it was before the cessation was declared.

Do not suppose, however, that the preclear, if he has been neglectful, recalcitrant[53] or generally uncooperative before, will now embrace therapy as a chastened[54] patient. Far from the case, he is now at least as difficult to work as he was before *plus* some additional antagonism engendered by the cessation order.

In such a case the auditor is damned if he does and double-damned if he doesn't. But there is a way out of this. The phenomenon of "transference," where the patient simply transfers his griefs to the practitioner, is not the mechanism here at work; transference is a different thing, bred of a thirst for attention and a feeling of needed support in the world. Transference can be expected to keep up forever if permitted; the patient of a doctor, for instance, may go on and on having illnesses just to keep the doctor around. Transference may occur in Dianetic therapy, the patient may lean on the auditor solidly, beg the auditor for advice, appear to hold out engrams in an effort to keep the auditor working hard and available and interested; all this is the result of a sympathy computation and is aberrated conduct. The clever auditor will not give advice or attempt to run anyone's life, for a person works well only as a self-determined organism. In Dianetic therapy, no matter what the attitude of the patient, no matter how great his "desires to be ill" or his transference of burden, no

---

53. recalcitrant: disobedient, resisting authority or discipline.
54. chasten: to restrain from excess; subdue.

matter about even his vicious remarks to the auditor during sessions, the condition cannot obtain forever. Basic personality is trying to get through; "I" is trying to integrate self. Even indifferent work will eventually release enough charge from a case and reduce enough engrams to bring a higher stability to the patient. Basic personality gets stronger and stronger and therefore more self-reliant. The introversion occasioned by continual effort to reach the interior world of the engram bank deintensifies and extroversion comes more and more into being as the case advances. The way out is to work the patient smoothly and well and one day he will be well released or clear. But meanwhile, if you stop therapy on anyone, don't be surprised at anything that happens; you can only remedy it by resuming the case.

Auditor Evaluation

The auditor must do much evaluation to himself. *He does not evaluate or force upon his preclear any computation.* If the preclear computes that this was what was making him ill, then this is what the auditor accepts. Explaining to the preclear what it was in the engram which affected him so and so is not only a waste of time but also makes the preclear confused. The reason an auditor evaluates is to make sure he is not accepting imagined data or incomplete data as engrams.

An incident will not lift unless the data in it is correct: this is automatic. Change just one syllable in the incident and it will stick. Or, if it seems to go away, it will be back. So there is no fear that any incident which decreases with recounting is incorrect. The data in it must be more or less correct or it would not so reduce. Thus the auditor who challenges incidents, data or otherwise plays god is going to have a thoroughly fouled up case on his hands before he goes very far, and he is going to have a subject who is not progressing. If the subject begins to run an engram where Mama is having intercourse with five Eskimos, let him run it and never, never, never, never tell him that you feel it was untrue. If you tell the subject you think he is imagining things, you may give him a serious setback. Tell him you think Mama had her reasons and you have sided with the opposition: you are not attacking the engram, you are helping Mama attack the subject. To criticize, correct or otherwise judge the preclear has no slightest part in Dianetics and will do more to slow up a case than any other single action. An auditor who challenges the material given him may be practicing witchcraft or Chinese acupuncture[55] or shamanism or voodoo,[56] but he is not practicing Dianetics. And he will not get results. One remark to the subject such as, "I think that you are mistaken in believing your mother would try to abort you," or "I feel that you are imagining it," may set your preclear back fifty hours. The auditor does not criticize or judge the preclear, nor does he evaluate for the preclear that person's material.

Auditing is all done privately and to oneself. If the patient has just recounted his fifth prenatal train wreck, you may be sure you have run into a lie factory in some engram. The wrong way to go about correcting this is communicating it to the preclear. The right way to go about it is to find the lie factory, an engram containing such a remark as, "Tell me anything! Tell me anything. I don't care so long as you say something. But for God's sakes don't tell me the truth, I can't stand it!" Or, "You can't tell him the truth. It would hurt too much." There

---

55. acupuncture: pricking the tissues of the body with fine needles to relieve pain or as a local anesthetic.

56. voodoo: a form of religion based on belief in witchcraft and magical rites, practiced by some people in the West Indies and America.

are a thousand forms of lie factory. And they are not too uncommon.

Never tell the preclear why you are looking for anything. If you say you want a lie factory, the lie factory will make up a lie factory. If you say you want an emotional charge, you will inhibit any emotional charge from discharging. Simply make a quiet estimate of the situation, reduce everything which seems valid and keep on trying to get the reason why the case is not functioning as well as possible.

The test for validity of an engram is not *plot*. Plot is worthless. Engrams are just collections of remarks contained in periods of "unconsciousness." It makes no difference whatever whether these remarks agree with the way the auditor thinks a life should be run or the way a preclear should look up to his parents. Plot is something writers put in stories. Auditors have nothing to do with it. An engram is basically illogical and irrational; don't try to read rationality into one! If the parents were known to be fine, upstanding members of the community and the engrams seem to indicate that Mama nightly played the prostitute, accept the engrams.

Validity is very simply established. Ask these questions of the engram:

1. Does it have a somatic?

2. Does the somatic undulate, which is to say, undergo a running change?

3. Does it reduce? (If it does not, the content the preclear is running is wrong or the engram is way up the chain and has others before it.)

4. Does the engramic content agree with the patient's aberration?

5. Does the somatic agree with psychosomatic ills the patient is known to have had?

6. Does it bring relief to the patient? And this last is more important than all the rest.

Because mental healers of the past have grandly said, "Oh, this does not fit with *my* idea of how life is run" is no reason an auditor should run Dianetics off the rails. Mental healers of yesteryear did not get results. Dianetics gets results: and one of the most important reasons why Dianetics gets results is that it is not trying to warp life to fit Dianetics but is applying Dianetics to life. Many new and startling things will come to the notice of the auditor. His motto, as seen on an ancient English crest where a ninety-foot raven stood upon a castle, could read, "Be surprised at nothing."

The Kinsey report did not begin to tell the story you, as an auditor, will get in Dianetics. Because the mother, by herself, is neither the face she showed Junior nor the face she showed society, and because Mother and Father, by themselves, do not conduct themselves as they might be supposed to have done in society is insufficient reason to force a preclear to go on being an aberree.

Continually in the psychiatric texts we come upon patients who tried to tell psychiatrists about prenatal life and who were told, with droll solemnity that the incidents were imaginary. Patients who had been given up on all fronts by all existing schools because their data was not tailored to fit the belief of those schools have recovered fully and achieved optimum mental condition, well above that of their former mentors, with Dianetics, partially because Dianetics does not set itself above the facts of life. He not only requires the patient to face reality by running the engrams but he also requires himself to face reality by accepting the fact that whatever the content, if it fits *any* of the above conditions listed, it is valid in therapy.

Auditing means to listen; it also means to compute. Computing on a case consists of establishing where the patient departs from optimum rationality in his conduct of life but, more important, where physically painful and painful emotion engrams exist and how they can be approached and reduced.

Patients discover some astonishing things about their parents and relatives when they are in therapy. Often they discover, like one patient who had believed he had daily been beaten by his father that life was actually much better than it had seemed.

Premarital conception cases are very common, with the patient yet unborn discovering himself at his parents' wedding. And these cases are often very difficult to resolve since they contain so much secrecy in their engrams.

The lie factory mechanisms will often try to give Mama extra lovers and try to make Papa into a raving beast, but a lie factory is very easy to detect: the incidents brought forth do not run like engrams: the second time over their content is widely changed, they do not have somatics and their content is not aberrative.

In short, the test is whether or not one has an actual engram, not whether or not the engram makes sense. For Father could well have been a raving beast in a boudoir and Mother could well have had coitus with the boarders: and Father could well have been a tame lamb for all the reputation Mother gave him postbirth and Mother could well have been a frigid prude despite the wild tales the preclear might have heard. The truth will come out in the reduction but its truth is no concern of the auditor's beyond getting up engrams.

First, last and always, get engrams, get them as early as possible for pain, later for emotion, get them, erase them, discharge them, clear them! That they did not compute as true data was what drove the aberree into being an aberree. Leave plot to writers: our task is therapy.

But don't "buy garbage": ask for the somatic, see if it varies as the preclear utters the words. Test for engrams. And devil take the plot.

CHAPTER TEN

Dianetics—Past and Future

The History of Dianetics

The history of Dianetics would be the history of a voyage of discovery, of an exploration into new and nearly uncharted realms, *terra incognita,* the human mind, a land which lies an inch behind your forehead.

The voyage has taken many years and the labor has been long, but we have charts now and can go and return at will.

Observations of savage and civilized races in this and far climes formed the foundation for the anthropological research: the writings of a few men in the last four thousand years formed the scholarly pilots. The ancient Hindu writings, the work of the early Greeks and Romans including Lucretius,[1] the labors of Francis Bacon, the researches of Darwin and some of the thoughts of Herbert Spencer compose the bulk of the philosophic background. Inevitable absorption from our current culture provided much unnoticed information. The remainder has been what the navigator calls, "off the chart."

In 1935 some of the basic research was begun: in 1938 the primary axioms were discovered and formulated. For the next several years these axioms were tested in the laboratory of the world. The war interrupted the work, as wars will, being chaos, but shortly after the cessation of actual hostilities, research was renewed.

---

1. Lucretius: Titus Lucretius Carus: (96?–55 B.C.) Roman philosophical poet.

Within a year the fundamentals of this science as they applied to the human mind had been integrated. They were tested on a long series of random patients and each test further refined the work, but each application brought specific results.

Five years after the initial resumption of labor, in 1950, the work was prepared for release, all tests having brought forth the conclusion that Dianetics *is* a science of mind, that it *does* disclose hitherto unknown laws about thought and that it has worked on every type of inorganic mental and organic psychosomatic illness. Further, in the refinement of form attained, it was proven possible for the work to be used easily by people not lengthily trained.

The goal we have here reached is a science which is workable and which can be worked with success by briefly taught individuals. This goal has not hitherto been attained or even approached.

Once one has gained a foothold on unknown lands, more things become known to him and with each new datum his horizon further widens, including broader bodies of knowledge. Dianetics cures, and cures without failure. And there are further goals.

Education, medicine, politics and art and, indeed, all branches of human thought, are clarified with Dianetics. And even so that is not enough.

Dianetics has, as yet, a brief history: it has a strong youth: it forecasts a better tomorrow. Before it is much older it will have included even more within its scope. The history of Dianetics is scarce begun.

Plan A included the perfection of the science, its testing on patients of all kinds and, finally, the dissemination of Dianetics as pertaining to therapy. That plan ends with the release of this book.

Plan B includes a further research into life force, an attempt at resolution of some of the ills not yet embraced such as cancer and diabetes, and the perfection of techniques discovered and their dissemination. That will end Plan B.

Plan C includes an effort to discover a higher echelon of universal origin and destination, if the problem is one of origin and destination, and the factors and forces involved to the end of securing a better understanding and useful application of the knowledge so gained, if gained, and if so gained, its dissemination.

A portion of Plan B is the organization of a foundation so that the research can be more swiftly accomplished.

The history of Dianetics has just begun. What other things begin with the origin of a science of mind only tomorrow can tell.

Judiciary Dianetics

This brief summary of Judiciary Dianetics is included in this present work as an aid to the auditor.

Judiciary Dianetics covers the field of adjudication[2] within the society and amongst the societies of man. Of necessity it embraces jurisprudence[3] and its codes and establishes precision definitions and equations for the establishment of equity. It is the science of judgment.

Jurisprudence and its adjudications are constructed on the cornerstones of *right* and *wrong, good* and *evil*. Definition of these is inherent in Dianetics: by these definitions a correct solution can be reached with regard to any action or actions of man.

The fundamental test of rationality is the ability to

---

2. adjudicate: to judge and pronounce a decision upon, to settle judicially.

3. jurisprudence: the study of law or of a particular part of law.

differentiate *right* from *wrong*. The fundamental factors in establishing censure are *good* and *evil*. Without precision definition of these four factors any structure of law or judgment is rendered forceless and becomes involved through its introduction of arbitrary factors which seek to adjudicate by introducing errors to nullify errors. Penal codes which will answer all needs can only be written when precision, scientific definitions exist for the four factors, and civil equity which will not lead to injustice can only then be established and formulated.

The problems of jurisprudence and, indeed, all judgment, are inextricably interwoven with the problems of behavior.

An ideal society would be a society of unaberrated persons, clears, conducting their lives within an unaberrated culture: for either the person or the culture may be aberrated. The aberrations of the culture enter into the equations of conduct as irrational factors both from the door of education and of social customs and jurisprudence. It is not enough that an individual be himself unaberrated, for he discovers himself within the confines of a society which itself has compounded its culture into many unreasonable prejudices and customs.

The establishment of actual source for wrong and evil is a fundamental problem of all jurisprudence. The actual source unfortunately lies in the irrationalities of those in past generations who, working with limited knowledge and oppressed by their environs, sought solutions with equations which contained false and indefinite factors. These generations, long entombed, cannot be brought to bar.[4] We are the heirs to all the ages of the past and that is good: but we are heirs as well to all the irrationalities of the past and that is evil. Under such

---

4. brought to bar: held accountable.

circumstances and in the absence of broad reason, adjudication by the auditor of the preclear as relates to evil or wrong actions cannot be performed with accuracy. The criminal and the insane, the hypochondriac and the wife-beater, the merciless dictator who seeks to shake the world and the street cleaner who only sits and weeps are all, each one, gripped and driven by their own sources of unreason, by the world which has entered into the hidden depths of their pain-wracked minds and which, in the form of social aberration, pounds against them from without.

The auditor is interested in what has been done *to*, not done *by* his patient; for whatever the patient has done is forever beyond recall and was not the source but was only the manifestation of his griefs.

Given a society of unaberrated persons, given a culture from which has been deleted all unreason, then and only then can man be truly responsible for his acts, then and only then. But we must take the shadow of the responsibility now for the fact of it. A man does not *have* to surrender to his engrams.

Perhaps at some distant date only the unaberrated person will be granted civil rights before law. Perhaps the goal will be reached at some future time when only the unaberrated person can attain to and benefit from citizenship. These are desirable goals and would produce a marked increase in the survival ability and happiness of man.

Even now the codes of jurisprudence can be reformed and it can be ascertained with precision whether the act which brought the individual before law was an aberrated act, or stemmed from an aberration of culture, or was an act which was committed to the detriment of another or of society. Surely the process of punishment can be refined so as to sentence the individual not to further aberration as a prisoner or a ruined man but to a higher plane of reason through the deletion of the aberration.

The past acts of an individual who has been cleared should be stricken from his record even as his illnesses have been, for with the cause removed there can be no point in retribution unless society itself is so aberrated that it desires to operate on sadistic principles.[5] There is more than idealism here, for it can be shown that aberration in individuals and the society rises in progressive ratio to the amount of punishment employed.

Efforts to resolve problems of jurisprudence which yet did not embrace precision definitions for *right* and *wrong, good* and *evil,* had recourse only to a principle known in Dianetics as the introduction of an arbitrary. Broad, unchangeable rules were thrust into problems in an effort to resolve them and yet each new rule further drove reason aside so that more rules were needed. An arbitrary structure is one in which one error has been observed and an effort has been made to correct it by introducing another error. In progressive complexity, new errors must be introduced to nullify the evil effects of old errors. A culture, to say nothing of jurisprudence, grows complex and unwieldy in progressive ratio to the number of new evils it must introduce in an effort to nullify old evils. At last there can be no reason; there can be but force and where there lives no reason and yet lives force, there is naught but the maelstrom of an insane rage. Where there dwells an insane rage, still unresolved, there must at length come apathy; and apathy, dwindling down, inevitably reaches death.

We are here at a bridge between one state of man

---

5. Our present society is not aberrated in this respect: the insane man is not held guilty or responsible *for* his acts. Lacking definition of a precise scientific nature for insanity and failing to recognize that all irrational acts are temporary insanity, the society has not been able to carry out its fundamental intention.

and a next. We are above the chasm which divides a lower from a higher plateau and this chasm marks an artificial evolutionary step in the progress of man.

The auditor is at that bridge; when cleared he will be at its higher end. He will watch much traffic cross. He may see customs, laws, organizations and societies attempt to avoid the bridge but, being swept along, tumble into a nothingness below.

In his attitude toward his preclears or toward society at large, he can gain nothing by reprimanding and judging past error in the light of current sentience. Not only can he gain nothing but he can inhibit progress. It is a remorseless fact that the attack upon unreason has begun. Attack unreason, not the society or the man.

Dianetics and War

The social organisms which we call states and nations behave and react in every respect as though they were individual organisms. The culture has its analytical mind, the combined sentience of its citizens in general and its artists, scientists and statesmen in particular. The social standard memory bank is the data accumulated along the generations. And the social organism has as well its reactive mind as represented by the prejudices and irrationalities of the entire group. This reactive mind is served by an engram bank wherein lie past painful experiences and which dictates reactive action on certain subjects whenever those subjects are restimulated in the society. This, all too briefly, is an analogy used in Political Dianetics.

The social organism behaves in a manner which can be graphed on the tone scale; it has its survival dynamic and its suppressors, its internal suppression due to engrams and its urge toward an infinity of optimum duration. Criminals, traitors and zealots constitute, for instance, internal engrams which suppress the survival potential on the tone scale.

There is a precision definition for each social level as related to the tone scale. A free society working in complete cooperation toward common goals would be a tone 4 society. A society hindered by arbitrary restrictions and oppressive laws would be a tone 2 society. A society managed and dictated to by the whims of one man or a few men would be a tone 1 society. A society governed by the mystery and superstition of some mystic body would be a tone 0 society. The potential of survival in each case can be seen anywhere in history. Any golden age is a tone 4. Oppressive practices, individual greeds and miscalculation in general reduce the society by introducing into it dissatisfied elements. To cope with these, in the past, further oppression has been used. The survival of the society reduced further. With more oppression came new engrams and so down the tone scale slipped the chances of long survival. And with this reduction of potential came pain as the lower zones were entered.

Societies rise and fall on the tone scale. But there is a danger point below which a society cannot go without reacting as would an individual so suppressed: the society reaches a break point and goes mad. This point is around 2.0.

The quarrel of society with society, nation with nation, has many causes, all of them more or less irrational. There have been many times when one society was forced to crush another less sentient than itself. But with each clash, new engrams were born both in the international scene and within the societies themselves.

War is an international tone 1. It is no more rational than any individual who, reaching a general and chronic tone 1, is placed in an institution or, temporarily tone 1, commits some crime and is thereafter imprisoned. But there is no gaoler[6] to societies; there is at this time only death and so they die and so they have died.

Before this time no tool could be employed by a nation but force when faced with another nation gone mad. By contagion of aberration, both nations then went mad. No nation ever fully won a war. No nation ever finally triumphed by force of arms. No nation ever averted war by posing threat or exhibiting defense.

Man is now faced, by these pyramiding hatreds, with weapons so powerful that man himself may vanish from the earth. There is no problem in the control of these weapons. They explode when and where man tells them to explode. The problem is in the control of man.

There is no national problem in the world today which cannot be resolved by reason alone. All factors inhibiting a solution of the problem of war and weapons are arbitrary factors and have no more validity than the justified explanations of a thief or murderer.

The farmer of Iowa has no quarrel with the storekeeper of Stalingrad. Those who say such quarrels exist *lie*.

There are no international concerns which cannot be resolved by peaceable means, not in the terms of supranational[7] government, but in the terms of reason.

Jockeying with indefinable ideologies, playing with mass ignorance, nonexistent entities like nightmares march the world in the form of the Gods of Ism.

No self-interest can be so great as to demand the slaughter of mankind. He who would demand it, he who would not by every rational means avert it, is insane. There is *no* justification for war.

---

6. gaoler: jailer.
7. supranational: of, for, involving or over all or a number of nations.

Behind the curtains of language and different customs, populaces are taught to recognize no kinship with other populaces. Taught by their own terrors and governed by their own aberrations, leaders hold up other isms as detestable things.

There is no perfect political state on earth today, there is not even a good definition of a perfect political creed. States are the victims of internal and external aberrations.

Dianetics addresses war because there is in fact a race between the science of mind and the atom bomb. There may be no future generation to know which won.

Rationality alone can guide man past these threats to his extinction.

Insanity does not exist without a confusion of definitions and purpose. The solution to the international problem does not lie in the regulation or curtailment of weapons nor yet in the restraints of men. It lies in the definition of political theory and policy in such terms that there can be no mistaking the clear processes; it lies in the establishment of rational goals toward which societies can collectively and individually work; and it lies in an intersocial competition of gains so great that none become dispensable to any other.

Man's primary fight is not with man—that is insanity. Man's primary fight is with those elements which oppress him as a species and bar his thrust toward high goals. Man's fight is with the elements, with space and time, and with species which are destructive to him. He has hardly begun his conquest. He is just now armed with tools enough and science enough to make good his conquest of the universe. He has no time to bicker and indulge in tantrums and yah-yah[8] across back fences about atom bombs.

---

8. yah-yah: slang term for bickering.

The harnessing of atomic power puts other worlds within his reach. Why haggle for this one? The late discoveries in the field of photosynthesis bid fair[9] to feed and clothe him royally even though he number a thousand times his present two billions on earth. For what reason can he quarrel? Why?

Two rational men will enter into a contest of gain and worth and production. Are these mighty nations, these powerful, fearful, thundering "giants," actually small and poorly educated, barely sane little boys screaming insults at each other over the possession of a dead cat? What of armies? Armies die. If might makes right, then Rome still rules the world. Who fears now this archaeological curiosity that was Rome?

There is a higher goal, a better goal, a more glorious victory than gutted towns and radiation-burned dead. There is freedom and happiness and plenty and a whole universe to be won.

He who would not see it is far from worthy to rule. He who would indulge his hates is too insane to advise.

How much can man conquer? He loses if he conquers man. He wins if he conquers his own fears and conquers then the stars.

Attack the natural enemies of man, attack them well, and war of man with man cannot thereafter be a problem. This is rationality.

Dianetics is not interested in saving the world, it is interested only in preventing the world from being saved. One more time would be fatal! Dianetics is not against fighting; it defines what may be fought. Those things include the sources of man's travail within the individual, within the society and the enemies of all mankind. Man, bewildered, has not known his enemies. They are visible now; attack!

---

9. bid fair: to seem likely (to be or do something).

The Future of Therapy

In twenty or a hundred years the therapeutic technique which is offered in this volume will appear to be obsolete. Should this not prove to be the case, then the author's faith in the inventiveness of his fellow man will not have been justified. We have here something which has not before existed, an invariably working science of mind. The application methods cannot but be refined.

All sciences begin with the discovery of basic axioms. They progress as new data are discovered and as the scope of the science is widened. Various tools and techniques rise up continually, improved and re-improved. The basic axioms, the initial discoveries of Dianetics, are such solid scientific truths that they will be altered but little. The data discovered by those axioms is already large and daily expanding. The techniques of using that data as represented in this volume will, before much more time elapses, be modified and improved. Their virtue just now is that these techniques work and produce good, solid, scientific results.

Once upon a time somebody set up the basic principles which had to do with fire. There had not been controlled fire before. Cooking, heating and finally metallurgy[10] made a new culture. The basic principles of fire are not much altered. The techniques employed in handling fire soon after it was discovered by man would be considered somewhat obsolete to us now. We have matches and lighters and fuels today, but just after fire was understood and began to be used, the bow-drill fire-maker and flint and steel would have been considered marvelous inventions: even so, man was already using fire and had been using it with profit for some time both

---

10. metallurgy: the scientific study of the properties of metals and alloys, the art of working metals or of extracting them from their ores.

as a weapon and as a household utility when the bow-drill and flint and steel were discovered or invented.

In the case of the wheel, basic principles were laid down which have not altered to this day. The first workable wheel must have been a rather unwieldy affair. But compared to *no* wheel, it was a miracle.

Thus with Dianetic therapy. The basic principles, axioms and general discoveries of Dianetics form an organization not before possessed by man. Not unlike the first fires and the first wheels, the therapy technique can be enormously improved. It works now; it can be used now with safety and effectiveness.

There are two definite drawbacks to this present technique. It demands more skill of the auditor than should be necessary and it is not as swift as it could be. The auditor should not be required to do any computing whatever and, indeed, a therapy technique could be envisioned where no auditor at all was necessary, for he is vital at the present time. A complete clear should take but a handful of hours. The problems here are those of improvement in terms of less skill required and less work.

One might say that it is an imposition upon a mathematician and philosopher to require him to resolve all the problems himself and to put forth all improvements. Indeed, it is an imposition that he be required to develop any technique of application at all, for there should be in any society an apportionment of labor.

When the basic axioms and computations were finished, it was impossible to release them for there were none to whom such research could be released for application. Thus the work had to be carried out to its furthest extent of not only experimentation but the development and proof of the techniques of application.

One might here use an analogy of bridge engineering. Let us suppose that two plateaus exist, one higher than the other, with a canyon between them. An engineer sees that if the canyon could be crossed by traffic, the hitherto unused higher plateau, being much more fertile and pleasant, would become the scene of a new culture. He sets himself the task of building a bridge. It had been supposed that no bridge could be built across the canyon, and indeed, since those on the lower plateau could not see the higher level, the existence of the higher plateau itself was denied. The engineer, by evolving new principles of bridge building and discovering new significance in his materials, manages to throw a bridge across the canyon. He himself crosses and he inspects the plateau carefully; others cross over his bridge and examine the new terrain with delight. Still more and more cross the bridge. The bridge is solid and, if not wide, can yet safely be negotiated. It has not been built for heavy, fast traffic. But it contains the basic principles and axioms by which the canyon can be spanned again and again. Many people begin to approach the canyon and look up.

What sort of an opinion would you have of the society on the lower plateau if they but moaned and wept and argued and gave no hand at all in the matter of widening the bridge or making new bridges?

*   *   *

In this handbook we have the basic axioms and a therapy which works.

For God's sake, get busy and build a better bridge!

Dianetics: The Bridge to the Future

Like the volcano on its now classic cover, *Dianetics* exploded into a troubled world in 1950 with the raw power of hope for mankind.

To millions of people, recovering from the devastation of World War II, the book provided rational answers, a hope of moving onwards, a chance to put their lives back in order.

Man was apparently capable of creating his own monsters—the atomic bomb had become a symbol of his ability to destroy himself and every living thing around him. Help most certainly did not exist in the complex psychiatric texts researched in the death camps of Nazi Germany. Their ice picks and electric shock machines were only further evidence of man's inhumanity to man.

Dianetics provided the possibility of personal triumph— a chance to win over the forces of evil, whether in a global context or within the private universe of each individual's attempt to achieve his goals for self-betterment.

The book sold out overnight. It was a resounding success—because it answered not only man's search for inner peace and happiness, but confronted, head-on, each individual's responsibilities for his fellow man, and gave practical ways to overcome the seemingly impossible task of setting mankind back on the road to a better world.

Thirty-six years later, its impact on the world is continuing and expanding. This year *Dianetics* is again a New York Times bestseller after thirty-six years in print, an unheard of phenomenon in the publishing world. Now in its sixtieth printing since 1950, when it caused a national stir staying on the New York Times for twenty-six weeks,

Dianetics is still one of the most talked about books in America. Can you change the world with a book? In L. Ron Hubbard's own words, "Ideas and not battles mark the forward progress of mankind." This is the mission of *Dianetics: The Modern Science of Mental Health*—to build a bridge between the suffering and pain of a world gone mad, to a better world: "A world without insanity, without criminals and without war—this is the goal of Dianetics."

That bridge has been strengthened and widened over the past thirty-six years with each book purchased, with each person who has read and applied it to his life and those around him. It has been the march of millions of individuals that has made *Dianetics* the phenomenon it has become.

For that is the audience selected by the book—not the military industrial complex who would see a country destroyed for the sake of the improved value of their stocks and bonds—but the common ordinary man who is striving for honest values: the future survival of his environment, his family and his fellow man.

That promise has been validated by millions of people from all points of the globe. The stories of its success are sufficient to build a mountain of hope, and each personal story is evidence of an individual mountain conquered.

To experience the excitement and expectation firsthand, let us turn back to those stories told by the earliest readers of what came to be known as "The Book."

In the May 1950 issue of the magazine *Astounding Science Fiction,* L. Ron Hubbard presented a sneak preview of *Dianetics* in an article entitled, "Dianetics: The Evolution of a Science."

The magazine sold out within a few days. Some two thousand letters arrived within the first two weeks, almost all of them orders for the forthcoming book. "We encounter a bit of a problem. Most of the letters this month were, of course, concerned with Dianetics," wrote the editor of *Astounding Science Fiction.*

One reader wrote:

"This is truly astounding. Dianetics!

"One sunny afternoon at seven thousand feet in the flak-shredded air over Dieppe,[1] I looked over my left shoulder across two hundred yards of open space and watched the dancing devils of flame spurt from the leading edge of the wings of an FW-190,[2] knowing that each flash might well be my last impression in this life as I busied myself with the mechanics of getting out of the line of fire in my little Spitfire.[3]

"And on another sunny morning in French Morocco, I 'drove' my P-39[4] over the brow of a low hill at roughly three hundred miles per hour and dipped its nose to find an unmapped high-tension line directly in my path, to feel the hot breath of Hell in the shock and flash that followed, and to wonder—seriously—if I had lived through the experience, even as I did so.

"I've weaved and dodged the vicious, impersonal bursts of antiaircraft fire over France and the Channel, trying not to guess when or whether the lads on the earth below would load the shell with 'my number' on it.

"But nothing I have ever done, read, heard, seen, felt or sensed in any way has affected me as profoundly as this material on Dianetics. For the very first time, I find myself justified in the use of words like awesome, electrifying, earth-shaking.—H. J. Robb"

The editor's note tacked to the bottom of Mr. Robb's letter read, *"It will be history."* Thirty-six years later, his promise has been borne out. *Dianetics* has been on best-seller lists from the moment these letters persuaded the

---

1. Dieppe: city in northern Framce on the English Channel.

2. FW-190: German fighter aircraft of World War II.

3. Spitfire: British fighter aircraft of World War II.

4. P-39: American fighter aircraft of World War II.

publisher that it would have to be *rushed* into publication ahead of schedule to satisfy the demands of its waiting audience.

When *Dianetics* reached the bookstores on May 9, 1950, it sparked a grass-roots fire. Headlines in the *Los Angeles Daily News* called *Dianetics* "THE BOOK" and proclaimed that it was "Taking U.S. by storm" and causing the "Fastest growing movement in the U.S." A daily Dianetics series written by a staff reporter tried to keep up with the pace as the book swept across the country. "THE BOOK" quickly rose to the top of the *New York Times* and other best-seller lists, and stayed there for months. There were six printings in just seven months.

Demands for training in Dianetics techniques poured in to Mr. Hubbard. He began giving instruction to people in his home in Elizabeth, New Jersey, and thus the first Hubbard Dianetic Research Foundation was formed.

Ann Saunders describes those early days: " 'Dianetics: The Evolution of a Science' . . . totally changed my life. The article came out a month before the book *Dianetics* appeared in the bookstore. Daily I went to the bookstore to find if the book was available. I read all of *Dianetics* and insisted that my friends read it also. A friend of mine audited me literally out of the book.

"The first session was fantastic. For the first time in my life I became aware of the fact that I was and could become truly free of this mess of pain and confusion and really live 100 percent. As a side effect I got rid of migraine headaches which had plagued me and effectively ruined my life."

Ann called the publisher to find out where L. Ron Hubbard was, and found his home address in Elizabeth, New Jersey. She arrived on his doorstep and went to work immediately for the Hubbard Dianetic Research Foundation as receptionist, telephone operator, registrar, typist and anything else that was needed, while learning to audit Dianetics techniques.

As popularity of the book continued to rage, six Dianetics centers reaching from the Atlantic coast to Hawaii sprang up. Hubbard spent most of 1950 traveling throughout the country giving lectures and demonstrations of Dianetics auditing, to meet the growing demand.

In August, he spoke to a crowd of over six thousand at the Shrine Auditorium in Los Angeles and within days had established the Los Angeles Hubbard Dianetic Research Foundation. In December, he gave a series of fifteen-minute lectures on over 126 radio stations. On the West Coast they were broadcast daily, Monday through Friday, and covered the subject of "Group Dianetics" and how Dianetics technology could be put to use to help handle the individual's, the community's and the nation's problems.

John McCormick, who attended the Shrine Auditorium lecture and regular Sunday morning lectures by Mr. Hubbard at a theater in Hollywood, said, "I read this [Dianetics] through three times in one weekend. I was totally revitalized and knew this was the data missing in my previous attempts to handle life . . . I could hardly wait to use it."

The first person John audited was a young lady who became his wife a year later (and remains so to this day).

Today, thirty-six years later, Ann and John are still enthralled by the adventure of Dianetics technology, sharing it with friends, family—with everyone they encounter.

Dianetics has become a best seller not just in the U.S., but throughout the world. It has already been published in thirteen languages and is currently being translated into many more, from South America to Asia, as demand for the book expands. More than 7.5 million copies have been sold. In one recent eight-month period alone, more than one million copies were sold.

Dianetics has been with us for thirty-six years, but it is still new news to the majority of the population of earth. Despite the fact that there are still many millions of people who have not read the book personally, the subject has touched their lives in other ways.

Dianetics technology has gradually become the accepted methodology in many different spheres of activity. In newspapers, national magazines and research journals, evidence of this impact appears daily.

For example, before Dianetics, it was unheard of to attribute certain illnesses to prenatal influences. But as an immediate result of the book, more than forty articles appeared in the early fifties supporting the idea of prenatals. Doctors, for example, now fully accept the influence of prenatals on a variety of conditions such as "physical" ills, alcohol abuse and drug addiction.

In hospitals throughout the world, Hubbard's guidelines regarding silence during operations have been adopted. A British journal reports that three scientists from leading universities have found that what anesthetized persons hear can affect them. Widespread national headlines confirm that patients hear *whatever* is said around them while under anesthetics and can suffer ill effects from these remarks.

To prevent shocks to a child that could leave permanent damage, removable only by Dianetics therapy, Hubbard in 1951 advised silence in the delivery room and the laying of the newborn on the mother's abdomen before the cord is cut.

One of the world's leading obstetricians, Frederick Leboyer, wrote in 1974, "As for hearing, nothing could be simpler: be silent . . . This apprenticeship of silence— so indispensable for mothers—is just as important for those who perform the delivery: the obstetricians, the attendants."

In a natural birth, Leboyer said, "The baby emerges . . . and we settle the child immediately on its mother's stomach. What better place could there be? . . . To sever the umbilicus⁵ when the child has scarcely left the mother's

---

5. umbilicus: the umbilical cord.

womb is an act of cruelty whose ill effects are immeasurable."[6]

When a Dianeticist publishing a book on pregnancy and childbirth asked Leboyer if she could quote him in her book, Leboyer responded: "I shall feel most honored being quoted together with Hubbard, whose work I greatly admire."

Fortunately for the health of countless children, Hubbard not only did the pioneering research, he also found a prevention and a remedy for aberrative effects of shocks received prenatally or during birth. "Preventive Dianetics" has today been adopted by thousands of parents, with the resulting happy children a testament to Hubbard's writings some thirty-six years ago. A new generation of "Dianetics children" is being born.

Over the past thirty-six years, evidence of the results of *Dianetics* has been collected, story by story, and now thousands of documents fill rooms, file cabinets and archives throughout the world. Validation of Dianetics exists in the form of graphs and test scores, individual testimonials, films, tapes and personal histories.

In Book One, Chapter Two, Hubbard describes the state called Clear—"the optimum individual." Clears demonstrate the ability to think clearly and to actively achieve their goals. The first people who arrived at Hubbard's home in Elizabeth, New Jersey, demanded to know "Where are the Clears?"

Today, documented by their shining success stories, Clears number in the tens of thousands. Their influence is felt in business, law, economics, the arts, childcare, the health professions—indeed, every aspect of society. Every day of their lives, Clears find themselves able to experience a state of spiritual well-being, happiness and self-confidence to which man has aspired for centuries.

Indeed, the figure of "tens of thousands" refers only to those Clears who are actually "certified," i.e., who have

---

6. Fredrick Leboyer, *Birth Without Violence*. Paris, 1974.

reported in to a Hubbard Guidance Center (an auditing center) and who now exist on record. There are probably many thousands more who have achieved this state through auditing with the *Dianetics* book, but who have not yet been officially validated.

Because Dianetics gives the basic truths about the human mind and human understanding, it reaches people of all nationalities, cultural beliefs and sociological backgrounds.

A computer consultant from Florida decided to travel across the country and the world offering workshops based on the techniques in the book. While in Zimbabwe, he delivered a workshop where Dianetics counseling using the *Dianetics* book was offered simultaneously in three languages—Urdu, Swahili and English—in one large room. The secretary general of the eight-thousand-member society of traditional healers—once called "witch doctors"—attended the workshop and was so impressed with the workability of *Dianetics* that he decided he wanted all his members trained in Dianetics techniques. People in such diverse countries as Somalia, Nigeria and Pakistan have also discovered the miracles of Dianetics technology.

Transcending her own cultural barriers—and fears—a mother of six children who is Clear decided to do volunteer work at a juvenile prison with hard-core gang members. She has received awards, done talk shows and has been written about in a local newspaper for the compassion and care she brought to her work. One of the youths she counseled told her that he wanted to kill another boy who had shot his brother. She used Dianetics techniques to help him find the root of his desire for vengeance and overcome it. As a result, she helped prevent a murder—and no doubt others. Four of her own children are now Clear.

Personal suffering does not have to involve violence to cause pain. Indeed, the individuals who write and talk about their successes with *Dianetics* remind one of that first letter writer, Harry Robb, who described the "dancing devils of flame" spurting from the wings of the attack plane. "Dancing devils" can take many forms—fears, traumas, failures, losses. A man from Dallas has always been active in community affairs, and is the person others in his neighborhood always turn to for advice. Then he lost trust in himself and so felt guilty when other people kept coming to him for help. As a result of Dianetics counseling, he has now not only gained renewed belief in himself, he feels he has better answers for *other* people. "Now I feel I can really help them." He wants to share with others the idea that there *is* another dimension to life.

If one were to pick a theme that emerges from these and other successes—it might be the achievement of personal goals, whether in sports, the arts or in business.

An Australian football player was told he would never play again due to a severe neck injury. After three years of painkillers, X-rays and expensive treatments, he had lost his motivation and his zest for life. Then he got Dianetics counseling and within nine months returned to his old team and again became one of its top players.

The products produced by artists who have used Dianetics techniques would fill hundreds of studios, galleries and concert halls. In their success stories, these artists often comment that reading *Dianetics,* using its techniques or becoming Clear causes a dramatic increase in their abilities to perform, their stability and their creative and spiritual power.

A concert pianist touring the world writes about how he obtained a copy of *Dianetics* in 1950 in Paris. "When I read the book, I reread and reread and reread it. I almost knew by heart whole sections." He began by auditing his friends and then himself became one of the first Clears. "I knew that things had changed all along. I made gains the whole time. I was more myself, more in command of my life; I made decisions where before

I had had indecisions." Thirty-six years later, he is still using Dianetics technology.

Hubbard has written, "A culture is only as great as its dreams, and its dreams are dreamed by artists." As more and more creative artists use Dianetics technology, a renaissance in the arts has indeed been sparked amongst them.

In business, the president of a major computer software company says that *Dianetics* helped her unlock her talents. She runs her company *and* handles her responsibilities as a wife, as a mother of two boys and as a contributor to charitable and school activities. "Could I have done it without *Dianetics?* Very possibly, but I'd probably be 'burned out.' With my responsibilities, I have to be 'on' at all times. Through reading *Dianetics* I came to understand the dynamics of self, familial and group relationships. Now I can perform at peak without falling victim to tunnel vision or 'burn out.' By applying Dianetics techniques I've also been able to unlock tremendous energy and find resources within myself. I have a balanced, happy and productive life."

The board chairman of a company ranked in the top five hundred corporations chosen by *Inc. Magazine* attributed his success in large part to the application of Dianetics technology. "It was through Dianetics technology," he explained, "that I first gained insight into the workings of the human mind, and once I understood that, everything else was easy. The technology has helped me in my relationship with my family, friends and employees. The rewards have been abundant."

By addressing the individual himself, by knowing and understanding the tremendous potential of the human spirit and its capacity to develop, Dianetics auditors around the world have gotten what could only be termed incredible results.

One night, while studying Dianetics technology in Manhattan, a young actor received a call from his mother.

"Your brother-in-law has drowned. He was pronounced dead on arrival at a small hospital in upstate New York. They've got him hooked up to tubes . . ."

Two and a half hours later, he and a friend arrived at a tiny hospital in the Catskills. He introduced himself to the nurse on duty in intensive care and explained that he was trained as a Dianetics counselor and wanted to help his brother-in-law, Ricky. The outlook was gloomy. Ricky had been underwater for five minutes and his chances of surviving were slim. The auditor began administering Dianetics techniques to him, and, little by little, throughout the long, dark night, he began to recover. First he could only reply by a faint flutter of his eyelids, then the blink became stronger.

"Then he started having fits of anger, along about 3 A.M., and I was afraid he was going to rip off the tubes. But I kept at it."

Finally Ricky was actually able to squeeze his brother-in-law's hand, so hard, in fact, that it hurt. The Dianetics counseling was continued until about 6:30 in the morning. "He opened his eyes, with no glaze, and he was calm. I looked down at him, and said, 'You see me, don't you?' He violently nodded his head, as if to say, 'You bet your life.' And I said, 'It's a good thing you see me, because I've been sitting here for hours.' Ricky laughed, and I cried."

Ricky fully recovered and today leads a normal life. As for his auditor, the young actor: "I became convinced of the absolute workability of Dianetics technology. I had studied other philosophies, but here was something that was real, that worked, not every once in a while but every time, if applied exactly."

Whether they have saved lives, healed marriages, boosted confidence or helped a person achieve his lifelong goals with Dianetics technology, these people who are using Dianetics truths and principles are adventurers. "They like to go out and do things," says an engineer who came into Dianetics because of his love of "the knife between my teeth on the bow of the boat, slushing through icebergs, icicles off my beard." And he goes on, "These people blow through their stops and fears. It's just an ever-expanding sphere of life."

Some thirty-four years after the first famous Los Angeles lecture, an auditing workshop was held at the Shrine Auditorium. With the same sense of expectancy as their earlier counterparts, the attendees learned to audit in two intensive days of study. They spent hours auditing their friends and family members and openly discussed the results: "I personally feel much calmer, more relaxed and surer of tomorrow than ever before in my life. A heavy burden has been lifted."

Another person wrote that same day: "I am getting better. I feel that every day is a better day."

He knew more than he said. With Dianetics technology, each day is indeed a better day. And as each person reads *Dianetics* he is challenged by the author's final demand on the closing page of the book. "For God's sake," he wrote, "get busy and build a better bridge." That bridge becomes stronger and better as each new person picks up the book and decides to use it to improve not only his life, but the lives of those around him.

And the analogy Hubbard drew at that time, of the bridge across the canyon, taking those who travel across it to a higher level than could be seen or imagined by those below, comes into closer and closer view.

For the heights to which mankind can now rise have only been hinted at.

The adventure is only beginning.

The Editors

About the Author

L. Ron Hubbard is acclaimed by millions as the foremost writer of self-betterment books in the world today. His non-fiction works alone have sold millions of copies. One major reason is that his writing expresses a firsthand knowledge of the basics of life and ability—a knowledge gained not by being on the sidelines of life, but by living it to the fullest.

"To really know life, you've got to be a part of life," L. Ron Hubbard said. "You must get down and look; you must get into the nooks and crannies of existence; you have to rub elbows with all kinds of men before you can finally establish what man is."

He did exactly that. From the open ranges of his home state of Montana to the hills of China, from the frigid coast of Alaska to the jungles of South Pacific islands, whether working with men on explorations or teaching inexperienced naval crews to survive the ravages of a world war, Ron truly learned what man and life are all about.

Armed with a keen intellect, boundless energy, limitless curiosity and a unique approach to philosophy and science which emphasized workability and practicality over all else, Ron embarked upon his study of life and its mysteries while still in his teens.

Traveling extensively throughout Asia and the Pacific, he saw firsthand the use of Far Eastern philosophies. And on a voyage from Seattle to Washington, D.C. he was also befriended by a student of Sigmund Freud, who subsequently taught him the meager amount of knowledge that existed in the Western school of mental healing.

Later, when attending college in the United States, Ron saw that man had no working knowledge of the mind—no way to increase a person's ability to overcome the mental barriers of his life. He observed Western civilization advancing in the physical sciences with no corresponding advance in the humanities. Man's understanding of himself and knowledge of the mind had not moved forward from the level of "knowledge" possessed by a medicine man in the jungles of North Borneo.

Ron began to investigate this serious gap in man's knowledge about the underlying principles of life, financing his research through his fiction writings.

He became one of the most prolific and well-known authors of the heyday of popular adventure and science fiction in the 1930s and 1940s, interrupted only by his service in the U.S. Navy during World War II.

Partially disabled at the war's end, Ron continued his research, making breakthroughs and developing techniques that enabled him and others to regain their health and to achieve greater happiness and ability. It was from this research that the basic tenets of Dianetics technology were codified.

In 1948, he wrote *Dianetics: The Original Thesis*. This manuscript summarized the previously uncharted landscape of the mind of man. Here was something completely new—a workable technology of the mind that could produce results where others believed results were not possible.

Ron's first description of his discoveries was copied and passed from hand to hand. As copies of the manuscript circulated, Ron began to get a steadily increasing flow of letters asking for further information and more applications of his new subject. He soon found he was spending all his time answering letters and decided to write a comprehensive text on the subject.

When *Dianetics: The Modern Science of Mental Health* was published in May 1950, it marked the beginning of a new era for man. It was the first book of its kind—a practical textbook on the mind that any layman could read, apply and immediately use to experience increased awareness, relief from unwanted physical conditions, and a new life. An excited public began to use the astounding technology of Dianetics processing daily. They began to audit each other with consistent success and results. This was indeed a practical technology that anyone could use to achieve results, something sadly lacking in any past practices of "mental healing."

Soon after the release of this phenomenal best-seller, Ron was in demand for lectures and further briefings on Dianetics.

He was called upon to expand the subject and to answer an ever-increasing flood of questions. Ron launched into further research and kept his public informed of his new discoveries through a series of lectures and a flood of published bulletins, magazines and books.

To this day, *Dianetics: The Modern Science of Mental*

Health has continued to be a best-seller. Nearly eight million copies have been sold since its release in 1950.

It was L. Ron Hubbard's lifelong purpose to complete his research into the nature of man and his relationship to life—a goal he fully achieved. However, Ron always considered that it was not enough that he alone should benefit from the results of his research. He took great care to record every detail of his discoveries in assimilable and applicable form so that others could share the wealth of knowledge he alone had uncovered.

"I like to help others," L. Ron Hubbard has said, "and count it as my greatest pleasure in life to see a person free himself of the shadows which darken his days.

"These shadows look so thick to him, and weigh him down so, that when he finds they are shadows and that he can see through them, walk through them and be again in the sun, he is enormously delighted. And I am afraid I am just as delighted as he is."

For the next thirty-six years he devoted himself to helping others and developing techniques to ensure the route to a higher level of understanding could be traveled by all. He asked that the technology that he developed be made available. Thousands of his taped lectures and writings, delineating this priceless technology and its application to individuals and organizations, fill library shelves on every continent. He created and made known the knowledge and technology necessary to change the face of civilization on earth.

"A civilization without crime, war or insanity, where the able can prosper and honest beings can have rights, and where man is free to rise to greater heights," is how Ron described his dream for society.

The technology L. Ron Hubbard has made available from his research makes this dream attainable. Applying that technology is all that needs to be done to achieve it.

With his research fully completed, L. Ron Hubbard departed his body on January 24, 1986. His physical departure was by no means an end to his work; on the contrary, it marks a beginning of a new and unprecedented expansion of his life's achievements through the efforts of the millions of his friends who are forwarding his dream.

Glossary

aberration: a departure from rational thought or behavior. From the Latin, *aberrare*, to wander from; Latin, *ab*, away, *errare*, to wander. It means basically to err, to make mistakes, or more specifically to have fixed ideas which are not true. The word is also used in its scientific sense. It means departure from a straight line. If a line should go from A to B, then if it is "aberrated" it would go from A to some other point, to some other point, to some other point, to some other point, to some other point and finally arrive at B. Taken in its scientific sense, it would also mean the lack of straightness or to see crookedly as, in example, a man sees a horse but thinks he sees an elephant. Aberrated conduct would be wrong conduct, or conduct not supported by reason. When a person has engrams, these tend to deflect what would be his normal ability to perceive truth and bring about an aberrated view of situations which then would cause an aberrated reaction to them. *Aberration* is opposed to sanity, which would be its opposite. This is the most fundamental level of aberration: "If the food smells good, go away from it!" This is directly against the survival intention of the organism.

aberree: was sometimes used in the early days of Dianetics to designate an aberrated person.

abreact: *psychoanalysis.* to release (repressed emotions) by acting out the situation causing the conflict.

ACTH: a hormone that was sometimes used to combat symptoms of rheumatoid arthritis; it stimulates the production of other hormones in the body.

acupuncture: Chinese practice of pricking the tissues of the body with fine needles to relieve pain or as a local anesthetic.

ad absurdum: to the point of ridiculousness.

adjudicate: to judge and pronounce a decision upon, to settle judicially.

Aesculapian: of or relating to medicine or the art of healing. (Aesculapius: *Roman mythology*. The god of medicine and healing.)

affinity: the attraction which exists between two human beings, or between a human being and another life organism.

Alexander: Alexander III, known as Alexander the Great: (356–323 B.C.) king of Macedonia (ancient kingdom located in what is now Greece and Yugoslavia).

alloy: to weaken or spoil by adding something that reduces value or pleasure.

ally: in Dianetics it basically means someone who protects a person who is in a weak state and becomes a very strong influence over the person. The weaker person, such as a child, even partakes the characteristics of the ally so that one may find that a person who has, for instance, a bad leg, has it because a protector or ally in his youth had a bad leg. The word is from French and Latin and means to bind together.

ally computation: little more than a mere idiot calculation that anyone who is a friend can be kept a friend only by approximating the conditions wherein the friendship was realized. It is a *computation* on the basis that one can only be safe in the vicinity of certain people and that one can only be in the vicinity of certain people by being sick or crazy or poor and generally disabled.

altitude: by *altitude* is meant a difference in level of prestige— one on a higher altitude carries conviction to one on a lower altitude merely because of altitude. The auditor may find himself unable to gain sufficient *altitude* with some patients to work them smoothly and he may have so much altitude with others that they believe everything he says. When he has too little altitude, he is not believed; when he has too much, he is believed too well.

altruistic: having unselfish concern for the welfare of others.

ambivalent: also called multivalence: *valens* means "powerful" in Latin. It is the second half of *ambivalent* "power in two directions" (*ambi-* is Latin for "both"). *Multivalence* means

561

"many powerfuls." It embraces the phenomena of split personality, the strange differences of personality in people in one and then another situation. *see also* **valence**

ambiversion: a condition or character trait that includes elements of both introversion and extroversion.

amniotic fluid: the fluid surrounding the embryo or fetus.

amniotic sac: the membrane sac enclosing the developing fetus and amniotic fluid.

amulet: something worn on the body because of its supposed magic power to protect against injury or evil; a charm.

analytical mind: the conscious aware mind which thinks, observes data, remembers it and resolves problems. It would be essentially the conscious mind as opposed to the unconscious mind. In Dianetics the analytical mind is the one which is alert and aware and the reactive mind simply reacts without analysis.

analyzer: *see* **analytical mind**

anemia: a deficiency in the oxygen-carrying material of the blood resulting in a paleness, generalized weakness, etc.

Aristotle: (384–322 B.C.) Greek philosopher.

arthritis: a condition causing inflammation, pain and stiffness in the joints.

articulate: well formulated; clearly presented.

astigmatism: a defect in an eye or lens preventing proper focusing.

attention unit: a quantity of awareness. Any organism is aware to some degree. A rational or relatively rational organism is aware of being aware. Attention units could be said to exist in the mind in varying quantity from person to person.

attenuate: to lessen in severity, value, amount, intensity, etc.; weaken.

auditing: the application of Dianetics processes and procedures to someone by an auditor. To *audit* is both to listen and to compute.

auditor: 1. a person trained and qualified in applying Dianetics processes and procedures to individuals for their betterment; called an auditor because *auditor* means "one who listens." 2. a person who is authorized to audit [to check or examine] accounts.

Auditor's Code: a collection of rules (do's and don'ts) that an auditor follows while auditing someone, which assures that the preclear will get the greatest possible gain out of the processing he is having.

autonomic nervous system: a system of nerves in the body that functions more or less automatically and regulates the function of the heart, lungs, intestines, glands and other internal organs.

averse: not willing or inclined; reluctant, opposed (*to*).

bacillus: loosely, any of the bacteria, especially those causing a disease.

Bacon, Francis: (1561–1626) English philosopher and author.

bank: *see* **reactive mind**

Bara, Theda: stage name of Theodosia Goodman (1890–1955), U.S. actress.

barber basin medicine: refers to the practice of surgery by barbers in earlier centuries. Generally untrained in medical procedures, their "treatments" were very painful with severe infections and often death resulting from unsanitary conditions.

Barrymore: famous family of stage and motion-picture actors: Maurice Barrymore and children Lionel, Ethyl and John.

basic: the first engram on any chain of similar engrams; *basic* is simply earliest.

basic-basic: the first engram after conception, the basic of all chains by sole virtue of being the first moment of pain.

basic personality: the basic self, the individual himself.

Bedlam: hospital of St. Mary of Bethlehem, London, an insane asylum.

Benzedrine: (trademark) an amphetamine, a drug used as a stimulant.

Bergson, Henri: (1859–1941) French philosopher. Awarded Nobel Prize for literature (1927).

bid fair: to seem likely (to be or do something).

biochemistry: the chemistry of living organisms.

Blood and Sand: title of a silent movie featuring Rudolph Valentino.

boil-off: becoming groggy and seeming to sleep; some period of the person's life wherein he was unconscious has been slightly restimulated.

bosun: a ship's petty officer in charge of rigging, boats, anchors, etc.

bouncer: an engramic command (such as "Can't stay here" or "Get out!") which sends the preclear up the track toward present time.

brace and bit: a tool for boring, consisting of a removable drill (bit) in a rotating handle (brace).

bracket: to place shots both short of the target and beyond it in order to find the range.

brought to bar: held accountable.

Bund: a street running along the waterfront in Shanghai.

buoyant: lighthearted, cheerful.

bursitis: inflammation of a bursa, a pouch between joints or between muscles or skin, etc., and bones, for lessening friction.

Caligula: (A.D. 12–41) Roman emperor (37–41). Reign marked by extreme cruelty and tyranny.

caliper: a compass for measuring the diameter of tubes or of round objects.

canceler: a contract with the patient that whatever the auditor says will not become literally interpreted by the patient or used by him in any way. It prevents accidental positive suggestion.

capricious: characterized by or subject to whim; impulsive and unpredictable.

case: all the content of the reactive mind.

catarrh: inflammation of a mucous membrane, especially of the nose or throat, causing an increased flow of mucous.

censure: to criticize severely.

cervix: a neck-shaped, anatomical structure, as the narrow outer end of the uterus.

chain: a series of incidents of similar nature or similar subject matter.

charge: harmful energy or force accumulated and stored in the reactive mind, resulting from the conflicts and unpleasant experiences that a person has had.

charlatan: a person who falsely claims to be an expert.

chary: cautious, wary.

chasten: to restrain from excess; subdue.

chattel: a movable possession (as opposed to a house or land).

Cheops: first king of Fourth Dynasty of Egypt (reigned circa 2900–2877 B.C.).

circuit: a part of an individual's bank (a colloquial name for the reactive mind) that behaves as though it were someone or something separate from him and that either talks to him or goes into action of its own accord, and may even, if severe enough, take control of him while it operates. A tune that keeps going around in someone's head is an example of a circuit.

clear: the clear is an unaberrated person. He is rational in that he forms the best possible solutions he can on the data he has and from his viewpoint. The clear has no engrams which can be restimulated to throw out the correctness of computation by entering hidden and false data. Clear is the goal in Dianetics therapy, a goal which some patience and a little study will bring about.

coach-and-four: a coach pulled by four horses.

cohabit: to live together in a sexual relationship when not legally married.

comatic: of a coma (a period of deep, prolonged unconsciousness usually resulting from a severe injury or illness).

compulsion: an irresistible impulse to act irrationally.

concourse: an act of coming or flowing together.

condenser: a device storing a charge of electricity. Also called a capacitor.

Confucianism: the system of morality taught by Confucius, a Chinese philosopher (551?–479? B.C.).

conjunctivitis: inflammation of the conjunctiva, the mucous membrane lining the inner eyelid and part of the eye.

consecrate: to set apart or declare as holy.

cordite: a smokeless explosive used as a propellant in bullets and shells.

corn-and-games: late in Roman history, the leaders of the Roman government and commerce gave away free food and staged free games (circuses) for the populace of Rome.

coronary: of the arteries supplying blood to the heart.

cow: to subdue by frightening with threats or force.

craven: cowardly.

crow: to express gleeful triumph.

cry havoc: to warn of great, impending danger.

cyanide: a very poisonous chemical substance.

cytology: the scientific study of cells.

Dalton, Jack: member of an outlaw gang in the nineteenth-century American West; also a character in early westerns.

Dante: originally Durante, Alighieri: (1265–1321) Italian poet. Wrote *Divina Commedia*, recounting an imaginary journey by the author through hell, purgatory and paradise.

debauchery: indulgence in harmful or immoral pleasures.

deck: to decorate, to dress up.

deep analysis: depth therapy: a form of psychotherapy that attempts to work through unconscious conflicts to resolve problems in behavior.

demon: a mental mechanism set up by an engram which takes over a portion of the analyzer and acts as an individual being. A bona fide demon is one who gives thoughts voice or echoes the spoken word interiorly or who gives all sorts of complicated advices like a real, live voice exteriorly.

denyer: a species of command which, literally translated, means that the engram doesn't exist. "I'm not here," "This is getting nowhere," "I must not talk about it," "I can't remember," etc. A command which makes the preclear feel there is no incident present.

dermatitis: inflammation of the skin.

dervish: a member of any various Moslem orders of ascetics (ones who lead a life of austere self-discipline, especially as an act of religious devotion or penance), some of which employ whirling dances and the chanting of religious formulas to produce a collective ecstasy.

designing: crafty, conniving.

diabetes: a disease in which sugar and starch are not properly absorbed by the body.

Dianetics: man's most advanced school of the mind. *Dianetics* means "through the soul" (from Greek *dia*, through, and *noos*, soul). *Dianetics* is further defined as "what the soul is doing to the body." It is a way of handling the energy of which life is made in such a way as to bring about a greater efficiency in the organism and in the spiritual life of the individual.

dipsomaniac: a person suffering from an uncontrollable craving for alcohol.

donjon: the fortified main tower of a castle.

dramatis personae: the characters in a play or story.

dramatization: the duplication of an engramic content, entire or in part, by an aberree in his present-time environment. Aberrated conduct is entirely dramatization. When dramatizing, the individual is like an actor playing his dictated part and going through a whole series of irrational actions. The degree of dramatization is in direct ratio to the degree of restimulation of the engrams causing it.

dross: inferior, trivial or worthless matter.

Dr. Sententious: made-up name for an "authority." Sententious: putting on an air of wisdom, dull and moralizing.

Drunkard: a play written by William H. Smith and "A Gentleman" in the late 1800s, a moral domestic drama of American life.

D.T.'s: delirium tremens: a form of delirium (a disordered state of mind) with tremors and terrifying delusions.

dub-in: imaginary recall.

dynamic: the urge, thrust and purpose of life—Survive!—in its four manifestations: self, sex, group and mankind.

dynamic principle of existence: survival. The goal of life can be considered to be infinite survival. Man, as a life form, can be demonstrated to obey in all his actions and purposes the one command: "Survive!" It is not a new thought that man is surviving. It is a new thought that man is motivated *only* by survival.

ectoplasm: the luminous substance believed to emanate from a spiritualistic medium.

effusion: a pouring forth.

egocentric: self-centered.

Ellis, Henry Havelock: (1859–1939) English criminologist and psychologist. Conducted studies in psychology and sociology of sex.

embryo: 1. an early or undeveloped stage of something. 2. a child in the womb in the first eight weeks of its development.

Emersonian: of Ralph Waldo Emerson: (1803–82) American essayist and poet.

encyst: to enclose in or as if in a cyst or sac.

endocrine: designating or of any gland producing one or more internal secretions that are introduced directly into the bloodstream and carried to other parts of the body whose functions they regulate or control.

engram: a mental image picture of an experience containing pain, unconsciousness, and a real or fancied threat to survival. It is a recording in the reactive mind of something which actually happened to an individual in the past and which contained pain and unconsciousness, both of which are recorded in the mental image picture called an engram. It must, by definition, have impact or injury as part of its content. These engrams are a complete recording, down to the last accurate detail, of every perception present in a moment of partial or full unconsciousness.

engram bank: a colloquial name for the reactive mind.

engram command: any phrase contained in an engram.

enjoin: to order, to command.

erase: to cause an engram to "vanish" entirely by recountings, at which time it is filed as memory and experience.

erudition: exhibition of knowledge not easily understood by the average person.

estrogen: a sex hormone or other substance capable of developing and maintaining female characteristics of the body.

exodontistry: the extraction of teeth.

fan-tan: a Chinese betting game in which the players lay wagers on the number of pieces that will remain when a hidden pile of them has been divided by four.

Farragut, David Glasgow: (1801–70) American admiral.

fetish: anything to which foolishly excessive respect or devotion is given.

fetus: in man, the offspring in the womb from the end of the third month of pregnancy until birth.

fidelity: accuracy.

file clerk: Dianetics auditor's slang for the mechanism of the mind which acts as a data monitor. Auditors can get instant or "flash" answers direct from the file clerk to aid in contacting incidents. Technically, the name of the *file clerk* might be "bank monitor units" but the phrase is too unwieldy.

flash answer: the first thing which comes into a person's head when a question is asked of him.

foible: a harmless peculiarity in a person's character.

forgetter mechanism: a forgetter mechanism is "Put it out of my mind," "If I remembered it I would go mad," "Can't remember," and just plain "I don't know," as well as the master of the family of phrases, "Forget it!" Any engram command which makes the individual believe he can't remember.

fuse: a short length of wire designed to melt and thus break a circuit if the current exceeds a safe level.

Galen: second-century A.D. physician.

galvanometer: an instrument for detecting and measuring small electric currents.

gaoler: jailer.

garner: to acquire or earn.

Gaslight: a play by Patrick Hamilton (later called *Angel Street*) in which a man tries to drive his wife insane.

gauge: thickness or diameter, as of sheet metal or wire.

Gauls: any of the Celtic-speaking people of Gaul, ancient region in western Europe consisting of what is now mainly France and Belgium.

Gay Nineties: the 1890s, a period of sudden affluence in the U.S. brought on by the industrial revolution.

glad-hand: a hearty welcome, especially when insincere.

Goldi: a Mongoloid people of eastern Siberia.

gonad: a bodily organ that produces gametes (mature sperm or eggs capable of participating in fertilization).

Grand Coulee Dam: a large, concrete dam located on the Columbia River in central Washington.

gregarious: living in herds or flocks.

grippe: influenza.

grouper: species of command which, literally translated, means that all incidents are in one place on the time track: "I'm jammed up," "Everything happens at once," "Everything comes in on me at once," "I'll get even with you," etc.

G-2: military intelligence section of the Army or Marine Corps.

Hamlet: hero of a play of the same name by William Shakespeare.

harlot: a prostitute.

harridan: a disreputable, shrewish old woman.

Harvey, William: (1578–1657) English physician and anatomist, discoverer of the mechanics of blood circulation.

hebephrenia: *psychiatry.* a form of aberration characterized by childish or silly behavior.

Hegelian: after Hegel, Georg Wilhelm Friedrich: (1770–1831) German philosopher.

hew: to chop or cut with an ax or sword, etc.

Hindu trinity: Hindu representation of the three manifestations of the Supreme Being—Brahma, Vishnu and Siva—each with a specific cosmic function: Brahma was associated with creation; Vishnu was associated with preservation and renewal; and Siva with destruction and disintegration.

Hippocrates: (460?–370? B.C.) Greek physician, known as "the father of medicine."

histamine: a chemical compound in body tissues that causes many allergic reactions.

holder: any engram command which makes an individual remain in an engram knowingly or unknowingly. These include such things as "Stay here," "Sit right there and think about it," "Come back and sit down," "I can't go," "I mustn't leave," etc.

Hume, David: (1711–76) Scottish philosopher and historian.

hurrah's nest: state of utmost confusion; a mess.

hyoscine: same as scopolamine, an alkaloid used in medicine as a sedative, hypnotic and sometimes with other drugs to relieve pain.

hypnoanalysis: the use of hypnosis or hypnotic drugs in combination with psychoanalytic techniques.

hypochondriac: a person who continually shows unnecessary anxiety about his health.

iatrogenic: means illness generated by doctors. An operation during which the doctor's knife slipped and accidentally harmed the patient might cause an iatrogenic illness or injury since the fault would have been with the surgeons.

idyllic: peaceful and happy.

impedimenta: encumberances, baggage.

inductive: of or using induction, logical reasoning that a general law exists because particular cases that seem to be examples of it exist.

injunction: an order or command that something must or must not be done.

in kind: in the same manner or with something equivalent.

in re: in regard to.

insidious: spreading or developing or acting inconspicuously but with harmful effect.

insulin shock: a state of collapse caused by a decrease in blood sugar resulting from the administration of excessive insulin.

inversion: acute awareness of self.

jub-jub bird: imaginary creature from the poem "Jabberwocky" by Lewis Carroll.

jurisprudence: the study of law or of a particular part of law.

Keats, John: (1795–1821) English poet.

keep: the strongest, innermost part or central tower of a medieval castle.

key-in: the moment an earlier upset or painful incident has been restimulated. A moment when the environment around the awake but fatigued or distressed individual is itself similar to the dormant engram. At that moment the engram becomes active. It is keyed-in and can thereafter be dramatized.

key out: the engram drops away without being erased.

Kinsey, Alfred C.: U.S. zoologist, studied human sexual behavior in the U.S.

kleptomaniac: a person suffering from an uncontrollable tendency to steal things, with no desire to use or profit by them.

Korzybski, Alfred: (1879–1950) American scientist and writer. Developed the subject of general semantics, a methodology that attempts to improve human behavior through a critical use of words and symbols.

Kraepelin, Emil: (1856–1926) German psychiatrist. Divided mental disturbances into various classifications.

Krafft-Ebing, Baron Richard von: (1840–1902) German neurologist and psychiatrist.

lead: an electrical conductor (usually a wire) conveying current from a source to a place of use.

Lesbos: Greek island in the Aegean Sea. The word *lesbian* derives from the ancient Greek name of this island, from the eroticism and homosexuality attributed to Sappho (ancient Greek poetess) and her followers.

Leucippus: Greek philosopher of fifth century B.C.

lie factory: technically, a phrase contained in an engram demanding prevarication [the telling of lies]—it was originally called a *fabricator*.

lock: an analytical moment in which the perceptics of the engram are approximated, thus restimulating the engram or bringing it into action, the present-time perceptics being erroneously interpreted by the reactive mind to mean that the same condition which produced physical pain once before is now again at hand.

Locke, John: (1632–1704) English philosopher.

loose: lacking conventional moral restraint in sexual behavior.

Lorentz-FitzGerald-Einstein equations: mathematical equations in the field of physics, developed by Albert Einstein, Hendrik Lorentz and George Francis FitzGerald.

Lucretius: Titus Lucretius Carus: (96?–55 B.C.) Roman philosophical poet.

lugubrious: very sad or mournful, especially in a way that seems exaggerated or ridiculous.

Macbeth: title character of a play by Shakespeare, tortured by his guilt for murders he committed rising to power in Scotland.

maelstrom: an agitated or tumultuous state of affairs.

mange: a skin disease affecting hairy animals, caused by a parasite and characterized by intense itching, scabs and loss of hair.

manic-depressive: an individual who, because of a phrase or a restimulation—no more no less—climbs way up the tone scale; there is just a small peak, and he hits this peak and then dives off it again and goes on with the engram.

Mauser: a brand of military or hunting rifles.

mawkish: sentimental in a sickly way.

Maxwell, James Clerk: (1831–79) Scottish physicist.

Mazda and Ahriman: the deities in Zoroastrianism, the religious system of the Persians before their conversion to

Islam. Mazda is the spirit of universal good and Ahriman is his archrival as the spirit of evil.

media-media: average.

memory: anything which, perceived, is filed in the standard memory bank and can be recalled by the analytical mind.

Mesmer, Franz Anton: (1734–1815) Austrian physician who developed the practice of mesmerism—hypnotism.

metallurgy: the scientific study of the properties of metals and alloys, the art of working metals or of extracting them from their ores.

metaphysics: a branch of philosophy that deals with the nature of existence and of truth and knowledge.

mien: a person's manner or bearing.

militate: to be directed (*against*); operate or work (*against* or, rarely, *for*): said of facts, evidence, actions, etc.

misdirector: any engram command which makes the patient move in a way or direction on the track which is contrary to instructions of the auditor or the desires of the analytical mind of the patient.

Moloch: the god of the ancient Phoenicians to whom children were sacrificed in the Old Testament.

monomanic: one who suffers from an obsession with one idea or interest.

morphine: a drug made from opium, used for relieving pain.

motor strip: the mind's control system through the motor controls. There are two panels on each side of the skull, one on top of the other, and they control opposite sides of the body. One of the panels on each side is where the thoughts register, and the other panel is where the muscle control is set up.

myelin sheathing: the fatty layer of tissues coating the nerves.

myopia: inability to see clearly what is far away—nearsightedness.

mysticism: any doctrine that asserts the possibility of attaining knowledge of spiritual truths through intuition acquired by fixed meditation.

narcosynthesis: the practice of inducing sleep with drugs and then talking to the patient to draw out buried thoughts.

Nation, Carry: (1846–1911) American temperance agitator.

neuron: the structural and functional unit of the nervous system.

neurosis: an emotional state containing conflicts and emotional data inhibiting the abilities or welfare of the individual.

neurotic: the *neurotic* has thorough concern about the future to the degree that he has many more fears about the future than he has goals in the future. He spends much of his time pondering the past.

Newton, Isaac: (1642–1727) English mathematician and astronomer. Discoverer of the law of gravitation.

Nineveh: capital of the ancient empire of Assyria, situated on the east bank of the Tigris River, opposite modern Mosul, Iraq.

obstetrical: of or regarding obstetrics, the branch of medicine and surgery that deals with childbirth.

ocular: of or relating to the sense of sight.

odor: repute; esteem.

Old Man of the Sea: character in the story of "Sindbad the Sailor" in *The Arabian Nights*. A seemingly harmless old man, he climbs onto the shoulders of the obliging Sindbad and refuses to get off. He clings there for many days and nights until Sindbad escapes by getting him drunk.

olfactory: of or relating to the sense of smell.

omnipresent: present everywhere at the same time, widely or constantly met with.

opium: a drug made from the juice of certain poppies, smoked or chewed as a stimulant or narcotic, and used in medicine as a sedative.

orthopedics: the branch of medicine dealing with the correction of deformities in bones or muscles.

pagan: not Christian, Moslem or Jewish.

pallid: faint in color; pale.

palsy: paralysis, especially with involuntary tremors.

panacea: a remedy for all kinds of diseases or troubles.

pander: to minister to others' passions or prejudices for selfish ends.

parathyroid: a hormone regulating calcium levels in the body.

Parcheesi: a trademark for a board game based on the game of pachisi (ancient game of India similar to backgammon).

paresis: partial paralysis, affecting muscular movement but not sensation.

Pasteur, Louis: (1822–95) French chemist and bacteriologist. Proved that decay and putrefaction are caused by bacteria; developed serums and vaccines for such diseases as cholera and rabies.

Pasturella pestis: organism causing bubonic plague.

paternity: the state of being a father; fatherhood.

pathological: of or concerned with a disease.

pathology: the scientific study of diseases of the body.

patter: the jargon of a particular group.

Pavlov, Ivan Petrovich: (1849–1936) Russian physiologist; noted for behavioral experiments on dogs.

peptic ulcer: an open sore in the stomach.

perceptic: any sense message such as a sight, sound, smell, etc.

phenobarbital: a medicinal drug used to calm the nerves and induce sleep.

Philip: Philip II: (382–336 B.C.) king of Macedonia, father of Alexander the Great.

phlebotomy: the act or practice of bloodletting as a therapeutic measure.

pillory: to hold up to public ridicule or scorn.

pituitrin: the various substances secreted by the pituitary gland, located at the base of the brain, which have important influences on growth and bodily functions.

platitude: a commonplace remark, especially if uttered solemnly as if it were new.

portend: to be an indication of; signify.

post: the starting gate at a racetrack.

postulate: something assumed to be true, especially as a basis for reasoning.

poultice: a hot, soft, moist mass, as of flour, herbs, mustard, etc. Sometimes spread on cloth, applied to a sore or inflamed part of the body.

preclear: from pre- clear, a person not yet clear; generally a person being audited, who is thus on the road to clear; a person who, through Dianetics processing, is finding out more about himself and life.

predisposition: a state of mind or body that renders a person liable to act or behave in a certain way or to be subject to certain diseases.

prefrontal lobes: portion of the brain directly behind the forehead.

prefrontal lobotomy: *psychiatry.* an operation in which the white fibers joining the prefrontal and frontal lobes to the interior region of the brain are severed.

prenatal: existing or taking place before birth.

prerelease: any patient who is entered into therapy to accomplish a release from his chief difficulties, psychosomatic or aberrational.

prescience: knowledge of events or actions before they happen.

present time: the *time* which is now and becomes the past as rapidly as it is observed. It is a term loosely applied to the environment existing in now. When we say someone should be in *present time* we mean he should be in communication with his environment. We mean, further, that he should be in communication with his environment as it exists, not as it existed.

procreate: to bring (a living thing) into existence by the natural process of reproduction.

promiscuous: having sexual relations with many people.

proviso: something that is insisted upon as a condition of an agreement.

psychic: of the soul or mind.

psychometry: same as psychometrics: measurement of psychological variables, as intelligence, aptitude and emotional disturbance.

psychosis: any major form of mental affliction or disease.

psychosomatic: *psycho* of course refers to mind and *somatic* refers to body; the term *psychosomatic* means the mind making the body ill or illnesses which have been created physically within the body by derangement of the mind.

punk: poor in quality or condition.

Q: symbol used to represent an undefined, but observable as existing, form of energy or force.

quinine: a bitter medicinal drug used to treat malaria and in tonics.

rationalization: justified thought—the excuses one makes to explain his irrational behavior.

reactive mind: a portion of a person's mind which works on a totally stimulus-response basis, which is not under his volitional control, and which exerts force and the power of command over his awareness, purposes, thoughts, body and actions. Stored in the reactive mind are engrams, and here we find the single source of aberrations and psychosomatic ills.

recalcitrant: disobedient, resisting authority or discipline.

recriminate: to accuse in return.

reduce: to take all the charge or pain out of an incident. This means to have the preclear recount the incident from beginning to end (while returned to it in reverie) over and over again, picking up all the somatics and perceptions present just as though the incident were happening at that moment. To *reduce* means, technically, to render free of aberrative material as far as possible to make the case progress.

release: a release is an individual from whom have been released the current or chronic mental and physical difficulties and painful emotion.

remonstrate: to make a protest.

repeater technique: the repetition of a word or phrase in order to produce movement on the time track into areas of disturbed thought containing that word or phrase. After the auditor has placed the patient in reverie, if he discovers the patient, for instance, insists he "can't go anyplace," the auditor makes him repeat the phrase. Repetition of such a phrase, over and over, sucks the patient back down the track and into contact with an engram which contains it.

repression: a command that the organism must not do something.

restimulation: the reactivation of a past memory due to similar circumstances in the present approximating circumstances of the past.

restimulator: an approximation of the reactive mind's content or some part thereof continually perceived in the environment of the organism.

returning: the person can "send" a portion of his mind to a past period on either a mental or combined mental and physical basis and can reexperience incidents which have taken place in his past in the same fashion and with the same sensations as before.

reverie: the state of reverie is actually just a name. It is a label introduced to make the patient feel that his state has altered and that he has gone into a state where his memory is very good or where he can do something he couldn't ordinarily do before. The actuality is that he is able to do it all the time anyway. It is not a strange state. The person is wide awake, but merely by asking him to close his eyes he is technically in reverie.

revile: to criticize angrily in abusive language.

rheostat: an electrical instrument used to control current by varying resistance.

Rohmer, Sax: pseudonym of Arthur Sarsfield Ward: (1883–1959) English author of *Dr. Fu Manchu.*

Ross, Ronald: (1857–1932) British physician.

Rousseau, Jean Jacques: (1712–78) French political philosopher and author.

sadism: enjoyment of inflicting or watching cruelty.

salvo: fire at with a number of guns or artillery pieces at one time.

sanitaria: plural of sanitarium: an establishment for treating chronic diseases.

schizophrenic: the original definition of *schizophrenic* or "scissor personality" was in observation of shift of identity; an idea that one is two persons.

Schopenhauer, Arthur: (1788–1860) German philosopher. Chief expounder of pessimism.

self-determinism: is the state wherein the individual can or cannot be controlled by his environment according to his own choice. He is confident in his interpersonal relationships. He reasons but does not need to react.

sensory strip: the *sensory strip* could be considered the "mental" side of the switchboard, and the *motor strip* the physical side. *See also* **motor strip**

shaman: a priest or witch doctor among certain peoples, claiming to have sole contact with the gods, etc.

short shrift: unsympathetic treatment.

signal: not average or ordinary; remarkable; notable.

sinusitis: inflammation of one or more sinus cavities in the skull.

solicitous: anxious and concerned about a person's welfare or comfort.

somatic: the word *somatic* means bodily or physical. Because the word *pain* is restimulative, and because the word *pain* has in the past led to a confusion between physical pain and mental pain, the word *somatic* is used in Dianetics to denote physical pain or discomfort of any kind.

somatic strip: the sequential physical record of pain or discomfort of any kind from conception to present time, which locates moments in time for the individual.

sonic: recall by hearing a past sound with the "mind's ear."

sonorous: resonant, giving a deep, powerful sound.

Spartans: the citizens of Sparta, a city in ancient Greece, who would permit a child to live only if he showed potential of becoming an asset to the state.

specious: seeming to be good, sound, correct, logical, etc., without really being so; plausible but not genuine.

Spencer, Herbert: (1820–1903) English philosopher. One of few modern thinkers to attempt a systematic account of all cosmic phenomena, including mental and social principles.

standard memory bank: recordings of everything perceived throughout the lifetime up to present time by the individual except physical pain, which is not recorded in the analytical mind but is recorded in the reactive mind.

stigma: a mark of shame, a stain on a person's good reputation.

stimuli: plural of stimulus: something that rouses a person or thing into activity or energy or that produces a reaction in an organ or tissue of the body.

Stoic: a member of a Greek school of philosophy, founded by Zeno about 308 B.C., holding that human beings should be free from passion and calmly accept all occurrences as the unavoidable result of divine will.

strychnine: a bitter, highly poisonous substance, used in very small doses as a stimulant.

sulfa: any of a group of chemical compounds with antibacterial properties.

suppressor: the exterior forces which reduce the chances of the survival of any form.

supranational: of, for, involving or over all or a number of nations.

syllogism: a form of reasoning in which a conclusion is reached from two statements, as in *"All men must die; I am a man; therefore, I must die."*

sylvan: relating to or characteristic of forests.

symbiote: any entity of life or energy which assists an individual or man in his survival.

symbiotic: the living together of similar or dissimilar organisms for mutual benefit.

tabloid: a newspaper usually half the normal size, with many pictures and short, often sensational, news stories.

tacit consent: in the case of two preclears working on each other, each one assuming in his turn the auditor's role, a condition can arise where each prevents the other from contacting certain engrams. This is tacit consent. A husband and wife may have a mutual period of quarrels and unhappiness. Engaged upon clearing each other, working alternately as auditor, they avoid, unknowingly, but by reactive computation, the mutual period, thus leaving in place painfully emotional engrams.

tactile: of or using the sense of touch.

talisman: an object supposed to bring good luck.

technology: the methods of application of an art or science as opposed to mere knowledge of the science or art itself.

telepathy: communication from one mind to another without the use of speech or writing or gestures, etc.

temporize: to effect a compromise; negotiate.

termagant: a shrewish, bullying woman.

terra incognita: an unknown land; a region or subject of which nothing is known.

testosterone: a male sex hormone.

thalamus: the interior region of the brain where sensory nerves originate.

θ: theta, the eighth letter in the Greek alphabet. Greek for thought or life or the spirit.

three-thousand-cycle note: a ringing sound with three thousand vibrations, or cycles, per second.

thyroid: a hormone that regulates the body's growth and development.

time track: the time span of the individual from conception to present time on which lies the sequence of events of his life.

token: a very special kind of restimulator; any object, practice or mannerism which one or more allies used. By identity thought the ally is survival, anything the ally used or did is, therefore, survival.

tome: a large or scholarly book.

tone scale: a scale which shows the emotional tones of a person. These, ranged from the highest to the lowest, are, in part, serenity (the highest level), enthusiasm (as we proceeded downward), conservatism, boredom, antagonism, anger, covert hostility, fear, grief, apathy.

Torquemada, Tomás de: (1420?–98) Spanish Dominican monk. Organized the Inquisition in Spain, became notorious for the severity of his judgments and the cruelty of his punishments.

track: *see* **time track**

tractable: easy to manage or deal with; docile.

transference: *psychoanalysis.* the process in and by which a person's feelings, thoughts and wishes shift from one person to another, especially this process in psychoanalysis with the analyst made the object of the shift.

transorbital leukotomy: *psychiatry.* an operation which, while the patient is being electrically shocked, thrusts an ordinary dime store ice pick into each eye and reaches up to rip the analyzer apart.

treat: to deal with a subject in writing or speech; speak or write (*of*).

trounce: to beat.

truck: dealings; business.

tuberculosis: an infectious wasting disease affecting various parts of the body.

utopian: of or like utopia, any idealized place, state or situation of perfection.

vacillate: to waver, to keep changing one's mind.

valence: personality. The term is used to denote the borrowing of the personality of another. A preclear "in his father's valence" is acting as if he were his father.

valence shift: getting the preclear moving around from one valence to the other.

valence wall: a sort of protective mechanism by which the charge of the case is compartmented to permit the individual to work at least some of the time.

vector: a physical quantity with both magnitude and direction, such as a force or velocity.

vignette: a short description or character sketch.

visio: recall by seeing a past sight with the "mind's eye."

vivisect: to perform surgical experiments on living animals.

voodoo: a form of religion based on belief in witchcraft and magical rites, practiced by some people in the West Indies and America.

welter: a disorderly mixture.

yah-yah: slang term for bickering.

zygote: the first cell of a new individual.

Index

More Books
by L. Ron Hubbard

All the following books by L. Ron Hubbard can help you to have a sense of mental well-being and real peace of mind. Any of these books can be ordered direct from the publisher or any Scientology[1] church or organization listed in the back of this book.

Basic Dianetics books

The Dynamics of Life—An Introduction to Dianetics Discoveries • L. Ron Hubbard's concise introduction to the subject of Dianetics spiritual healing technology. Learn how the *reactive mind* was discovered and how physical and emotional pains you've suffered can suppress the strong life forces (dynamics) you naturally possess. Available at bookstores everywhere.

Dianetics: The Evolution of a Science • This book tells the story of how Dianetics technology was developed and how you can *use* Dianetics breakthroughs to realize your own true capabilities. Available at bookstores everywhere.

Self Analysis • *Self Analysis* is a simple and very popular self-help volume designed for use a few minutes each day, by anyone. Use *Self Analysis* to unlock a stronger, more confident "you" simply by recalling past pleasures you've enjoyed. Available at bookstores everywhere.

Science of Survival • Is there a way to know in advance how people will react to you and your goals? How do you

---

1. Scientology: Scientology® applied religious philosophy, the study of the human spirit in its relationship to the physical universe and its living forms. Note: Dianetics technology is the forerunner of Scientology and is today in extensive use by Scientology churches and organizations all over the world.

know someone you meet or work with is really honest, trustworthy or reliable before finding out the hard way? Is there any way to predict these traits? Yes! Read *Science of Survival* and you'll not only have a real, self-assured knowledge of human behavior, you'll also be pretty hard to fool.

The Basic Dianetics Picture Book • A visual aid for a quicker understanding and explanation of Dianetics technology. Learn the structure of the reactive mind and how negative mental pictures can interfere with your self-confidence and ability to think clearly.

Basic Scientology books

Scientology: The Fundamentals of Thought • The attitude with which we approach life is an all-important factor of our success or failure in life. With this introductory book to Scientology principles, you can gain a positive outlook on life. Available at bookstores everywhere.

The Problems of Work • *The Problems of Work* is a remarkable study of the daily conflicts in the working world. By studying and using L. Ron Hubbard's principles, you, too, can turn a challenging situation into a golden opportunity. The book is instructive, easy to understand and offers solutions you can put to use *today*. Available at bookstores everywhere.

Scientology: A New Slant on Life • A series of popular essays by L. Ron Hubbard including "Two Rules for Happy Living," "Marriage," "How to Live with Children," "The Man Who Succeeds," "Communication" and many more.

The Basic Scientology Picture Book • A visual aid to a better understanding of the basic principles of Scientology applied religious philosophy and its relationship to life.

Introduction to Scientology Ethics • This book by L. Ron Hubbard presents practical guidelines for honest and ethical behavior that you can use to achieve your goals in life and find personal fulfillment.

Books about the Purification Rundown

Purification: An Illustrated Answer to Drugs • Drugs and chemical deposits stop spiritual and personal betterment. This illustrated book tells about the amazing Purification Rundown, a program designed to rid your body of accumulated drugs and toxic chemicals and open the way for spiritual improvement.

Purification Rundown Delivery Manual • This book is used by anyone who does the famous Purification Rundown. It is designed to help a person through the program to the best possible result.

Books to help you help others

The Volunteer Minister's Handbook • A practical how-to book that can help anyone deal with community, business, group or even personal problems. This handbook covers such vital topics as drug abuse, study problems, marriage counseling, handling group cooperation and much more.

Introductory and Demonstration Processes and Assists • How can you help someone improve his enthusiasm for living? How can you improve someone's self-confidence on the job? Mastery of this book will give you confidence in helping others deal with life.

The Way to Happiness • The world's first common-sense, nonreligious moral code. Twenty-one principles of conduct based on observation and knowledge of the nature of man. Buy it in packets of twelve booklets, read it and give it to your friends. Also available as a beautiful, hardbound gift book. Ask for it at bookstores everywhere.

Advanced Dianetics books

Dianetics 55! • Learn the rules of better communication that can help you live a more fulfilling life. Here, L. Ron

Hubbard deals with the fundamental principles of communication and how you can master these to achieve your goals in life.

Child Dianetics • Have you all but given up on handling children? Do temper tantrums leave you at a loss for what to do? Parents who read *Child Dianetics* and apply its simple exercises to their children will find out something can be done!

Research and Discovery Series • This is a very large series of books covering the research and development record of Dianetics technology. This is material never before published. Follow along as L. Ron Hubbard refines and streamlines Dianetics technology and builds a better bridge!

Notes on the Lectures • In the rush of excitement following the release of *Dianetics: The Modern Science of Mental Health*, L. Ron Hubbard was in demand all over the world as a speaker. He has given over three thousand lectures. This book is compiled from lectures given in the fall of 1950. Here, Hubbard expands upon aspects of Dianetics processing and application of Dianetics principles to groups.

Handbook for Preclears • For use as a self-help volume or to apply to others, this book is designed to increase personal ability and peace of mind.

Advanced Procedure and Axioms • Advanced Dianetics discoveries and techniques comprising a research breakthrough by L. Ron Hubbard beyond the field of the mind, and a new codification of the basic principles of existence.

Advanced Scientology books

The Phoenix Lectures • This book gives an in-depth look at the roots of Scientology philosophy and how it was developed. The influence of earlier great philosophies and religious leaders is covered in detail. An enlightening look at the infinite potentialities of man.

The Creation of Human Ability • A handbook containing many advanced processes for use by Scientology auditors, with full clarification of the major philosophical and technical breakthroughs by L. Ron Hubbard from which these techniques were derived.

Scientology 0-8: The Book of Basics • A comprehensive look at many basic Scientology principles, including charts which detail man's true potentials.

Scientology 8-80 • This book gives a real understanding of how life energy can be released to unlock a being's abilities and self-confidence.

Scientology 8-8008 • L. Ron Hubbard describes procedures designed to increase the abilities of man to heights only dreamed of before now.

All About Radiation • Bluntly informative, this book describes observations and discoveries concerning the mental effects of radiation and their handling. A very important book with today's concern about nuclear power plants and nuclear weapons.

Control and the Mechanics of Start-Change-Stop • This book covers various aspects of the subject of control, plus procedures to help a person recover his ability to control the parts of his life.

Scientology: Clear Procedure • Advanced procedures to help a person achieve a state of mental well-being never before achieved in man.

Axioms and Logics • The basic axioms upon which Scientology procedures are based. Vital to an understanding of life and the components of human existence.

The Book of Case Remedies • The trained auditor's and student's manual covering preclear difficulties and their remedies.

Mission Into Time • A fascinating account of a unique research expedition into both space and time, searching for evidence of *past life recall*.

Have You Lived Before This Life? • Do people live more than once? Have we existed in past eras? Many researchers claim that we have. But is this really true? Trained auditors tested a series of forty-one cases. Their fascinating findings are given in this book.

611

A History of Man • A fascinating look at the possible genetic background and history of the human race—revolutionary concepts guaranteed to intrigue you and challenge many basic assumptions about man's true power, potential and abilities.

Technical Bulletins of Dianetics and Scientology • Twelve volumes, containing all of L. Ron Hubbard's technical bulletins and issues from 1950 to 1979. Almost any question a person may have concerning Dianetics and Scientology technology can be answered directly from the pages of these books, which also include a 250-page master subject index containing over twenty thousand entries!

Philadelphia Doctorate Course Lectures • A famous lecture series given in 1952 in which Ron explains man's relationship to the physical universe. High-quality cassette tapes and transcripts of these lectures, each with a glossary and complete index.

Books for the workplace

Organization Executive Course • Composed of eight large-format volumes, the *Organization Executive Course* is a collection of memos, letters and essays of L. Ron Hubbard, setting forth his unique philosophy of organization. The principles in these volumes have been successfully applied to many businesses with stellar results, and by individuals to increase their self-confidence and job security.

Management Series • What are the basic, underlying laws of success in any organization? The *Management Series* contains what every manager, executive or office worker needs to know to deal intelligently with finance, personnel, on-the-job training programs and how to effectively deal with a volume of reports and data and *use* that data flow to their advantage.

Modern Management Technology Defined—Hubbard Dictionary of Administration and Management • A comprehensive dictionary containing the entire range of business terminology, including such areas as personnel management, communication within the group, financial management and data evaluation.

How to Live Though an Executive • This book is the first real executive survival manual. Here's the way out for any executive who's swamped with information, reports, memos, meetings and other demands on his time. The problems of communication and passing information can make or break an executive, and with this book the solutions are simple.

Policy Subject Index • A study guide and index to the *Organization Executive Course* and the *Management Series* volumes; indexes the writings contained in these volumes by title.

Dianetics and Scientology study aids

The Study Tapes • In today's world, you have to learn fast to keep up. But the growth of new technology and new skills can seem overwhelming. You need to be able to read and understand information *rapidly. The Study Tapes* by L. Ron Hubbard will give you the way to quickly learn any new subject and retain what you learn. *The Study Tapes* are recorded on high-quality cassette tapes and come with an indexed transcription booklet for easy study and fast reference. Get your set today!

Dianetics and Scientology Technical Dictionary • A full dictionary of Dianetics and Scientology terms, defines fully the technical terms that will be encountered in the preceding books.

Basic Dictionary of Dianetics and Scientology • A simple dictionary of terms, ideal for the new Scientologist™ or for explaining Dianetics and Scientology principles to your friends and relatives.

Books about the E-Meter

The Book Introducing the E-Meter • This is a basic booklet that introduces you to the Hubbard™ Electrometer or E-Meter, an instrument which measures emotional reaction by tiny impulses generated by thought. The Hubbard Electrometer is often used today in Dianetics and Scientology processing.

The Book of E-Meter Drills • This book teaches one all phases of E-Meter operation with hands-on exercises.

E-Meter Essentials • More advanced aspects of E-Meter use, plus the mental phenomena behind many E-Meter readings.

Understanding the E-Meter • This is a large, illustrated book that fully explains the basics of the E-Meter, how it works and how it can measure the electrical activity of thought. Any question about the operation of the E-Meter can be handled with this book.

Reference materials

The Background and Ceremonies of the Church of Scientology • This book contains the Creed of the Church, church services, sermons and many ceremonies as originally given in person by L. Ron Hubbard, Founder of Scientology.

What Is Scientology? • Here is a definitive collection of facts and figures, on and about what millions consider to be the most extraordinary phenomenon of our time. What is Scientology all about? What makes it the fastest growing religious philosophy in the world today? The answers to these and many other questions on the subject are contained in this book.

FOR MORE INFORMATION ABOUT DIANETICS OR TO ORDER BOOKS AND CASSETTES

CALL: 1-800-367-8788

Is there such a thing as a hotline that doesn't believe in giving advice? What about a hotline for able individuals to help them solve their *own* problems?

"If we take a man and keep giving him advice," L. Ron Hubbard has said, "we don't necessarily wind up with a resolution of his problems. But if, on the other hand, we put him in a position where he had higher intelligence, where his reaction time was better, where he could confront life better, where he could identify the factors in his life more easily, then he's in a position where he can solve his own problems."

Call the unique new hotline and referral service with operators trained in Dianetics technology. Callers find someone they can trust to talk to about a problem, and they are referred to their nearest Dianetics center for more information if they are interested.

You can also order Dianetics books and cassettes by calling this number.

Call this toll-free number 7 days a week from 9 a.m. to 11 p.m. Pacific Standard Time.

Hear

Best-selling Author
L. Ron Hubbard's

INTRODUCTION
TO DIANETICS
Cassette

You've read the book *Dianetics*. Now listen to the author of *Dianetics*, L. Ron Hubbard, as he further explains Dianetics principles in this newly released cassette lecture—a vital companion to the book *Dianetics*.

Here is the story of how L. Ron Hubbard came to discover the principles of Dianetics technology, how he uncovered the reactive mind, and how he developed the techniques described in the book, to bring individuals to the state of Clear.

Learn more about how you can use Dianetics technology to create a happier and more fulfilling life for yourself, friends and family.

Order this lecture now for only $9.95.

See next page for details.

Order THIS LECTURE TODAY!

Send the following information to:

Bridge Publications, Inc.
Dept. Dn 85
1414 North Catalina Street
Los Angeles, CA 90027

1. Your check or money order for $9.95, plus $1.00 for postage and handling

   or, if you want to charge your order,

   Your VISA or MasterCard number, expiration date and your signature

2. Your name, address, city, state and zip code

   Or, call 1-800-367-8788 and order your cassette by phone today!

Discover Greater Happiness and Well-Being

Read These Dianetics Books by L. Ron Hubbard

Self Analysis by L. Ron Hubbard
Dianetics tests and exercises in a practical home study manual. Just a half hour spent with this book every night can help you increase confidence, improve your abilities and find greater peace of mind. Includes a special evaluation chart, self-administered tests, two discs for use in the exercises and 150 pages of self-analysis lists.
$9.00 ($11.00 Canadian)

Dianetics: The Evolution of a Science by L. Ron Hubbard
L. Ron Hubbard reveals the story of his journey into the hidden depths of the human mind—a journey that produced his pioneering research and knowledge about the mind and life. Today, Dianetics technology is used by people all over the world to live happier and more fulfilling lives. Find out how Dianetics can work for you.
$7.00 ($9.00 Canadian)

The Dynamics of Life by L. Ron Hubbard
Hubbard's concise introduction to the subject of Dianetics technology. "The basic individual," says Hubbard, "is not a buried unknown or a different person, but an intensity of all that is best and most able in the person." With Dianetics technology, an individual can release his own powerful "dynamics of life" to live a better and happier life.
$7.00 ($9.00 Canadian)

Learn More About Dianetics and How It Can Benefit You

Attend a Course or Workshop in Your Area

Dianetics techniques, as described in this book, are used throughout the world by thousands of people every day to live happier lives and help others. These principles and techniques have been proven workable throughout years of rigorous application and testing.

There are centers where you can learn about Dianetics technology in most major cities throughout the world. A full list of addresses appears at the end of this book. Here you can listen to trained Dianetics lecturers, get all of your questions answered, meet other interested people and experience Dianetics counseling for yourself.

The Dianetics services available at these centers include the following:

Free Introductory Dianetics Auditing Session—Experience Dianetics auditing as described in this book and find out for yourself how it can help you overcome barriers and live a happier and more fulfilling life.

Dianetics Lecture—Hear an experienced Dianetics lecturer, and get all of your questions answered. Learn more about the basic principles of Dianetics technology and how it can be applied to help people gain confidence and control in life.

Free Dianetics Film—See actual Dianetics auditing sessions and their impressive and very real results in an exciting half-hour film. This film provides an excellent introduction to Dianetics principles and shows their application in life.

Free Dianetics Personality Test—How well do you know yourself? What are your strong points? Where do you need improvement? A free Dianetics personality test can help you discover more about yourself and your life and start you on the road to personal betterment.

Dianetics Extension Course—Now you can learn more about Dianetics right in your own home with the Dianetics Extension Course. Trained Dianetics supervisors will review your lessons by mail and help you gain greater knowledge and understanding.

Essentials of Dianetics Course—For the serious student of Dianetics technology, this in-depth course teaches you how to apply the principles of this book under a trained Dianeticist. You actually give and receive Dianetics auditing as described in this book. Discover how to effectively handle the reactive mind and help others to a happier life.

Dianetics Workshop—Meet and work with other interested Dianeticists in this exciting workshop. Learn from experienced Dianetics workshop leaders and experience, with fellow students, the application of Dianetics techniques. Give and receive Dianetics auditing and discover its workability in overcoming barriers to confidence and happiness.

Hubbard Dianetics Auditor Course—The professional level course in Dianetics auditing techniques. Learn to use Dianetics technology to professional standards so you can help friends, family and anyone to become well and happy. You can become a professional at handling the basic causes of pain, upset and irrational behavior. Plenty of demonstrations, drills and practical application make it easy to learn and apply Dianetics.

How to Find a Dianetics Auditor

Skilled, professional Dianetics auditors can be contacted at any of the following Scientology churches or organizations.

Dianetics is the forerunner of Scientology applied religious philosophy and is in extensive use by Scientology churches and organizations throughout the world.

If you would like more information about Dianetics processing or want to learn more about processing others, contact your nearest Scientology church or organization today.

United States of America

Albuquerque
Church of Scientology of New Mexico
1210 San Pedro NE
Albuquerque, New Mexico 87110

Ann Arbor
Church of Scientology of Ann Arbor
301 North Ingalls Street
Ann Arbor, Michigan 48104

Austin
Church of Scientology of Texas
2200 Guadalupe
Austin, Texas 78705

Boston
Church of Scientology of Boston
448 Beacon Street
Boston, Massachusetts 02115

Buffalo
Church of Scientology Buffalo
47 West Huron Street
Buffalo, New York 14202

Chicago
Church of Scientology of Illinois
6424 North Hermitage
Chicago, Illinois 60626

Cincinnati
Church of Scientology of Ohio
3352 Jefferson Avenue
Cincinnati, Ohio 45220

Columbus
Church of Scientology of Central Ohio
167 East State Street
Columbus, Ohio 43215

Denver
Church of Scientology of Colorado
375 South Navajo Street
Denver, Colorado 80223

Detroit
Church of Scientology of Michigan
302 South Main Street
Royal Oak, Michigan 48067

Honolulu
Church of Scientology of Hawaii
1100 Alakea St., #301
Honolulu, Hawaii 96813

Kansas City
Church of Scientology of Kansas City
3742 Broadway, Suite 203
Kansas City, Missouri 64111

Las Vegas
Church of Scientology of Nevada
846 East Sahara Avenue
Las Vegas, Nevada 89104

Long Island
Church of Scientology
of Long Island
46 Islip Avenue
Islip, New York 11751

Los Angeles and vicinity
Church of Scientology of Los Angeles
4810 Sunset Boulevard
Los Angeles, California 90027

Church of Scientology Orange County
1451 Irvine Boulevard
Tustin, California 92680

Church of Scientology Pasadena
99 East Colorado Boulevard
Pasadena, California 91105

Church of Scientology
Valley Organization
10335 Magnolia Boulevard
North Hollywood, California 91601

Church of Scientology
Western United States
American Saint Hill Organization
1413 North Berendo Street
Los Angeles, California 90027

Church of Scientology
Western United States
American Saint Hill Foundation
1413 North Berendo Street
Los Angeles, California 90027

Church of Scientology
Western United States
Advanced Organization of Los Angeles
1306 North Berendo Street
Los Angeles, California 90027

Miami
Church of Scientology of Florida
120 Giralda Avenue
Coral Gables, Florida 33134

Minneapolis
Church of Scientology
of Minnesota
3019 Minnehaha Avenue S
Minneapolis, Minnesota 55406

New Haven
Church of Scientology of New Haven
909 Whalley Avenue
New Haven, Connecticut 06515

New York City
Church of Scientology of New York
227 West 46th Street
New York City, New York 10036

Orlando
Church of Scientology of Orlando
710A East Colonial
Orlando, Florida 32803

Philadelphia
Church of Scientology of Pennsylvania
1315 Race Street
Philadelphia, Pennsylvania 19107

Phoenix
Church of Scientology of Arizona
4450 North Central Avenue, #102
Phoenix, Arizona 85012

Portland
Church of Scientology of Portland
215 South East 9th Avenue
Portland, Oregon 97214

Sacramento
Church of Scientology of Sacramento
825 15th Street
Sacramento, California 95814-2096

San Diego
Church of Scientology of San Diego
2409 Fourth Avenue
San Diego, California 92101

San Francisco
Church of Scientology of San Francisco
83 McAllister Street
San Francisco, California 94102

San Jose
Church of Scientology
of Stevens Creek
4340 Stevens Creek Boulevard
Suite 180
San Jose, California 95129

Santa Barbara
Church of Scientology Santa Barbara
524 State Street
Santa Barbara, California 93101

Seattle
Church of Scientology
of Washington State
2004 Westlake
Seattle, Washington 98121

St. Louis
Church of Scientology of Missouri
5606 Delmar
St. Louis, Missouri 63112

Tampa
Church of Scientology of Tampa
4809 North Armenia Avenue
Suite 215
Tampa, Florida 33603

Church of Scientology
Flag Service Organization
210 South Fort Harrison Avenue
Clearwater, Florida 33516

Washington, D.C.
Founding Church of Scientology
2125 "S" Street N.W.
Washington, D.C. 20008

Canada

Edmonton
Church of Scientology of Alberta
10349 82nd Avenue
Edmonton, Alberta
Canada T6E 1Z9

Kitchener
Church of Scientology of Kitchener
8 Water Street North
Kitchener, Ontario
Canada N2H 5A5

Montreal
Church of Scientology of Montréal
4489 Papineau Street
Montréal, Québec
Canada H2H 1T7

Ottawa
Church of Scientology Ottawa
309 Cooper Street, 5th Floor
Ottawa, Ontario
Canada K2P 0G5

Quebec
Church of Scientology of Québec
226 1/2 St-Joseph est
Québec, Québec
Canada G1K 3A9

Toronto
Church of Scientology of Toronto
696 Yonge Street
Toronto, Ontario
Canada M4Y 2A7

Vancouver
Church of Scientology
of British Columbia
401 West Hastings Street
Vancouver, British Columbia
Canada V6B 1L5

Winnipeg
Church of Scientology of Winnipeg
978 Banning Street
Winnipeg, Manitoba
Canada R3E 2J2

United Kingdom

Birmingham
Scientology Birmingham
3 St. Mary's Row
Moseley, Birmingham
England B13 8HW

East Grinstead
Saint Hill Foundation
Saint Hill Manor
East Grinstead, West Sussex
England RH19 4JY

Advanced Organization Saint Hill
Saint Hill Manor
East Grinstead, West Sussex
England RH19 4JY

Edinburgh
Hubbard Academy
of Personal Independence
20 Southbridge
Edinburgh, Scotland EH1 1LL

London
Church of Scientology in London
68 Tottenham Court Road
London W1E 4YZ, England

Manchester
Church of Scientology Manchester
258/260 Deansgate
Manchester, England M3 4BG

Plymouth
Church of Scientology in Plymouth
41 Ebrington Street
Plymouth, Devon
England PL4 9AA

Sunderland
Scientology Sunderland
51 Fawcett Street
Sunderland, Tyne and Wear
England SR1 1UA

Austria

Vienna
Church of Scientology Austria
(Scientology-Kirche Österreich)
Mariahilfer Strasse 88A/II/2
A-1070 Vienna, Austria

Belgium

Brussels
Church of Scientology of Belgium
45A, Rue de l'Ecuyer
1000 Bruxelles, Belgium

Denmark

Aarhus
Church of Scientology Jylland
Guldsmedegade 17, 2
8000 Aarhus C.
Denmark

Copenhagen
Church of Scientology Copenhagen
Store Kongensgade 55
1264 Copenhagen K, Denmark

Church of Scientology Denmark
Vesterbrogade 23 A – 25
1620 Copenhagen V, Denmark

Church of Scientology
Advanced Organization Saint Hill
   for Europe and Africa
Jernbanegade 6
1608 Copenhagen V, Denmark

France

Angers
Church of Scientology Angers
10–12, rue Max Richard
49000 Angers, France

Clermont-Ferrand
Church of Scientology
   Clermont-Ferrand
18, rue André Moinier
63000 Clermont-Ferrand
France

Lyon
Church of Scientology Lyon
3, place des Capucins
69001 Lyon, France

Paris
Church of Scientology of Paris
65, rue de Dunkerque
75009 Paris, France

St. Etienne
Eglise de Scientology
39, rue Georges Teissier
42000 St. Etienne
France

Germany

Berlin
Church of Scientology Berlin e.V.
Sonnenallee 32
1000 Berlin 44, Germany

Düsseldorf
Scientology Düsseldorf
Oststrasse 55
4000 Düsseldorf 1
West Germany

Hamburg
Church of Scientology Hamburg e.V.
Gerhofstrasse 18
2000 Hamburg 36
West Germany

Munich
Church of Scientology München e.V.
Beichstrasse 12
D-8000 München 40
West Germany

Greece

Athens
Applied Philosophy Center
   of Greece (KEFE)
Ippokratous 175B
11472 Athens, Greece

Israel

Tel Aviv
Scientology Israel
158, Disengoff Street
Tel Aviv, Israel

Italy

Brescia
Church of Scientology Brescia
Corso Magenta 32C
25100 Brescia, Italy

Lissone
Church of Scientology Lissone
Via Lambro, 15
20052 Monza, Italy

Milan
Church of Scientology Milano
Via Zurigo, 3
20147 Milano, Italy

Novara
Dianetics Institute Novara
Via Rosseli 10
28100 Novara, Italy

Padua
Associazione di Dianetics
e Scientology Padova
Via Pietro d'Abano 1
35100 Padova, Italy

Pordenone
Associazione di Dianetics
e Scientology Pordenone
Viale Cossetti 18
33170 Pordenone, Italy

Rome
Associazione di Dianetics
e Scientology di Roma
Via del Pantheon, 57
00168 Roma, Italy

Turin
Dianetics Institute Torino
Via Garibaldi, 26
10121 Torino, Italy

Verona
Associazione di Dianetics
e Scientology di Verona
Vicolo Dietro S. Andrea 10
37100 Verona, Italy

Netherlands

Amsterdam
Church of Scientology Amsterdam
Nieuwe Zijds Voorburgwal 271–287
1012 RL Amsterdam
Netherlands

Norway

Oslo
Church of Scientology
Waldemar Thranes Gt. 86B
0175 Oslo 1, Norway

Portugal

Lisbon
Instituto de Dianética Lisboa
Travessa Da Trindade 12–4
1200 Lisboa, Portugal

Spain

Barcelona
Dianética
Calle Pau Claris 85, Pral 1ª
08010 Barcelona, Spain

Madrid
Asociación civil de Dianética
Montera 20
Madrid 14, Spain

Sweden

Gothenburg
Church of Scientology Göteborg
Norra Hamngatan 4
S-411 14 Göteborg, Sweden

Malmö
Church of Scientology Malmö
Stortorget 27-29
S-211 34 Malmö, Sweden

Stockholm
Church of Scientology Stockholm
Kammakargatan 46
S-111 60 Stockholm, Sweden

Switzerland

Basel
Church of Scientology Basel
Hardstrasse 95
4052 Basel, Switzerland

Bern
Church of Scientology Bern
Effingerstrasse 25
CH-3008 Bern, Switzerland

Geneva
Church of Scientology Genève
4, rue du Léman
1201 Genève, Switzerland

Zurich
Church of Scientology Zürich
Badenerstrasse 294
CH-8004 Zürich, Switzerland

Australia

Adelaide
Church of Scientology Adelaide
28 Waymouth Street
Adelaide, South Australia 5000
Australia

Brisbane
Church of Scientology Brisbane
106 Edward Street, 1st Floor
Brisbane, Queensland 4000, Australia

Canberra
Church of Scientology A.C.T.
23 East Row, Rooms 2 & 3
Civic, Canberra
A.C.T. 2601, Australia

Melbourne
Church of Scientology Melbourne
44 Russell Street
Melbourne, Victoria 3000
Australia

Perth
Church of Scientology Perth
39-41 King Street
Perth, Western Australia 6000
Australia

Sydney
Church of Scientology Sydney
201 Castlereagh Street
Sydney, New South Wales 2000
Australia

Church of Scientology
Advanced Organization Saint Hill
   Australia, New Zealand and Oceania
201 Castlereagh Street, 3rd Floor
Sydney, New South Wales 2000
Australia

New Zealand

Auckland
Church of Scientology of New Zealand
44 Queen Street, 2nd Floor
Auckland 1, New Zealand

Africa

Bulawayo
Church of Scientology in Zimbabwe
74 Abercorn Street
Bulawayo, Zimbabwe

Cape Town
Church of Scientology in South Africa
5 Beckham Street
Gardens
Cape Town 8001, South Africa

Durban
Church of Scientology in South Africa
57 College Lane
Durban 4001, South Africa

Harare
Church of Scientology Harare
151A Victoria Street
Harare, Zimbabwe

Johannesburg
Church of Scientology in South Africa
Security Building, 2nd Floor
95 Commissioner Street
Johannesburg 2001
South Africa

Johannesburg (cont.)
Church of Scientology
   Johannesburg North
101 Huntford Building
Cnr. Hunter & Fortesque Rds.
Yeoville 2198
Johannesburg, South Africa

Port Elizabeth
Church of Scientology Port Elizabeth
2 St. Christopher
27 Westbourne Road
6001 Port Elizabeth
South Africa

Pretoria
Church of Scientology in South Africa
"Die Meent Arcade"
   2nd Level, Shop 43b
266 Pretorius Street
Pretoria 0002
South Africa

Latin America

Colombia

Bogotá
Centro Cultural de Dianética
Carrera 19 No. 39–55
Apartado Aereo 92419
Bogotá, D.E. Colombia

Mexico

Estado de Mexico
Instituto Tecnologico
   de Dianética, A.C.
Reforma 530, Lomas
México, D.F., cp. 11000

Guadalajara
Organización Cultural de Dianética
   Guadalajara, A.C.
Av. Lopez Mateos Nte. 329
Guadalajara, Jalisco, México

Mexico City
Asociación Cultural Dianética, A.C.
Hermes No. 46
Colonia Crédito Constructor
03940 México 19, D.F.

Instituto de Filosofia Aplicada, A.C.
Dinamarca 63
Colonia Juárez
06600 México D.F.

Instituto de Filosofia Aplicada, A.C.
Plaza Rio de Janeiro No 52
Colonia Roma
06700 México D.F.

Mexico City (cont.)
Organización, Desarrollo
 y Dianética, A.C.
Providencia 1000
Colonia Del Valle
03100 México D.F.

Centro de Dianética de Polanco, A.C.
Mariano Escobedo 524
Colonia Anzures
11590 México D.F.

Venezuela

Valencia
Asociación Cultural Dianética
 de Venezuela, A.C.
Ave. 101 No. 150–23
Urbanizacion La Alegria
Apartado Postal 833
Valencia, Venezuela

Celebrity Centre® Churches

Hamburg
Celebrity Centre
Church of Scientology
Mönckebergstrasse 5
2000 Hamburg 1, West Germany

Las Vegas
Church of Scientology
Celebrity Centre Las Vegas
3430 East Tropicana, Suite 50
Las Vegas, Nevada 89121

Los Angeles
Church of Scientology
Celebrity Centre International
5930 Franklin Avenue
Hollywood, California 90028

New York
Church of Scientology
Celebrity Centre New York
65 East 82nd Street
New York, New York 10028

Paris
Church of Scientology
Celebrity Centre Paris
69, rue Legendre
75017 Paris
France

Portland
Church of Scientology
Celebrity Centre Portland
709 South West Salmon Street
Portland, Oregon 97205

**To obtain more Dianetics or Scientology
books, contact any of the following
publishers:**

Bridge Publications, Inc.
1414 North Catalina Street
Los Angeles, California 90027

New Era Publications ApS
Store Kongensgade 55
1264 Copenhagen K, Denmark

Publicaciones de Filosofia Aplicada,
S.A.
Alabama No. 105
Colonia Napoles
03810 México 18, D.F.